Engineering Optimization

Engineering Optimization

A modern approach

Ranjan Ganguli

Department of Aerospace Engineering
Indian Institute of Science, Bangalore

Universities Press

Universities Press (India) Private Limited

Registered Office
3-6-747/1/A & 3-6-754/1, Himayatnagar, Hyderabad 500 029 (A.P), India
e-mail: *www.universitiespress.com*

Distributed by
Orient Blackswan Private Limited

Registered Office
3-6-752, Himayatnagar, Hyderabad 500 029 (A.P), India

Other Offices
Bangalore / Bhopal / Bhubaneshwar / Chennai /Ernakulam / Guwahati
Hyderabad / Jaipur / Kolkata /Lucknow / Mumbai / New Delhi / Patna

First published 2011
Reprint 2013

ISBN: 978 81 7371 739 0

Typeset in Times 10.6/12.6 by
Krishtel eMaging Solutions Pvt.ltd.,
Chennai 600 017

Printed at
Orion Printers Private Limited
Hyderabad 500 004

Published by
Universities Press (India) Private Limited
3-6-747/1/A & 3-6-754/1, Himayatnagar,
Hyderabad 500 029 (A.P), India

This book is dedicated to my parents
Shri Ramendra Chandra Ganguli and Smt. Ratna Ganguli

Contents

Preface

This book describes various optimization methods which are useful for the engineering student. The focus of the book is on nonlinear optimization and more attention is given on approaches such as response surface and genetic algorithm, which have become popular in the past decade. To the best of my knowledge, no book on engineering optimization covers the important area of response surface methods. This approach is very important for moving optimization from academic settings to industry, where multidisciplinary analysis requiring solutions by complex computer programs is the norm. Response surface methods help in decoupling the analysis problem from the optimization problem and will help make optimization pervasive in engineering design. They also help in addressing the important issues of robustness in design and numerical noise.

A sound schooling in optimality criterion methods and numerical techniques for gradient-based optimization is provided. Optimality criteria methods have become important with the increased use of metamodeling methods, where objectives and constraints are replaced by simple analytical functions. The availability of symbolic manipulation software also makes it easy to use the optimality criteria methods. The book approaches optimization from a modern perspective, where surrogate modelling and non-gradient based algorithms are assuming increasing importance. It also provides an in-depth coverage of the classical methods which are useful for pedagogical reasons, though they are available through various software libraries.

The book also provides a thorough instruction in the concepts of optimization such as necessary and sufficient conditions of optimality, gradient-based unconstrained methods, 1D methods and selected constrained optimization methods including linear programming. The concepts and methods in the book are explained using solved examples. At many places, the examples and problems have been selected to be somewhat difficult. For example, for some of the functions used in this book, analytical 1D search is non-trivial and the student is forced to use zero-order methods. Another feature of this book is the detailed derivation and discussions of the different versions of the conjugate-gradient and quasi-Newton methods. Most books on engineering optimization present these methods to students through ready-to-use formulas but do not explain how these formulas were derived. I have tried to bridge the gap between "nonlinear programming" and "engineering optimization" in this book while retaining a level of mathematical simplicity which is amenable to an engineering student. Issues such as rates of convergence of algorithms, finite difference and analytical derivatives, automatic differentiation, orthogonal arrays for sparse sampling of design spaces and the importance of preventing singular Hessian in the

Newton method are addressed. Multimodal functions are also addressed and motivate the need for genetic algorithms.

I believe that the best way to learn optimization methods is by solving problems manually, followed by computer programming. In fact, optimization courses are very useful in increasing the mathematical and computer proficiency of engineering students and preparing them for project work and graduate study. Therefore, at several places in this book, simple proofs of some of the algorithms are provided. The book contains many problems which are useful for home assignments and project work. After reading this book, the student should be well-prepared to handle engineering design optimization in the industry and to pursue further research work in this area.

I am grateful to Professor Shapour Azarm at the University of Maryland for introducing me to this subject when I was a graduate student in the early 1990s. I have also been strongly influenced by Professor Jasbir Arora's book on optimal design from which I learnt the subject and whose pedagogical style of providing examples for each new concept or method I have tried to follow in this book. I am grateful to many students and research assistants at the Indian Institute of Science who took my course on "Engineering Optimization". Takers for this course are students from various engineering departments and occasionally, students of science and management studies. A part of the course is taught with the help of the University of Toulouse under the Indo-French Cyber University Program. A short course on this topic was given at Konkuk University in Seoul, Korea. I thank all the students in these courses for their questions and suggestions. In particular, I am grateful to Avinash Rai, P. Beena, V. N. Guruprakash, P. Raghudas and several students for solving some of the example problems. Though I have tried my best to check the examples and problems, some errors may have crept in. Please email any corrections, suggestions and constructive criticism to me at drganguli@gmail.com.

Ranjan Ganguli
Bangalore
October 2010

1 Basic Concepts

In all systems of knowledge, there is a desire to find the best possible solution for a given problem. Optimization is the branch of applied mathematics that deals with finding the best or optimal solution. In cases where many factors come into play in a physical problem, optimization of these factors is required to find the particular solution which gives the best result for a combination of these factors. Thus, optimization techniques are concerned with finding the best or *optimal* value of a quantity which can depend on many other variable factors. The need to find the best solution exists in all branches of knowledge, hence, the application of optimization methods is widespread—including all branches of engineering and science and also business and management where it is studied as a specialization in operations research. However, the posing of a practical design problem as an optimization problem requires considerable expertise and domain knowledge. Once this has been achieved, an array of tools can be used to solve it. This array of optimization methods is the main focus of this book. Basic concepts in optimization and some required mathematics are introduced in this chapter.

1.1 Statement of the Optimization Problem

The optimization problem is always expressed in a formal and standard form. This decouples the process of formulation of the optimization problem from its solution. A constrained optimization problem can be defined in the standard form as follows:[1]

Find the design variable vector **x** which *minimizes* the *objective function*

$$f(\mathbf{x}) = f(x_1, x_2, x_3, \ldots, x_n) \tag{1.1}$$

subject to *m inequality* constraints

$$g_i(\mathbf{x}) \le 0 \qquad i = 1, 2, 3, \ldots, m \tag{1.2}$$

and *p equality* constraints

$$h_j(\mathbf{x}) = 0 \qquad j = 1, 2, 3, \ldots, p. \tag{1.3}$$

Here $\mathbf{x}$ is a vector of size $n \times 1$ (sometimes called the *design vector*) and contains the *design variables* of the problem. Equations (1.1), (1.2) and (1.3) define a vast array of practical optimization problems. Studying these carefully leads to several important observations as discussed in this section.

1. In some cases, there may be no constraints, which results in an unconstrained optimization problem. However, most optimal design problems are constrained optimization problems. Despite this, studying unconstrained engineering problems is useful since many constrained optimization methods are based on extensions of unconstrained optimization methods. It is also possible to convert constrained optimization problems to unconstrained optimization problems using penalty methods, where a term is added to the objective function so that it is penalized for constraint violations.
2. The number of independent equality constraints must be less than the number of design variables, that is, $p < n$. If $p = n$, then the equality constraints can be solved to get a solution. If $p > n$, there are more equations than unknowns. Such an over-determined system of equations either means that there are redundant equality constraints or the formulation is inconsistent.
3. There is no restriction on the number of inequality constraints.
4. If $f(\mathbf{x}), h_j(\mathbf{x}), g_i(\mathbf{x})$ are *all* linear in terms of $\mathbf{x}$, we have a linear programming problem.
5. If any of $f(\mathbf{x}), h_j(\mathbf{x}), g_i(\mathbf{x})$ are nonlinear in terms of $\mathbf{x}$, we have a nonlinear programming problem.
6. $G_j(\mathbf{x}) \geq 0$ can be written as $g_j(\mathbf{x}) = -G_j(\mathbf{x}) \leq 0$. Thus we multiply the relation by -1 to convert a $\geq$ to a $\leq$ type problem.
7. The set of all feasible designs is called the constraint set and defined as

$$S = \{\mathbf{x} | h_j(\mathbf{x}) = 0;\ j = 1, p;\ g_i(\mathbf{x}) \leq 0;\ i = 1, m\}.$$

   The constraint set defines the feasible region. The optimal point must lie in the feasible region.
8. An inequality constraint $g_i(\mathbf{x}) \leq 0$ is said to be active at a design point $\mathbf{x}^*$ if it is satisfied at equality i.e., $g_i(\mathbf{x}^*) = 0$. For a feasible solution, an inequality constraint may or may not be active. However, all equality constraints are active for a feasible design.
9. A design variable is called discrete if its value must be selected from a given finite set of values. For example,
   (a) piezoceramic patches of thicknesses [0.25, 0.50, 0.75, 1.00, 1.25 mm, …, etc.] may be commercially available.
   (b) composite ply angles should be limited to [$\pm 45^\circ / \pm 90^\circ / 0^\circ$] for ease of manufacturing.
10. A design variable is called an integer if it has an integer value. For example,
   (a) number of bolts used in a mechanical system.
   (b) number of blades in a helicopter rotor.

(c) number of engines in an airplane.
(d) number of materials available for design (steel = 1, aluminum = 2, ...).
(e) number of airfoil sections available for wing design (NACA0012 = 1, NACA0015 = 2, ...).

11. Integer and discrete design variables lead to additional complications for optimization problems. Problems with integer design variables are called integer programming problems.

1.1.1 Graphical optimization

Some simple optimization problems can be solved graphically. First, we plot the constraints and identify the feasible region. Next, we plot the contours of the objective function such that the point in the feasible region where the objective reaches a minimum value can be found. However, the graphical approach is limited to 1D and 2D problems though it can be used in some cases for 3D problems.

1.1.2 Classification of optimization methods

There are two main types of optimization methods. The first type of method is based on the *optimality criteria* and is also called the *indirect method*. The second type of method is based on an *iterative search* of the design space and is also called the *direct method*. In this chapter, we will study the indirect methods which require definition of the optimality criteria. Later chapters focus on the direct method.

1.2 Basic Definitions

Optimality criteria are conditions that a function must satisfy at its minimum point. The minimum can be global or local (Figure 1.1) as defined in the following.[1–6]

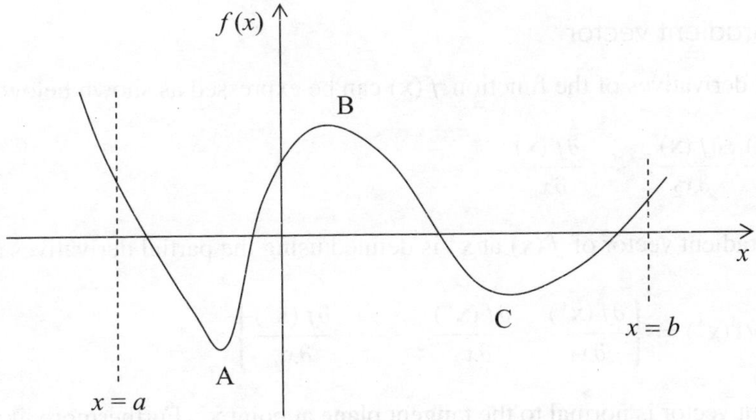

Figure 1.1 *Local and global minimum of a function*

1.2.1 Global minimum

A function of n variables, $f(\mathbf{x})$, has a global minimum at $\mathbf{x}^*$ if $f(\mathbf{x}^*) \leq f(\mathbf{x})$ for all $\mathbf{x}$ in the feasible region. If the strict inequality holds, then $\mathbf{x}^*$ is a strong global minimum.

1.2.2 Local minimum

A function of n variables, $f(\mathbf{x})$, has a local minimum at $\mathbf{x}^*$ if $f(\mathbf{x}^*) \leq f(\mathbf{x})$ holds in a small neighbourhood of $\mathbf{x}^*$ in the feasible region. For the bounded function shown in Figure 1.1, point A is a global minimum, point B is the global maximum and C is a local minimum.

1.2.3 Weierstrass theorem

The Weierstrass theorem gives a test which can be used to determine whether a function has a global minimum point. The theorem is as follows:[1]

> *Let $f(\mathbf{x})$ be a continuous function on a nonempty feasible set S which is closed and bounded. Then $f(\mathbf{x})$ has a global minimum in S.*

The concepts of *closed sets* and *bounded sets* need to be defined to use this theorem.

1. A set S is closed if it includes all its boundary points. Moreover, any sequence of points in the set has a subsequence that converges to a point in the set.
2. A set S is bounded if for any point $\mathbf{x} \in S$ inside the set, $\mathbf{x}^{\mathrm{T}}\mathbf{x} < c$, where c is a finite number.

If the Weierstrass theorem is satisfied, the existence of a global minimum is guaranteed. However, even if it is not satisfied, a global minimum may still exist. Unfortunately, the theorem does not help in actually finding the global minimum and only predicts its likely existence.

The concepts of gradient vector and Hessian matrix of a multivariate function are extremely important in optimization. These concepts are defined in the following sections.

1.2.4 Gradient vector

The partial derivatives of the function $f(\mathbf{x})$ can be expressed as shown below:

$$\frac{\partial f(\mathbf{x})}{\partial x_1}, \frac{\partial f(\mathbf{x})}{\partial x_2}, \ldots, \frac{\partial f(\mathbf{x})}{\partial x_n}. \tag{1.4}$$

Then the gradient vector of $f(\mathbf{x})$ at $\mathbf{x}^*$ is defined using the partial derivatives as,

$$\mathbf{c} = \nabla \mathbf{f}(\mathbf{x}^*) = \left\{ \frac{\partial f(\mathbf{x}^*)}{\partial x_1} \quad \frac{\partial f(\mathbf{x}^*)}{\partial x_2} \quad \cdots \quad \frac{\partial f(\mathbf{x}^*)}{\partial x_n} \right\}^{\mathrm{T}}. \tag{1.5}$$

The gradient vector is normal to the tangent plane at point $\mathbf{x}^*$. Furthermore, it points to the direction of *maximum increase* of the function. Therefore, $-\nabla \mathbf{f}(\mathbf{x}^*)$ points in the direction of *maximum decrease* of function $f(\mathbf{x}^*)$.

1.2.5 Hessian matrix

If $f(\mathbf{x})$ is assumed twice differentiable, the Hessian matrix can be obtained as defined below:

$$\mathbf{H} = \begin{bmatrix} \frac{\partial^2 f}{\partial x_1^2} & \frac{\partial^2 f}{\partial x_1 \partial x_2} & \cdots & \frac{\partial^2 f}{\partial x_1 \partial x_n} \\ \frac{\partial^2 f}{\partial x_2 \partial x_1} & \frac{\partial^2 f}{\partial x_2^2} & \cdots & \frac{\partial^2 f}{\partial x_2 \partial x_n} \\ \vdots & \vdots & \ddots & \vdots \\ \frac{\partial^2 f}{\partial x_n \partial x_1} & \frac{\partial^2 f}{\partial x_n \partial x_2} & \cdots & \frac{\partial^2 f}{\partial x_n^2} \end{bmatrix}. \tag{1.6}$$

Furthermore, partial derivatives of the twice differentiable function satisfy the rule:

$$\frac{\partial^2 f}{\partial x_i \partial x_j} = \frac{\partial^2 f}{\partial x_j \partial x_i} \qquad i = 1, \ldots, n, \; j = 1, \ldots, n. \tag{1.7}$$

From the definition of the Hessian in (1.6), it is clear that this just implies that the Hessian is a symmetric matrix:

$$\mathbf{H} = \mathbf{H}^{\mathrm{T}}. \tag{1.8}$$

Example 1.1 Find the gradient and Hessian of the following function at point (1, 1):

$$f(x) = x_1^4 + x_2^4 + 4x_1^3 x_2^3.$$

Solution: The gradient is given by:

$$\mathbf{c} = \begin{Bmatrix} \frac{\partial f}{\partial x_1} \\ \frac{\partial f}{\partial x_2} \end{Bmatrix} = \begin{Bmatrix} 4x_1^3 + 12x_1^2 x_2^3 \\ 4x_2^3 + 12x_2^2 x_1^3 \end{Bmatrix}.$$

At point (1, 1), the gradient becomes

$$\mathbf{c} = \begin{Bmatrix} 16 \\ 16 \end{Bmatrix}.$$

To calculate the Hessian, we need to get the second derivatives.

$$\mathbf{H} = \begin{bmatrix} 12x_1^2 + 24x_1 x_2^3 & 36x_1^2 x_2^2 \\ 36x_1^2 x_2^2 & 12x_2^2 + 24x_2 x_1^3 \end{bmatrix}.$$

At point (1, 1), the Hessian becomes

$$\mathbf{H} = \begin{bmatrix} 36 & 36 \\ 36 & 36 \end{bmatrix}.$$

The gradient and the Hessian occur frequently in optimization because they are used to represent a multivariate function in the Taylor series expansion.

1.3 Taylor Series Expansion

The use of approximations of functions is very important in optimization. The Taylor series is a local approximation of the function about a given point which is obtained using its derivatives. The Taylor series can be used to derive the optimality conditions.

A single variable function, $f(x)$, is expanded about the point $x = x^*$:

$$f(x) = f(x^*) + \frac{df(x^*)}{dx}(x - x^*) + \frac{1}{2}\frac{d^2 f(x^*)}{dx^2}(x - x^*)^2 + \underbrace{R}_{\text{Higher-order terms}}. \tag{1.9}$$

The approximation is valid for x close to x^* if the higher-order terms are neglected.

The Taylor series enables us to find an approximation to a function at a given point in terms of its value and the value of its derivatives at another point. For most functions, the infinite Taylor series will converge. However, what is of interest in optimization is the fact that the first few terms can capture the behaviour of a function *locally*. A special case of the Taylor series occurs when $x^* = 0$ and is called the Maclaurin series given as

$$f(x) = f(0) + \frac{df(0)}{dx}x + \frac{1}{2}\frac{d^2 f(0)}{dx^2}x^2 + R. \tag{1.10}$$

Let us return to the Taylor series and let $d = x - x^*$ (a small change in point x^*). Then (1.9) can be written as given below:

$$f(x^* + d) = f(x^*) + \frac{df(x^*)}{dx}d + \frac{1}{2}\frac{d^2 f(x^*)}{dx^2}d^2 + R. \tag{1.11}$$

For a function of two variables:

$$\begin{aligned} f(x_1, x_2) = {} & f(x_1^*, x_2^*) + \frac{\partial f}{\partial x_1}(x_1 - x_1^*) + \frac{\partial f}{\partial x_2}(x_2 - x_2^*) \\ & + \frac{1}{2}\left[\frac{\partial^2 f}{\partial x_1^2}(x_1 - x_1^*)^2 + 2\frac{\partial^2 f}{\partial x_1 \partial x_2}(x_1 - x_1^*)(x_2 - x_2^*) \right. \\ & \left. + \frac{\partial^2 f}{\partial x_2^2}(x_2 - x_2^*)^2\right] + R. \end{aligned} \tag{1.12}$$

All derivatives are calculated at point (x_1^*, x_2^*). Using summation notation, (1.12) can be written as

$$f(x_1, x_2) = f(x_1^*, x_2^*) + \sum_{i=1}^{2} \underbrace{\frac{\partial f}{\partial x_1}}_{\text{Component of gradient}}(x_i - x_i^*) + \frac{1}{2}\sum_{i=1}^{2}\sum_{j=1}^{2} \underbrace{\frac{\partial^2 f}{\partial x_i \partial x_j}}_{\text{Component of Hessian}}(x_i - x_i^*)(x_j - x_j^*) + R. \tag{1.13}$$

Thus, we can write the Taylor series for a function of n variables in matrix notation as

$$f(\mathbf{x}) = f(\mathbf{x}^*) + \nabla \mathbf{f}^{\mathrm{T}}(\mathbf{x} - \mathbf{x}^*) + \frac{1}{2}(\mathbf{x} - \mathbf{x}^*)^{\mathrm{T}}\mathbf{H}(\mathbf{x} - \mathbf{x}^*) + R. \tag{1.14}$$

Setting, $\mathbf{d} = \mathbf{x} - \mathbf{x}^*$ in (1.14), we get

$$f(\mathbf{x}^* + \mathbf{d}) = f(\mathbf{x}^*) + \nabla \mathbf{f}^{\mathrm{T}}\mathbf{d} + \frac{1}{2}\mathbf{d}^{\mathrm{T}}\mathbf{H}\mathbf{d} + R. \tag{1.15}$$

Now the change in function value is given by

$$\Delta f = f(\mathbf{x}^* + \mathbf{d}) - f(\mathbf{x}^*). \tag{1.16}$$

Putting (1.16) into (1.15) yields

$$\Delta f = \nabla \mathbf{f}^{\mathrm{T}}\mathbf{d} + \frac{1}{2}\mathbf{d}^{\mathrm{T}}\mathbf{H}\mathbf{d} + R. \tag{1.17}$$

Example 1.2 Obtain an approximate estimate of $f(x) = \cos x$ around point $x^* = 0$ and around point $x^* = \pi/2$ using the first two derivatives.

Solution: We need the first and second derivatives for the Taylor series expansion:

$$\frac{df}{dx} = -\sin x, \qquad \frac{d^2 f}{dx^2} = -\cos x.$$

$$\cos x \approx \cos(0) - \sin(0)[x - 0] + \frac{1}{2}(-\cos(0))(x - 0)^2 = 1 - \frac{1}{2}x^2.$$

Now consider, $f(x) = \cos x$ around point $x^* = \pi/2$.

$$\cos x \approx \cos\left(\frac{\pi}{2}\right) - \sin\left(\frac{\pi}{2}\right)\left[x - \frac{\pi}{2}\right] + \frac{1}{2}\left(-\cos\left(\frac{\pi}{2}\right)\right)\left(x - \frac{\pi}{2}\right)^2 = \frac{\pi}{2} - x.$$

Thus, the Taylor series expansion is *local* and differs from point to point for most functions. Methods derived from the Taylor series are good locally. Appreciating the local nature of the Taylor series expansions is very important, and this is again brought out in the following example.

Example 1.3 Expand the function $f(x) = 3x_1^3 x_2$ in a Taylor series about (1, 1) and (1, 0).

Solution:

$$f(\mathbf{x}) = 3x_1^3 x_2 \quad \text{at} \quad \mathbf{x}^* = (1, 1).$$

$$\mathbf{c} = \begin{Bmatrix} \frac{\partial f}{\partial x_1} \\ \frac{\partial f}{\partial x_2} \end{Bmatrix} = \begin{bmatrix} 9x_1^2 x_2 \\ 3x_1^3 \end{bmatrix} = \begin{bmatrix} 9 \\ 3 \end{bmatrix}.$$

$$\mathbf{H} = \begin{bmatrix} 18x_1 x_2 & 9x_1^2 \\ 9x_1^2 & 0 \end{bmatrix} = \begin{bmatrix} 18 & 9 \\ 9 & 0 \end{bmatrix}.$$

$$\bar{f}(x) = 3 + \begin{bmatrix} 9 \\ 3 \end{bmatrix}^{T} \begin{bmatrix} (x_1 - 1) \\ (x_2 - 1) \end{bmatrix} + \frac{1}{2} \begin{bmatrix} (x_1 - 1) \\ (x_2 - 1) \end{bmatrix}^{T} \begin{bmatrix} 18 & 9 \\ 9 & 0 \end{bmatrix} \begin{bmatrix} (x_1 - 1) \\ (x_2 - 1) \end{bmatrix}.$$

$$\bar{f}(x) = 9x_1^2 + 9x_1x_2 - 18x_1 - 6x_2 + 9.$$

The expansion gives a second-order polynomial approximation of function $3x_1^3x_2$ about point $\mathbf{x}^* = (1, 1)$. Now, find the expansion about (1, 0).

$$f(\mathbf{x}) = 3x_1^3x_2 \quad \text{at} \quad \mathbf{x}^* = (1, 0).$$

$$\mathbf{c} = \begin{Bmatrix} \frac{\partial f}{\partial x_1} \\ \frac{\partial f}{\partial x_2} \end{Bmatrix} = \begin{bmatrix} 9x_1^2x_2 \\ 3x_1^3 \end{bmatrix} = \begin{bmatrix} 0 \\ 3 \end{bmatrix}.$$

$$\mathbf{H} = \begin{bmatrix} 18x_1x_2 & 9x_1^2 \\ 9x_1^2 & 0 \end{bmatrix} = \begin{bmatrix} 0 & 9 \\ 9 & 0 \end{bmatrix}.$$

$$\bar{f}(x) = 0 + \begin{bmatrix} 0 \\ 3 \end{bmatrix}^{T} \begin{bmatrix} (x_1 - 1) \\ (x_2 - 0) \end{bmatrix} + \frac{1}{2} \begin{bmatrix} (x_1 - 1) \\ (x_2 - 0) \end{bmatrix}^{T} \begin{bmatrix} 0 & 9 \\ 9 & 0 \end{bmatrix} \begin{bmatrix} (x_1 - 1) \\ (x_2 - 0) \end{bmatrix}.$$

$$\bar{f}(x) = 9x_1x_2 - 6x_2.$$

The expansion gives a second-order approximation of function $3x_1^3x_2$ about point $\mathbf{x}^* = (1, 0)$. Again, this example reminds us that the Taylor series is local and the methods based on the Taylor series expansion, such as gradient-based methods, are all local in nature.

Before studying general functions for optimization, it is useful to look at some special classes of functions called quadratic forms. The knowledge of quadratic forms is needed for understanding second-order optimality conditions. Many optimization algorithms are developed for quadratic functions and then extended to general nonlinear functions. This approach works because most nonlinear functions work like quadratic forms in a local sense

1.4 Quadratic Forms

The quadratic form is a nonlinear function having *only second-order terms*. For example,

$$F(\mathbf{x}) = x_1^2 + 2x_2^2 + 7x_3^2 + 2x_1x_2 + 4x_2x_3 + 14x_3x_1 \tag{1.18}$$

is a quadratic form. The general expression for a quadratic form can be written as[1]

$$F(\mathbf{x}) = \frac{1}{2}\sum_{i=1}^{n}\sum_{j=1}^{n} p_{ij}x_ix_j. \tag{1.19}$$

Expanding (1.19) yields the following:

$$\begin{aligned} F(\mathbf{x}) = \frac{1}{2}[&(p_{11}x_1^2 + p_{12}x_1x_2 + \cdots + p_{1n}x_1x_n) \\ &+ (p_{21}x_2x_1 + p_{22}x_2^2 + \cdots + p_{2n}x_2x_n) \\ &+ \cdots + (p_{n1}x_nx_1 + \cdots + p_{nn}x_n^2)]. \end{aligned} \tag{1.20}$$

If p_{ij} and x_i are given, then $F(\mathbf{x})$ is a scalar and is called a *quadratic* form because all terms are second-order terms.

The quadratic form can be written in matrix notation. To do so, consider

$$\mathbf{y} = \mathbf{P}\mathbf{x}. \tag{1.21}$$

Here $\mathbf{P}$ is a $n \times n$ matrix and $\mathbf{x}$ and $\mathbf{y}$ are $n \times 1$ vectors. Now (1.19) can be written as:

$$F(\mathbf{x}) = \frac{1}{2}\sum_{i=1}^{n} x_i \left(\sum_{j=1}^{n} p_{ij}x_j\right) = \underbrace{\frac{1}{2}\sum_{i=1}^{n} x_i y_i}_{\text{dot product}}. \tag{1.22}$$

Combining (1.21) and (1.22), we can write

$$F(\mathbf{x}) = \frac{1}{2}\mathbf{x}^{\mathrm{T}}\mathbf{y} \Rightarrow F(\mathbf{x}) = \frac{1}{2}\mathbf{x}^{\mathrm{T}}\mathbf{P}\mathbf{x}. \tag{1.23}$$

Matrix $\mathbf{P}$ is called the matrix of the quadratic form and contains information about its mathematical nature.

$F(\mathbf{x})$ in (1.20) can be rewritten as shown below:

$$\begin{aligned}F(\mathbf{x}) = \frac{1}{2}\{&[p_{11}x_1^2 + p_{22}x_2^2 + \cdots + p_{nn}x_n^2]\\ &+ [(p_{12} + p_{21})x_1x_2 + (p_{13} + p_{31})x_1x_3 + \cdots + (p_{1n} + p_{n1})x_1x_n]\\ &+ [(p_{23} + p_{32})x_2x_3 + (p_{24} + p_{42})x_2x_4 + \cdots + (p_{2n} + p_{n2})x_2x_n]\\ &+ \cdots + [(p_{n-1,n} + p_{n,n-1})x_{n-1}x_n]\}.\end{aligned} \tag{1.24}$$

Here we have separated the *square* terms corresponding to the diagonal terms of the $\mathbf{P}$ matrix from the other terms. For $i \neq j$, the coefficient of x_ix_j is $(p_{ij} + p_{ji})$. Define :

$$a_{ij} = \frac{1}{2}(p_{ij} + p_{ji}) \Rightarrow a_{ij} + a_{ji} = p_{ij} + p_{ji} \tag{1.25}$$

for all i and j coefficients of matrix $\mathbf{A}$. Replacing the ps by as, we can write

$$F(\mathbf{x}) = \frac{1}{2}\mathbf{x}^{\mathrm{T}}\mathbf{P}\mathbf{x} = \frac{1}{2}\mathbf{x}^{\mathrm{T}}\mathbf{A}\mathbf{x}. \tag{1.26}$$

From (1.26), we can see that the value of the quadratic form does not change when $\mathbf{P}$ is replaced by $\mathbf{A}$. However, $\mathbf{A}$ is always *symmetric*, since

$$\left.\begin{aligned} a_{ij} &= \frac{1}{2}(p_{ij} + p_{ji})\\ a_{ji} &= \frac{1}{2}(p_{ji} + p_{ij})\end{aligned}\right\rangle \text{ equal.} \tag{1.27}$$

There can be many $\mathbf{P}$ matrices, but *there is only one* $\mathbf{A}$ *matrix for a quadratic form.* Asymmetric matrices are not very useful for getting a mathematical insight into the problem. Symmetric matrices tell us more about the matrix.

Example 1.4 Express the following quadratic form as a symmetric matrix:

$$F(x_1, x_2, x_3) = \frac{1}{2}(5x_1^2 + x_1x_2 - 12x_1x_3 + 10x_2^2 - 7x_2x_3 + x_3^2).$$

Solution: We first express the equation in matrix form:

$$F(\mathbf{x}) = \frac{1}{2}[x_1x_2x_3]\begin{bmatrix} 5 & 1 & -12 \\ 0 & 10 & -7 \\ 0 & 0 & 1 \end{bmatrix}\begin{Bmatrix} x_1 \\ x_2 \\ x_3 \end{Bmatrix} = \frac{1}{2}\mathbf{x}^{\mathrm{T}}\mathbf{P}\mathbf{x}.$$

$$p_{11} = 5,\ p_{22} = 10,\ p_{33} = 1,\ p_{12} = 1,\ p_{13} = -12,\ p_{23} = -7.$$

However, **P** is asymmetric. We need to find **A**.

$$p_{12} + p_{21} = 1 + 0 = 1, \quad a_{12} = 0.5.$$

$$p_{13} + p_{31} = -12 + 0 = -12, \quad a_{13} = -6.$$

$$p_{23} + p_{32} = -7 + 0 = -7, \quad a_{23} = -3.5.$$

$$F(\mathbf{x}) = \frac{1}{2}[x_1x_2x_3]\begin{bmatrix} 5 & 0.5 & -6 \\ 0.5 & 10 & -3.5 \\ -6 & -3.5 & 1 \end{bmatrix}\begin{Bmatrix} x_1 \\ x_2 \\ x_3 \end{Bmatrix} = \frac{1}{2}\mathbf{x}^{\mathrm{T}}\mathbf{A}\mathbf{x}.$$

The nature of a quadratic form is revealed by the values (positive and/or negative) that it can take. Important properties such as the positive definiteness of a matrix can be deduced from the quadratic form.

1.4.1 Form of a matrix

Matrix **A** can be classified depending on the sign of the quadratic form. The matrix is:[6]

1. Negative semidefinite if $(1/2)\mathbf{x}^{\mathrm{T}}\mathbf{A}\mathbf{x} \le 0$ for all $\mathbf{x}$ except at least one $\mathbf{x} \neq 0$ with $\mathbf{x}^{\mathrm{T}}\mathbf{A}\mathbf{x} = 0$.
2. Negative definite if $(1/2)\mathbf{x}^{\mathrm{T}}\mathbf{A}\mathbf{x} < 0$ for all $\mathbf{x}$ except $\mathbf{x} = 0$.
3. Positive semidefinite if $(1/2)\mathbf{x}^{\mathrm{T}}\mathbf{A}\mathbf{x} \ge 0$ for all $\mathbf{x}$ except at least one $\mathbf{x} \neq 0$ with $\mathbf{x}^{\mathrm{T}}\mathbf{A}\mathbf{x} = 0$.
4. Positive definite if $(1/2)\mathbf{x}^{\mathrm{T}}\mathbf{A}\mathbf{x} > 0$ except for $\mathbf{x} = 0$.
5. Indefinite if $(1/2)\mathbf{x}^{\mathrm{T}}\mathbf{A}\mathbf{x}$ is positive for some $\mathbf{x}$ and negative for others.

Many physical quantities such as energy are often positive, and therefore quadratic forms representing these quantities yield positive definite matrices.

Example 1.5 Determine the form of the matrices given below.

$$\text{(a)}\quad \mathbf{A} = \begin{bmatrix} 2 & 0 & 0 \\ 0 & 4 & 0 \\ 0 & 0 & 13 \end{bmatrix} \qquad \text{(b)}\quad \mathbf{A} = \begin{bmatrix} 1 & -1 & 0 \\ -1 & 1 & 0 \\ 0 & 0 & 1 \end{bmatrix}$$

Solution:

(a)

$$\mathbf{x}^{\mathrm{T}}\mathbf{A}\mathbf{x} = [x_1 x_2 x_3]\begin{bmatrix} 2 & 0 & 0 \\ 0 & 4 & 0 \\ 0 & 0 & 13 \end{bmatrix}\begin{Bmatrix} x_1 \\ x_2 \\ x_3 \end{Bmatrix}$$

$$= [x_1 x_2 x_3]\begin{Bmatrix} 2x_1 \\ 4x_2 \\ 13x_3 \end{Bmatrix} = 2x_1^2 + 4x_2^2 + 13x_3^2 > 0$$

unless $x_1 = x_2 = x_3 = 0(\mathbf{x} = 0)$.

Therefore, the form of the matrix **A** is positive definite.

(b)

$$\mathbf{x}^{\mathrm{T}}\mathbf{A}\mathbf{x} = [x_1 x_2 x_3]\begin{bmatrix} 1 & -1 & 0 \\ -1 & 1 & 0 \\ 0 & 0 & 1 \end{bmatrix}\begin{Bmatrix} x_1 \\ x_2 \\ x_3 \end{Bmatrix}$$

$$= [x_1 x_2 x_3]\begin{Bmatrix} x_1 - x_2 \\ -x_1 + x_2 \\ x_3 \end{Bmatrix} = x_1^2 - 2x_1x_2 + x_2^2 + x_3^2$$

$$= (x_1 - x_2)^2 + x_3^2 \geq 0$$

for all **x**.

However, $\mathbf{x}^{\mathrm{T}}\mathbf{A}\mathbf{x} = 0$ when $(x_1 - x_2)^2 + x_3^2 = 0$.

Therefore, the matrix is not positive definite but positive semidefinite, if $x_3 = 0$, $x_1 = x_2$. For example, 1, 1, 0; 2, 2, 0; ... ; 10, 10, 0 are possible values of x.

Finding the form of a matrix from its quadratic form requires algebraic manipulations and can be cumbersome. A direct approach to evaluate the form of a matrix comes from its eigenvalues.

1.4.2 Eigenvalue check for the form of a matrix

Let $\lambda_i, i = 1, 2, \ldots, n$ be n eigenvalues of a symmetric $n \times n$ matrix **A** associated with the quadratic form $F(\mathbf{x}) = (1/2)\mathbf{x}^{\mathrm{T}}\mathbf{A}\mathbf{x}$. Then,

1. **A** is positive definite if $\lambda_i > 0, i = 1, n$ are strictly positive.
2. **A** is positive semidefinite if $\lambda_i \geq 0, i = 1, n$ are nonnegative.
3. **A** is negative definite if $\lambda_i < 0, i = 1, n$ are strictly negative.
4. **A** is negative semidefinite if $\lambda_i \leq 0, i = 1, n$ are nonpositive.
5. **A** is indefinite if some $\lambda_i < 0$ and some other $\lambda_i > 0$.

Example 1.6 Determine the form of the following matrix using the eigenvalue approach.

$$\text{(a)} \quad \mathbf{A} = \begin{bmatrix} -2 & 4 & -7 \\ 4 & -4 & 0 \\ -7 & 0 & -1 \end{bmatrix} \qquad \text{(b)} \quad \mathbf{B} = \begin{bmatrix} 1 & -1 & 0 \\ -1 & 1 & 0 \\ 0 & 0 & 1 \end{bmatrix}$$

Solution:

(a) Eigenvalues of **A** are given by

$$\begin{vmatrix} 2-\lambda & 4 & -7 \\ 4 & -4-\lambda & 0 \\ -7 & 0 & -1-\lambda \end{vmatrix} = 0.$$

$$\lambda_1 = 6.28, \lambda_2 = -10.05, \lambda_3 = -3.22.$$

The form is indefinite.

(b) Eigenvalues of $\mathbf{B} = \begin{bmatrix} 1 & -1 & 0 \\ -1 & 1 & 0 \\ 0 & 0 & 1 \end{bmatrix}$ are obtained using

$$\begin{vmatrix} 1-\lambda & -1 & 0 \\ -1 & 1-\lambda & 0 \\ 0 & 0 & 1-\lambda \end{vmatrix} = 0.$$

$$\lambda_1 = 0, \lambda_2 = 1, \lambda_3 = 2.$$

Thus, the form is positive semidefinite since there are nonnegative eigenvalues.

1.4.3 Differentiation of the quadratic form

$$F(\mathbf{x}) = \frac{1}{2}\sum_{i=1}^{n}\sum_{j=1}^{n} a_{ij}x_i x_j. \tag{1.28}$$

$$\frac{\partial F(\mathbf{x})}{\partial x_i} = \sum_{j=1}^{n} a_{ij}x_j \Rightarrow \nabla \mathbf{F}(\mathbf{x}) = \mathbf{Ax}. \tag{1.29}$$

$$\frac{\partial^2 F(\mathbf{x})}{\partial x_j \partial x_i} = a_{ij} \Rightarrow \mathbf{H} = \mathbf{A}. \tag{1.30}$$

Components a_{ij} of the matrix **A** are the *components of the Hessian matrix associated with the quadratic form.*

With the basic concepts of the gradient, Hessian, Taylor series expansion and quadratic forms behind us, we are in a position to lay out the necessary and sufficient conditions for optimization.

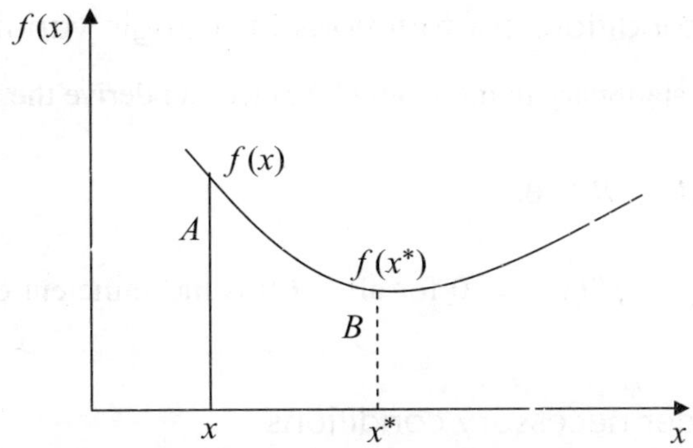

Figure 1.2 *Minimum point of a single-variable function*

1.5 Optimality Criteria for Unconstrained Optimization

Necessary conditions must be satisfied at the optimum point. A point cannot be optimum if it does not satisfy the necessary conditions. However, satisfaction of necessary conditions does not guarantee an optimum. If a candidate optimum point satisfies the sufficient conditions, we have an optimum point.

The problem we are addressing is: Minimize $f(\mathbf{x})$ without any constraints on $\mathbf{x}$. We first look at the single-variable case and then at the multivariable case.

1.5.1 Necessary conditions for optimality of functions of one variable

Expand the function in a Taylor series:

$$f(x) = f(x^*) + f'(x^*)d + \frac{1}{2}f''(x^*)d^2 + R \tag{1.31}$$

$$\Delta f = f'(x^*)d + \frac{1}{2}f''(x^*)d^2 + R. \tag{1.32}$$

Let x^* be a local minimum point of a function shown in Figure 1.2, and x be another point in its vicinity.

By definition, the function value at the minimum point must be lower than that at a nearby point. Then, we can write:

$$\Delta f = f(x) - f(x^*) \geq 0. \tag{1.33}$$

Assuming d is small (*local* approximation), the first-order term in (1.32) dominates,

$$f'(x^*)d \geq 0. \tag{1.34}$$

However, $d = x - x^*$ can be either positive or negative. Therefore, for (1.34) to be true,

$$f'(x^*) = 0. \tag{1.35}$$

Points satisfying $f'(x^*) = 0$ can be *local minimum, maximum* or neither maximum nor minimum (*inflection or saddle points*). In general, they are called *stationary points*.

1.5.2 Sufficient conditions for functions of a single variable

Since $f'(x^*) = 0$ at a stationary point, from (1.32) we can derive the following:

$$\Delta f = \frac{1}{2} f''(x^*) d^2 + R \geq 0. \tag{1.36}$$

Since $d \neq 0$ and $d^2 \geq 0$, $f''(x^*) > 0$ for all $d \neq 0$ is the sufficient condition for a local minimum point.

1.5.3 Second-order necessary conditions

Even if $f''(x^*) > 0$ is not satisfied, x^* can be a minimum point. For example, $f''(x^*) = 0$ is possible. However, x^* cannot be a minimum unless $f''(x^*) \geq 0$. If $f''(x^*) = 0$, we need to evaluate higher-order derivatives at the stationary point. For example, $f'''(x^*)$ must be zero at the stationary point (necessary condition) and $f^{iv}(x^*) > 0$ for x^* to be a local minimum. As a rule, *the lowest non-zero derivative must be even ordered for a stationary point and positive for a local minimum point.*[1]

Example 1.7 Determine the local minimum of the following functions: (a) $f(x) = \sin x$ and (b) $f(x) = x^3 - x^2 - x - 1$.

Solution:

(a)

$$f(x) = \sin x.$$

$$f'(x) = \cos x, \quad f''(x) = -\sin x.$$

$$f'(x) = 0 \Rightarrow \cos x = 0, \qquad x = \pm\frac{\pi}{2}, \pm\frac{3\pi}{2}, \pm\frac{5\pi}{2}, \pm\frac{7\pi}{2} \cdots$$

$$f''(x) = -\sin x > 0 \quad \text{at} \quad x = \frac{3\pi}{2}, \frac{7\pi}{2}, \ldots -\frac{\pi}{2}, -\frac{5\pi}{2}, \ldots$$

The minimum value of sin x is -1 at these points. There are infinite local minima. This is a *multimodal* optimization problem where more than one local minimum exists.

(b)

$$f(x) = x^3 - x^2 - x - 1.$$

$$f'(x) = 3x^2 - 2x - 1 = 0 \Rightarrow x^* = -\frac{1}{3}, 1$$

$$f''(x) = 6x - 2.$$

$$f''(1) = 4 > 0 \quad \text{(minimum)}$$

$$f''\left(-\frac{1}{3}\right) = -4 < 0 \quad \text{(maximum)}$$

1.5.4 Optimality conditions for a function of several variables

We can easily generalize the concepts introduced in 1D to n dimensions. The Taylor series for a multivariate function is given by:

$$f(\mathbf{x}) = f(\mathbf{x}^*) + \nabla \mathbf{f}(\mathbf{x}^*)^{\mathrm{T}}\mathbf{d} + \frac{1}{2}\mathbf{d}^{\mathrm{T}}\mathbf{H}(\mathbf{x}^*)\mathbf{d} + R \tag{1.37}$$

$$\Delta f = f(\mathbf{x}) - f(\mathbf{x}^*) = \nabla \mathbf{f}(\mathbf{x}^*)^{\mathrm{T}}\mathbf{d} + \frac{1}{2}\mathbf{d}^{\mathrm{T}}\mathbf{H}(\mathbf{x}^*)\mathbf{d} + R. \tag{1.38}$$

If $\mathbf{x}^*$ is a local minimum of f, $\Delta f \geq 0$. From (1.38), this is possible for all possible $\mathbf{d}$ only if the following condition is true:

$$\nabla \mathbf{f}(\mathbf{x}^*) = 0. \tag{1.39}$$

The gradient vector becoming zero is the *necessary condition* and gives the *stationary points*. Again, from (1.38) we can see that the *stationary point is a local minimum if*

$$\mathbf{d}^{\mathrm{T}}\mathbf{H}(\mathbf{x}^*)\mathbf{d} > 0. \tag{1.40}$$

Equation (1.40) represents a positive definite quadratic form. A *positive definite Hessian* matrix is a *sufficient condition* for the existence of a *local minimum* of the function.

Example 1.8 Find the local minimum of $f(\mathbf{x}) = x_1^2 + 2x_2^2 + \mathrm{e}^{-x_1-x_2}$.

Solution: We calculate the gradient and set it to zero:

$$\nabla \mathbf{f} = \begin{bmatrix} 2x_1 - \mathrm{e}^{-x_1-x_2} \\ 4x_2 - \mathrm{e}^{-x_1-x_2} \end{bmatrix} = \begin{Bmatrix} 0 \\ 0 \end{Bmatrix}.$$

The resulting two equations yield:

$$2x_1 - 4x_2 = 0 \quad \text{or} \quad x_1 = 2x_2.$$

Putting this into the first equation, $2x_1 - \mathrm{e}^{-x_1-x_2} = 0$, yields

$$\ln(4x_2) + 3x_2 = 0.$$

This equation can be solved numerically to get $x_2^* = 0.15638$. The stationary point is thus

$$\mathbf{x}^* = \begin{Bmatrix} 0.31276 \\ 0.15638 \end{Bmatrix}.$$

The Hessian is calculated as

$$\mathbf{H} = \begin{bmatrix} 2 + \mathrm{e}^{-x_1-x_2} & \mathrm{e}^{-x_1-x_2} \\ \mathrm{e}^{-x_1-x_2} & 4 + \mathrm{e}^{-x_1-x_2} \end{bmatrix}.$$

At the stationary point, the Hessian becomes

$$\mathbf{H} = \begin{bmatrix} 2.6255 & 0.6255 \\ 0.6255 & 4.6255 \end{bmatrix}.$$

The eigenvalues of the Hessian are 2.446 and 4.805, which are both positive. Therefore, the Hessian is positive definite and the stationary point i local minimum

Example 1.9 Find the stationary points of the following function and investigate their nature using second-order conditions:

$$f(x) = \frac{x_1^3 + x_2^3}{6} - \frac{x_1^2}{2} - x_2^2 + 1.$$

Solution: The gradient of the function can be obtained; it is given by

$$\mathbf{c} = \begin{Bmatrix} \frac{\partial f}{\partial x_1} \\ \frac{\partial f}{\partial x_2} \end{Bmatrix} = \begin{Bmatrix} \frac{x_1^2}{2-x_1} \\ \frac{x_2^2}{2-x_2} \end{Bmatrix} = \begin{Bmatrix} x_1\left(\frac{x_1}{2-1}\right) \\ x_2\left(\frac{x_2}{2-2}\right) \end{Bmatrix} = \begin{Bmatrix} 0 \\ 0 \end{Bmatrix}.$$

Solving the above equation yields more than one possible solution: (0, 0), (0, 4), (2, 0) and (2, 4). This results in four possible Hessian matrices. Let us first calculate the Hessian matrix:

$$\mathbf{H} = \begin{bmatrix} x_1 - 1 & 0 \\ 0 & x_2 - 2 \end{bmatrix}.$$

For $\mathbf{x}^* = (0, 0)$, we get $\mathbf{H} = \begin{bmatrix} -1 & 0 \\ 0 & -2 \end{bmatrix}$, which yields eigenvalues -1 and -2. Therefore, the stationary point $\mathbf{x}^* = (0, 0)$ corresponds to a negative definite Hessian and is a maximum point. At this point, the function value is $f(0, 0) = 1$.

For $\mathbf{x}^* = (0, 4)$, we get $\mathbf{H} = \begin{bmatrix} -1 & 0 \\ 0 & 2 \end{bmatrix}$, which yields eigenvalues -1 and 2. Therefore, the stationary point $\mathbf{x}^* = (0, 4)$ corresponds to an indefinite Hessian and is a point of inflection. At this point, the function value is $f(0, 4) = -4.33$.

For $\mathbf{x}^* = (2, 0)$, we get $\mathbf{H} = \begin{bmatrix} 1 & 0 \\ 0 & -2 \end{bmatrix}$, which yields eigenvalues 1 and -2. Therefore, the stationary point $\mathbf{x}^* = (2, 0)$ corresponds to an indefinite Hessian and is a point of inflection. At this point, the function value is $f(2, 0) = 0.33$.

For $\mathbf{x}^* = (2, 4)$, we get $\mathbf{H} = \begin{bmatrix} 1 & 0 \\ 0 & 2 \end{bmatrix}$, which yields eigenvalues 1 and 2. Therefore, the stationary point $\mathbf{x}^* = (2, 4)$ corresponds to a positive definite Hessian and is a minimum point. At this point, the function value is $f(2, 4) = -5$.

Example 1.10 Find the minimum point of the Rosenbrock function

$$f = 100(x_2 - x_1^2)^2 + (1 - x_1)^2.$$

Solution: We first calculate the gradient and set it equal to zero

$$\frac{\partial f}{\partial x_1} = -400x_1x_2 + 400x_1^3 - 2 + 2x_1 = 0.$$

$$\frac{\partial f}{\partial x_2} = 200(x_2 - x_1^2) = 0.$$

The second equation immediately yields $x_2 = x_1^2$. Putting this into the first equation yields $2x_1 - 2 = 0$ or $x_1 = 1$. Then we also get $x_2 = 1$. Thus $\mathbf{x}^* = (1, 1)$ is a stationary point of the Rosenbrock function. We need to find if this is also a minimum point. So, we calculate the Hessian matrix as follows:

$$\mathbf{H} = \begin{bmatrix} -400x_2 + 1200x_1^2 & -400x_1 \\ -400x_1 & 200 \end{bmatrix}.$$

At the stationary point (1, 1), the Hessian is defined as follows:

$$\mathbf{H} = \begin{bmatrix} 802 & -400 \\ -400 & 200 \end{bmatrix}.$$

The eigenvalues of the Hessian are obtained as 1001.6 and 0.4, which are both positive. The Hessian is positive definite at (1, 1) which is a minimum point.

Example 1.11 Find the minimum point of

$$f = 3x_1 + \frac{100}{x_1 x_2} + 5x_2.$$

Solution: The gradient is set to zero to get the stationary points:

$$\frac{\partial f}{\partial x_1} = 3 - \frac{100}{x_1^2 x_2} = 0.$$

$$\frac{\partial f}{\partial x_2} = -\frac{100}{x_1 x_2^2} + 5 = 0.$$

Simplifying these two equations yields the following conditions:

$$x_1^2 x_2 = \frac{100}{3}.$$

$$x_1 x_2^2 = 20.$$

Getting $x_1 = 20/x_2^2$ from the second equation and putting into the first equation yields

$$\frac{400}{x_2^3} = \frac{100}{3} \quad \text{or} \quad x_2 = \sqrt[3]{12} = 2.289.$$

Then we get:

$$x_1 = \frac{20}{x_2^2} = 3.817.$$

The stationary point is thus $x^* = (3.817, 2.289)$. We now need to find if this is a minimum point. To do so, we calculate the Hessian:

$$\mathbf{H} = \begin{bmatrix} \frac{200}{x_1^3 x_2} & \frac{100}{x_1^2 x_2^2} \\ \frac{100}{x_1^2 x_2^2} & \frac{200}{x_1 x_2^3} \end{bmatrix}.$$

At $x^* = (3.817, 2.289)$, the Hessian becomes

$$\mathbf{H} = \begin{bmatrix} 1.571 & 1.3099 \\ 1.3099 & 4.369 \end{bmatrix}.$$

The eigenvalues of the Hessian are then obtained as 1.0535 and 4.8865, which are both positive. The Hessian is thus positive definite, and $x^* = (3.817, 2.289)$ is a minimum point.

1.6 Optimality Criteria for Constrained Optimization

Recall the constrained optimization problem: Find the design variables $\mathbf{x} = \{x_1, x_2, \dots, x_n\}$ which can minimize the function:

$$f(\mathbf{x}) = f(x_1, x_2, \dots, x_n). \tag{1.41}$$

The optimization is subject to constraints given by the $(p+m)$ equations:

$$h_i(\mathbf{x}) = 0, \qquad i = 1, \dots, p. \tag{1.42}$$

$$g_j(\mathbf{x}) \le 0, \qquad j = 1, \dots, m. \tag{1.43}$$

We need to determine if any necessary conditions exist for finding a solution to the problem defined by (1.41), (1.42) and (1.43). Such a condition would allow us to find the optimal design variables: $\mathbf{x}^* = \{x_1^*, x_2^*, \dots, x_n^*\}$. First, we consider the case with only equality constraints and then expand the problem to include inequality constraints. Before discussing the necessary conditions, the concept of a regular point needs to be introduced.

1.6.1 Regular point

Consider minimizing $f(\mathbf{x})$ subject to $h_i(\mathbf{x}) = 0, i = 1, p$. A point $\mathbf{x}^*$ satisfying all $h(\mathbf{x}^*) = 0$ is called a *regular point* of the design space if $f(\mathbf{x})$is *differentiable* at $\mathbf{x}^*$ and the *gradient vectors of all constraints* at the point $\mathbf{x}^*$ are *linearly independent*. If inequality constraints are included, then the active inequality constraints also have to be linearly independent for a regular point.[1]

1.6.2 Necessary conditions: Equality constraints

The Lagrange function is defined using the objective and constraint function and the Lagrange multiplier v. For a problem with only one equality constraint, the Lagrange function can be written as given below:

$$L(\mathbf{x}, v) = f(\mathbf{x}) + vh(\mathbf{x}). \tag{1.44}$$

Since (1.44) can be considered to be a function of variables $\mathbf{x}$ and v, the necessary condition for a minimum is given by setting the gradient of the Lagrange function to zero.

$$\nabla L(\mathbf{x}^*) = 0 \tag{1.45}$$

From (1.44) and (1.45), we can write down a set of conditions, as shown below:

$$\nabla f(\mathbf{x}^*) + v\nabla h(\mathbf{x}^*) = 0$$

$$\nabla f(\mathbf{x}^*) = -v\nabla h(\mathbf{x}^*). \tag{1.46}$$

At the candidate minimum point, gradients of the cost and constraint functions are along the same line and proportional to each other. The Lagrange multiplier, v, is the proportionality constraint.

Also,

$$\frac{\partial L(\mathbf{x}^*, \mathbf{v}^*)}{\partial v_j} = h_j(\mathbf{x}^*) = 0 \qquad j = 1 \cdots p. \tag{1.47}$$

The necessary condition for the equality-constrained problem is that the Lagrange function be stationary both with respect to **x** and **v**.

Example 1.12 A fuel cylinder is also used to generate power by putting a solar power film on its surface. Find the radius (R) and length (l) of a cylinder with maximum volume such that the surface area is given by S.

Solution: The objective is to maximize the volume while the surface area is kept fixed. The volume of the cylinder is given by $\pi R^2 l$ and surface area is given as $S = 2\pi R^2 + 2\pi Rl$. Thus, we want to minimize:

$$f = -\pi R^2 l.$$

Subject to the equality constraint:

$$h = 2\pi Rl + 2\pi R^2 - S = 0.$$

We form the Lagrange function:

$$L = f + vh = -\pi R^2 l + v(2\pi Rl + 2\pi R^2 - S).$$

Taking the gradient of the Lagrange function, we get

$$\frac{\partial L}{\partial R} = -2\pi Rl + v(2\pi l + 4\pi R) = 0.$$

$$\frac{\partial L}{\partial \ell} = -\pi R^2 + v(2\pi R) = 0.$$

$$\frac{\partial L}{\partial v} = 2\pi Rl + 2\pi R^2 - S = 0.$$

Solving for the design variables and Lagrange multiplier, yields the expressions given below:

$$R^* = \left(\frac{S}{6\pi}\right)^{1/2}.$$

$$l^* = \left(\frac{2S}{3\pi}\right)^{1/2} = 2R^*.$$

$$v^* = \left(\frac{S}{24\pi}\right)^{1/2} = \frac{R^*}{2}.$$

To summarize, the optimal design in this problem is a cylinder whose diameter equals the length.

1.6.3 Necessary conditions: Inequality constraints

Consider the inequality constraints given by the set of m equations: $g_i(\mathbf{x}) \le 0\ i = 1, m$. The inequality is transformed to equality by adding a positive number.

$$g_i(x) + s_i^2 = 0, \qquad i = 1, m. \tag{1.48}$$

Here s_i is called a slack variable and can have any real value. Obviously,

$$s_i^2 \ge 0, \qquad i = 1, m. \tag{1.49}$$

The Lagrange function can then be defined as given below:

$$L = f(\mathbf{x}) + \sum_{i=1}^{p} v_i h_i(\mathbf{x}) + \sum_{j=1}^{m} u_j (g_j(\mathbf{x}) + s_j^2), \quad i = 1, p;\ j = 1, m. \tag{1.50}$$

The Lagrange multipliers for each inequality constraint must be nonnegative.

$$u_j \ge 0, \qquad j = 1, m. \tag{1.51}$$

If the inequality constraint is inactive at the optimum, $u_j = 0$. If the inequality constraint is active, then $(g_j(\mathbf{x}) = 0)$ and $u_j \ge 0$.

Example 1.13 Find the optimal point for the following problem using optimality criteria.
Minimize $f(x_1, x_2) = (x_1 - 5)^2 + (x_2 - 5)^2$
subject to $g(x_1, x_2) = x_1 + x_2 - 1 \le 0$.

Solution: We form the Lagrange function:

$$L = (x_1 - 5)^2 + (x_2 - 5)^2 - u(x_1 + x_2 - 1 + s^2).$$

Next, we set the gradient of the Lagrange function to zero:

$$\frac{\partial L}{\partial x_1} = 2(x_1 - 5) + u = 0.$$

$$\frac{\partial L}{\partial x_2} = 2(x_2 - 5) + u = 0.$$

$$\frac{\partial L}{\partial u} = x_1 + x_2 - 1 + s^2 = 0.$$

$$\frac{\partial L}{\partial s} = 2us = 0.$$

Now, we consider the various possibilities created by the switching condition $us = 0$.

Case 1: $s = 0 \Rightarrow us = 0$.

$$2(x_1 - 5) + u = 0.$$

$$2(x_2 - 5) + u = 0.$$

$$x_1 + x_2 - 1 = 0.$$

Solving these equations yields, $x_1 = 0.5, x_2 = 0.5, s = 0, u = 9$. This solution corresponds to a case where the inequality is active.

Case 2: $u = 0 \Rightarrow us = 0.$

$$2(x_1 - 5) = 0.$$

$$2(x_2 - 5) = 0.$$

$$x_1 + x_2 - 1 + s^2 = 0.$$

Solving these equations yields, $x_1 = 5, x_2 = 5, s^2 = -9, u = 0$. However, $s^2 = -9$ is not possible. Therefore, this is not a valid solution.

Case 3: $u = 0, s = 0 \Rightarrow us = 0.$

$$2(x_1 - 5) = 0.$$

$$2(x_2 - 5) = 0.$$

$$x_1 + x_2 - 1 = 0.$$

Here, the first two equations yield, $x_1 = x_2 = 5$. However, this does not satisfy the third equation $x_1 + x_2 - 1 = 0$. Thus, this is not a valid solution.

We see that only case 1 is a valid solution and is therefore a candidate optimum point,

$$\mathbf{x}^* = (0.5, \quad 0.5).$$

At this point, $g(x_1, x_2) = 0.5 + 0.5 - 1 = 0$ and $f(x_1, x_2) = (-4.5)^2 + (-4.5)^2 = 40.5$.

1.6.4 Karusch–Kuhn–Tucker (KKT) first-order necessary conditions

Let $\mathbf{x}^*$ be a regular point of the constraint set that is a local minimum for $f(\mathbf{x})$ subject to the constraints $h_i(\mathbf{x}) = 0;\ i = 1, \ldots, p$ and $g_j(\mathbf{x}) \leq 0;\ j = 1, \ldots, m$. The Lagrangian can then be written in matrix form as given below:[1]

$$L(\mathbf{x}, \mathbf{v}, \mathbf{u}, \mathbf{s}) = f(\mathbf{x}) + \mathbf{v}^{\mathrm{T}}\mathbf{h}(\mathbf{x}) + \mathbf{u}^{\mathrm{T}}(\mathbf{g}(\mathbf{x}) + \mathbf{s}^2), \tag{1.49}$$

or in summation form:

$$L(\mathbf{x}, \mathbf{v}, \mathbf{u}, \mathbf{s}) = f(\mathbf{x}) + \sum_{i=1}^{p} v_j h_i(\mathbf{x}) + \sum_{i=1}^{m} u_i (g_i(\mathbf{x}) + s_i^2). \tag{1.50}$$

The KKT condition states that there exist Lagrange multipliers, $\mathbf{v}^*$ ($p \times 1$ vector) and $\mathbf{u}^*$ ($m \times 1$ vector), such that the Lagrangian is stationary with respect to x_j, v_i, u_i, and s_i, that is,

$$\frac{\partial L}{\partial x_j} = \frac{\partial f}{\partial x_j} + \sum_{i=1}^{p} v_i^* \frac{\partial h_i}{\partial x_j} + \sum_{i=1}^{m} u_i^* \frac{\partial g_i}{\partial x_j} = 0 \qquad j = 1, \ldots, n \tag{1.51}$$

$$\begin{aligned}
h_i(\mathbf{x}^*) &= 0 \qquad i = 1, \ldots, p \\
g_i(\mathbf{x}^*) + s_i^2 &= 0 \qquad i = 1, \ldots, m \\
s_i^2 &\geq 0 \qquad i = 1, \ldots, m \\
u_i^* s_i &= 0 \qquad i = 1, \ldots, m \\
u_i^* &\geq 0 \qquad i = 1, \ldots, m
\end{aligned} \tag{1.52}$$

and all derivatives are evaluated at point $\mathbf{x}^*$. These are the KKT necessary conditions for obtaining the stationary points of a multivariate function with equality and inequality constraints. There are $n + 2m + p$ unknowns and equations in (1.51) and (1.52). The equations $u_i^* s_i = 0$ are called the *switching conditions.* The KKT conditions have a geometrical interpretation. Equation (1.51) can be written as follows:

$$-\frac{\partial f}{\partial x_i} = \sum_{i=1}^{p} v_i^* \frac{\partial h_i}{\partial x_j} + \sum_{i=1}^{m} u_i^* \frac{\partial g_i}{\partial x_j} \qquad j = 1, \ldots, n. \tag{1.53}$$

At the stationary point, negative gradient (steepest descent) direction of the objective function is a linear combination of the gradient of the constraints. The Lagrange multipliers are the scalar parameters of this linear combination.

Example 1.14 Minimize $f(\mathbf{x}) = (x_1 - 3)^2 + (x_2 - 3)^2$ subject to $x_1 + x_2 \leq 4$ and $x_1 - 3x_2 = 1$.

Solution: Construct the Lagrange function as

$$L(\mathbf{x}) = (x_1 - 3)^2 + (x_2 - 3)^2 + v(x_1 - 3x_2 - 1) + u(x_1 + x_2 - 4 + s^2).$$

Calculate the gradient of the Lagrange function and set it equal to zero.

$$\frac{\partial L}{\partial x_1} = 2(x_1 - 3) + v + u = 0.$$

$$\frac{\partial L}{\partial x_2} = 2(x_2 - 3) - 3v + u = 0.$$

$$\frac{\partial L}{\partial v} = x_1 - 3x_2 - 1 = 0.$$

$$\frac{\partial L}{\partial u} = x_1 + x_2 - 4 + s^2 = 0.$$

$$\frac{\partial L}{\partial s} = 2us = 0.$$

Let us now consider the different cases resulting from the switching conditions.

Case 1: $u = 0 \Rightarrow us = 0.$

$$2(x_1 - 3) + v = 0.$$

$$2(x_2 - 3) - 3v = 0.$$

$$x_1 - 3x_2 - 1 = 0.$$

$$x_1 + x_2 - 4 + s^2 = 0.$$

Solving these four equations, we get $x_1 = 3.7$, $x_2 = 0.9$, $v = -1.4$ and $s^2 = -0.6$. However, $s^2 = -0.6$ is not a valid solution.

Case 2: $s = 0 \Rightarrow us = 0.$

$$2(x_1 - 3) + v + u = 0.$$

$$2(x_2 - 3) - 3v + u = 0.$$

$$x_1 - 3x_2 - 1 = 0.$$

$$x_1 + x_2 - 4 = 0.$$

These equations can be solved to yield $x_1 = 3.25, x_2 = 0.75, v = -1.25$ and $u = 0.75$. This is a valid solution, as $u > 0$ and corresponds to the inequality constraint being active.

Case 3: $s = u = 0 \Rightarrow us = 0.$

$$2(x_1 - 3) + v = 0.$$

$$2(x_2 - 3) - 3v = 0.$$

$$x_1 - 3x_2 - 1 = 0.$$

$$x_1 + x_2 - 4 = 0.$$

Solving the last two equations yields $x_1 = 3.25, x_2 = 0.75$. Putting $(3.25, 0.75)$ in $2(x_1 - 3) + v = 0$, yields $v = -0.5$. However, putting $(3.25, 0.75)$ in $2(x_2 - 3) - 3v = 0$, yields $v = -1.5$. Thus, there is a contradiction and the solution is not a valid solution.

Based on the cases, we see that $\mathbf{x} = (3.25, 0.75)$ represents a candidate minimum point. Obviously, the equality constraint is satisfied at this point as $x_1 - 3x_2 = 3.25 - 3.0.75 = 0$. Also, the inequality constraint is active $x_1 + x_2 - 4 = 3.25 + 0.75 - 4 = 0$. The function value at the candidate minimum point is $f = (3.25 - 3)^2 + (0.75 - 3)^2 = 5.125$.

Example 1.15 Minimize the function $f = x_1^2 + (x_2 + 3)^2$ subject to the constraint, $x_2 \geq e^{2x_1}$.

Solution: The constraint equation can be written in standard form as $e^{2x_1} - x_2 \leq 0$. From this, form the Lagrange function:

$$L = x_1^2 + (x_2 + 3)^2 + u(e^{2x_1} - x_2 + s^2).$$

Taking the gradients and setting them to zero yields:

$$\frac{\partial L}{\partial x_1} = 2x_1 + u2e^{2x_1} = 0.$$

$$\frac{\partial L}{\partial x_2} = 2(x_2 + 3) - u = 0.$$

$$\frac{\partial L}{\partial u} = e^{2x_1} - x_2 + s^2 = 0.$$

$$\frac{\partial L}{\partial s} = 2us = 0.$$

We now look at the cases due to the switching conditions:

Case 1: $s = 0 \Rightarrow us = 0.$

$$x_1 + ue^{2x_1} = 0.$$

$$2x_2 - u + 6 = 0.$$

$$e^{2x_1} - x_2 = 0.$$

Eliminating u from the first two equations yields:

$$x_1 + 2x_2e^{2x_1} + 6e^{2x_1} - x_2 = 0.$$

Putting $x_2 = e^{2x_1}$ in the above equation gives:

$$x_1 + 2e^{4x_1} + 6e^{2x_1} = 0.$$

This can be solved numerically, to yield $x_1 = -0.9474$. Then we get, $x_2 = e^{2x_1} = 0.1503$. The point $(-0.9474, 0.1503)$ corresponds to a candidate minimum point. The inequality constraint is active at this point and the function value is $f = 10.82$.

Case 2: $u = 0 \Rightarrow us = 0.$

$$x_1 = 0.$$

$$2x_2 + 6 = 0.$$

$$e^{2x_1} - x_2 + s^2 = 0.$$

The first two equations yield $x_1 = 0$, $x_2 = -3$. Putting these into the third equation yields $s^2 = -4$, which is not a valid solution.

Case 3: $u = 0, s = 0 \Rightarrow us = 0.$

$$x_1 = 0.$$

$$2x_2 + 6 = 0.$$

$$e^{2x_1} - x_2 = 0.$$

The first two equations yield $x_1 = 0, x_2 = -3$. Putting these into the third equation, $e^0 + 3 = 1 + 3 = 4 \neq 0$. Thus, this case is not a valid solution. The only valid KKT point is given by $(-0.9474, 0.1503)$.

The KKT conditions give candidate optimal points. However, they are necessary but not sufficient conditions and do not give any information about the point being a global minimum. For some problems called convex problems, it is easy to show that the local minimum is also the global minimum.

1.7 Convexity

Global solutions for optimization problems can be found when the objective function is a convex function and the feasible region is a convex set. A set S is convex if for any elements x and y of S, the following condition holds good:[1]

$$\alpha x + (1-\alpha)y \in S \tag{1.54}$$

for all $0 \le \alpha \le 1$. Geometrically, (1.54) means that the convex set should be such that if x and y are in S, the line segment connecting x and y is also in S. Some examples of convex and nonconvex sets are shown in Figure 1.3.

A function f is *convex* on a convex set S if it satisfies

$$f(\alpha x + (1-\alpha)y) \le \alpha f(x) + (1-\alpha) f(y), \tag{1.55}$$

for $0 \le \alpha \le 1$ for all $x, y \in S$. Geometrically, (1.55) means that the line segment connecting points $(x, f(x))$ and $(y, f(y))$ lies on or above the graph of the function, as shown in Figure 1.4. A function is *strictly convex* if $f(\alpha x+(1-\alpha)y) < \alpha f(x)+(1-\alpha)f(y)$ for all $x \neq y$ and $0 < \alpha < 1$, where $x, y \in S$.

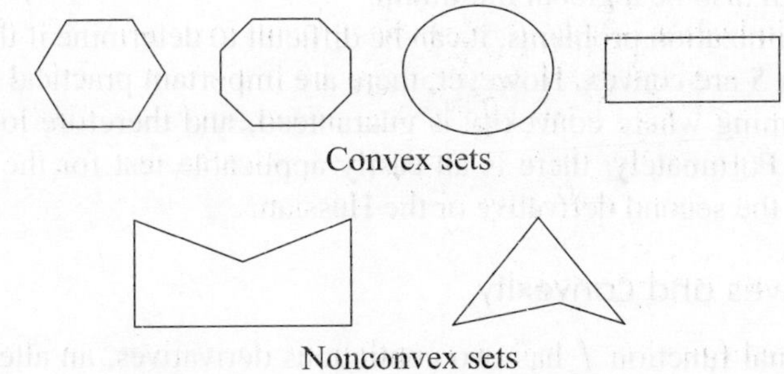

Figure 1.3 *Convex and nonconvex sets*

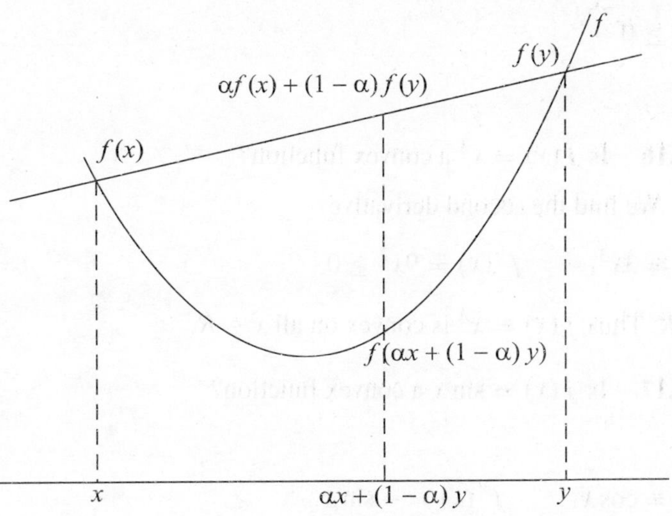

Figure 1.4 *Illustration of convexity of a function*

A function is *concave* on S if it satisfies:

$$f(\alpha x + (1-\alpha)y) \geq \alpha f(x) + (1-\alpha)f(y), \tag{1.56}$$

for $0 \leq \alpha \leq 1$ for all $x, y \in S$. It can be seen from the definitions in (1.55) and (1.56) that linear functions are both convex and concave. Therefore, every set defined by a system of linear constraints is a convex set.

A *convex programming* problem is of the form: Minimize,

$$f(x) \quad x \in S, \tag{1.57}$$

where S is a convex set and f is a convex function on S. Now, we can state the following theorem:[1]

> *If x^* is a local minimizer of a convex programming problem, then x^* is also a global minimizer.*

If the objective function is strictly convex, then x^* is the unique global minimizer. Thus, if one can show that an optimization problem is a convex programming problem, then any local minimum will also be a global minimum.

For general optimization problems, it can be difficult to determine if the function f and the feasible region S are convex. However, there are important practical problems such as in linear programming where convexity is guaranteed, and therefore local minimum are global minimum. Fortunately, there is an easily applicable test for the convexity of the function based on the second derivative or the Hessian.

1.7.1 Derivatives and convexity

If a one-dimensional function f has two continuous derivatives, an alternative definition of convexity can be given which is much easier to check. This is stated as follows:

A function with two continuous derivatives is convex if and only if

$$f''(x) \geq 0 \tag{1.58}$$

for all S.

Example 1.16 Is $f(x) = x^4$ a convex function?

Solution: We find the second derivative

$$f'(x) = 3x^3, \qquad f''(x) = 9x^2 \geq 0$$

for all $x \in R$. Thus $f(x) = x^4$ is convex on all $x \in R$.

Example 1.17 Is $f(x) = \sin x$ a convex function?

Solution:

$$f'(x) = \cos x, \qquad f''(x) = -\sin x.$$

Since $f''(x) = -\sin x$ can be both positive and negative, $f(x) = \sin x$ is not convex.

In the multidimensional case, convexity requires that the Hessian matrix for the function must be positive semidefinite, that is, at each point $\mathbf{x} \in S$

$$\mathbf{y}^{\mathrm{T}}\mathbf{H}(\mathbf{x})\mathbf{y} \geq 0 \tag{1.59}$$

for all $\mathbf{y}$.

Example 1.18 Is $f(x_1, x_2) = 4x_1^2 + 12x_1x_2 + 9x_2^2$ convex?

Solution:

$$\mathbf{y}^{\mathrm{T}}\mathbf{H}\mathbf{y} = (y_1 \quad y_2)\begin{pmatrix} 8 & 12 \\ 12 & 18 \end{pmatrix}\begin{pmatrix} y_1 \\ y_2 \end{pmatrix} = 8y_1^2 + 24y_1y_2 + 18y_2^2 = 2(2y_1 + 3y_2)^2 \geq 0.$$

Therefore, the function is convex.

In the one-dimensional case, if a function satisfies $f''(x) > 0$ for all $x \in S$, it is strictly convex on S.

Example 1.19 Show that $f(x) = x^2$ is strictly convex.

Solution:

$$f'(x) = 2x, \qquad f''(x) = 2 > 0.$$

Thus, $f(x) = x^2$ is strictly convex for all x.

In the multidimensional case, if the Hessian matrix $\mathbf{H}(\mathbf{x})$ is positive definite for all $x \in S$ then the function is strictly convex on S.

1.7.2 Second-order conditions

If a function $f(\mathbf{x})$ is convex in a convex-feasible region then the KKT conditions are necessary as well as sufficient for a global minimum. Note that in this case, first-order KKT conditions are also sufficient conditions.

For a general constrained optimization problem, let $\mathbf{x}^*$ be a KKT point. The second derivative of the Lagrange function at this point is given as follows:[1]

$$\nabla^2 L = \nabla^2 f + \sum_{i=1}^{p} v_i^* \nabla^2 h_i + \sum_{i=1}^{m} u_i^* \nabla^2 g_i. \tag{1.60}$$

Now we define a nonzero feasible direction $\mathbf{d} \neq 0$ such that

$$\nabla^2 h_i^{\mathrm{T}}\mathbf{d} = 0, \tag{1.61}$$

$$\nabla^2 g_i^{\mathrm{T}}\mathbf{d} = 0,$$

where (1.61) are valid for all equalities and for inequalities which have $u_i > 0$. If for any i, $u_i = 0$, the following inequality may be written:

$$\nabla^2 g_i^{\mathrm{T}}\mathbf{d} \leq 0. \tag{1.62}$$

Then, we can state that for $\mathbf{x}^*$ to be an isolated local minimum,

$$\mathbf{d}^{\mathrm{T}}\nabla^2 L(\mathbf{x}^*)\mathbf{d} > 0. \tag{1.63}$$

If the Hessian of the Lagrangian is positive definite at $\mathbf{x}^*$, then (1.63) is satisfied. However, if $\nabla^2 L(\mathbf{x}^*)$ is not positive definite, $\mathbf{x}^*$ can still be an isolated local minimum. In such cases, $\mathbf{d} \neq 0$ must be calculated using the constraints in (1.61) and (1.62), and then the condition $\mathbf{d}^{\mathrm{T}}\nabla^2 L(\mathbf{x}^*)\mathbf{d} > 0$ must be tested.

1.8 Examples in Engineering

In this chapter, we have discussed some of the basics of optimization theory. Before closing, we look at two problems in engineering mechanics and show how a practical design problem may be framed as an optimization problem and then put into the standard optimization form.[1]

Example 1.20 Formulate the problem for minimum weight design of a tubular column as an optimization problem. Such columns are widely used for bearing loads in structural engineering. Consider the column to be cantilevered (fixed at the root and free at the top), having a length L and a circular tube cross-section with inner radius of R_1 and outer radius of R_2. The column must be able to support a load P without buckling or overstressing. To keep the cost down, the thickness of the column should be one-tenth the mean radius, at most. Once the problem is formulated, replace the physical design variables by $x_1, x_2, \ldots, x_n$ and any constants by $c_1, c_2, \ldots, c_n$. Put the problem in the standard form where it appears like a mathematical optimization problem.

Solution: Figure 1.5 shows a schematic diagram of the tubular column. The problem involves minimizing the weight with constraints on strength and column geometry.

The mass of the column is calculated using the formula:

$$f = \rho L A = \pi\rho L(R_2^2 - R_1^2).$$

There is a possibility that the column can fail due to crushing. The crushing constraint can be represented by this inequality:

$$\sigma = \frac{P}{A} \le \sigma_a.$$

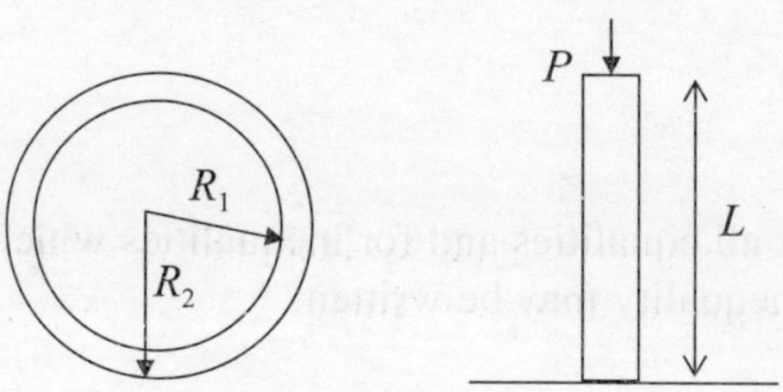

Figure 1.5 *Representation of the tabular column*

Here σ_a is the maximum stress that can be allowed under an axial load. The above constraint can be expressed in terms of the column geometry parameters:

$$\frac{P}{\pi(R_2^2 - R_1^2)} - \sigma_a \le 0.$$

It is also possible that the column can fail by buckling under the applied load P. The buckling load constraint may be written as follows:

$$P \le \frac{\pi^2 EI}{4L^2},$$

where $I = (\pi/4)(R_2^4 - R_1^2)$ is the area moment of inertia of the cross-section. Thus the buckling constraint is given by the following inequality.

$$P \le \frac{\pi^3 EI}{16L^2}(R_2^2 - R_1^2).$$

Since optimization algorithms may take the values of the design variables to unrealistic levels, lower and upper bounds should be applied to some constraints, thereby,

$$R_1^{(\min)} \le R_1 \le R_1^{(\max)}.$$

$$R_2^{(\min)} \le R_2 \le R_2^{(\max)}.$$

$$L^{(\min)} \le L \le L^{(\max)}.$$

In addition, we should ensure mathematically that the outer radius is larger than the inner radius:

$$R_2 \ge R_1.$$

Finally, we need to put a constraint on wall thickness. The mean radius is the following.

$$\bar{R} = \frac{R_1 + R_2}{2}.$$

The wall thickness is given by $t = R_2 - R_1$. Thus the constraint that the wall should be thin can be put as follows.

$$\frac{t}{\bar{R}} = \frac{R_2 - R_1}{\frac{(R_1+R_2)}{2}} \le \frac{1}{10}.$$

The problem has now been converted from a physical problem to a mathematical problem. It can be written in the standard form as follows.

Minimize:

$$f(L, R_1, R_2) = \pi\rho L(R_2^2 - R_1^2),$$

subject to the constraints:

$$g_1(R_1, R_2) = \frac{P}{\pi(R_2^2 - R_1^2)} - \sigma_a \le 0$$

$$g_2(R_1, R_2, L) = P - \frac{\pi^3 EI}{16L^2}(R_2^2 - R_1^2) \le 0$$

$$g_3(R_2) = R_2^{(\min)} - R_2 \le 0$$

$$g_4(R_2) = R_2 - R_2^{(\max)} \le 0$$

$$g_5(R_1) = R_1^{(\min)} - R_1 \le 0$$

$$g_6(R_1) = R_1 - R_1^{(\max)} \le 0$$

$$g_7(R_1, R_2) = \frac{2(R_2 - R_1)}{R_1 + R_2} - \frac{1}{10} \le 0.$$

At this stage, the problem is in the standard form and can be solved by various optimization algorithms. To avoid having problems during the computation when using numerical methods, it is a good idea to normalize all constraints such that their values are similar. This can be done by dividing the inequalities by any positive number, keeping in mind that such an operation does not change the inequality. Any constants in the objective function can be removed by redefining the objective function.

Minimize:

$$\bar{f}(L, R_1, R_2) = \frac{f(L, R_1, R_2)}{\pi\rho} = L(R_2^2 - R_1^2),$$

subject to the conditions:

$$\bar{g}_1(R_1, R_2) = \frac{P}{\pi\sigma_a(R_2^2 - R_1^2)} - 1 \le 0$$

$$g_2(R_1, R_2, L) = 1 - \frac{\pi^3 EI}{16PL^2}(R_2^2 - R_1^2) \le 0$$

$$g_3(R_2) = 1 - \frac{R_2}{R_2^{(\min)}} \le 0$$

$$g_4(R_2) = \frac{R_2}{R_2^{(\max)}} - 1 \le 0$$

$$g_5(R_1) = 1 - \frac{R_1}{R_1^{(\min)}} \le 0$$

$$g_6(R_1) = \frac{R_1}{R_1^{(\max)}} - 1 \le 0$$

$$g_7(R_1, R_2) = \frac{20(R_2 - R_1)}{R_1 + R_2} - 1 \le 0.$$

However, to use optimization algorithms, it is a good idea to place the problem in the standard form in terms of mathematical design variables. Let $x_1 = L$, $x_2 = R_1$ and $x_3 = R_2$ be the design variables in mathematical form. Then the optimization problem becomes the following.

Minimize:

$$\bar{f}(x_1, x_2, x_3) = x_1(x_3^2 - x_2^2),$$

subject to the conditions:

$$\bar{g}_1(x_2, x_3) = \frac{c_1}{(x_3^2 - x_2^2)} - 1 \leq 0$$

$$g_2(x_1, x_2, x_3) = 1 - \frac{c_2}{x_1^2}(x_3^2 - x_2^2) \leq 0$$

$$g_3(x_3) = 1 - \frac{x_3}{x_3^{(\min)}} \leq 0$$

$$g_4(x_3) = \frac{x_3}{x_3^{(\max)}} - 1 \leq 0$$

$$g_5(x_2) = 1 - \frac{x_2}{x_2^{(\min)}} \leq 0$$

$$g_6(x_2) = \frac{x_2}{x_2^{(\max)}} - 1 \leq 0$$

$$g_7(x_{21}, x_3) = \frac{20(x_3 - x_2)}{x_2 + x_3} - 1 \leq 0$$

where the two constants c_1 and c_2 are given by:

$$c_1 = \frac{P}{\pi \sigma_a}, \qquad c_2 = \frac{\pi^3 EI}{16P}.$$

Now the problem has been decoupled from its origin in engineering and has been cast as an optimization problem.

Example 1.21 A beam of rectangular cross-section is subjected to a maximum shear force, V, and a bending moment, M. The fundamental frequency of the beam is ω. The maximum allowable values of bending and shear stresses are σ_a and τ_a, respectively, and the minimum permitted value of the fundamental frequency is ω_a. The bending stress, shear stress and fundamental frequency of the beam are given by the following formulas:

$$\sigma = \frac{6M}{bd^2}, \qquad \tau = \frac{3V}{2bd}, \qquad \omega = 3.516\sqrt{\frac{Ed^2}{12\rho L}}.$$

The allowable stresses on the beam are $\sigma_a = 10\,\text{MPa}$, $\tau_a = 2\,\text{MPa}$, and the minimum natural frequency is $\omega_a = 2400\,\text{rad/s}$. All forcing frequencies acting on the structure are below this value and this bound assures that the phenomenon of resonance does not take place. Also, $L = 1\,\text{m}$, $\rho = 7850\,\text{kg/m}^3$, $E = 210\,\text{GPa}$. We want to design a minimum weight beam under a loading of $M = 40\,\text{kNm}$ and $V = 150\,\text{kN}$. Pose this as an optimization problem and express it in a purely mathematical form.

Solution: The weight of the beam is given by the following equation:

$$f_1(b, d) = \rho b d L.$$

The design variables in this problem are b and d. The constraint equations may be written as follows:

$$\sigma = \frac{6.40 \cdot 10^3}{bd^2} = \frac{240000}{bd^2} \leq 10 \cdot 10^6.$$

$$\tau = \frac{3.150 \cdot 10^3}{2bd} = \frac{225000}{bd} \leq 2 \cdot 10^6.$$

$$\omega = 3.516\sqrt{\frac{210 \cdot 10^9 d^2}{12.7850 \cdot 1^2}} = 5249.68d \leq 2400.$$

Further simplifications of these three inequalities yields

$$1 - 41.66bd^2 \leq 0.$$

$$1 - 8.89bd \leq 0.$$

$$2.1872d - 1 \leq 0.$$

Now, the objective function mathematically depends only on b and d and may be written as $f(b, d) = bd$. We define variables $x_1 = b$, $x_2 = d$. Then, the mathematical optimization problem for beam design may be written.

Minimize:

$$f(x_1, x_2) = x_1 x_2,$$

subject to the following conditions:

$$1 - 41.66x_1x_2^2 \leq 0$$

$$1 - 8.89x_1x_2 \leq 0$$

$$2.1872x_2 - 1 \leq 0.$$

We can see that the problem is a nonlinear constrained optimization problem with two design variables and can be solved by the methods discussed in this chapter.

Problems

1. Expand e^x as a Maclaurin series. Estimate the value of $e^{0.5}$, e^2 and e^5 using this series to get 1 per cent accuracy with respect to the exact values. How many terms are required to achieve this accuracy level? Repeat the problem by using a Taylor series expansion of e^x about $x = 2.5$? Comment on your results.

2. Expand $f = \sqrt{x}$ about $x = 1, 2$ and 4 to second order. Plot the function and the approximation and comment on your results.
3. Expand the following function in a Taylor series about $(1, 1)$ up to two terms:

$$f(\mathbf{x}) = x_1 e^{(x_1 + x_2^3)}.$$

4. Expand the following function in a Taylor series about $(1, 2)$ up to two terms:

$$f(\mathbf{x}) = x_1^4 + x_2^4 + 4x_1^3 x_2^3.$$

5. Expand the Rosenbrock function $f(\mathbf{x}) = 100(x_2 - x_1^2)^2 + (1 - x_1)^2$ about $(1, 1)$ as a Taylor series retaining (a) two terms and (b) three terms. Compare these approximations in the vicinity of $(1, 1)$ with the actual function. Comment on your results.
6. Find a cubic polynomial with a minimum at 5 and a maximum at -5.
7. Find the stationary points of the following function and determine if they are minima, maxima or points of inflection:

$$f(x) = x^4 - 6x^3 + 3x^2 + 10x.$$

Verify your results graphically.

8. What are the stationary points of the function f as a function of the scalar c.

$$f(\mathbf{x}) = cx_1^2 + \frac{1}{2}x_2^2 - 2x_1 x_2 - 4x_2.$$

For what value or values of c is the point a minima, maxima or a point of inflection?

9. Find the stationary points of the function:

$$f(x_1, x_2) = (x_1^2 - x_2^2)e^{-(x_1^2 + x_2^2)}.$$

Determine whether the points are minima, maxima or points of inflection. Plot the function to verify your results. Conduct an exhaustive search of the design space by creating a grid in terms of the two design variables, and write a computer program to find the minimum and maximum points. Comment on your results.

10. Solve the following problem using optimality criteria:
Minimize $f(x_1, x_2) = x_1^4 + x_2^4$ subject to $x_1 + 8x_2 = 32$.
11. Solve the following problem using optimality criteria:
Minimize e^x subject to $1 - x^2 \geq 0$.
12. Minimize $f(\mathbf{x}) = x_1^2 + 15x_2^2 - x_1 x_2$ subject to $x_1 + x_2 - 4 = 0$.
13. Minimize $f(\mathbf{x}) = x_1^2 + 15x_2^2 - x_1 x_2$ subject to $x_1 + x_2 \geq 4$.
14. Consider the problem:
Minimize $f(\mathbf{x}) = x_2$,
subject to the conditions:

$$x_1^2 + x_2^2 \geq 1$$

$$x_1^2 + x_2^2 \leq 4$$

Graphically show the feasible region and find the minimum point. Solve the problem using KKT conditions and verify your answer with the graph.

15. Solve for candidate minimum points using KKT conditions.
Minimize x_1,
subject to the conditions:

$$x_1^2 + x_2^2 \le 4$$

$$x_1^2 \ge 1.$$

16. Solve for candidate minimum points using KKT conditions.
Minimize x_1,
subject to the conditions:

$$(x_1 + 1)^2 + x_2^2 \ge 1$$

$$x_1^2 + x_2^2 \le 2.$$

17. Solve the following problem for candidate minimum points.
Minimize $x_1 + x_2$,
subject to the conditions:

$$(x_1 - 1)^2 + x_2^2 \le 2$$

$$(x_1 + 1)^2 + x_2^2 \ge 2.$$

18. Solve the problem using KKT conditions,

$$f(\mathbf{x}) = x_1 x_2 x_3,$$

subject to the conditions:

$$\frac{x_1}{2} + \frac{x_2}{3} + \frac{x_3}{4} \le 1.$$

19. Consider a linear programming problem and minimize

$$f(\mathbf{x}) = \mathbf{c}^{\mathrm{T}}\mathbf{x},$$

subject to $\mathbf{Ax} \ge \mathbf{b}$.
Write the KKT conditions.

20. Minimize:

$$f(\mathbf{x}) = x_1 x_2,$$

subject to

$$\frac{x_1}{a} + \frac{x_2}{b} = 1.$$

21. Find if the following functions are convex.

(a) $f(x, y) = x^4 + y^6$
(b) $f(x, y) = x^2 y^2$
(c) e^{x^2}
(d) $\sqrt{1 + x^2}$

22. Show that the intersection of two convex sets is a convex set.
23. Does the following represent a convex programming problem?
Minimize:

$$f = \mathrm{e}^{-x^2},$$

subject to the condition: $x \geq 1$.
24. Find the minimum point of the generalized Rosenbrock function given below:

$$f(\mathbf{x}) = a(x_2 - x_1^2)^2 + (1 - x_1)^2.$$

Here $a > 0$.
25. Find the minimum point of the following function:

$$f(\mathbf{x}) = \frac{3}{2}x_1^2 + 2x_2^3 + \frac{3}{2}x_3^2 + x_1x_3 + 3x_2x_3 - 3x_1 - x_3 + 10.$$

26. Find the four minimum points for the modified Himmelblau function given below:

$$f(\mathbf{x}) = (x_1^2 + x_2 - 11)^2 + (x_1 + x_2^2 - 7)^2.$$

Plot the function and check your result.
27. Consider the Matlab peaks function:

$$f(x, y) = 3(1 - x)^2\mathrm{e}^{-x^2-(y+1)^2} - 10\left(\frac{x}{5} - x^3 - y^5\right)\mathrm{e}^{-x^2-y^2} - \frac{\mathrm{e}^{-(x+1)^2-y^2}}{3}.$$

Find the minimum point of the function. Plot the function and check your result.
28. Find the minimum point for the following function:

$$f(\mathbf{x}) = x_1^2 + 2x_2^2 + 3x_3^2 + \cdots + nx_n^2 + \mathrm{e}^{-x_1-x_2-x_3-\cdots-x_n}.$$

Obtain a general result for the necessary condition and then obtain results for $n =$ 3, 10, 50, 100 and 500.
29. Find the stationary points of the following function using optimality criteria. Check if they are minimum points, maximum points or points of inflection:

$$f = 100(x_2 - x_1^2)^2 + (1 - x_1)^2 + 90(x_4 - x_3^2)^2 + (1 - x_3)^2$$
$$+ 10.1[(x_2 - 1)^2 + (x_4 - 1)^2] + 19.8(x_2 - 1)(x_4 - 1).$$

30. Solve the column design problem in Example 1.20 for the following numerical values using the KKT conditions. Verify your results graphically. $P = 150\,\mathrm{kN}$, $L = 5.2\,\mathrm{m}$, $E = 210\,\mathrm{Gpa}$, $\sigma_a = 250\,\mathrm{MPa}$, $\rho = 7850\,\mathrm{kg/m^3}$ and the move limits are given by:

$$0.2 \leq R_1 \leq 0.6\,\mathrm{m}$$

$$0.2 \leq R_2 \leq 0.6\,\mathrm{m}.$$

31. Solve the beam design problem in Example 1.21 using the KKT conditions and verify the results graphically.

2 Direct One-Dimensional Search

In Chapter 1, we discussed indirect methods in optimization which were based on the optimality criteria. Though these methods are typically applicable to simple analytical functions, they can also be very useful when solving optimization problems using the response surface methods, where the relationship between objective function and design variables obtained from a complex computer code is expressed by polynomial approximations. However, for many problems, the direct search approach is a fast and convenient numerical method. In this chapter, we introduce the direct search method and discuss a vital element of the direct search method—the one-dimensional search.

2.1 General Numerical Optimization Algorithm

The numerical optimization proceeds iteratively using the following general design variable update rule to move from iteration k to $k+1$.[4]

$$\mathbf{x}^{(k+1)} = \mathbf{x}^{(k)} + \Delta\mathbf{x}^{(k)}. \tag{2.1}$$

The change in design variable may be written as

$$\Delta\mathbf{x}^{(k)} = \alpha_k \mathbf{d}^{(k)}. \tag{2.2}$$

Here $\mathbf{d}^{(k)}$ is the search direction and α_k is a positive scalar called the step size in the search direction. Figure 2.1 shows how the candidate optimal point moves from point A to point B and then from point B to point C by moving α_k along the vector $\mathbf{d}^{(k)}$.

2.1.1 Descent condition

We want to select $\mathbf{d}^{(k)}$ such that the function decreases from iteration k to $k+1$.

$$f(\mathbf{x}^{(k+1)}) < f(\mathbf{x}^{(k)}). \tag{2.3}$$

$$\Rightarrow f(\mathbf{x}^{(k)} + \Delta\mathbf{x}^{(k)}) < f(\mathbf{x}^{(k)}). \tag{2.4}$$

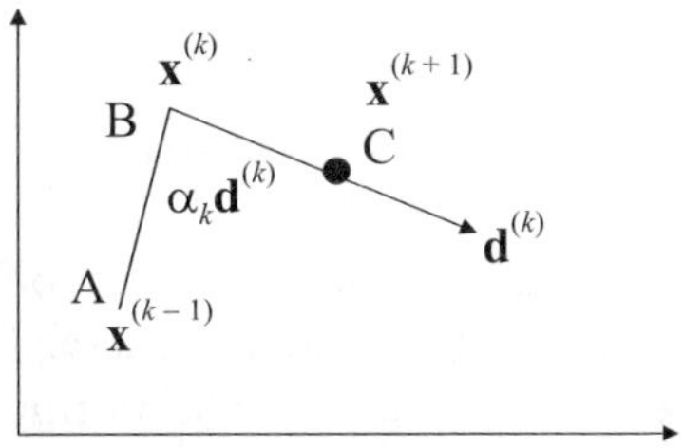

Figure 2.1 *Descent direction and line search*

Using a linear Taylor series approximation of the right-hand side in (2.4) yields the following condition:

$$f(\mathbf{x}^{(k)}) + \alpha_k(\mathbf{c}^{(k)} \cdot \mathbf{d}^{(k)}) < f(\mathbf{x}^{(k)})$$
$$\Rightarrow \alpha_k(\mathbf{c}^{(k)} \cdot \mathbf{d}^{(k)}) < 0. \tag{2.5}$$

Since $\alpha_k > 0$, the descent condition is yielded by (2.5) as given below:

$$\mathbf{c}^{(k)} \cdot \mathbf{d}^{(k)} < 0. \tag{2.6}$$

The descent condition must be satisfied by a search direction obtained from any optimization algorithm.

Example 2.1 Show that $\mathbf{d}^{(k)} = -\mathbf{c}^{(k)}$ is a descent direction.

Solution: $\mathbf{c}^{(k)} \cdot \mathbf{d}^{(k)} = -\mathbf{c}^{(k)} \cdot \mathbf{c}^{(k)} < 0.$

This is the basis of the steepest descent algorithm which will be discussed further in Chapter 3.

When a gradient-based search algorithm for minimization is proposed, one should first check if it satisfies the descent condition.

2.1.2 Step-size determination

The iterative formula $\mathbf{x}^{(k+1)} = \mathbf{x}^{(k)} + \alpha_k\mathbf{d}^{(k)}$ is based on finding a search direction $\mathbf{d}^{(k)}$ which satisfies the descent condition $\mathbf{c}^{(k)} \cdot \mathbf{d}^{(k)} < 0$ and an appropriate positive step size α_k. We first look at the determination of α_k: this process is called the step-size determination or one-dimensional search.

Assume that the search direction $\mathbf{d}^{(k)}$ has been found at point $\mathbf{x}^{(k)}$. Then

$$f(\mathbf{x}^{(k+1)}) = f(\mathbf{x}^{(k)} + \alpha_k\mathbf{d}^{(k)}) = f(\alpha). \tag{2.7}$$

If $\mathbf{x}^{(k)}$ is not a minimum point, then

$$f(\mathbf{x}^{(k+1)}) < f(\mathbf{x}^{(k)}). \tag{2.8}$$

However,

$$f(\mathbf{x}^{(k)}) = f(\mathbf{x}^{(k)} + 0\mathbf{d}^{(k)}) = f(0). \tag{2.9}$$

Substituting (2.7) and (2.9) into (2.8), we can write

$$f(\alpha) < f(0). \tag{2.10}$$

From (2.10), we can deduce that if $\mathbf{x}^{(k)}$ is not a minimum point, then it is possible to find a descent direction $\mathbf{d}^{(k)}$ and move along it by distance α such that the function value is further reduced. As Figure 2.2 shows, the descent condition implies that the one-dimensional search problem in optimization must have a minimum point at some $\alpha > 0$ unless $\mathbf{x}^{(k)}$ is a minimum point; in which case, $\alpha = 0$.

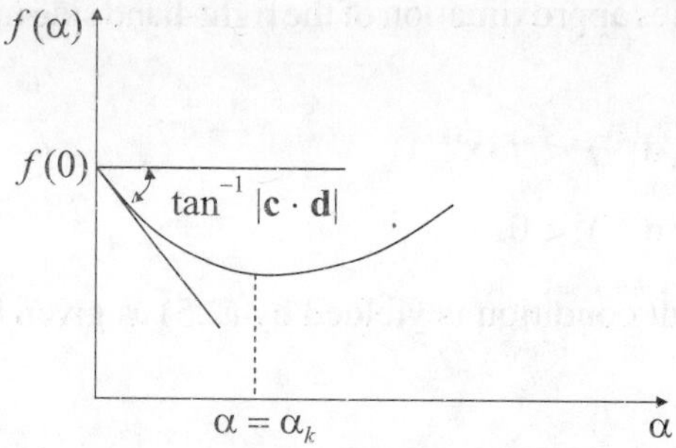

Figure 2.2 *Graphical representation of one-dimensional search in optimization*

2.1.3 Analytical methods to calculate step size

If the analytical expression of $f(\alpha)$ is available, we can use the necessary and sufficient conditions for minimization derived in Chapter 1. The necessary condition is that $f'(\alpha) = 0$ and the sufficient condition is that $f''(\alpha) > 0$.

2.1.4 Line search termination criteria

The line search should be terminated when the minimum point of $f(\alpha)$ has been found. We shall see that this condition leads to an important relationship between the gradient vector and the search direction of the optimization problem. Consider,

$$f(\mathbf{x}^{(k+1)}) = f(\mathbf{x}^{(k)} + \alpha_k \mathbf{d}^{(k)}) = f(\alpha). \tag{2.11}$$

Differentiating (2.11) with respect to α,

$$\frac{df(\mathbf{x}^{(k+1)})}{d\alpha} = \frac{df(\mathbf{x}^{(k+1)})}{d\mathbf{x}} \frac{d(\mathbf{x}^{(k+1)})}{d\alpha} = \mathbf{c}^{(k+1)} \cdot \mathbf{d}^{(k)} = 0. \tag{2.12}$$

Chain-rule differentiation is used to obtain the line search termination condition and shows that the search direction in the kth iteration must be normal to the gradient at the $(k+1)$th iteration. This criterion can be used to terminate the line search criteria when numerical step search methods are used. Also note that

$$f'(0) = \mathbf{c}^{(k+1)}(\alpha = 0) \cdot \mathbf{d}^{(k)}(\alpha = 0) = \mathbf{c}^{(k)} \cdot \mathbf{d}^{(k)} < 0. \tag{2.13}$$

We can see from (2.13) that at $\alpha = 0$, the slope $f'(0) < 0$, as can be seen from Figure 2.2.

Example 2.2 Determine whether $\mathbf{d} = (-2, 2)$, $\mathbf{d} = (2, -2)$ and $\mathbf{d} = (1, 0)$ are descent directions at $\mathbf{x} = (1, 1)$ for the function $f(\mathbf{x}) = (x_1 - 2)^2 + x_2^2$.

Solution: Now, $\mathbf{d}$ is a descent direction if $\mathbf{c} \cdot \mathbf{d} < 0$

$$\mathbf{c} = \begin{Bmatrix} \frac{\partial f}{\partial x_1} \\ \frac{\partial f}{\partial x_2} \end{Bmatrix} = \begin{Bmatrix} 2(x_1 - 2) \\ 2x_2 \end{Bmatrix} = \begin{Bmatrix} -2 \\ 2 \end{Bmatrix}.$$

$$\mathbf{c} \cdot \mathbf{d} = (-2 \quad 2) \begin{pmatrix} -2 \\ 2 \end{pmatrix} = 8 > 0.$$

Thus, $\mathbf{d} = (-2, 2)$ is not a descent direction. Now consider the direction $\mathbf{d} = (2, -2)$.

$$\mathbf{c} \cdot \mathbf{d} = (-2 \quad 2) \begin{pmatrix} 2 \\ -2 \end{pmatrix} = -8 < 0.$$

Thus, $\mathbf{d} = (2, -2)$ is a descent direction. It can also be seen that $\mathbf{d} = (2, -2)$ corresponds to the direction of steepest descent as $\mathbf{d} = -\mathbf{c}$.

Now consider $\mathbf{d} = (1, 0)$,

$$\mathbf{c} \cdot \mathbf{d} = (-2 \quad 2) \begin{pmatrix} 1 \\ 0 \end{pmatrix} = -2 < 0.$$

Thus, $\mathbf{d} = (1, 0)$ is also a descent direction. For a given function and point, many different descent directions are possible.

Example 2.3 For the function $f(\mathbf{x}) = 0.1x_1^2 + x_2^2 - 10$, find the step size, given the search direction $\mathbf{d} = (-1, 0)$ and the current point $\mathbf{x} = (5, 1)$.

Solution: We should first determine whether $\mathbf{d} = (-1, 0)$ is a descent direction.

$$\mathbf{c} = \begin{Bmatrix} \frac{\partial f}{\partial x_1} \\ \frac{\partial f}{\partial x_2} \end{Bmatrix} = \begin{Bmatrix} 0.2x_1 \\ 2x_2 \end{Bmatrix} = \begin{Bmatrix} 1 \\ 2 \end{Bmatrix}.$$

Therefore, $\mathbf{c} \cdot \mathbf{d} = (1 \; 2)\begin{pmatrix} -1 \\ 0 \end{pmatrix} = -1 < 0$ is a descent direction. The next design point is,

$$\mathbf{x}^{(k+1)} = \mathbf{x}^{(k)} + \alpha \mathbf{d}^{(k)}.$$

$$\begin{Bmatrix} x_1 \\ x_2 \end{Bmatrix}^{(k+1)} = \begin{Bmatrix} 5 \\ 1 \end{Bmatrix} + \alpha \begin{Bmatrix} -1 \\ 0 \end{Bmatrix} = \begin{Bmatrix} 5 - \alpha \\ 1 \end{Bmatrix}.$$

$$x_1 = 5 - \alpha, \qquad x_2 = 1.$$

$$f(\mathbf{x}) = 0.1x_1^2 + x_2^2 - 10 = 0.1(5 - \alpha)^2 + 1 - 10$$

$$= 0.1\alpha^2 - \alpha - 6.5 = f(\alpha).$$

We need to find the value of α which minimizes $f(\alpha)$,

$$f'(\alpha) = 0.2\alpha - 1 = 0 \Rightarrow \alpha = 5$$

$$f''(\alpha) = 0.2 > 0 \Rightarrow \text{minimum point, convex function}$$

$$\begin{Bmatrix} x_1 \\ x_2 \end{Bmatrix}^{(k+1)} = \begin{Bmatrix} 5 \\ 1 \end{Bmatrix} + 5 \begin{Bmatrix} -1 \\ 0 \end{Bmatrix} = \begin{Bmatrix} 0 \\ 1 \end{Bmatrix}.$$

We can now check some of the values to see how the function simplifies in the descent direction.

$$f(\mathbf{x}^{(k+1)}) = -9, \qquad f(\alpha = 5) = -9$$

$$f(\mathbf{x}^{(k)}) = -6.5, \qquad f(\alpha = 0) = -6.5$$

$$f'(0) = -1.$$

Thus, we see that the function decreases after the iteration. We also note the equivalence between the one-dimensional problem and the multivariate problem, and the fact that $f(\alpha) < f(0)$ and $f'(0) < 0$.

2.2 Numerical Methods to Calculate Step Size

For most real optimization problems, it is not possible to explicitly obtain the function $f(\alpha)$. Therefore, a numerical method must be used to find α_k to minimize $f(\mathbf{x})$ along the direction $\mathbf{d}^{(k)}$. One-dimensional search methods allow us to determine the minimizer of a function over a closed interval (α_l, α_u). They typically assume that the function is *unimodal*. A unimodal function is one that has a unique minimum in the interval of interest. The assumption of a unimodal function is reasonable if we have selected a descent direction. We want to determine the location of the minimum within (α_l, α_u) which is called the *interval of uncertainty*, shown in Figure 2.3. Thus, we have[1]

$$I = \alpha_u - \alpha_l \tag{2.14}$$

The aim of the one-dimensional search is to reduce the interval of uncertainty I until it is less than a small number ε, i.e., $I < \varepsilon$. Once the interval has been sufficiently reduced,

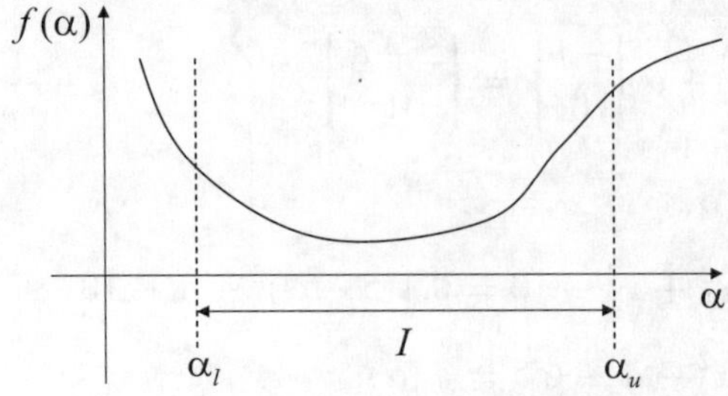

Figure 2.3 *Interval of uncertainty*

$\alpha^* = 0.5(\alpha_l + \alpha_u)$ is chosen as the minimum point of $f(\alpha)$. Methods based on reducing the interval of uncertainty are called *interval-reducing methods.* Most interval-reducing methods are zero-order methods in which gradient evaluation is not needed for the calculation. The simplest such method is the *equal-interval search.*

2.3 Equal-Interval Search

In this method, we start with an interval $\alpha = [0, \bar{\alpha}]$ and divide it into equal intervals of size δ each. We evaluate $f(\alpha)$ at several points on a uniform grid where δ is a small number. These points are then given by $\alpha = \delta, 2\delta, 3\delta, \ldots (q-1)\delta, q\delta, (q+1)\delta, \ldots$ as shown in Figure 2.4.

Compare values at every set of three successive points $q-1$, q and $q+1$. There are two possible cases:

1. If $f(q\delta) > f((q+1)\delta)$, then the minimum point has not yet been surpassed.
2. If $f(q\delta) < f((q+1)\delta)$, then the minimum point has been surpassed.

If the condition (1) is true, then the function evaluation should be continued until condition (2) becomes true. If the condition (2) is true, then the minimum of the function is to be found either between $q-1$ and q or q and $q+1$. These two possibilities are shown in Figure 2.5. The minimum is therefore *bracketed* between $q-1$ and $q+1$.

$$\alpha_l = (q-1)\delta, \qquad \alpha_u = (q+1)\delta. \tag{2.15}$$

$$I = \alpha_u - \alpha_l = 2\delta. \tag{2.16}$$

The interval of uncertainty has been reduced from $I = \bar{\alpha}$ to $I = 2\delta$. To further reduce the interval of uncertainty, the following two steps must be carried out:

1. Restart the search process from $\alpha = \alpha_l$ to $\alpha = \alpha_u$ and use a finer grid in δ, say $r\delta$, where $r \ll 1$.

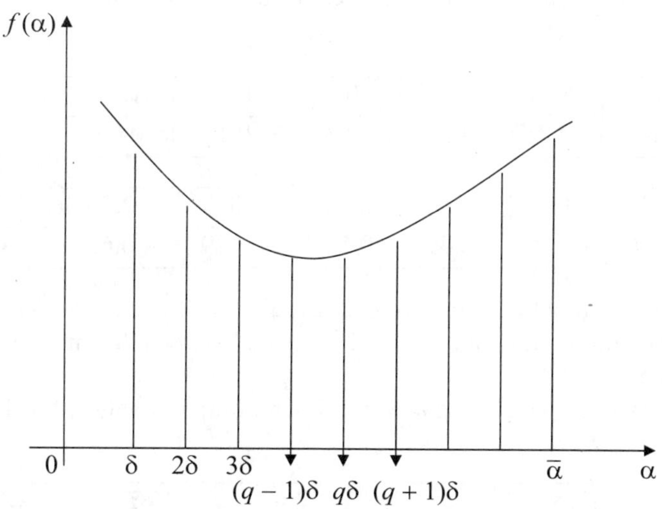

Figure 2.4 *Illustration of equal-interval search method*

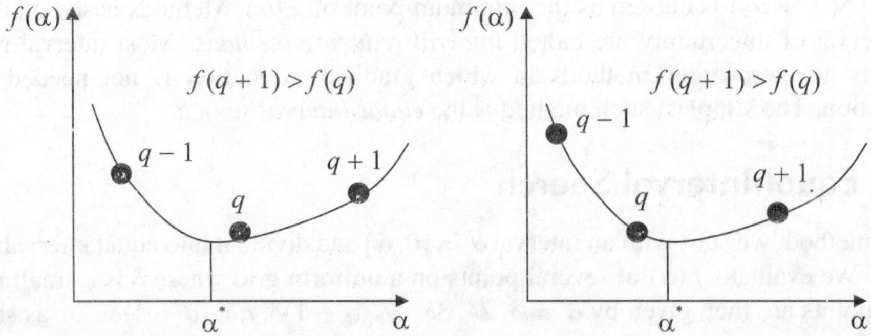

Figure 2.5 *Bracketing the minimum in equal-interval search*

2. Again bracket the minimum point. If $I < \varepsilon$ then stop, else go to 1 with the new lower and upper bounds.

Though it is simple conceptually, this method is not efficient because it can take many function evaluations before we finally arrive at the minimum. It is good to start with a large δ (coarse grid) and quickly bracket the minimum point. After that, the finer grids can be used to further zoom in on the minimum point. Although we have discussed the method given above with the point $\bar{\alpha}$ as a requirement, the algorithm can proceed without any $\bar{\alpha}$. This is because the bracketing of the minimum will be done between $(q-1)\delta$ and $(q+1)\delta$. Therefore, the equal-interval method can be used once δ has been selected. However, the appropriate selection of δ for different functions and problems is a challenge and the efficiency of the method strongly depends on this selection.

Example 2.4 Find the minimum point of the function $f(\alpha) = 2 - \alpha - \ln(3.638 - \alpha)$ using the equal-interval search.

Solution: Let us select $\delta = 0.25$ to do the initial bracketing. The values of the function for this coarse grid are shown below (Entries for α and $f(\alpha)$ in the grid are presented in two rows due to lack of space.):

α	0	0.25	0.5	0.75	1.0	1.25
$f(\alpha)$	0.71	0.53	0.36	0.19	0.03	−0.12

1.5	1.75	2.0	2.25	**2.5**	**2.75**	**3**
−0.26	−0.39	−0.49	−0.58	−0.629	−0.631	−0.55

We can see that the function value decreases until $\alpha = 3$. Thus, $q+1 \rightarrow 3$ and $q \rightarrow 2.75$, $q-1 \rightarrow 2.5$. The minimum point is now bracketed between 2.5 and 3 and the interval of uncertainty is 0.5.

In the next iteration, we choose $\delta = 0.05$. The function values for this finer grid are shown below:

α	2.5	2.55	**2.6**	**2.65**	**2.7**
$f(\alpha)$	−0.62927	−0.63434	**−0.6273**	**−0.63793**	**−0.63599**

Note that we stop the iterations as soon as the function value shows an increase. Now we have, $q+1 \rightarrow 2.7$ and $q \rightarrow 2.65$, $q-1 \rightarrow 2.6$. The minimum point is now bracketed between 2.6 and 2.7 and the interval of uncertainty is 0.1.

In the next iteration, we choose $\delta = 0.01$. We now get the function values as shown below:

α	2.6	2.61	2.62	**2.63**	**2.64**	**2.65**
$f(\alpha)$	−0.637296	−0.637615	−0.637840	**−0.637968**	**−0.637998**	**−0.637927**

Now we have, $q+1 \rightarrow 2.65$ and $q \rightarrow 2.64$, $q-1 \rightarrow 2.63$. The minimum point is now bracketed between 2.63 and 2.65 and the interval of uncertainty is 0.02.

Let us perform a final iteration to find the minimum. We select $\delta = 0.005$ and get the following function values.

α	2.63	**2.635**	**2.64**	**2.645**
$f(\alpha)$	−0.6379682	**−0.6379955**	**−0.6379980**	**−0.6379754**

Now we have, $q+1 \rightarrow 2.645$ and $q \rightarrow 2.64$, $q-1 \rightarrow 2.635$. The minimum point is now bracketed between 2.635 and 2.645 and the interval of uncertainty is 0.01. We can continue to further refine the grid to reduce the interval of uncertainty, or we can stop at this point and take the minimum point as $\alpha^* \approx (\alpha_{q+1} + \alpha_{q-1})/2 = 2.64$, which is close to 2.368, the exact solution.

The level of refinement we should do in a one-dimensional search depends on the optimization algorithm being used to calculate the search direction **d**. Some algorithms require an *accurate* line search while others are robust to a *sloppy* line search. Many function evaluations can be saved if the optimization algorithm can tolerate a sloppy line search.

2.4 Golden-Section Search

We can intuitively see that the equal-interval search could be improved by taking larger steps at each interval until the minimum is bracketed. A variable-interval search method like the *golden-section search* is one such method where the step sizes increase as α increases, and the minimum is bracketed. In the golden-section search, r in $r\delta$ is selected as the golden ratio = 1.618, which is an approximation to three decimal places for the irrational number. We take a small detour to explain the golden ratio.

The *golden ratio* is a number which occurs in many places in number theory. It is also called the *divine proportion* or the *golden mean*. This number is often encountered when taking the ratio of distances in geometric figures such as the pentagon, decagon etc. For example, consider the definition given by Euclid in 300 BC who defined it using a line segment. Consider the line segment AB shown in Figure 2.6. Find a point C between A and B such that

$$\tau = \frac{\text{AC}}{\text{CB}} = \frac{\text{AB}}{\text{AC}}. \tag{2.17}$$

Then we get

$$\tau = \frac{\tau + 1}{\tau}. \tag{2.18}$$

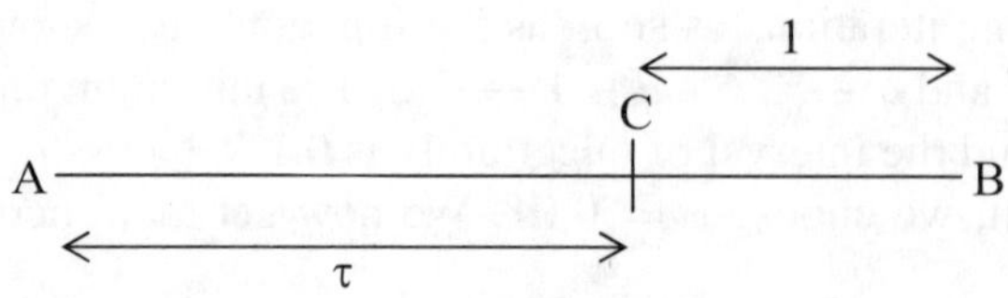

Figure 2.6 *Euclid's line section definition of the golden ratio*

This leads to

$$\tau^2 - \tau - 1 = 0. \tag{2.19}$$

We can solve this equation to get the value

$$\tau = \frac{1+\sqrt{5}}{2}. \tag{2.20}$$

We calculate the golden ratio using (2.20) and find that it equals 1.61803399 to eight decimal places.

The golden ratio can also be obtained from the Fibonacci sequence.

$$F_n = F_{n-1} + F_{n-2}, \qquad n = 2, 3, 4 \ldots$$

$$F_0 = 1, \qquad F_1 = 1. \tag{2.21}$$

The Fibonacci sequence is: 1, 1, 2, 3, 5, 8, 13, 21, 34, 55, 85, ... An interesting property of this sequence is that the ratio of subsequent numbers in the sequence converges to a fixed number at infinity,

$$\frac{F_n}{F_{n-1}} \to \frac{\sqrt{5}+1}{2} = 1.618 \quad as\ n \to \infty. \tag{2.22}$$

The reciprocal of the golden ratio may also be calculated:

$$\frac{F_{n-1}}{F_n} \to \frac{2}{\sqrt{5}+1} = 0.618 \quad \text{as } n \to \infty. \tag{2.23}$$

There are many such situations where the golden ratio occurs in mathematics. We now return to the golden-section method. The basic philosophy of the golden-section search method is as follows.

1. Start at $\alpha = 0$. Evaluate $f(\alpha)$ at $\alpha = \delta$, where $\delta > 0$ is a small number. Again, the user must select an appropriate δ.
2. Take an increment 1.618δ in the step size and evaluate functions at the following points and compare them

$$q = 0; \qquad \alpha_0 = \delta \tag{2.24}$$

$$q = 1; \qquad \alpha_1 = \delta + 1.618\delta = 2.618\delta = \sum_{j=0}^{1} \delta(1.618)^j \tag{2.25}$$

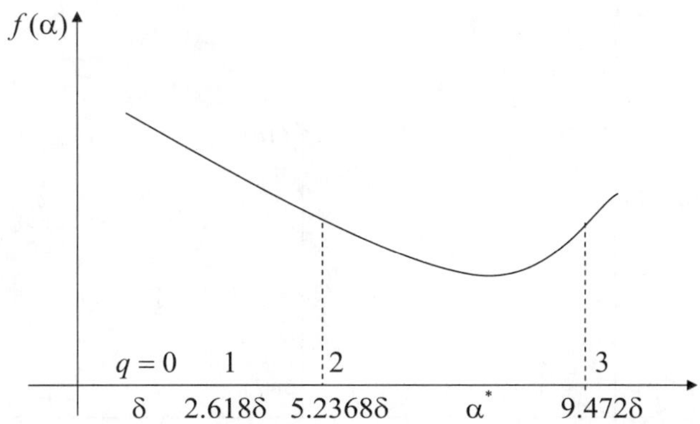

Figure 2.7 *Illustration of the golden-section search*

$$q = 2; \qquad \alpha_2 = 2.618\delta + 1.618(1.618\delta) = 5.236\delta = \sum_{j=0}^{2} \delta(1.618)^j$$

$$\vdots$$

$$q; \qquad \sum_{j=0}^{q} \delta(1.618)^j, \quad q = 0, 1, 2, \ldots \tag{2.26}$$

The golden-section search accelerates as the steps unfold: $(\delta, 2.618\delta, 5.236\delta, 9.4718\delta, \ldots)$ while the equal-interval search moves forward with a constant velocity $(\delta, 2\delta, 3\delta, 4\delta, \ldots)$. Thus, the golden-section search can bracket the minimum point more efficiently as can be seen from Figure 2.7. However, the initial interval of uncertainty obtained by the golden-section search is likely to be larger than that obtained by the equal-interval search.

Let us assume that the function at α_{q-1} is smaller than at α_{q-2} and α_q, i.e.,[1]

$$f(\alpha_{q-1}) < f(\alpha_{q-2}) \quad \text{and} \quad f(\alpha_{q-1}) < f(\alpha_q). \tag{2.27}$$

This situation is shown in Figure 2.8. The minimum point then lies between α_{q-2} and α_q and we can write the new interval bounds:

$$\alpha_u = \alpha_q = \sum_{j=0}^{q} \delta(1.618)^j. \tag{2.28}$$

$$\alpha_l = \alpha_{q-2} = \sum_{j=0}^{q-2} \delta(1.618)^j. \tag{2.29}$$

Now, the interval of uncertainty is

$$I = \alpha_u - \alpha_l. \tag{2.30}$$

$$I = \sum_{j=0}^{q} \delta(1.618)^j - \sum_{j=0}^{q-2} \delta(1.618)^j. \tag{2.31}$$

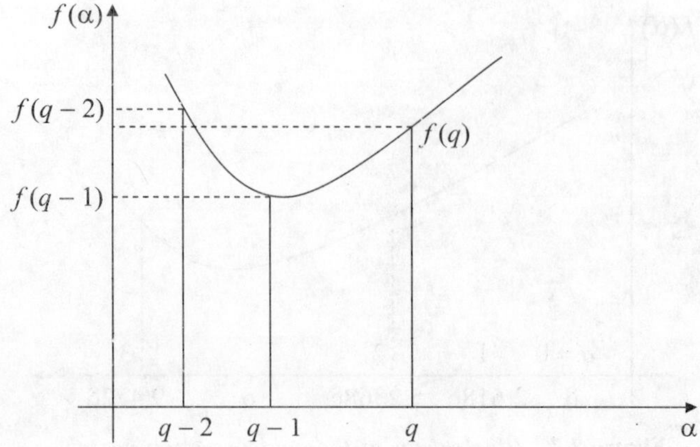

Figure 2.8 *Bracketing the minimum in the golden-section search*

$$I = \delta(1.618)^q + \delta(1.618)^{q-1}.$$

$$I = \delta(1.618)^{q-1}[1 + 1.618].$$

$$I = 2.618(1.618)^{q-1}\delta. \tag{2.32}$$

Note from (2.32) that as q becomes large, the interval of uncertainty will increase in width. Once the interval has been bracketed, it needs to be reduced.

2.4.1 Reduction in the interval of uncertainty

Let α_a and α_b be two points located at a distance τI from either end as shown in Figure 2.9. Comparing values of $f(\alpha_l)$ and $f(\alpha_u)$, either the left or right of (α_a, α_b) will get discarded. There are two possible cases:

1. If $f(\alpha_a) > f(\alpha_b)$, then (α_a, α_u) is the new interval.
2. If $f(\alpha_a) < f(\alpha_b)$, (α_l, α_b) is the new interval.

These situations are shown in Figure 2.10.

Assume that the right-hand side gets discarded, so α_l^1 and α_u^1 are the new lower and upper bounds of the minimum.

Then,

$$I^1 = \tau I. \tag{2.33}$$

Since $f(\alpha_u^1)$ is known,

$$\tau I^1 = (1 - \tau)I. \tag{2.34}$$

From (2.33) and (2.34), we get

$$\tau(\tau I) = (1 - \tau)I, \tag{2.35}$$

or

$$\tau^2 + \tau - 1 = 0$$

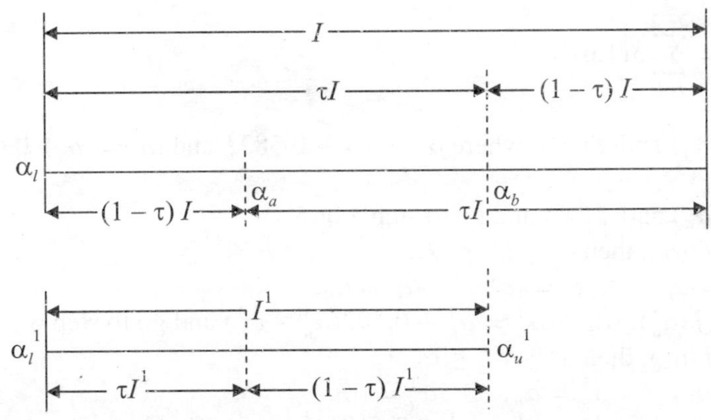

Figure 2.9 *Reduction in interval of uncertainty in the golden-section search*

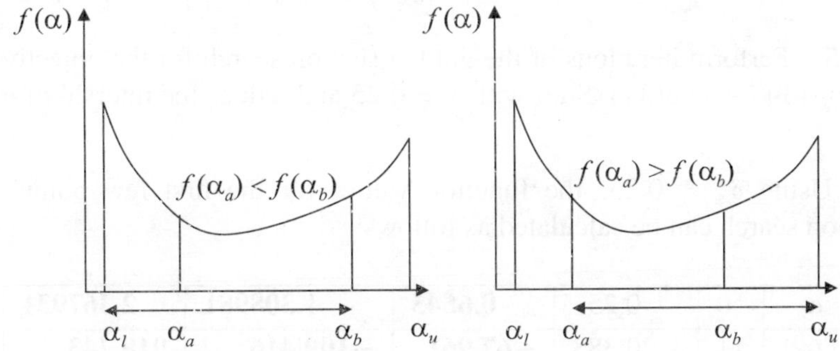

Figure 2.10 *Interval reduction in the golden-section method*

$$\rightarrow \tau = \frac{\sqrt{5}-1}{2} = \frac{\sqrt{5}+1}{\sqrt{5}+1}\frac{\sqrt{5}-1}{2} = \frac{2}{\sqrt{5}+1} = 0.618. \quad (2.36)$$

The positive root of the above quadratic equation is the one with physical significance in this problem and is the reciprocal of the golden ratio.

Thus the two points (α_a, α_b) are located at $0.618I$ or $0.382I$ from either end of the interval.

2.4.2 Golden-section search algorithm

1. For a small step size δ is α, let q be the smallest integer which satisfies

$$f(\alpha_{q-1}) < f(\alpha_{q-2}) \quad \text{and} \quad f(\alpha_{q-1}) < f(\alpha_q),$$

where $\alpha_q = \sum_{j=0}^{q} \delta(1.618)^j$.

The upper and lower bounds on α^*, indicated by α_u and α_l, are then given as follows:

$$\alpha_u = \sum_{j=0}^{q} \delta(1.618)^j,$$

$$\alpha_l = \sum_{j=0}^{q-2} \delta(1.618)^j.$$

2. Compute $f(\alpha_a)$ and $f(\alpha_b)$, where $\alpha_a = \alpha_l + 0.382I$ and $\alpha_b = \alpha_l + 0.618I$, where $I = \alpha_u - \alpha_l$.
3. Compare $f(\alpha_a)$ and $f(\alpha_b)$ and go to step 4 or 5.
4. If $f(\alpha_a) < f(\alpha_b)$, then $\alpha_l \le \alpha^* \le \alpha_b$.
   Thus $\alpha_l^1 = \alpha_l, \quad \alpha_u^1 = \alpha_b, \quad \alpha_b^1 = \alpha_a$.
   Compute $f(\alpha_a^1)$, where $\alpha_a^1 = \alpha_l^1 + 0.382(\alpha_u^1 - \alpha_l^1)$ and go to step 6.
5. If $f(\alpha_a) > f(\alpha_b)$, then $\alpha_a \le \alpha^* \le \alpha_u$.
   Set $\alpha_l^1 = \alpha_a, \quad \alpha_u^1 = \alpha_u, \quad \alpha_a^1 = \alpha_b$.
   Compute $f(\alpha_b^1)$, where $\alpha_b^1 = \alpha_l^1 + 0.618(\alpha_u^1 - \alpha_l^1)$. Go to step 6.
6. If $I^1 = \alpha_u^1 - \alpha_l^1 < \varepsilon$, let $\alpha^* = (\alpha_u^1 + \alpha_l^1)/2$ and stop.
   If not, then delete superscript on $\alpha_l^1, \alpha_a^1, \alpha_b^1$ and α_u^1 and return to step 3.

Example 2.5 Perform iterations of the golden-section search for the objective function $f(\alpha) = 10 - 130\alpha + \exp(3\alpha)$. Start with $\delta = 0.25$ and reduce the interval of uncertainty to 0.25.

Solution: Using $\delta = 0.25$, the function values for the first few points using the golden-section search can be calculated as follows:

α	0	0.25	**0.6545**	**1.308981**	**2.367931**
$f(\alpha)$	11	−20.383	**−67.961**	**−109.416**	**918.743**

We clearly see that the function value decreases and then increases which leads to the bracketing of the minimum with $q-2 \to 0.6545$, $q-1 \to 1.308981$ and $q \to 2.367931$. The initial interval of uncertainty is 1.713431. We need to reduce this to 0.25.

We can now refine the interval as shown below.

$\alpha_l = 0.6545$	$\alpha_a = 1.308981$	$\alpha_b = 1.7134$	$\alpha_u = 2.367931$
$f(\alpha_l) = -67.9608$	$f(\alpha_a) = -109.416$	$f(\alpha_b) = -41.992$	$f(\alpha_u) = 918.7427$

We can see that $f(\alpha_a) < f(\alpha_b)$ here, and from step 4 of the golden-section search algorithm, $\alpha_l^1 = \alpha_l = 0.6545$, $\alpha_u^1 = \alpha_b = 1.7134$ and $\alpha_b^1 = \alpha_a = 1.308981$. Also, we can calculate $\alpha_a^1 = \alpha_l^1 + 0.382(\alpha_u^1 - \alpha_l^1) = 1.059$.

The interval of uncertainty has now been reduced to 1.0589 and the new bounds of the interval are shown below:

$\alpha_l = 0.6545$	$\alpha_a = 1.059$	$\alpha_b = 1.308981$	$\alpha_u = 1.7134$
$f(\alpha_l) = -67.9608$	$f(\alpha_a) = -103.695$	$f(\alpha_b) = -109.416$	$f(\alpha_u) = -41.992$

We want to refine the interval again. Clearly, now we have $f(\alpha_a) > f(\alpha_b)$ here and thus we need to perform step 5 of the golden-section search algorithm. This leads to $\alpha_l^1 = 1.059$, $\alpha_a^1 = 1.308981$, $\alpha_u^1 = 1.7134$ and $\alpha_b^1 = 1.463419$.

The interval of uncertainty is now reduced to 0.654, and the new points for the interval are given below.

$\alpha_l = 1.059$	$\alpha_a = 1.308981$	$\alpha_b = 1.463419$	$\alpha_u = 1.7134$
$f(\alpha_l) = -103.695$	$f(\alpha_a) = -109.416$	$f(\alpha_b) = -99.583$	$f(\alpha_u) = -41.992$

Let us refine the interval again. We have $f(\alpha_a) < f(\alpha_b)$, and therefore use step 4 from the golden-section search algorithm. This leads to $\alpha_l^1 = 1.059$, $\alpha_u^1 = 1.463419$ and $\alpha_b^1 = 1.308981$. Also, we can calculate $\alpha_a^1 = 1.213488$. The interval of uncertainty is now 0.4044 and the new points are given below.

$\alpha_l = 1.059$	$\alpha_a = 1.213488$	$\alpha_b = 1.308981$	$\alpha_u = 1.4634$
$f(\alpha_l) = -103.695$	$f(\alpha_a) = -109.644$	$f(\alpha_b) = -109.416$	$f(\alpha_u) = -99.583$

We can now see that the golden section is closing in on the minimum point which lies between 1.059 and 1.4634. Again we see that we have $f(\alpha_a) < f(\alpha_b)$ and so step 4 of the golden-section search algorithm can be used. This leads to $\alpha_l^1 = 1.059$, $\alpha_u^1 = 1.308981$ and $\alpha_b^1 = 1.213488$. Also, we can calculate $\alpha_a^1 = 1.154493$. The interval of uncertainty is now 0.2499 and satisfies the convergence criterion for this problem. The new points are given below.

$\alpha_l = 1.059$	$\alpha_a = 1.154493$	$\alpha_b = 1.213488$	$\alpha_u = 1.30898$
$f(\alpha_l) = -103.695$	$f(\alpha_a) = -108.156$	$f(\alpha_b) = -109.644$	$f(\alpha_u) = -109.416$

We can continue the process to reduce the interval of uncertainty. At the current iteration, we can get the approximation to the minimum as follows:

$$\alpha^* \approx \frac{\alpha_l + \alpha_u}{2} = 1.2317.$$

This is not too far from the exact solution of 1.256.

2.5 Polynomial Interpolation

Zero-order methods such as the equal-interval search and golden-section search can take too many function evaluations during the line search process. Function evaluations take up considerable computer time, especially for real-life problems where function calculations require running a computational simulation code.

Any continuous function on a given interval can be approximated as closely as desired by a polynomial of sufficiently high order. We have seen this in the Taylor series expansion of continuous functions. The minimum point of a low-order polynomial can be found easily. Polynomial interpolation is an efficient method for one-dimensional search and is implemented in many optimization codes. We will see in Chapter 6 that the response surface methods in optimization use multivariate polynomials to approximate functions.

2.5.1 Quadratic curve fitting

All continuous functions appear quadratic within a sufficiently small interval about the minimum point. Therefore, any such function can be approximated by a general quadratic curve, using the expression:

$$q(\alpha) = a_0 + a_1\alpha + a_2\alpha^2. \tag{2.34}$$

To get a quadratic expression that is a close approximation of the function, we need to evaluate the function at three points. These three points can be selected as the lower and upper limits of the interval and an intermediate point, such as the mid-point of the interval: $(\alpha_l, \alpha_u, \alpha_i)$. The situation is illustrated in Figure 2.11. Since these three points satisfy the equation of the curve, they can be used to define three equations, as shown below:[1]

$$\begin{aligned} a_0 + a_1\alpha_l + a_2\alpha_l^2 &= f(\alpha_l) \\ a_0 + a_1\alpha_u + a_2\alpha_u^2 &= f(\alpha_u) \\ a_0 + a_1\alpha_i + a_2\alpha_i^2 &= f(\alpha_i). \end{aligned} \tag{2.35}$$

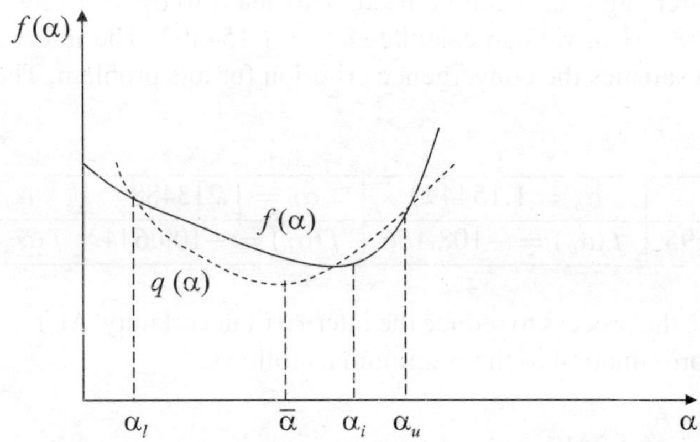

Figure 2.11 *Illustration of the polynomial-interpolation method*

In these equations, a_0, a_1 and a_2 are the three constants used to characterize the curve, as given in (2.34). They can be obtained by solving the set of equations, and we get

$$\begin{aligned} a_2 &= \frac{1}{(\alpha_u - \alpha_i)}\left[\frac{f(\alpha_u) - f(\alpha_l)}{\alpha_u - \alpha_l} - \frac{f(\alpha_i) - f(\alpha_l)}{\alpha_i - \alpha_l}\right] \\ a_1 &= \frac{f(\alpha_i) - f(\alpha_l)}{\alpha_i - \alpha_l} - a_2(\alpha_l + \alpha_i) \\ a_0 &= f(\alpha_l) - a_1\alpha_l - a_2\alpha_l^2. \end{aligned} \tag{2.36}$$

Once the coefficients a_0, a_1 and a_2 are known, we can calculate $q(\alpha)$ and obtain the necessary and sufficient conditions for a minimum in the usual manner, by postulating the following conditions for a minimum point:

$$q(\alpha) = a_0 + a_1\alpha + a_2\alpha^2$$

$$\frac{dq}{d\alpha} = a_1 + 2a_2\alpha = 0 \Rightarrow \bar{\alpha} = -\frac{a_1}{2a_2}$$

$$\frac{d^2q}{d\alpha^2} = 2a_2 > 0. \tag{2.37}$$

If the algorithm is proceeding along a descent direction and we have chosen the three points for quadratic interpolation such that the minimum is bracketed within them, then the minimum of the quadratic approximation should be close to the actual minimum. For example, if an interval method is used to bracket the minimum, the points (α_l, α_u) can be used as the extreme points for quadratic interpolation with the value in between as the third point. While the minimum of the quadratic function may be close to the actual minimum, an iterative procedure can be used to further refine the interval of uncertainty.

2.5.2 Quadratic-interpolation algorithm

1. Locate initial interval (α_l, α_u) by selecting a value of δ. Use a zero-order method with a relatively large δ.
2. Select α_i as an intermediate point in (α_l, α_u). If zero-order methods have bracketed the minimum to $q-1$, q and $q+1$ points, one can select the qth point as the intermediate point without requiring a function evaluation. Otherwise, calculate $f(\alpha_i)$.
3. Find a_0, a_1 and a_2 for quadratic fit, and evaluate $\bar{\alpha}$ and $f(\bar{\alpha})$ value at optimal point of quadratic fit.
4. If $\alpha_i < \bar{\alpha}$, go to 4a or 4b. Else go to 4c or 4d. (Illustrated in Figure 2.12)

   (4a) If $f(\alpha_i) < f(\bar{\alpha})$, then $\alpha_l \le \alpha^* \le \bar{\alpha}$.

   $$\alpha_l^1 = \alpha_l, \qquad \alpha_u^1 = \bar{\alpha}, \qquad \alpha_i^1 = \alpha_i. \quad \text{Go to step 7.}$$

   (4b) If $f(\alpha_i) > f(\bar{\alpha})$, then $\alpha_i \le \alpha^* \le \alpha_u$.

   $$\alpha_l^1 = \alpha_i, \qquad \alpha_i^1 = \bar{\alpha}, \qquad \alpha_u^1 = \alpha_u. \quad \text{Go to step 7.}$$

   (4c) If $f(\alpha_i) < f(\bar{\alpha})$, then $\bar{\alpha} \le \alpha^* \le \alpha_u$.

   $$\alpha_l^1 = \bar{\alpha}, \qquad \alpha_i^1 = \alpha_i, \qquad \alpha_u^1 = \alpha_u. \quad \text{Go to step 7}$$

   (4d) If $f(\alpha_i) > f(\bar{\alpha})$, then $\alpha_l \le \alpha^* \le \alpha_i$.

   $$\alpha_l^1 = \alpha_l, \qquad \alpha_i^1 = \bar{\alpha}, \qquad \alpha_u^1 = \alpha_i. \quad \text{Go to step 7.}$$

7. If two successive estimates of the minimum point of $f(\alpha)$ are sufficiently close, then stop. Otherwise, delete superscripts on $\alpha_l^1, \alpha_i^1, \alpha_u^1$ and return to step 2.

The quadratic-fit method is popular; however, it can fail to make sufficient progress or become ill-conditioned due to the denominator terms in (2.36) and (2.37) becoming too small. In such cases, a shift to the equal-interval search is recommended. Such an approach of falling back on a robust but less-efficient approach is called a *safeguard technique* and is typically built into professional software.

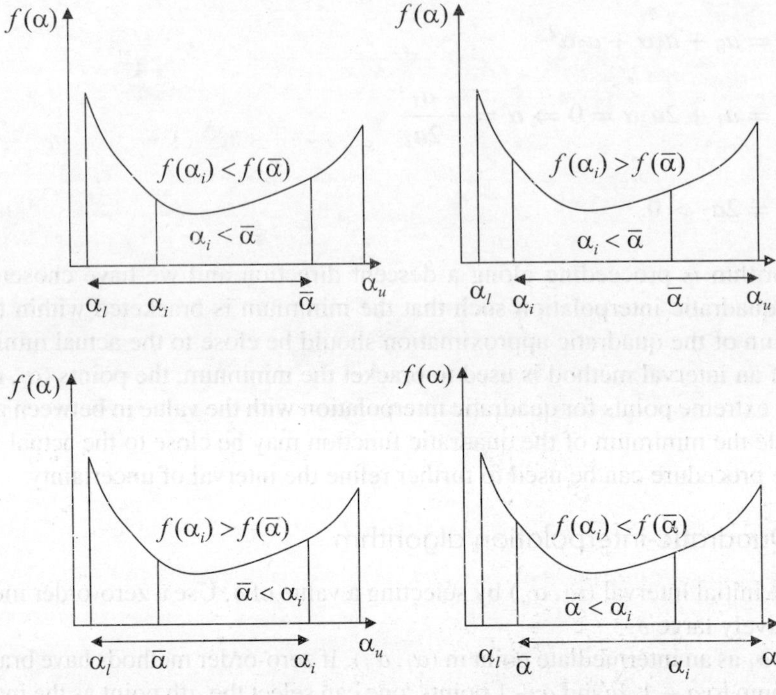

Figure 2.12 *Interval reduction in the quadratic-approximation method*

Example 2.6 Bracket the minimum of the function $f(\alpha) = 10 - 130\alpha + \exp(3\alpha)$ using the golden-section search with $\delta = 0.25$. Then, perform two iterations of the quadratic search to reduce the interval of uncertainty.

Solution: For the variable, $\delta = 0.25$, the function values for the first few points can be calculated using the golden-section search as shown in the table below:

α	0	0.25	**0.6545**	**1.308981**	**2.367931**
$f(\alpha)$	11	−20.383	**−67.961**	**−109.416**	**918.743**

We clearly see that the function value first decreases and then increases which leads to the bracketing of the minimum with $q-2 \rightarrow 0.6545$, $q-1 \rightarrow 1.308981$ and $q \rightarrow 2.367931$. The initial interval of uncertainty is 1.713431.

To perform the quadratic search, we can fit a quadratic function through the three points, $\alpha_l = 0.6545$, $\alpha_i = 1.308981$ and $\alpha_u = 2.36731$. The coefficients of the quadratic fit are calculated as $a_0 = 373.0553$, $a_1 = -795.827$ and $a_2 = 293.1025$. This leads to the minimum of the quadratic being $\bar{a} = 1.066$ and the function value $f(\bar{\alpha}) = -104.132$. Now we perform the checks corresponding to step 4 of the quadratic-search algorithm. Here, $\alpha_i > \bar{\alpha}$ and $f(\alpha_i) < f(\bar{\alpha})$, which corresponds to step 4c of the algorithm. The new interval then becomes $\alpha_l^1 = \bar{\alpha} = 1.0666$, $\alpha_i^1 = \alpha_i = 1.308981$ and $\alpha_u^1 = \alpha_u = 2.36931$. The new interval of uncertainty is 1.301 and the new points are given below:

$\alpha_l = 1.066635$	$\alpha_i = 1.308981$	$\alpha_u = 2.367931$
$f(\alpha_l) = -104.132$	$f(\alpha_i) = -109.416$	$f(\alpha_u) = 918.743$

We perform another iteration to reduce the interval of uncertainty. The first step is to obtain the quadratic fit through the three new points. This yields the coefficients $a_0 = 620.7999$, $a_1 = -1496.58$ and $a_2 = 785.8862$. The minimum point for the quadratic function is $\bar{a} = 1.205367$ and the function value at this point is $f(\bar{\alpha}) = -109.505$. We immediately notice that $\alpha_i > \bar{\alpha}$ and $f(\alpha_i) > f(\bar{\alpha})$ which corresponds to step 4d of the quadratic-search algorithm. Performing this step, the new points are obtained as $\alpha_l' = 1.0666$, $\alpha_i^1 = 1.205367$ and $\alpha_u^1 = 1.308981$. The interval of uncertainty is now reduced to 0.242. We can obtain an approximate value of the minimum at this point as $\alpha^* \approx (\alpha_l + \alpha_u)/2 = 1.1878$. Compare this to the exact solution of 1.256. Further iterations can be performed to reduce the interval of uncertainty.

2.6 Inexact Line Search

The numerical methods discussed for line search until now are exact line search methods, since they try to find the exact local minima to a given level of accuracy. However, for practical optimization problems, it is better to spend the function evaluations and computer resources in the optimization iterations $(k-1, k, k+1, \dots)$ than in trying to find the exact value of α_k. Therefore, many commercial optimization algorithms use the inexact line search methods for finding a value of α_k which satisfies the descent condition.

We want to find the step size $\alpha_k > 0$ such that the objective function value decreases. Such a step size exists if $\mathbf{c}^{(k)} \cdot \mathbf{d}^{(k)} < 0$. Armijo's rule is a simple inexact line search method.

2.6.1 Armijo's rule

Armijo's rule is based on a straight line represented by[1]

$$l(\alpha) = f(0) + \alpha(\rho f'(0)), \tag{2.38}$$

where $0 < \rho < 1$. At $\alpha = 0$, this function has a value $f(0)$ and is represented by the horizontal dotted line in Figure 2.13. Since $\alpha > 0$, $\rho > 0$, $f'(0) < 0$ at other points, the function represents a line starting from $f(0)$, sloping downwards and intersecting the function $f(\alpha)$ as shown in Figure 2.13. This can also be seen from the fact that $dl/d\alpha = \rho f'(0) < 0$.

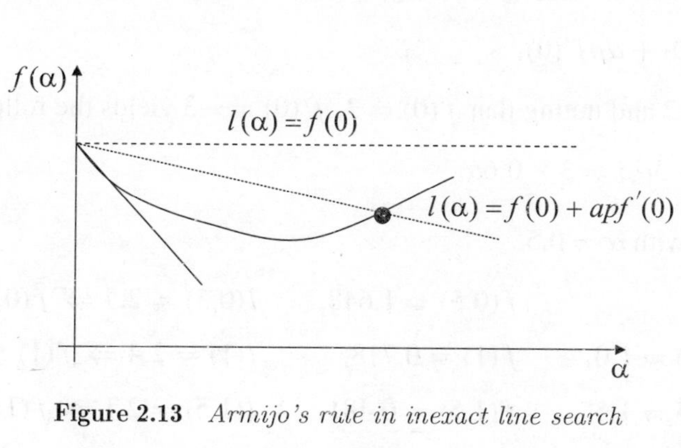

Figure 2.13 *Armijo's rule in inexact line search*

For a given value of α and ρ, the line in Figure 2.13 should intersect with the curve at a value of $f(\alpha) < f(0)$ for the step size to qualify as a descent step.

2.6.2 Armijo's rule algorithm

1. Start with an initial guess of $\alpha > 0$ and assume a typical value of $\rho = 0.2$.
2. Check if the selected step size satisfies the condition given below:

$$f(\alpha) \leq f(0) + \alpha(\rho f'(0)).$$

This implies that the line crosses the function below the horizontal line defined by $f = f(0)$.

(a) If $f(\alpha) \leq f(0) + \alpha(\rho f'(0))$, then check if

$$f(\eta\alpha) \leq f(0) + \eta\alpha(\rho f'(0)) \text{ is satisfied for } \eta = 2, 3, 4, \ldots.$$

This step effectively increases the values of the step size as $\eta\alpha$ increases and for some $\eta\alpha$, the step size will no longer reduce the function relative to $f(0)$. Select the largest η where $f(\eta\alpha) \leq f(0) + \eta\alpha(\rho f'(0))$ is satisfied.

(b) If $f(\alpha) > f(0) + \alpha(\rho f'(0))$, then check if

$$f\left(\frac{\alpha}{\eta}\right) \leq f(0) + \frac{\alpha}{\eta}(\rho f'(0)) \text{ is satisfied for } \eta = 2, 3, 4, \ldots.$$

This step effectively decreases the values of the step size as α/η decreases and for some α/η, the step size will reduce the function relative to $f(0)$. Select the smallest η for which $f(\alpha/\eta) \leq f(0) + (\alpha/\eta)(\rho(0))$ is satisfied.

Example 2.7 Find the minimum of $f(\alpha) = 2 - 4\alpha + e^{\alpha}$ using inexact line search. Use an initial guess of 0.5 and 6 and also use $\rho = 0.2$.

Solution: We know that the exact solution of this problem is

$$f'(\alpha) = -4 + e^{\alpha} \Rightarrow \alpha = \ln 4 = 1.3862.$$

$$f''(\alpha) = e^{\alpha} > 0 \quad \text{for } \alpha > 0.$$

To construct the line according to Armijo's rule,

$$l(\alpha) = f(0) + \alpha\rho f'(0).$$

Selecting $\rho = 0.2$ and noting that $f(0) = 3$, $f'(0) = -3$ yields the following condition:

$$l(\alpha) = 3 - 3\alpha\rho = 3 - 0.6\alpha.$$

Case 1: Start with $\alpha = 0.5$.

$\alpha = 0.5,\quad f(0.5) = 1.648,\quad l(0.5) = 2.7 \Rightarrow f(0.5) \leq l(0.5).$

$\alpha = 2 \cdot 0.5 = 1.0,\quad f(1) = 0.718,\quad l(1) = 2.4 \Rightarrow f(1) \leq l(1).$

$\alpha = 3 \cdot 0.5 = 1.5,\quad f(1.5) = 0.481,\quad l(1.5) = 2.1 \Rightarrow f(1.5) \leq l(1.5).$

$$\alpha = 4 \cdot 0.5 = 2, \qquad f(2) = 1.389, \qquad l(2) = 1.8 \Rightarrow f(2) \le l(2).$$

$$\alpha = 5 \cdot 0.5 = 2.5, \qquad f(2.5) = 4.18, \qquad l(2.5) = 1.5 \Rightarrow f(2.5) > l(2.5).$$

Thus, $\alpha = \eta \cdot 0.5 = 2$ is the highest value where the condition $f(\eta\alpha) \le f(0) + \eta\alpha(\rho f'(0))$ is true and is selected as *optimal*. Note that

$$f(2) = 1.389$$

$$f(0) = 3$$

$$f(2) < f(0).$$

Case 2: Start with $\alpha = 6$.

$$\alpha = 6, \qquad f(6) = 381.4, \qquad l(6) = -0.6 \Rightarrow f(6) > l(6).$$

$$\alpha = \frac{6}{2} = 3, \qquad f(3) = 10.08, \qquad l(3) = 1.2 \Rightarrow f(3) > l(3).$$

$$\alpha = \frac{6}{3} = 2, \qquad f(2) = 1.389, \qquad l(2) = 1.8 \Rightarrow f(2) < l(2).$$

Thus, $\alpha = 6/\eta = 6/3 = 2$ is the lowest value where the condition $f(\eta\alpha) \le f(0) + \eta\alpha(\rho f'(0))$ is true and is selected as *optimal*.

This example is illustrated in Figure 2.14.

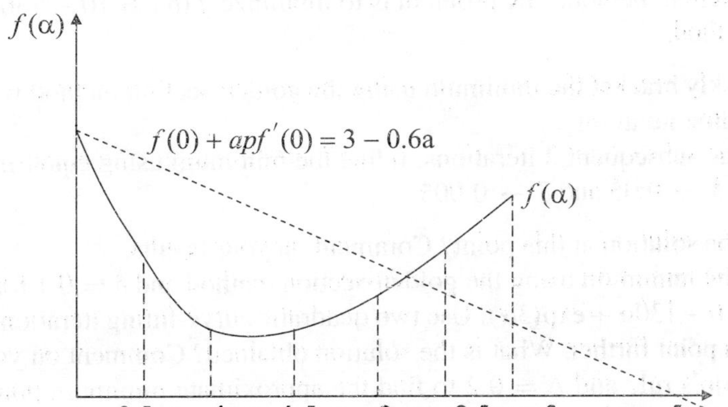

Figure 2.14 *Example illustrating Armijo's rule in one-dimensional search*

There are other more sophisticated line search methods which are often used in commercial software for computational efficiency. We can also see that it is possible to construct hybrid methods which combine two different one-dimensional search methods. Note that there are some methods like the conjugate-gradient method which will be discussed in Chapter 3 which work well if the line search is exact. Other methods which will be discussed in Chapter 4 are more robust and work well with inexact line search. The derivation of the gradient-based methods should be carefully studied to see if an exact line search criterion is assumed.

Problems

1. Consider the one-dimensional function given by

$$f(\alpha) = e^{-\alpha} + \alpha^2.$$

   (a) Use the equal-interval method to bracket the minimum with $\delta = 0.1$.
   (b) What is the interval of uncertainty?
   (c) What is the approximate minimum?

2. Minimize the following function using the equal-interval search method with a starting $\delta = 0.1$:

$$f(\alpha) = 10 - 130\alpha + \exp(3\alpha).$$

   Reduce the interval to $\delta = r\delta$ for the future iterations. Perform two more iterations and use $r = 0.1$.

3. Minimize the function

$$f(\alpha) = 10 - 130\alpha + \exp(3\alpha)$$

   using the golden-section method with a starting $\delta = 0.1$. Bracket the minimum and perform two iterations to reduce the interval of uncertainty. How does the golden-section method compare with the equal-interval search used in Problem 2?

4. Develop a simple hybrid method which combines equal-interval search with the golden-section method. The problem is to minimize $f(\alpha) = 10 - 130\alpha + \exp(3\alpha)$. In the method,

   (a) quickly bracket the minimum using the golden-section method with $\delta = 0.1$ in the first iteration.

   (b) in the subsequent 2 iterations, refine the minimum using equal-interval search and $\delta \to 0.05$ and $\delta \to 0.005$.

   What is the solution at this point? Comment on your results.

5. Bracket the minimum using the golden-section method and $\delta = 0.1$ for the function $f(\alpha) = 10 - 130\alpha + \exp(3\alpha)$. Use two quadratic curve-fitting iterations to refine the minimum point further. What is the solution obtained? Comment on your results.

6. Use Armijo's rule and $\rho = 0.2$ to find the approximate minimum point of $f(\alpha) = 10 - 130\alpha + \exp(3\alpha)$, starting from $\alpha = 0.2$. How does the solution compare to the *exact* line searches and the exact analytical solution? Repeat the problem starting from $\alpha = 5.6$.

7. Write a computer program to implement the equal-interval search. Starting from a $\delta = 0.1$, minimize the function $f(\alpha) = 10 - 130\alpha + \exp(3\alpha)$ to an accuracy of five decimal places relative to the exact analytical solution. Reduce δ to one-tenth the value in subsequent iterations, that is, use $\delta = 0.1, 0.01, 0.001, \ldots$. How many function evaluations are needed?

8. Write a computer program to implement the golden-section search. Starting from a $\delta = 0.1$, minimize the function $f(\alpha) = 10 - 130\alpha + \exp(3\alpha)$ to an accuracy of five decimal places relative to the exact analytical solution. How many function evaluations are needed?

9. Write a computer program to implement the golden-section method and the quadratic-search method. Use the golden-section search to bracket the minimum while starting with a $\delta = 0.3$. Then, minimize the function $f(\alpha) = 10 - 130\alpha + \exp(3\alpha)$ using the quadratic search to an accuracy of five decimal places relative to the exact analytical solution. How many function evaluations are needed?
10. Repeat Problem 8 using a $\delta = 0.05$ with the golden-section search to bracket the minimum. How many function evaluations are needed to converge to five decimal places relative to the optimum? What do you learn by comparing Problems 8 and 9 and the current problem?
11. Consider the function $f(\alpha) = \alpha^2 + e^{-\alpha}$. Find the minimum point using the golden-section search and the equal-interval search computer programs. Stop when the interval of uncertainty is below 0.00001. Compare the function evaluations needed by each algorithm.
12. Consider the function $f(\alpha) = \alpha + e^{-\alpha}$. Find the minimum point using the golden-section search and the equal-interval search computer programs. Stop when the interval of uncertainty is below 0.00001. Compare the function evaluations needed by each algorithm.
13. Using the programs for golden-section search, find the minimum of the following function to an accuracy of five decimal places:

$$f(x) = x^2 + \frac{a}{x} \quad a = 1, 10, 100, 1000.$$

Comment on your results about selection of the value for δ.

14. Use the program for equal-interval search to find the minimum of the following function to an accuracy of five decimal places:

$$f(x) = 4x^4 - x^3 + 5x^2 - 16x + 10.$$

Compare the result with that obtained using a computerized algorithm for Armijo's rule.

15. Only using a pocket calculator, bracket the minimum of the function:

$$f(x) = e^x - 300x^3.$$

Then, use your quadratic approximation program to refine the minimum to an interval of uncertainty of 0.001.

16. Again, use a pocket calculator to bracket the minimum of the function:

$$f(x) = x^2 - 4x + 20.$$

Using the end-point of the interval of uncertainty and the minimum predicted by Armijo's rule, fit a quadratic function. How does the minimum of this quadratic compare with the exact solution? Refine the minimum further with the quadratic function program.

17. Consider the Rosenbrock function:

$$f(\mathbf{x}) = 100(x_2 - x_1^2)^2 + (1 - x_1)^2.$$

If $\mathbf{x}^{(0)} = (0, 0)$ and $\mathbf{d}^{(0)} = (-2, 0)$, do we have a descent direction? If so, find the one-dimensional problem and analytically calculate the step size.

18. Consider Wood's function, given below:

$$f(\mathbf{x}) = 100(x_2 - x_1^2)^2 + (1 - x_1)^2 + 90(x_4 - x_3^2)^2 + (1 - x_3)^2$$
$$+ 10.1[(x_2 - 1)^2 + (x_4 - 1)^2] + 19.8(x_2 - 1)(x_4 - 1).$$

If $\mathbf{x}^{(k)} = (-3, -1, -3, -1)$, and a search direction is partially given as $\mathbf{d}^{(k)} = (1, 2, 3, y)$, find the appropriate y so that this will be a descent direction.

3 Gradient-Based Methods

In this chapter, we study some methods of determining the search direction **d**—the steepest-descent and conjugate-gradient methods. These methods are based on finding the direction **d** defined on the space spanned by vectors n, such that $f(\mathbf{x})$ decreases rapidly along the direction specified by this vector **d**. The steepest-descent and conjugate-gradient methods are first-order methods and use the first derivative or gradient of the objective function. Second-order methods make use of the second derivative or Hessian of the objective function and will be discussed in the next chapter.

3.1 Properties of the Gradient Vector

The gradient vector of a function plays an important part in all gradient-based methods. Such methods tend to be fast and efficient in a local sense and are widely used for problems with a large number of design variables. It is therefore worthwhile to study the main properties of the gradient vector.

The first property of the gradient vector **c** of a function $f(\mathbf{x})$ at point $\mathbf{x}^{(k)}$ is that it is orthogonal (normal) to the tangent plane, in other words, $\mathbf{c} \cdot \mathbf{T} = 0$, on the surface which is defined by the equation $f(\mathbf{x}) =$ constant. To see this, consider a curve C on the surface $f(x_1, x_2, \ldots, x_n) =$ constant.

Let s be any parameter along C. Then, a tangent vector **T** along C at $\mathbf{x}^{(k)}$ is

$$\mathbf{T} = \left[\frac{\partial x_1}{\partial s}\,\frac{\partial x_2}{\partial s}\cdots\frac{\partial x_n}{\partial s}\right]^{\mathrm{T}}. \tag{3.1}$$

Since $f(\mathbf{x}) =$ constant on the surface, $df/ds = 0$ (directional derivative of f), or

$$\frac{df}{ds} = \frac{\partial f}{\partial x_1}\cdot\frac{\partial x_1}{\partial s} + \cdots + \frac{\partial f}{\partial x_n}\cdot\frac{\partial x_n}{\partial s} = 0. \tag{3.2}$$

Alternatively, the above equation can be written as follows:[1]

$$\mathbf{c}\cdot\mathbf{T} = 0. \tag{3.3}$$

Example 3.1 Verify that the gradient vector for $f(\mathbf{x}) = x_1^2 + 2x_2^2 - \mathrm{e}^{-x_1 - x_2}$ is normal to the tangent at $\mathbf{x}^{(0)} = (1, 0)$.

Solution: The gradient vector is given by

$$\mathbf{c} = \begin{Bmatrix} \dfrac{\partial f}{\partial x_1} \\ \dfrac{\partial f}{\partial x_2} \end{Bmatrix} = \begin{Bmatrix} 2x_1 + e^{-x_1-x_2} \\ 4x_2 + e^{-x_1-x_2} \end{Bmatrix}.$$

At (1, 0), the gradient becomes

$$\mathbf{c} = \begin{Bmatrix} 2 + e^{-1} \\ e^{-1} \end{Bmatrix} = \begin{Bmatrix} 2.368 \\ 0.368 \end{Bmatrix}.$$

The norm of the gradient is given by

$$\|\mathbf{c}\| = \sqrt{2.368^2 + 0.368^2} = 2.396.$$

Therefore, the unit vector along the gradient is given by

$$\hat{\mathbf{c}} = \frac{\mathbf{c}}{\|\mathbf{c}\|} = \begin{Bmatrix} 0.988 \\ 0.153 \end{Bmatrix}.$$

Next, we need to find a tangent vector on the surface where $f(\mathbf{x}) =$ constant at the point (1, 0). The tangent vector can be obtained by calculating $(\partial x_1/\partial s, \partial x_2/\partial s)$. Consider the surface $f(\mathbf{x}) = x_1^2 + 2x_2^2 - e^{-x_1-x_2} =$ constant. Differentiating this curve with respect to s yields the following condition:

$$2x_1 \frac{\partial x_1}{\partial s} + 4x_2 \frac{\partial x_2}{\partial s} + e^{-x_1-x_2} \frac{\partial x_1}{\partial s} + e^{-x_1-x_2} \frac{\partial x_2}{\partial s} = 0.$$

At (1, 0) this becomes

$$2\frac{\partial x_1}{\partial s} + e^{-1}\frac{\partial x_1}{\partial s} + e^{-1}\frac{\partial x_2}{\partial s} = 0.$$

This can be simplified to give the expression:

$$2.368\frac{\partial x_1}{\partial s} + 0.368\frac{\partial x_2}{\partial s} = 0 \Rightarrow \frac{\partial x_2}{\partial s} = -6.434\frac{\partial x_1}{\partial s}.$$

Now we can write

$$\mathbf{T} = \left(\frac{\partial x_1}{\partial s} \quad \frac{\partial x_2}{\partial s} \right) = \left(\frac{\partial x_1}{\partial s} \quad -6.434\frac{\partial x_1}{\partial s} \right).$$

The norm of the tangent vector can be calculated using the formula:

$$\|\mathbf{T}\| = \sqrt{\left(\frac{\partial x_1}{\partial s}\right)^2 + \left(-6.434\frac{\partial x_1}{\partial s}\right)^2} = 6.511\frac{\partial x_1}{\partial s}.$$

From the above calculations, the tangent unit vector at (1, 0) is finally obtained. It has the expression:

$$\hat{\mathbf{T}} = \frac{\mathbf{T}}{\|\mathbf{T}\|} = \begin{pmatrix} 0.153 \\ -0.988 \end{pmatrix}.$$

Finally, we take the dot product of the gradient and tangent unit vectors

$$\hat{\mathbf{c}} \cdot \hat{\mathbf{T}} = 0.988 \times 0.153 - 0.153 \times 0.988 = 0.$$

Thus, we see that the gradient and tangent vectors are normal to each other.

The second property of the gradient is that it represents a direction of *maximum increase* of $f(\mathbf{x})$ at $\mathbf{x}^{(k)}$. To see this, let $\mathbf{u}$ be a unit vector which is not tangent to the surface and t be a parameter along the vector. The derivative of $f(\mathbf{x})$ in the direction $\mathbf{u}$ at $\mathbf{x}$ is defined as follows:[1]

$$\frac{df}{dt} = \lim_{\varepsilon \to 0} \frac{f(\mathbf{x} + \varepsilon \mathbf{u}) - f(\mathbf{x})}{\varepsilon}. \tag{3.4}$$

Using the Taylor series expansion:

$$f(\mathbf{x} + \varepsilon \mathbf{u}) = f(\mathbf{x}) + \varepsilon \left[u_1 \frac{\partial f}{\partial x_1} + u_2 \frac{\partial f}{\partial x_2} + \cdots + u_n \frac{\partial f}{\partial x_n} \right] + o(\varepsilon^2), \tag{3.5}$$

where u_i are components of unit vector $\mathbf{u}$ and $o(\varepsilon^2)$ contains the higher-order terms. Rewriting (3.5) by collecting similar terms together, we obtain:

$$f(\mathbf{x} + \varepsilon \mathbf{u}) - f(\mathbf{x}) = \varepsilon \sum_{i=1}^{n} u_i \frac{\partial f}{\partial x_i} + o(\varepsilon^2). \tag{3.6}$$

Using this form, (3.4) can be written as follows:

$$\frac{df}{dt} = \sum_{i=1}^{n} u_i \frac{\partial f}{\partial x_i} = \mathbf{c} \cdot \mathbf{u}. \tag{3.7}$$

The right-hand side of (3.7) represents a scalar product, which can be rewritten in the form:

$$\frac{df}{dt} = \|\mathbf{c}\| \, \|\mathbf{u}\| \cos\theta. \tag{3.8}$$

Consider the left-hand side of (3.8) at two extreme values, $\cos\theta = 1$ and $\cos\theta = -1$.

1. When $\theta = 0$, $\cos\theta = 1$, df/dt is a maximum, and $\mathbf{u}$ is along $\mathbf{c}$. This case corresponds to the *maximum rate of increase* of $f(\mathbf{x})$.
2. When $\theta = 180°$, $\cos\theta = -1$, df/dt is a minimum and $\mathbf{u}$ is opposite to $\mathbf{c}$. This case corresponds to the *maximum rate of decrease* of $f(\mathbf{x})$.

We thus come to a very important concept in optimization. At any design point, $\mathbf{x}^{(k)}$, the gradient vector, $\mathbf{c}^{(k)}$, represents the maximum rate of increase of $f(\mathbf{x})$ and $-\mathbf{c}^{(k)}$ represents the maximum rate of decrease of $f(\mathbf{x})$.

The third important property of the gradient is that the maximum rate of change of $f(\mathbf{x})$ at $\mathbf{x}$ is the magnitude of the gradient vector. Since $\mathbf{u}$ is a unit vector, the maximum value of df/dt is obtained from (3.8) as follows:

$$\max \left| \frac{df}{dt} \right| = \|\mathbf{c}\|. \tag{3.9}$$

However, for $\theta = 0$, $\mathbf{u}$ is the direction of the gradient vector. Thus, the magnitude of the gradient represents the maximum rate of change of the function $f(\mathbf{x})$ at $\mathbf{x}^{(k)}$.

The classical steepest-descent method discussed in the next section makes use of the gradient vector in finding the search direction.

3.2 Steepest-Descent Method

Let $f(\mathbf{x})$ be a function defined over the space spanned by vectors $\mathbf{x}$. We have already seen that the direction of steepest descent is given by the following equation:[3]

$$\mathbf{d} = -\mathbf{c}. \tag{3.10}$$

The choice of this direction of descent satisfies the condition for descent, namely, $\mathbf{c} \cdot \mathbf{d} = -\mathbf{c} \cdot \mathbf{c} < 0$. The criterion for termination of the algorithm is when $\|\mathbf{c}\| < \varepsilon$, which implies that the gradient has become very small. Alternatively, the algorithm can be stopped after performing the maximum number of iterations or when the designs show very little change between successive iterations.

An interesting property of the steepest-descent method is that successive directions of steepest descent are normal to one another:

$$\mathbf{d}^{(k)} \cdot \mathbf{d}^{(k+1)} = 0. \tag{3.11}$$

We can see this as follows. Recall the line search criteria derived in Chapter 2, as shown in (2.12):

$$\mathbf{c}^{(k+1)} \cdot \mathbf{d}^{(k)} = 0. \tag{3.12}$$

For the steepest-descent method, the condition to be satisfied is $\mathbf{d}^{(k)} = -\mathbf{c}^{(k)}$, and therefore

$$\mathbf{c}^{(k+1)} \cdot \mathbf{c}^{(k)} = \mathbf{d}^{(k+1)} \cdot \mathbf{d}^{(k)} = 0. \tag{3.13}$$

The equation $\mathbf{c}^{(k+1)} \cdot \mathbf{d}^{(k)} = 0$ can be used as a criterion for line search. However, due to round-off and truncation errors, this equality will not be satisfied exactly. Therefore, the inequality $\mathbf{c}^{(k+1)} \cdot \mathbf{d}^{(k)} < \varepsilon$ can be used. The steepest-descent method can be expressed as an algorithm which is given below.

3.2.1 The steepest-descent algorithm

1. Estimate a starting design, labelled, $\mathbf{x}^{(0)}$ and set iteration counter $k = 0$. Select the value of the convergence parameter $\varepsilon > 0$ as a small number of the order of, say, 10^{-5}.
2. Calculate the gradient vector $\mathbf{c}^{(k)}$, either analytically or using finite-difference methods. Calculate $\|\mathbf{c}^{(k)}\|$. If $\|\mathbf{c}^{(k)}\| < \varepsilon$, stop and set $\mathbf{x}^* = \mathbf{x}^{(k)}$.
3. Define the search direction at the current design point $\mathbf{x}^{(k)}$ through the equation
$$\mathbf{d}^{(k)} = -\mathbf{c}^{(k)}.$$
4. Select a step size α_k to minimize $f(\mathbf{x}^{(k)} + \alpha_k \mathbf{d}^{(k)})$ using 1D search.
5. Update the design in the following manner:
$$\mathbf{x}^{(k+1)} = \mathbf{x}^{(k)} + \alpha_k \mathbf{d}^{(k)}, \quad \text{set } k = k + 1 \text{ to go to step 2.}$$

Example 3.2 Perform two iterations of the steepest-descent method for the function

$$f(x_1, x_2) = x_1^2 + 2x_2^2 + e^{-x_1 - x_2}.$$

Use the coordinate (1, 2) as the starting design point.

Solution:

1. $\mathbf{x}^{(0)} = (1, 2) \rightarrow$ starting design. Set $k = 0$.
2. Calculate the gradient vector at the current design point as follows:

$$\mathbf{c}^{(0)} = \begin{Bmatrix} 2x_1 - e^{-x_1 - x_2} \\ 4x_2 - e^{-x_1 - x_2} \end{Bmatrix} = \begin{Bmatrix} 1.9502 \\ 7.9502 \end{Bmatrix}.$$

We should check if the design point is itself a stationary point. In such a case, $\|\mathbf{c}^{(0)}\| < \varepsilon$.

$$\|\mathbf{c}\| = 8.1859 > 0.$$

Since the norm of the gradient is nonzero, we need to find a descent direction to reduce the function value.

3. Set the search direction as the steepest-descent direction, $\mathbf{d}^{(0)} = -\mathbf{c}^{(0)} = \begin{Bmatrix} -1.9502 \\ -7.9502 \end{Bmatrix}$.
4. Calculate α to minimize $f(\mathbf{x}^{(0)} + \alpha \mathbf{d}^{(0)})$.

$$\mathbf{x}^{(0)} + \alpha \mathbf{d}^{(0)} = \begin{Bmatrix} 1 \\ 2 \end{Bmatrix} + \alpha \begin{Bmatrix} -1.9502 \\ -7.9502 \end{Bmatrix}$$

$$= \begin{Bmatrix} 1 - 1.9502\alpha \\ 2 - 7.9502\alpha \end{Bmatrix} = \mathbf{x}^{(1)} = \begin{Bmatrix} x_1 \\ x_2 \end{Bmatrix}^{(1)}$$

$$f(\mathbf{x}^{(0)} + \alpha \mathbf{d}^{(k)}) = (1 - 1.9502\alpha)^2 + 2(2 - 7.9502\alpha)^2 + e^{-3+9.9\alpha}$$

$$\Rightarrow f(\alpha) = 9 - 67.502\alpha + 260.4294\alpha^2 + 9.9e^{-3+0.9\alpha}.$$

The function $f(\alpha)$ is quite complicated and it is not easy to get an analytical solution for it. We can use the equal-interval search to get the optimal α. Starting with $\delta = 0.25$, we can bracket the minimum between 0 and 0.5. Performing further iterations, the minimum point is obtained as $\alpha^* = 0.24$, which is the optimal step size.

5. Update the design,

$$\mathbf{x}^{(1)} = \mathbf{x}^{(0)} + \alpha \mathbf{d}^{(0)} = \begin{Bmatrix} 1 \\ 2 \end{Bmatrix} + 0.24 \begin{Bmatrix} -1.9502 \\ -7.9502 \end{Bmatrix} = \begin{Bmatrix} 0.5319 \\ 0.0919 \end{Bmatrix}.$$

1. Set $k = k + 1 = 1$. Go to step 2 and use the notation 2a to represent the next iteration.

2a. Set $k = 1$ and calculate the gradient again:

$$\mathbf{c}^{(1)} = \begin{Bmatrix} 2x_1 - e^{-x_1 - x_2} \\ 4x_2 - e^{-x_1 - x_2} \end{Bmatrix} = \begin{Bmatrix} 0.5279 \\ -0.1680 \end{Bmatrix}$$

The norm of the gradient is now $\|\mathbf{c}\| = 0.5539 > 0$, which exhibits a reduction of about 93 percent from the starting value. However, the norm is not close to zero, so more iterations are needed to arrive at the answer.

3a. Set the search direction as the steepest-descent direction, $\mathbf{d}^{(1)} = -\mathbf{c}^{(1)} = \begin{Bmatrix} -0.5279 \\ 0.1680 \end{Bmatrix}$.

4a. Calculate α to minimize $f(\mathbf{x}^{(1)} + \alpha\mathbf{d}^{(1)})$:

$$\mathbf{x}^{(1)} + \alpha\mathbf{d}^{(1)} = \begin{Bmatrix} 0.5319 \\ 0.9195 \end{Bmatrix} + \alpha \begin{Bmatrix} -0.5279 \\ 0.1680 \end{Bmatrix}$$

$$= \begin{Bmatrix} 0.5319 - 0.5279\alpha \\ 0.9195 - 0.1680\alpha \end{Bmatrix} = \mathbf{x}^{(2)} = \begin{Bmatrix} x_1 \\ x_2 \end{Bmatrix}^{(2)}$$

$$f(\mathbf{x}^{(1)} + \alpha\mathbf{d}^{(1)}) = (0.5319 - 0.5279\alpha)^2 + 2(0.9195 - 0.1680\alpha)^2$$

$$+ \mathrm{e}^{-1.4514+0.6959\alpha} := f(\alpha).$$

We again use the equal-interval search to get the optimal value for α. Starting with $\delta = 0.25$, we can bracket the minimum between 0.25 and 0.75. Performing further iterations, the minimum point is obtained at $\alpha^* = 0.41$, which is the optimal step size.

5a. Update the design:

$$\mathbf{x}^{(2)} = \mathbf{x}^{(1)} + \alpha\, \mathbf{d}^{(1)} = \begin{Bmatrix} 0.5319 \\ 0.0919 \end{Bmatrix} + 0.41 \begin{Bmatrix} -0.5279 \\ 0.1680 \end{Bmatrix} = \begin{Bmatrix} 0.3155 \\ 0.1608 \end{Bmatrix}.$$

Set $k = k + 1 = 2$. Go to step 2 again. Let us call this step 2b.

2b. We set $k = 1$ and calculate the gradient again:

$$\mathbf{c}^{(2)} = \begin{Bmatrix} 2x_1 - \mathrm{e}^{-x_1-x_2} \\ 4x_2 - \mathrm{e}^{-x_1-x_2} \end{Bmatrix} = \begin{Bmatrix} 0.0099 \\ 0.0122 \end{Bmatrix}.$$

The norm of the gradient is now, $\|\mathbf{c}\| = 0.016 > 0$ with a considerable decrease from the last iteration. For the given function, the steepest-descent method converges quite fast.

The steepest-descent method, though classical and simple, suffers from some serious shortcomings which restrict its applications for practical problems. The main problem is that the method is slow. This happens primarily because information of the previous designs and search directions or gradients is not used. A substantial decrease in the objective function occurs within the first few iterations and the objective function decreases quite slowly in later iterations. This is also caused by the normal search directions which lead to approaching the optimal point through a zigzag path. However, the basic idea of using the gradient information to decide the search direction has led to more powerful methods such as the conjugate-gradient method, which will be discussed later in this chapter.

There are some other aspects of the steepest-descent method which are sometimes useful. Under some special conditions, it is possible to use a fixed step size with this method, which helps to avoid the line search.

$$\mathbf{x}^{(x+1)} = \mathbf{x}^{(k)} - \alpha\mathbf{c}^{(k)}. \tag{3.14}$$

This approach works for a quadratic function when the following condition holds:

$$0 < \alpha < \frac{2}{\lambda_{\max}(\mathbf{A})}. \tag{3.15}$$

Here $\mathbf{A}$ is the positive definite symmetric matrix corresponding to the quadratic function and $\lambda_{\max}$ is the largest eigenvalue of $\mathbf{A}$. From (3.14), we can see that an arbitrary small step size can sometimes lead to the convergence of the steepest-descent method. This is sometimes useful in situations where a 1D search code is not available.

Another interesting fact about the steepest-descent method is that it converges after just a single iteration in the case of a quadratic function whose matrix $\mathbf{A}$ has the condition number equal to 1. The condition number, which is being mentioned here for the first time in this text, is the ratio of the largest to the smallest eigenvalue of matrix $\mathbf{A}$.

$$\text{cond}(\mathbf{A}) = \frac{\lambda_{\max}}{\lambda_{\min}}. \tag{3.16}$$

It is of significance because for a nonquadratic function, the condition number of the Hessian matrix affects the convergence rates.

It is possible to scale the matrix to adjust the condition number. For a general function $f(\mathbf{x})$, define new variables that satisfy the condition:

$$\mathbf{x} = \mathbf{T}\mathbf{y}. \tag{3.17}$$

Then we get a new function $g(\mathbf{y}) = f(\mathbf{T}\mathbf{y})$. Here, $\mathbf{T}$ is a transformation matrix and should be selected such that the condition number of the Hessian is made close to one.

Example 3.3 Verify that the steepest-descent direction results in a greater decrease in the objective function $f(\mathbf{x}) = x_1^2 + 2x_2^2 - \mathrm{e}^{-x_1-x_2}$, $\mathbf{x}^{(0)} = (1, 0)$ compared to the Newton search direction given by $\mathbf{d} = -\mathbf{H}^{-1}\mathbf{c}$. Assume a step size $\alpha = 1$.

Solution: Let us first consider the steepest-descent search direction. The gradient of the function is given by the equation:

$$\mathbf{c} = \begin{Bmatrix} \dfrac{\partial f}{\partial x_1} \\ \dfrac{\partial f}{\partial x_2} \end{Bmatrix} = \begin{Bmatrix} 2x_1 + \mathrm{e}^{-x_1-x_2} \\ 4x_2 + \mathrm{e}^{-x_1-x_2} \end{Bmatrix}.$$

At (1, 0), we get the gradient as follows:

$$\mathbf{c} = \begin{Bmatrix} 2 + \mathrm{e}^{-1} \\ \mathrm{e}^{-1} \end{Bmatrix} = \begin{Bmatrix} 2.368 \\ 0.368 \end{Bmatrix}.$$

The steepest-descent search direction is then given by the expression:

$$\mathbf{d}_1 = -\mathbf{c} = \begin{Bmatrix} -2.368 \\ -0.368 \end{Bmatrix}.$$

The search direction yields the next point as shown below:

$$\mathbf{x}^{(1)} = \mathbf{x}^{(0)} + \alpha\mathbf{d}_1 = \begin{Bmatrix} 1 \\ 0 \end{Bmatrix} + 1\begin{Bmatrix} -2.368 \\ -0.368 \end{Bmatrix} = \begin{Bmatrix} -1.368 \\ -0.368 \end{Bmatrix}.$$

The function value at this new point is found to be -7.817. Compare this with the value of 0.6321 at the starting point.

Next, we look at the Newton search direction $\mathbf{d}_2 = -\mathbf{H}^{-1}\mathbf{c}$. The Hessian matrix for the function can be calculated as

$$\mathbf{H} = \begin{bmatrix} 2 - e^{-x_1-x_2} & -e^{-x_1-x_2} \\ -e^{-x_1-x_2} & 4 - e^{-x_1-x_2} \end{bmatrix}$$

At (1, 0), the Hessian can be determined, and is given by:

$$\mathbf{H} = \begin{bmatrix} 2 - e^{-1} & -e^{-1} \\ -e^{-1} & 4 - e^{-1} \end{bmatrix} = \begin{bmatrix} 1.632 & -0.368 \\ -0.368 & 3.632 \end{bmatrix}.$$

The inverse of the Hessian is the following:

$$\mathbf{H}^{-1} = \begin{bmatrix} 0.6271 & 0.0635 \\ 0.0635 & 0.2818 \end{bmatrix}.$$

The Newton search direction can now be calculated:

$$\mathbf{d}_2 = -\mathbf{H}^{-1}\mathbf{c} = -\begin{bmatrix} 0.6271 & 0.0635 \\ 0.0635 & 0.2818 \end{bmatrix}\begin{Bmatrix} 2.368 \\ 0.368 \end{Bmatrix} = \begin{Bmatrix} -1.5083 \\ -0.2541 \end{Bmatrix}.$$

This direction yields the new point, given by:

$$\mathbf{x}^{(1)} = \mathbf{x}^{(0)} + \alpha\mathbf{d}_2 = \begin{Bmatrix} 1 \\ 0 \end{Bmatrix} + 1\begin{Bmatrix} -1.5083 \\ 0.2541 \end{Bmatrix} = \begin{Bmatrix} -0.5083 \\ -0.2581 \end{Bmatrix}.$$

Putting this new design point into the function, yields a value of -1.756. Compare this with the starting value, 0.6321. Though the Newton direction also reduces the function value, the steepest-descent direction causes a greater reduction for this problem in the first iteration.

Example 3.4 Find the optimal step size for the steepest-descent method when applied to the quadratic function

$$f(\mathbf{x}) = \frac{1}{2}\mathbf{x}^T\mathbf{A}\mathbf{x} - \mathbf{b}^T\mathbf{x}.$$

Here $\mathbf{A}$ is a symmetric and positive definite matrix.

Solution: The gradient of the quadratic function is given by:

$$\mathbf{c} = \mathbf{A}\mathbf{x} - \mathbf{b}.$$

The necessary condition for optimality is given by the equation $\mathbf{c} = \mathbf{A}\mathbf{x} - \mathbf{b} = 0$, and the sufficient condition for minimum is given by the Hessian being positive definite. Since,

$$\mathbf{H} = \mathbf{A},$$

to obtain a minimum point, we require that matrix $\mathbf{A}$ is positive definite. For the steepest-descent algorithm, we have:

$$\mathbf{x}^{(k+1)} = \mathbf{x}^{(k)} + \alpha_k\mathbf{d}^{(k)} = \mathbf{x}^{(k)} - \alpha_k\mathbf{c}^{(k)}.$$

To find the optimal step size α_k, we put $\mathbf{x}^{(k+1)}$ into the quadratic function $f(\mathbf{x})$. This yields the expressions given below:

$$f(\mathbf{x})^{(k+1)} = \frac{1}{2}(\mathbf{x}^{(k)} - \alpha_k \mathbf{c}^{(k)})^{\mathrm{T}} \mathbf{A}(\mathbf{x}^{(k)} - \alpha_k \mathbf{c}^{(k)}) - \mathbf{b}^{\mathrm{T}}(\mathbf{x}^{(k)} - \alpha_k \mathbf{c}^{(k)}) = f(\alpha).$$

$$\frac{df}{d\alpha} = (\mathbf{x}^{(k)} - \alpha_k \mathbf{c}^{(k)})\mathbf{A}(-\mathbf{c}^{(k)}) - \mathbf{b}^{\mathrm{T}}(-\mathbf{c}^{(k)}) = 0$$

$$= \alpha \mathbf{c}^{(k)\mathrm{T}} \mathbf{A} \mathbf{c}^{(k)} - (\mathbf{x}^{(k)\mathrm{T}} \mathbf{A} - \mathbf{b}^{\mathrm{T}})\mathbf{c}^{(k)} = 0.$$

However, taking the transpose of the gradient for the quadratic function gives $\mathbf{x}^{\mathrm{T}}\mathbf{A} - \mathbf{b}^{\mathrm{T}} = \mathbf{c}^{\mathrm{T}}$. So we get:

$$\frac{df}{d\alpha} = \alpha \mathbf{c}^{(k)\mathrm{T}} \mathbf{A} \mathbf{c}^{(k)} - \mathbf{c}^{(k)\mathrm{T}} \mathbf{c}^{(k)} = 0.$$

Solving for α, we get the optimal step size:

$$\alpha_k = \frac{\mathbf{c}^{(k)\mathrm{T}} \mathbf{c}^{(k)}}{\mathbf{c}^{(k)\mathrm{T}} \mathbf{A} \mathbf{c}^{(k)}}.$$

Thus, for a quadratic function, we can obtain an analytical expression for the optimal step size.

Example 3.5 Consider the quadratic function with condition number equal to one:

$$f(x_1, x_2) = \frac{1}{2}(x_1 \quad x_2) \begin{bmatrix} a & 0 \\ 0 & a \end{bmatrix} \begin{pmatrix} x_1 \\ x_2 \end{pmatrix} + (b_1 \quad b_2) \begin{pmatrix} x_1 \\ x_2 \end{pmatrix}.$$

Show that the steepest-descent method converges in a single iteration for this function. Assume $a > 0$.

Solution: The algorithm for steepest descent from a starting design is given here:

$$\mathbf{x}^{(1)} = \mathbf{x}^{(0)} - \alpha \mathbf{c}^{(0)}.$$

Now, the step size for the quadratic function can be calculated using the following expression:

$$\alpha = \frac{\mathbf{c}^{(k)\mathrm{T}} \mathbf{c}^{(k)}}{\mathbf{c}^{(k)\mathrm{T}} \mathbf{A} \mathbf{c}^{(k)}} = \frac{(\mathbf{A}\mathbf{x}^{(0)} - \mathbf{b})^{\mathrm{T}}(\mathbf{A}\mathbf{x}^{(0)} - \mathbf{b})}{(\mathbf{A}\mathbf{x}^{(0)} - \mathbf{b})^{\mathrm{T}} \mathbf{A}(\mathbf{A}\mathbf{x}^{(0)} - \mathbf{b})}.$$

Putting the values for the given problem, we get for α:

$$\alpha = \frac{(ax_1 - b_1)^2 + (ax_2 - b_2)^2}{a[(ax_1 - b_1)^2 + (ax_2 - b_2)^2]} = \frac{1}{a}.$$

Thus, the new point gets defined by the equation:

$$\mathbf{x}^{(1)} = \mathbf{x}^{(0)} - \frac{1}{a}\mathbf{c}^{(0)}.$$

To write it out explicitly:

$$\begin{Bmatrix} x_1^{(1)} \\ x_2^{(2)} \end{Bmatrix} = \begin{Bmatrix} x_1^{(0)} \\ x_2^{(0)} \end{Bmatrix} - \frac{1}{a}\begin{Bmatrix} ax_1^{(0)} - b_1 \\ ax_1^{(0)} - b_1 \end{Bmatrix} = \begin{Bmatrix} \frac{b_1}{a} \\ \frac{b_2}{a} \end{Bmatrix}.$$

Since $\mathbf{Ax}^* = \mathbf{b}$, we also see that the following relation holds good between the components:

$$\begin{Bmatrix} x_1^* \\ x_2^* \end{Bmatrix} = \mathbf{A}^{-1}\mathbf{b} = \begin{bmatrix} a & 0 \\ 0 & a \end{bmatrix}^{-1}\begin{Bmatrix} b_1 \\ b_2 \end{Bmatrix} = \begin{Bmatrix} \frac{b_1}{a} \\ \frac{b_2}{a} \end{Bmatrix}.$$

Thus, we see that starting from any given point, the steepest-descent method converges in just a single iteration for a quadratic function with unit condition number.

Example 3.6 Consider the function defined below:

$$f(x_1, x_2) = \frac{1}{2}(x_1 \quad x_2)\begin{bmatrix} a & 0 \\ 0 & b \end{bmatrix}\begin{pmatrix} x_1 \\ x_2 \end{pmatrix}.$$

Perform a scaling of variables using $\mathbf{x} = \mathbf{Ty}$. Find the diagonal matrix $\mathbf{T}$, if possible, such that the function can be written in the following manner:

$$f(y_1, y_2) = \frac{1}{2}(y_1 \quad y_2)\begin{bmatrix} 1 & 0 \\ 0 & 1 \end{bmatrix}\begin{pmatrix} y_1 \\ y_2 \end{pmatrix}.$$

Solution: $\mathbf{T} = \begin{bmatrix} T_1 & 0 \\ 0 & T_2 \end{bmatrix}$.

$$f(\mathbf{x}) = \frac{1}{2}\mathbf{x}^{\mathrm{T}}\mathbf{Ax} = \frac{1}{2}(\mathbf{Ty})^{\mathrm{T}}\mathbf{A}(\mathbf{Ty}) = \frac{1}{2}\mathbf{y}^{\mathrm{T}}\mathbf{By} = f(\mathbf{y}).$$

Here,

$$\mathbf{B} = \mathbf{T}^{\mathrm{T}}\mathbf{AT} = \begin{bmatrix} T_1 & 0 \\ 0 & T_2 \end{bmatrix}\begin{bmatrix} a & 0 \\ 0 & b \end{bmatrix}\begin{bmatrix} T_1 & 0 \\ 0 & T_2 \end{bmatrix} = \begin{bmatrix} 1 & 0 \\ 0 & 1 \end{bmatrix}$$

Simplifying the above, we get an equation for the variables:

$$\begin{bmatrix} aT_1^2 & 0 \\ 0 & bT_2^2 \end{bmatrix} = \begin{bmatrix} 1 & 0 \\ 0 & 1 \end{bmatrix}.$$

This gives the solution

$$\mathbf{T} = \begin{bmatrix} \frac{1}{\sqrt{a}} & 0 \\ 0 & \frac{1}{\sqrt{b}} \end{bmatrix}.$$

Therefore, if $\mathbf{A}$ is a diagonal matrix, in general, we can use the following transformation to convert the matrix into one with condition number equal to 1:

$$\mathbf{T} = \begin{bmatrix} \frac{1}{\sqrt{H_{11}}} & 0 \\ 0 & \frac{1}{\sqrt{H_{22}}} \end{bmatrix}.$$

Such a problem can be solved very efficiently by the steepest-descent method.

Example 3.7 Show that eigenvectors of $\mathbf{A}$ can be used to convert the matrix into a diagonal matrix.

Solution: Consider the eigenvalue problem:

$$\mathbf{A}\boldsymbol{\varphi} = \lambda\boldsymbol{\varphi}.$$

Premultiply by $\boldsymbol{\varphi}^{\mathrm{T}}$:

$$\boldsymbol{\varphi}^{\mathrm{T}}\mathbf{A}\boldsymbol{\varphi} = \boldsymbol{\varphi}^{\mathrm{T}}\lambda\boldsymbol{\varphi} = \boldsymbol{\Lambda}.$$

Since the eigenvectors are orthogonal, the right-hand side becomes a diagonal matrix, which can be converted to a matrix with condition number equal to 1 by using the scaling in Example 3.6. However, this approach is not of any practical use as it is computationally expensive to calculate the eigenvectors of a matrix.

The steepest-descent method is a first-order method and shows linear convergence. Algorithms based on second-order information often show quadratic convergence. In the following section, the concept of rates of convergence is introduced so as to study and understand the meaning of the above statements.

3.3 Rates of Convergence

Most optimization algorithms calculate a sequence of solutions given by $\mathbf{x}^{(k+1)} = \mathbf{x}^{(k)} + \alpha_k\mathbf{d}^{(k)}$. The two main questions regarding any such algorithm are the following:

1. Does it converge?
2. How fast does it converge?

Typically, the cost of an algorithm is calculated using the number of steps required to arrive at a convergence or by counting the number of arithmetic operations required. This cost is called the computational complexity of the algorithm. For many practical optimization methods, the number of operations needed to find an exact solution can be very large. The rate of convergence is a measure which allows us to compare such algorithms.

Assume a sequence of points $x^{(k)}$ converging to an optimal solution x^*. The sequence of errors can be defined as follows:

$$\mathrm{e}_k = x^{(k)} - x^*. \tag{3.18}$$

If the algorithm convergences at some point, it follows that:

$$\lim_{k\to\infty} \mathrm{e}_k = 0. \tag{3.19}$$

The sequence $x_1, x_2, \ldots, x_k$ is said to converge to x^* at a rate r and rate constant c if[2]

$$\lim_{k\to\infty} \frac{\|\mathrm{e}_{k+1}\|}{\|\mathrm{e}_k\|^r} = c, \tag{3.20}$$

and $c < \infty$. For simplicity, we assume that the convergence behaviour is ideal, so that limits are not needed in the calculation. Then (3.20) can be written as follows:

$$\|\mathrm{e}_{k+1}\| = c\|\mathrm{e}_k\|^r. \tag{3.21}$$

Linear convergence occurs when $r = 1$, and (3.21) becomes

$$\|e_{k+1}\| = c\|e_k\|. \tag{3.22}$$

However, the behaviour of an algorithm with linear convergence depends on the value of the rate constant c. There are three possible cases:

1. When $0 < c < 1$, the norm of the error is reduced at every iteration by a constant factor.
2. If $c > 1$, then the sequence diverges.
3. When $c = 1$, the error does not decrease. The algorithm gets *stuck*.

There are several possibilities when $0 < c < 1$ for a convergent sequence depending on the value of c. For example, if $c = 0.1$ and $\|e_0\| = 1$, the sequence of error norms are $1, 10^{-1}, 10^{-2}, 10^{-3}, \ldots, 10^{-7}, \ldots$ which implies a seven-digit accuracy after seven iterations, which is a good result. However, if $c = 0.99$, the norm of the errors are $1, 0.99, 0.9801, 0.9703, 0.9606, 0.9510, 0.9415, 0.9321, \ldots$ and it takes about 1600 iterations to reduce the error to 10^{-7}.

If $r = 1$ and $c = 0$, the convergence is called superlinear and all cases where $r > 1$ are termed superlinear convergence, since, if

$$\lim_{k\to\infty} \frac{\|e_{k+1}\|}{\|e_k\|^r} = c < \infty, \tag{3.23}$$

then $\lim_{k\to\infty} \|e_{k+1}\|/\|e_k\| = \lim_{k\to\infty} (\|e_{k+1}\|/\|e\|^r)\|e_k\|^{r-1} = c \lim_{k\to\infty} \|e_k\|^{r-1} = 0$, only if $r > 1$ or $c = 0$. Also, if $r = 1$, then c must be zero. These cases constitute superlinear convergence.

Quadratic convergence occurs when $r = 2$. Algorithms with quadratic convergence are seen to converge very quickly. Consider the case where $r = 2$, $c = 1$, $\|e_0\| = 10^{-1}$. Then, the sequence of error norms becomes: $10^{-1}, 10^{-2}, 10^{-4}, 10^{-8}, \ldots$ and three iterations are sufficient for seven-digit accuracy.

Another important case occurs when $1 < r < 2$. This is another special case of superlinear convergence and is important because (1) it is qualitatively similar to quadratic convergence for the precision of most computer calculations, and (2) it can be achieved by algorithms that only calculate first derivatives, whereas to achieve quadratic convergence, it is necessary to compute second derivatives as well. When $r = 1.5$, $c = 1$ and $\|e_0\| = 10^{-1}$, the sequence of error norms is: $1\times10^{-1}, 3\times10^{-2}, 6\times10^{-3}, 4\times10^{-4}, 9\times10^{-6}, 3\times10^{-8}, \ldots$ five iterations are required for single-precision accuracy.

Example 3.8 Determine the rate of convergence and rate constant of the sequence, $2, 1.1, 1.01, 1.001, 1.0001, 1.00001 \ldots$

Solution: We can see that the general term for the sequence is $x_k = 1 + 10^{-k}$. The sequence converges to $x^* = 1$ and $e_k = x_k - x^* = 10^{-k}$. Thus we get the rate constant as

$$c = \lim_{k\to\infty} \frac{\|e_{k+1}\|}{\|e_k\|} = \lim_{k\to\infty} \frac{10^{-(k+1)}}{10^{-k}} = \frac{1}{10}.$$

The sequence therefore converges linearly with rate constant $1/10$. A lower value of rate constant results in faster convergence.

Example 3.9 Consider the sequence, 4, 2.5, 2.05, and 2.00060975, defined by,

$$x^{(k+1)} = \frac{1}{2}\left(x^{(k)} + \frac{4}{x^{(k)}}\right) = \frac{x^{(k)}}{2} + \frac{2}{x^{(k)}}.$$

Find the rate of convergence and the rate constant.

Solution: With $x^{(0)} = 4$, since $x^* \to 2$,

$$\begin{aligned} e_{k+1} &= x^{(k+1)} - x^* = \frac{x^{(k)}}{2} + \frac{2}{x^{(k)}} - 2 \\ &= \frac{1}{2x^{(k)}}(x^{(k)2} + 4 - 4x^{(k)}) = \frac{1}{2x^{(k)}}(x^{(k)} - 2)^2 = \frac{1}{2x^{(k)}} e_k^2 \end{aligned}$$

or $\lim_{k\to\infty} \|e_{k+1}\|/\|e_k\|^2 = 1/2|x^*| = 1/4$.

This sequence converges quadratically with rate constant 1/4. We can see the rapidity of convergence.

Example 3.10 Find the rate of convergence and rate constant of the sequence

$$\frac{1}{2}, \frac{1}{4}, \frac{1}{8}, \frac{1}{16}, \frac{1}{32}, \ldots.$$

Solution: The general term of the sequence is given by

$$x^{(k)} = \frac{1}{2^k} = 2^{-k}.$$

The optimal solution is $x^* = 0$. The error term is $e_k = x^{(k)} - x^* = 2^{-k}$ and

$$c = \lim_{k\to\infty} \frac{\|e_{k+1}\|}{\|e_k\|} = \lim_{k\to\infty} \frac{2^{-(k+1)}}{2^{-k}} = \frac{1}{2}.$$

Thus, the rate constant is 0.5 and the convergence rate is linear. However, since the rate constant is higher, the convergence is slow as compared to Example 3.8. Note that if we assumed a quadratic convergence rate, we would get

$$\lim_{k\to\infty} \frac{\|e_{k+1}\|}{\|e_k\|^2} = \lim_{k\to\infty} \frac{2^{-(k+1)}}{2^{-k}2^{-k}} = \frac{1}{2.2^{-k}} = \frac{1}{2^{-k+1}} = \text{not a constant.}$$

Thus, the sequence does not show quadratic convergence.

Example 3.11 Find the convergence rate and rate constant for the sequence defined by the general term $x^{(k)} = 3^{-k^2}$.

Solution: The sequence appears as $1/3, 1/81, 1/19683, \ldots$, and tends to $x^* = 0$. The error terms are given by $e_k = x^{(k)} - x^* = 3^{-k^2}$ and $e_{k+1} = 3^{-(k+1)^2} = 3^{-k^2-2k-1} = e_k 3^{-2k-1}$. Therefore,

$$\lim_{k\to\infty} \frac{\|e_{k+1}\|}{\|e_k\|} = \lim_{k\to\infty} \frac{1}{3^{2k+1}} = 0.$$

Since the rate constant is zero, this is a case of superlinear convergence.

In practical situations, ideal convergence behaviour is only observed in the limit and not at the initial iterations.

Example 3.12 Use the steepest-descent method for the function $f(\mathbf{x}) = x_1^2 + 2x_2^2$ starting from the point $\mathbf{x}^{(0)} = (1, 1)$. Find the rate constant.

Solution: The optimal point of this problem is obviously at $\mathbf{x}^* = (0, 0)$ and $f(\mathbf{x}^*) = 0$. The gradient of the function is given by

$$\mathbf{c} = \begin{pmatrix} 2x_1 \\ 4x_2 \end{pmatrix}.$$

The steepest-descent method then gives

$$\mathbf{x}^{(k+1)} = \mathbf{x}^{(k)} - \alpha \begin{pmatrix} 2x_1^{(k)} \\ 4x_2^{(k)} \end{pmatrix}.$$

The function value at the starting point $\mathbf{x}^{(0)} = (1, 1)$ is 3 and the gradient norm is 4.472. For the given starting point, we get

$$\mathbf{x}^{(1)} = \begin{pmatrix} 1 - 2\alpha \\ 1 - 4\alpha \end{pmatrix}$$

Putting this point in the function, we get the 1D problem

$$f(\alpha) = (1 - 2\alpha)^2 + 2(1 - 4\alpha)^2.$$

To get the optimal step size,

$$f'(\alpha) = -4(1 - 2\alpha) - 16(1 - 4\alpha) = 0.$$

$$\alpha = 0.2778.$$

The new design point and function value are obtained:

$$\mathbf{x}^{(1)} = \begin{pmatrix} 0.4444 \\ -0.1111 \end{pmatrix}, \qquad f(\mathbf{x}^{(1)}) = 0.2222.$$

Assuming linear convergence, the rate constant can be calculated:

$$\frac{f(x^{(1)}) - f(x^*)}{f(x^{(0)}) - f(x^*)} = \frac{0.2222 - 0}{3 - 0} = 0.074.$$

The second design point is

$$\mathbf{x}^{(2)} = \begin{pmatrix} 0.4444 - 0.8888\alpha \\ -0.1111 + 0.4444\alpha \end{pmatrix}.$$

Putting this value in the function, we get,

$$f(\alpha) = (0.4444 - 0.8888\alpha)^2 + 2(-0.1111 + 0.4444\alpha)^2.$$

The optimal step size is $\alpha = 0.4167$. The new design point and function value then take the value:

$$\mathbf{x}^{(2)} = \begin{pmatrix} 0.0740 \\ 0.0741 \end{pmatrix}; \qquad f(\mathbf{x}^{(2)}) = 0.0164.$$

The rate constant is then as given below.

$$\frac{f(x^{(2)}) - f(x^*)}{f(x^{(1)}) - f(x^*)} = \frac{0.0164 - 0}{0.2222 - 0} = 0.073.$$

We see that for the given problem, the steepest-descent method converges linearly with a rate constant of about 0.074.

In general, when the steepest-decent method is applied to a positive definite quadratic form and an exact line search method is used, the method converges linearly to the minimum $\mathbf{x}^*$. It has a rate constant which is given below:[2]

$$c = \frac{f(\mathbf{x}^{(k+1)}) - f(\mathbf{x}^*)}{f(\mathbf{x}^{(k)}) - f(\mathbf{x}^*)} \leq \left(\frac{\text{cond}(\mathbf{A}) - 1}{\text{cond}(\mathbf{A}) + 1}\right).$$

For Example 3.12, the condition number of **A** is 2 and the upper bound on the rate constant is given by:

$$c \leq \left(\frac{2-1}{2+1}\right)^2.$$

$$c \leq 0.1111.$$

We can see that as the condition number becomes higher, the rate constant become close to 1 and the steepest-descent method can become very slow. Thus, the rate constant plays an important role in the convergence of the algorithm, even when the convergence rate is fixed. In general, the steepest-descent method works reasonably well only when $\text{cond}(\mathbf{A}) \leq 50$. When $\text{cond}(\mathbf{A}) = 100$, the rate constant is about 0.96 which means that the steepest-descent method improves the solution by only 4 per cent in each iteration.

For a general function, $\mathbf{A} = \mathbf{H}^*$, which is the Hessian value at the optimal point.

3.4 Conjugate-Gradient Method

This method was proposed by Fletcher and Reeves in 1964 as an improvement over the steepest-descent method. As remarked earlier, in the steepest-decent method, consecutive steps are orthogonal which leads to the zigzag behaviour of the search directions. This tends to slow down the convergence of the steepest-descent method. The conjugate-gradient method, on the other hand, is very interesting, as a slight deflection of the search direction of the steepest-descent method results in a considerable improvement of convergence properties. Before describing the conjugate-gradient method, we need to define conjugate gradients, which are based on the concept of conjugate directions.

3.4.1 Conjugate directions

Consider a quadratic function:

$$f(\mathbf{x}) = \frac{1}{2}\mathbf{x}^{\mathrm{T}}\mathbf{A}\mathbf{x} - \mathbf{b}^{\mathrm{T}}\mathbf{x}. \tag{3.24}$$

Let **A** be a symmetric positive definite matrix of size $n \times n$ implying that there are n design variables. Then we say that directions $\mathbf{d}^{(1)}$ and $\mathbf{d}^{(2)}$ are **A**-conjugate if[4]

$$\mathbf{d}^{(1)\mathrm{T}}\mathbf{A}\mathbf{d}^{(2)} = 0. \tag{3.25}$$

In general, directions $\mathbf{d}^{(0)}, \mathbf{d}^{(1)}, \mathbf{d}^{(2)}, \ldots, \mathbf{d}^{(n-1)}$ are **A**-conjugate if for all $i \neq j$

$$\mathbf{d}^{(i)\mathrm{T}}\mathbf{A}\mathbf{d}^{(j)} = 0. \tag{3.26}$$

Example 3.13 Show that the conjugate directions are linearly independent if they are nonzero.

Solution: Consider k different conjugate directions, $\mathbf{d}^{(0)}, \mathbf{d}^{(1)}, \mathbf{d}^{(2)}, \ldots, \mathbf{d}^{(k)}$, where $k \leq n-1$.

Let $\alpha_0, \alpha_1, \alpha_2, \ldots, \alpha_k$ be scalars such that

$$\alpha_0\mathbf{d}^{(1)} + \alpha_1\mathbf{d}^{(2)} + \cdots + \alpha_k\mathbf{d}^{(k)} = 0.$$

Premultiply the above equation by $\mathbf{d}^{(j)\mathrm{T}}\mathbf{A}$, where $0 \leq j \leq k$:

$$\mathbf{d}^{(j)\mathrm{T}}\mathbf{A}(\alpha_0\mathbf{d}^{(1)} + \alpha_1\mathbf{d}^{(2)} + \cdots + \alpha_k\mathbf{d}^{(k)}) = 0.$$

Most terms on the left-hand side of the above equation will vanish due to conjugacy (3.26), yielding

$$\alpha_j\mathbf{d}^{(j)\mathrm{T}}\mathbf{A}\mathbf{d}^{(j)} = 0.$$

However, since **A** is positive definite:

$$\mathbf{d}^{(j)\mathrm{T}}\mathbf{A}\mathbf{d}^{(j)} > 0.$$

Thus, we must have all $\alpha_j = 0$, $j = 1, 2, \ldots, k$. This implies that the directions are linearly independent.

Example 3.14 Consider a quadratic function, with

$$\mathbf{A} = \begin{bmatrix} 3 & 1 \\ 0 & 2 \end{bmatrix}.$$

The first vector $\mathbf{d}^{(0)}$ is known as:

$$d^{(0)} = \begin{pmatrix} 1 \\ 0 \end{pmatrix}.$$

Find the conjugate vector.

Solution: We should first check for positive definiteness of **A**. The eigenvalues of **A** are obtained using the equation:

$$\begin{vmatrix} 3-\lambda & 1 \\ 0 & 2-\lambda \end{vmatrix} = 0.$$

Solving this leads to $\lambda = 2, 3$. Thus **A** is positive definite.

Let the conjugate vector be given by:

$$\mathbf{d}^{(1)} = \begin{pmatrix} d_1^{(1)} \\ d_2^{(1)} \end{pmatrix}.$$

Then,

$$\mathbf{d}^{(0)\mathrm{T}}\mathbf{A}\mathbf{d}^{(1)} = (1 \quad 0)\begin{bmatrix} 3 & 1 \\ 0 & 2 \end{bmatrix}\begin{pmatrix} d_1^{(1)} \\ d_2^{(1)} \end{pmatrix} = 0.$$

Alternatively,

$$3d_1^{(1)} + d_2^{(1)} = 0.$$

Let

$$d_2^{(1)} = 3, \qquad 3d_1^{(1)} = -3 \Rightarrow d_1^{(1)} = -1.$$

We thus get the conjugate direction as follows:

$$\mathbf{d}^{(1)} = \begin{pmatrix} -1 \\ 3 \end{pmatrix}.$$

Here, $\mathbf{d}^{(0)}$ and $\mathbf{d}^{(1)}$ are mutually $\mathbf{A}$-conjugate directions.

From the above problem, we can see that given a positive definite matrix $\mathbf{A}$ and a starting direction vector $\mathbf{d}^{(0)}$, we can find the conjugate directions. However, this approach to finding conjugate directions is tedious and *ad hoc*. Better approaches are proposed in the conjugate-gradient algorithm where the first direction is assumed as the steepest-descent direction. There are several different formulas for the conjugate-gradient method, proposed by different researchers. The most widespread is the Fletcher–Reeves formula which we use to describe the method next. We will discuss other methods in subsequent sections in this chapter.

In the conjugate-gradient method proposed by Fletcher and Reeves, the conjugate directions are defined as follows:[1]

$$\mathbf{d}^{(k)} = -\mathbf{c}^{(k)} + \beta_k \mathbf{d}^{(k-1)}, \tag{3.27}$$

where,

$$\beta_k = \left(\frac{\|\mathbf{c}^{(k)}\|}{\|\mathbf{c}^{(k-1)}\|} \right)^2. \tag{3.28}$$

We will show subsequently that these directions are conjugate for quadratic functions with positive definite and symmetric Hessians. Let us check if the descent condition is satisfied by the conjugate-gradient search direction. Recall that the descent direction should satisfy,

$$\mathbf{c}^{(k)} \cdot \mathbf{d}^{(k)} < 0. \tag{3.29}$$

For the conjugate directions,

$$\begin{aligned} \mathbf{c}^{(k)} \cdot \mathbf{d}^{(k)} &= \mathbf{c}^{(k)} \cdot (-\mathbf{c}^{(k)} + \beta_k \mathbf{d}^{(k-1)}) \\ &= -\mathbf{c}^{(k)} \cdot \mathbf{c}^{(k)} + \beta_k \mathbf{c}^{(k)} \cdot \mathbf{d}^{(k-1)} = -\mathbf{c}^{(k)} \cdot \mathbf{c}^{(k)} < 0, \end{aligned} \tag{3.30}$$

where the line-search termination criteria $\mathbf{c}^{(k+1)} \cdot \mathbf{d}^{(k)} = 0$ is used to set $\mathbf{c}^{(k)} \cdot \mathbf{d}^{(k-1)} = 0$ in (3.29). Note that conjugate-gradient method assures a descent condition only if an exact line search is used. We now write the algorithm for the Fletcher–Reeves version of the conjugate-gradient method.

3.4.2 A general conjugate-gradient algorithm

1. Estimate the starting design $\mathbf{x}^{(0)}$. Set $k = 0$ and select ε.
   Calculate $\mathbf{d}^{(0)} = -\mathbf{c}^{(0)}$.
   Check to see whether $\|\mathbf{c}^{(0)}\| < \varepsilon$. If this is true, then the starting point is a stationary point, stop now; if it is not, then perform an iteration of the steepest-descent method. Now set $k = 1$ and go to step 2.
2. Calculate $\mathbf{c}^{(k)}$.
   If $\|\mathbf{c}^{(k)}\| < \varepsilon$, stop the process, otherwise continue.
3. Calculate the new *conjugate direction* as follows:

$$\mathbf{d}^{(k)} = -\mathbf{c}^{(k)} + \beta_k \mathbf{d}^{(k-1)}.$$

4. Compute $\alpha_k = \alpha$ to minimize the function:

$$f(\mathbf{x}^{(k)} + \alpha \mathbf{d}^{(k)}).$$

5. Update the design in the following manner:

$$\mathbf{x}^{(k+1)} = \mathbf{x}^{(k)} + \alpha_k \mathbf{d}^{(k)}.$$

   Set $k = k + 1$ and go to step 2.

The first step of the conjugate-gradient method is the same as for the steepest-descent. Further steps are modified by using a scaled or *deflected direction*. The basic philosophy here is to deflect the search direction of the steepest-descent method from $\mathbf{d}^{(k)} = -\mathbf{c}^{(k)}$ to $\mathbf{d}^{(k)} = -\mathbf{c}^{(k)} + \mathbf{g}$, where $\mathbf{g}$ is an appropriate vector which prevents the zigzag behaviour of the steepest-descent method.

Since $\mathbf{c}^{(k)}$ and $\mathbf{c}^{(k-1)}$ are available at iteration k and the norm of the gradient is calculated at each iteration to check its convergence, the calculation of the conjugate gradient is a simple step. The conjugate-gradient method finds the minimum for positive definite quadratic forms having n design variables in n iterations, a fact which we shall prove later in this chapter. The conjugate-gradient method is ideally suited for second-order quadratic forms. For general functions, it is best to restart the iteration process after every $n + 1$ iterations for computational stability. In actual implementation, the conjugate-gradient method is often used for problems with a very large number of design variables. In such cases, the conjugate property of the directions can deteriorate even before the n iterations are over, due to roundoff errors. These errors cause the algorithm to deteriorate from its theoretical predictions. The less similar the function is to a quadratic function, the more rapidly the conjugate directions will cease to be conjugate. Also, for large-sized problems such as those with $n = 500$ or above, we may not want to wait for 500 iterations for a reasonable solution. Such problems can be alleviated by scaling the problem such that any ill-conditioning of the matrix $\mathbf{A}$ of the quadratic form (or the Hessian, in the case of a nonlinear function) is reduced.

Example 3.15 Minimize the function $f(x_1, x_2) = x_1^2 + 2x_2^2 + e^{-x_1-x_2}$ using the Fletcher–Reeves conjugate-gradient method. Use the starting point $\mathbf{x}^{(0)} = (1, 2)$.

Solution: The first iteration is the same for the steepest-descent and conjugate-gradient methods and has already been done in Example 3.2. At the end of the first iteration, we have the following:

$$\mathbf{x}^{(0)} = \begin{Bmatrix} 1 \\ 2 \end{Bmatrix}, \quad \mathbf{x}^{(1)} = \begin{Bmatrix} 0.5319 \\ 0.0919 \end{Bmatrix}, \quad \mathbf{c}^{(0)} = \begin{Bmatrix} 1.9502 \\ 7.9502 \end{Bmatrix},$$

$$\mathbf{c}^{(1)} = \begin{Bmatrix} 0.5279 \\ -0.1680 \end{Bmatrix}, \quad \mathbf{d}^{(0)} = \begin{Bmatrix} -1.9502 \\ -7.9502 \end{Bmatrix}, \quad \|\mathbf{c}^{(0)}\| = 8.1859.$$

We also see that $\|\mathbf{c}^{(1)}\| = 0.554 > 0$. We need to now calculate the conjugate-gradient search direction:

$$\beta_1 = \left(\frac{\|\mathbf{c}^{(1)}\|}{\|\mathbf{c}^{(0)}\|} \right)^2 = \left(\frac{0.5539}{8.1859} \right)^2 = 0.0046.$$

$$\mathbf{d}^{(1)} = -\mathbf{c}^{(1)} + \beta_1 \mathbf{d}^{(0)},$$

$$= \begin{Bmatrix} -0.5279 \\ 0.1680 \end{Bmatrix} + 0.0046 \begin{Bmatrix} -1.9502 \\ -7.9502 \end{Bmatrix} = \begin{Bmatrix} -0.5368 \\ 0.1316 \end{Bmatrix}.$$

We see that in the conjugate-gradient method, the search direction is slightly changed from that of the steepest-descent method. Using this search direction, we get the next design point:

$$\mathbf{x}^{(2)} = \mathbf{x}^{(1)} + \alpha \mathbf{d}^{(1)} = \begin{Bmatrix} 0.5319 \\ 0.0919 \end{Bmatrix} + \alpha \begin{Bmatrix} -0.5368 \\ 0.1316 \end{Bmatrix} = \begin{Bmatrix} 0.5319 - 0.5368\alpha \\ 0.0919 + 0.1316\alpha \end{Bmatrix}$$

Putting this design point into the function yields the following equation.

$$f(x_1, x_2) = (0.5319 - 0.5368\alpha)^2 + 2(0.0919 + 0.1316\alpha)^2 + e^{-0.6238+0.4052\alpha}$$
$$= f(\alpha).$$

The minimum of $f(\alpha)$ can be found using 1D search methods. First, using $\delta = 0.25$, we bracket the minimum between 0.25 and 0.75. Then we keep reducing the interval and get $\alpha^* = 0.41$ as the optimal point. The new design point becomes

$$\mathbf{x}^{(2)} = \begin{Bmatrix} 0.5319 - 0.5368\alpha \\ 0.0919 + 0.1316\alpha \end{Bmatrix} = \begin{Bmatrix} 0.3118 \\ 0.1459 \end{Bmatrix}.$$

The gradient value at this point is given by the expression:

$$\mathbf{c}^{(1)} = \begin{Bmatrix} 2x_1 - e^{-x_1-x_2} \\ 4x_2 - e^{-x_1-x_2} \end{Bmatrix} = \begin{Bmatrix} -0.009 \\ -0.049 \end{Bmatrix}.$$

The gradient norm is reduced to 0.05 in this iteration. Further iterations are required for convergence.

3.4.3 Other conjugate-gradient methods

There are some other versions of the conjugate-gradient method which use different formulas for β_k. In particular, two other formulas suggested by researchers are also quite popular, and computational results indicate that these methods can perform better than the Fletcher–Reeves formula. These formulas are given below:[4]

A. Polak–Ribiere method
This method is characterized by the following formula for β_k:

$$\beta_k = \frac{(\mathbf{c}^{(k)} - \mathbf{c}^{(k-1)})^{\mathrm{T}}\mathbf{c}^{(k)}}{\mathbf{c}^{(k-1)\mathrm{T}}\mathbf{c}^{(k-1)}}. \tag{3.31}$$

B. Hestenes–Stiefel method
This method uses the following variation for β_k:

$$\beta_k = \frac{(\mathbf{c}^{(k)} - \mathbf{c}^{(k-1)})^{\mathrm{T}}\mathbf{c}^{(k)}}{(\mathbf{c}^{(k)} - \mathbf{c}^{(k-1)})^{\mathrm{T}}\mathbf{d}^{(k-1)}}. \tag{3.32}$$

In some cases, the Polak–Ribiere method cycles infinitely without converging. However, for many general problems, the Polak–Ribiere method converges more quickly than the Fletcher–Reeves method. The convergence of the Polak–Ribiere method can be guaranteed by restarting the method if $\beta_k < 0$. In general, conjugate-gradient methods can be restarted when $\beta_k < 0$ simply by using the formula $\beta_k = \max(0, \beta_k)$ at each iteration.

In general, the line search in conjugate-gradient methods is much more important than for other methods. The proof that the conjugate-gradient direction is a descent direction uses the line search termination criteria. However, an important advantage of the conjugate-gradient method is low storage requirement, since it is based on vector algebra and does not use Hessian or approximate Hessian matrices as in the Newton and quasi-Newton methods which are discussed in Chapter 4.

3.4.4 Preconditioning

In practical implementations, a preconditioner is always recommended for conjugate-gradient methods. The preconditioner tries to reduce the *condition number* of the matrix of the quadratic form. Preconditioning makes the quadratic form more *circular* relative to its original *elliptical* form (think of the difference between $x_1^2 + x_2^2 = r^2$ and $x_1^2 + 100x_2^2 = r^2$). The eigenvalues of matrix **A** then become closer to each other. Note that the application of the conjugate-gradient method to minimize the positive definite quadratic form results in a solution of the linear system $\mathbf{Ax} = \mathbf{b}$. A preconditioner is a positive definite matrix **M** which changes the linear system to:[2]

$$\mathbf{M}^{-1}\mathbf{Ax} = \mathbf{M}^{-1}\mathbf{b}.$$

Here, the matrix **M** is chosen to bring the condition number of $\mathbf{M}^{-1}\mathbf{A}$ as close to one as possible. Now, if we select $\mathbf{M} = \mathbf{A}$, the condition number of $\mathbf{M}^{-1}\mathbf{A}$ will become unity. However, inverting **A** can be computationally expensive since we are talking of a very large problem size. A widely used and simple approach is to select **M** as a diagonal matrix since the inverse of a diagonal matrix can be easily found. A particularly simple choice is to use the diagonal terms of **A** to form the preconditioning matrix. This is known as *Jacobi preconditioning*.

For a general nonlinear function, the Hessian at the minimum point is an ideal preconditioner. However, this choice is impractical for most problems. An alternative is to use the diagonal of the Hessian at the design point, which is relatively cheaper to calculate. If any diagonal term of the Hessian becomes negative, we can replace it with the identity matrix which means that we skip preconditioning in that iteration.

More elaborate preconditioners based on Cholesky factorization of matrices exist. It is now accepted that for problems with a large number of design variables, conjugate-gradient methods should be used with a preconditioner.

Example 3.16 Consider a linear system which is defined by the following equation:

$$\begin{bmatrix} 10000 & 1000 \\ 1 & 2 \end{bmatrix} \begin{pmatrix} x_1 \\ x_2 \end{pmatrix} = \begin{pmatrix} 1 \\ 1 \end{pmatrix}.$$

Find a preconditioner for this problem, and calculate the reduction in the condition number of the matrix.

Solution: The eigenvalues of

$$\mathbf{A} = \begin{bmatrix} 10000 & 1000 \\ 1 & 2 \end{bmatrix}$$

are obtained using

$$\begin{vmatrix} 10000-\lambda & 1000 \\ 1 & 2-\lambda \end{vmatrix} = 0.$$

Solving for the eigenvalues yields $\lambda = 1.9, 10000.1$. Therefore, $\text{cond}(\mathbf{A}) = 5263$.

We select the diagonal preconditioner by the condition:

$$\mathbf{M} = \begin{bmatrix} 10000 & 0 \\ 0 & 2 \end{bmatrix},$$

where we have simply taken the diagonal elements of **A**.

Then,

$$\mathbf{M}^{-1}\mathbf{A} = \begin{bmatrix} 10000 & 0 \\ 0 & 2 \end{bmatrix}^{-1} \begin{bmatrix} 10000 & 1000 \\ 1 & 2 \end{bmatrix} = \begin{bmatrix} \frac{1}{10000} & 0 \\ 0 & \frac{1}{2} \end{bmatrix} \begin{bmatrix} 10000 & 1000 \\ 1 & 2 \end{bmatrix}$$

$$= \begin{bmatrix} 1 & 0.1 \\ 0.5 & 1 \end{bmatrix}.$$

Also,

$$\lambda = 1.2236, 0.7764$$

$$\text{cond}(\mathbf{M}^{-1}\mathbf{A}) = 1.58$$

We see that the condition number has decreased significantly.

3.5 Basic Conjugate-Gradient Algorithms for Quadratic Functions

The statement of the formulas for β_k for the various conjugate-gradient methods in the previous section may appear to be reminiscent of a magic trick. It is possible to get a much better appreciation of these formulas by considering their applications to quadratic functions. Consider the problem of minimizing the quadratic function of n design variables:

$$f(\mathbf{x}) = \frac{1}{2}\mathbf{x}^{\mathrm{T}}\mathbf{A}\mathbf{x} - \mathbf{b}^{\mathrm{T}}\mathbf{x}. \tag{3.33}$$

We assume $\mathbf{A}$ to be symmetric and positive definite. We will now show that starting from any point $\mathbf{x}^{(0)}$ and using $\mathbf{A}$-conjugate directions $\mathbf{d}^{(0)}, \mathbf{d}^{(1)}, \mathbf{d}^{(2)}, \ldots, \mathbf{d}^{(n-1)}$, the conjugate direction algorithm converges to $\mathbf{x}^*$ in exactly n iterations, or[4]

$$\mathbf{x}^{(n)} = \mathbf{x}^*. \tag{3.34}$$

The algorithm used has the form

$$\mathbf{x}^{(k+1)} = \mathbf{x}^{(k)} + \alpha_k \mathbf{d}^{(k)}. \tag{3.35}$$

Here,

$$\alpha_k = -\frac{\mathbf{c}^{(k)\mathrm{T}} \cdot \mathbf{d}^{(k)}}{\mathbf{d}^{(k)\mathrm{T}}\mathbf{A}\mathbf{d}^{(k)}}. \tag{3.36}$$

To derive this result, we use the fact that the $\mathbf{A}$-conjugate directions $\mathbf{d}^{(0)}, \mathbf{d}^{(1)}, \mathbf{d}^{(2)}, \ldots, \mathbf{d}^{(n-1)}$ are linearly independent. Consider that $\mathbf{x}^* - \mathbf{x}^{(0)}$ is a vector of size n representing the difference between the optimal design and the starting design. Such a vector can be written in terms of the conjugate directions which are linearly independent as follows:

$$\mathbf{x}^* - \mathbf{x}^{(0)} = \beta_0\mathbf{d}^{(0)} + \beta_1\mathbf{d}^{(1)} + \cdots + \beta_{n-1}\mathbf{d}^{(n-1)}. \tag{3.37}$$

Here, $\beta_0, \beta_1, \ldots, \beta_{n-1}$ are constants. Premultiplying both sides of (3.37) by $\mathbf{d}^{(k)\mathrm{T}}\mathbf{A}$ yields

$$\mathbf{d}^{(k)\mathrm{T}}\mathbf{A}(\mathbf{x}^* - \mathbf{x}^{(0)}) = \mathbf{d}^{(k)\mathrm{T}}\mathbf{A}(\beta_0\mathbf{d}^{(0)} + \beta_1\mathbf{d}^{(1)} + \cdots + \beta_{n-1}\mathbf{d}^{(n-1)}) = \beta_k\mathbf{d}^{(k)\mathrm{T}}\mathbf{A}\mathbf{d}^{(k)}. \tag{3.38}$$

All terms except the kth term in (3.38) vanish due to the $\mathbf{A}$-conjugate property of the directions. Thus, we get,

$$\beta_k = \frac{\mathbf{d}^{(k)\mathrm{T}}\mathbf{A}(\mathbf{x}^* - \mathbf{x}^{(0)})}{\mathbf{d}^{(k)\mathrm{T}}\mathbf{A}\mathbf{d}^{(k)}}. \tag{3.39}$$

Now,

$$\begin{aligned}\mathbf{x}^{(k)} &= \mathbf{x}^{(k-1)} + \alpha_{k-1}\mathbf{d}^{(k-1)} = \mathbf{x}^{(k-2)} + \alpha_{k-2}\mathbf{d}^{(k-2)} + \alpha_{k-1}\mathbf{d}^{(k-1)} \\ &= \mathbf{x}^{(0)} + \alpha_0\mathbf{d}^{(0)} + \alpha_1\mathbf{d}^{(1)} + \cdots + \alpha_{k-2}\mathbf{d}^{(k-2)} + \alpha_{k-1}\mathbf{d}^{(k-1)}.\end{aligned} \tag{3.40}$$

Thus, we get:

$$\mathbf{x}^{(k)} - \mathbf{x}^{(0)} = \alpha_0\mathbf{d}^{(0)} + \alpha_1\mathbf{d}^{(1)} + \cdots + \alpha_{k-2}\mathbf{d}^{(k-2)} + \alpha_{k-1}\mathbf{d}^{(k-1)}. \tag{3.41}$$

We can now write $\mathbf{x}^* - \mathbf{x}^{(0)}$ as follows:

$$\mathbf{x}^* - \mathbf{x}^{(0)} = (\mathbf{x}^* - \mathbf{x}^{(k)}) + (\mathbf{x}^{(k)} - \mathbf{x}^{(0)}). \tag{3.42}$$

We premultiply both sides of (3.42) by $\mathbf{d}^{(k)\mathrm{T}}\mathbf{A}$

$$\mathbf{d}^{(k)\mathrm{T}}\mathbf{A}(\mathbf{x}^* - \mathbf{x}^{(0)}) = \mathbf{d}^{(k)\mathrm{T}}\mathbf{A}(\mathbf{x}^* - \mathbf{x}^{(k)}) + \mathbf{d}^{(k)\mathrm{T}}\mathbf{A}(\mathbf{x}^{(k)} - \mathbf{x}^{(0)}). \tag{3.43}$$

We have obtained expressions for $\mathbf{x}^* - \mathbf{x}^{(k)}$ and $\mathbf{x}^{(k)} - \mathbf{x}^{(0)}$ earlier. Putting these in (3.43) yields

$$\begin{aligned}\mathbf{d}^{(k)\mathrm{T}}\mathbf{A}(\mathbf{x}^* - \mathbf{x}^{(0)}) &= \mathbf{d}^{(k)\mathrm{T}}\mathbf{A}(\mathbf{x}^* - \mathbf{x}^{(k)}) \\ &\quad + \mathbf{d}^{(k)\mathrm{T}}\mathbf{A}(\alpha_0\mathbf{d}^{(0)} + \alpha_1\mathbf{d}^{(1)} + \cdots + \alpha_{k-1}\mathbf{d}^{(k-1)}).\end{aligned} \tag{3.44}$$

Due to **A**-conjugacy, all the terms on the second expression in the right-hand side of (3.44) become zero and we are left with the following condition:

$$\mathbf{d}^{(k)\mathrm{T}}\mathbf{A}(\mathbf{x}^* - \mathbf{x}^{(0)}) = \mathbf{d}^{(k)\mathrm{T}}\mathbf{A}(\mathbf{x}^* - \mathbf{x}^{(k)}). \tag{3.45}$$

Now, using the fact that for a quadratic function $\mathbf{c}^{(k)} = \mathbf{A}\mathbf{x}^{(k)} - \mathbf{b}$ and $\mathbf{A}\mathbf{x}^* = \mathbf{b}$, we get

$$\mathbf{d}^{(k)\mathrm{T}}\mathbf{A}(\mathbf{x}^* - \mathbf{x}^{(0)}) = \mathbf{d}^{(k)\mathrm{T}}(\mathbf{A}\mathbf{x}^* - \mathbf{A}\mathbf{x}^{(k)}) = \mathbf{d}^{(k)\mathrm{T}}(\mathbf{b} - \mathbf{c}^{(k)} - \mathbf{b}) = -\mathbf{d}^{(k)\mathrm{T}}\mathbf{c}^{(k)}. \tag{3.46}$$

Let us return to the constants defined earlier in (3.39). We see that the numerator of the right-hand side of (3.39) is now known from (3.46) as $-\mathbf{d}^{(k)\mathrm{T}}\mathbf{c}^{(k)}$. Thus we get

$$\beta_k = -\frac{\mathbf{d}^{(k)\mathrm{T}}\mathbf{c}^{(k)}}{\mathbf{d}^{(k)\mathrm{T}}\mathbf{A}\mathbf{d}^{(k)}}. \tag{3.47}$$

We also note:

$$\mathbf{x}^* = \mathbf{x}^{(0)} + \beta_0\mathbf{d}^{(0)} + \beta_1\mathbf{d}^{(1)} + \cdots + \beta_{n-1}\mathbf{d}^{(n-1)}. \tag{3.48}$$

$$\mathbf{x}^{(k)} = \mathbf{x}^{(0)} + \alpha_0\mathbf{d}^{(0)} + \alpha_1\mathbf{d}^{(1)} + \cdots + \alpha_{k-1}\mathbf{d}^{(k-1)}. \tag{3.49}$$

Putting $k = n$ and subtracting (3.49) from (3.48) yields the following:

$$\mathbf{x}^* - \mathbf{x}^{(n)} = (\beta_0 - \alpha_0)\mathbf{d}^{(0)} + (\beta_1 - \alpha_1)\mathbf{d}^{(1)} + \cdots + (\alpha_{n-1} - \beta_{n-1})\mathbf{d}^{(n-1)}. \tag{3.50}$$

Thus, if we selected the step sizes $\alpha_i = \beta_i$ for $i = 1, 2, \ldots, n-1$, that is,

$$\alpha_k = -\frac{\mathbf{d}^{(k)\mathrm{T}}\mathbf{c}^{(k)}}{\mathbf{d}^{(k)\mathrm{T}}\mathbf{A}\mathbf{d}^{(k)}}, \tag{3.51}$$

we get from (3.50),

$$\mathbf{x}^* = \mathbf{x}^{(n)}. \tag{3.52}$$

This shows that the conjugate-gradient method converges in n iterations for a quadratic function.

We should point out that for general nonlinear functions which are not quadratic, the conjugate-gradient method is generally able to achieve a reasonable level of convergence within about $2n$ iterations.

3.6 Conjugate-Gradient Directions for Quadratic Functions

For quadratic functions, the conjugate-gradient method will work with any set of conjugate gradients selected for the matrix **A** for the given problem. However, we want to create a method which is independent of the matrix **A**, but still converges for quadratic functions in n iterations. Then we can use the algorithm for any general nonlinear function. This approach of developing an algorithm based on a quadratic function and then using it for a general optimization problem is often used to develop new optimization algorithms. The approach is reasonable, as many functions are *quadratic* locally and have positive definite Hessians near a minimum point. We now derive the conjugate-gradient method for quadratic problems and derive the formulas for the Fletcher–Reeves and other methods discussed earlier in this chapter.

Consider the quadratic function:

$$f(\mathbf{x}) = \frac{1}{2}\mathbf{x}^{\mathrm{T}}\mathbf{A}\mathbf{x} - \mathbf{b}^{\mathrm{T}}\mathbf{x}. \tag{3.53}$$

We assume **A** to be symmetric and positive definite. We select the first direction following the steepest-descent method.

$$\mathbf{d}^{(0)} = -\mathbf{c}^{(0)}. \tag{3.54}$$

The first design point thus becomes

$$\mathbf{x}^{(1)} = \mathbf{x}^{(0)} + \alpha_0\mathbf{d}^{(0)}, \quad \text{where } \alpha_0 = -\frac{\mathbf{d}^{(0)\mathrm{T}}\mathbf{c}^{(0)}}{\mathbf{d}^{(0)\mathrm{T}}\mathbf{A}\mathbf{d}^{(0)}}. \tag{3.55}$$

Let us select the conjugate direction $\mathbf{d}^{(1)}$ as a linear combination of the previous direction and the current gradient:

$$\mathbf{d}^{(1)} = -\mathbf{c}^{(1)} + \beta_0\mathbf{d}^{(0)}. \tag{3.56}$$

Premultiplying (3.56) by $\mathbf{d}^{(0)\mathrm{T}}\mathbf{A}$ yields:

$$\mathbf{d}^{(0)\mathrm{T}}\mathbf{A}\mathbf{d}^{(1)} = -\mathbf{d}^{(0)\mathrm{T}}\mathbf{A}\mathbf{c}^{(1)} + \beta_0\mathbf{d}^{(0)\mathrm{T}}\mathbf{A}\mathbf{d}^{(0)}. \tag{3.57}$$

For $\mathbf{d}^{(1)}$ to be **A**-conjugate, (3.57) must be zero which is possible if we select β_0 such that

$$-\mathbf{d}^{(0)\mathrm{T}}\mathbf{A}\mathbf{c}^{(1)} + \beta_0\mathbf{d}^{(0)\mathrm{T}}\mathbf{A}\mathbf{d}^{(0)} = 0. \tag{3.58}$$

Equation (3.58) yields the condition given below:

$$\beta_0 = \frac{\mathbf{d}^{(0)\mathrm{T}}\mathbf{A}\mathbf{c}^{(1)}}{\mathbf{d}^{(0)\mathrm{T}}\mathbf{A}\mathbf{d}^{(0)}}. \tag{3.59}$$

Consider now that the kth iteration is over and we have obtained $\mathbf{x}^{(k)}$ and $\mathbf{d}^{(k)}$. The next search direction is obtained as follows:

$$\mathbf{d}^{(k+1)} = -\mathbf{c}^{(k+1)} + \beta_k\mathbf{d}^{(k)}. \tag{3.60}$$

Again, we premultiply both sides by $\mathbf{d}^{(k)\mathrm{T}}\mathbf{A}$ and enforce the conjugacy condition.

$$\mathbf{d}^{(k)\mathrm{T}}\mathbf{A}\mathbf{d}^{(k+1)} = -\mathbf{d}^{(k)\mathrm{T}}\mathbf{A}\mathbf{c}^{(k+1)} + \beta_k \mathbf{d}^{(k)\mathrm{T}}\mathbf{A}\mathbf{d}^{(k)} = 0. \tag{3.61}$$

Equation (3.61) yields:

$$\beta_k = \frac{\mathbf{d}^{(k)\mathrm{T}}\mathbf{A}\mathbf{c}^{(k+1)}}{\mathbf{d}^{(k)\mathrm{T}}\mathbf{A}\mathbf{d}^{(k)}}. \tag{3.62}$$

Using this β_k and search directions $\mathbf{d}^{(k+1)} = -\mathbf{c}^{(k+1)} + \beta_k \mathbf{d}^{(k)}$, we can generate $\mathbf{A}$-conjugate directions $\mathbf{d}^{(0)}, \mathbf{d}^{(1)}, \mathbf{d}^{(2)}, \ldots, \mathbf{d}^{(n-1)}$. For a quadratic function with n design variables, we should converge in n iterations.

At this point, we can see that calculation of β_k in (3.62) requires knowledge of the matrix $\mathbf{A}$. While such a matrix is available for any quadratic function, for general nonlinear functions, no such matrix exists. Thus, the formula in (3.62) is useful for quadratic functions only and cannot be applied to general nonlinear functions. More general formulas are therefore obtained by removing the matrix $\mathbf{A}$ from the calculation of β_k using other equations. This approach leads to the formulas of Hestenes–Stiefel, Polak–Ribiere and Fletcher–Reeves presented earlier. For quadratic functions, these formulas give the same results but their performance can deviate significantly when used on general nonlinear functions.

3.6.1 Derivation of Hestenes–Stiefel formula

We start with the conjugate-gradient formula for β_k and slightly rewrite it as follows:

$$\beta_k = \frac{\mathbf{d}^{(k)\mathrm{T}}\mathbf{A}\mathbf{c}^{(k+1)}}{\mathbf{d}^{(k)\mathrm{T}}\mathbf{A}\mathbf{d}^{(k)}} = \frac{(\mathbf{d}^{(k)\mathrm{T}}\mathbf{A}\mathbf{c}^{(k+1)})\mathrm{T}}{\mathbf{d}^{(k)\mathrm{T}}\mathbf{A}\mathbf{d}^{(k)}} = \frac{\mathbf{c}^{(k+1)\mathrm{T}}\mathbf{A}\mathbf{d}^{(k)}}{\mathbf{d}^{(k)\mathrm{T}}\mathbf{A}\mathbf{d}^{(k)}}. \tag{3.63}$$

Here we have used the fact that the transpose of the scalar numerator remains unchanged. We would like to eliminate the term $\mathbf{A}\mathbf{d}^{(k)}$ from the calculation of β_k. To do so, consider

$$\mathbf{x}^{(k+1)} = \mathbf{x}^{(k)} + \alpha_k \mathbf{d}^{(k)}. \tag{3.64}$$

Premultiply the above equation by $\mathbf{A}$:

$$\mathbf{A}\mathbf{x}^{(k+1)} = \mathbf{A}\mathbf{x}^{(k)} + \alpha_k \mathbf{A}\mathbf{d}^{(k)}. \tag{3.65}$$

For a quadratic function, we can write

$$\mathbf{c}^{(k)} = \mathbf{A}\mathbf{x}^{(k)} - \mathbf{b}.$$

$$\mathbf{c}^{(k+1)} = \mathbf{A}\mathbf{x}^{(k+1)} - \mathbf{b}. \tag{3.66}$$

Thus, we can write from (3.65) and (3.66)

$$\mathbf{A}\mathbf{x}^{(k+1)} - \mathbf{A}\mathbf{x}^{(k)} = \mathbf{c}^{(k+1)} - \mathbf{c}^{(k)} = \alpha_k \mathbf{A}\mathbf{d}^{(k)}. \tag{3.67}$$

Thus we obtain the term $\mathbf{A}\mathbf{d}^{(k)}$:

$$\mathbf{A}\mathbf{d}^{(k)} = \frac{\mathbf{c}^{(k+1)} - \mathbf{c}^{(k)}}{\alpha_k}. \tag{3.68}$$

The result obtained in (3.68) is an exact one for quadratic functions. Using (3.68) in (3.63):

$$\beta_k = \frac{\mathbf{c}^{(k+1)\mathrm{T}}\mathbf{A}\mathbf{d}^{(k)}}{\mathbf{d}^{(k)\mathrm{T}}\mathbf{A}\mathbf{d}^{(k)}} = \frac{\mathbf{c}^{(k+1)\mathrm{T}}(\mathbf{c}^{(k+1)} - \mathbf{c}^{(k)})}{\mathbf{d}^{(k)\mathrm{T}}(\mathbf{c}^{(k+1)} - \mathbf{c}^{(k)})}. \tag{3.69}$$

The Hestenes–Stiefel formula is given by (3.69). We can use this formula for a general function as it does not need the **A** matrix. However, for a general function, the method may not converge in n iterations and the directions should be reset to the steepest-descent directions in the $(n+1)$th iteration. After that, the update formula can again be used.

3.6.2 Derivation of Polak–Ribiere formula

To get this formula, we will use the line search criteria $\mathbf{c}^{(k+1)} \cdot \mathbf{d}^{(k)} = 0$ to modify the Hestenes–Stiefel formula. Consider the denominator term of the formula in (3.69):

$$D = \mathbf{d}^{(k)\mathrm{T}}\mathbf{c}^{(k+1)} - \mathbf{d}^{(k)\mathrm{T}}\mathbf{c}^{(k)}. \tag{3.70}$$

Since both terms are scalar products, we can transpose the expression without changing its value:

$$D = \mathbf{c}^{(k+1)\mathrm{T}}\mathbf{d}^{(k)} - \mathbf{c}^{(k)\mathrm{T}}\mathbf{d}^{(k)}. \tag{3.71}$$

We immediately see that the first term $\mathbf{c}^{(k+1)\mathrm{T}}\mathbf{d}^{(k)}$ is zero if we invoke the line search criterion. *Note that here we are making it mandatory that we perform an exact line search.* The second term in (3.71) is now changed to put it in a form where only gradients are used. To do this, consider this equation:

$$\mathbf{d}^{(k)} = -\mathbf{c}^{(k)} + \beta_{k-1}\mathbf{d}^{(k-1)}. \tag{3.72}$$

Premultiply both sides of (3.72) by $\mathbf{c}^{(k)\mathrm{T}}$ to yield

$$\mathbf{c}^{(k)\mathrm{T}}\mathbf{d}^{(k)} = -\mathbf{c}^{(k)\mathrm{T}}\mathbf{c}^{(k)} + \beta_{k-1}\mathbf{c}^{(k)\mathrm{T}}\mathbf{d}^{(k-1)}. \tag{3.73}$$

Again, by the line search criteria, the term $\mathbf{c}^{(k)\mathrm{T}}\mathbf{d}^{(k-1)}$ in (3.73) becomes zero and we have obtained the expression for the term:

$$\mathbf{c}^{(k)\mathrm{T}}\mathbf{d}^{(k)} = -\mathbf{c}^{(k)\mathrm{T}}\mathbf{c}^{(k)}. \tag{3.74}$$

Substituting (3.74) in the Hestenes–Stiefel formula in (3.69) yields:

$$\beta_k = \frac{\mathbf{c}^{(k+1)\mathrm{T}}(\mathbf{c}^{(k+1)} - \mathbf{c}^{(k)})}{\mathbf{c}^{(k)\mathrm{T}}\mathbf{c}^{(k)}}. \tag{3.75}$$

This is the Polak–Ribiere formula. Note that this formula works well with exact line search. From its derivation, we know why this is so.

3.6.3 Derivation of Fletcher–Reeves formula

We start with the Polak–Ribiere formula in (3.75). Our intent is to simplify the numerator term in the formula. To do so, we start with the search direction:

$$\mathbf{d}^{(k)} = -\mathbf{c}^{(k)} + \beta_{k-1}\mathbf{d}^{(k-1)}. \tag{3.76}$$

Premultiply both sides of the above equation by $\mathbf{c}^{(k+1)\mathrm{T}}$.

$$\mathbf{c}^{(k+1)\mathrm{T}}\mathbf{d}^{(k)} = -\mathbf{c}^{(k+1)\mathrm{T}}\mathbf{c}^{(k)} + \beta_{k-1}\mathbf{c}^{(k+1)\mathrm{T}}\mathbf{d}^{(k-1)}. \tag{3.77}$$

The left-hand side term $\mathbf{c}^{(k+1)\mathrm{T}}\mathbf{d}^{(k)}$ becomes zero by invoking the line search criteria. Then we get,

$$\mathbf{c}^{(k+1)\mathrm{T}}\mathbf{c}^{(k)} = \beta_{k-1}\mathbf{c}^{(k+1)\mathrm{T}}\mathbf{d}^{(k-1)}. \tag{3.78}$$

This is the second term in the numerator of the Polak–Ribiere formula in (3.75) and we shall show that it is zero for quadratic functions.

Now, for a quadratic function:

$$\mathbf{A}(\mathbf{x}^{(k+1)} - \mathbf{x}^{(k)}) = \mathbf{A}\mathbf{x}^{(k+1)} - \mathbf{b} - (\mathbf{A}\mathbf{x}^{(k)} - \mathbf{b}) = \mathbf{c}^{(k+1)} - \mathbf{c}^{(k)}. \tag{3.79}$$

Thus,

$$\mathbf{c}^{(k+1)} = \mathbf{c}^{(k)} + \mathbf{A}\mathbf{x}^{(k+1)} - \mathbf{A}\mathbf{x}^{(k)}. \tag{3.80}$$

The equation for search direction is as follows:

$$\mathbf{x}^{(k+1)} = \mathbf{x}^{(k)} + \alpha_k\mathbf{d}^{(k)}. \tag{3.81}$$

Premultiplying both sides of the above equation by $\mathbf{A}$ yields the equation:

$$\mathbf{A}\mathbf{x}^{(k+1)} = \mathbf{A}\mathbf{x}^{(k)} + \alpha_k\mathbf{A}\mathbf{d}^{(k)} \tag{3.82}$$

or

$$\mathbf{c}^{(k+1)} = \mathbf{c}^{(k)} + \mathbf{A}\mathbf{x}^{(k+1)} - \mathbf{A}\mathbf{x}^{(k)} = \mathbf{c}^{(k)} + \alpha_k\mathbf{A}\mathbf{d}^{(k)}. \tag{3.83}$$

Now we have all the expressions to evaluate the term

$$\mathbf{c}^{(k+1)\mathrm{T}}\mathbf{d}^{(k-1)} = (\mathbf{c}^{(k)} + \alpha_k\mathbf{A}\mathbf{d}^{(k)})^{\mathrm{T}}\mathbf{d}^{(k-1)} = \mathbf{c}^{(k)\mathrm{T}}\mathbf{d}^{(k-1)} + \alpha_k\mathbf{d}^{(k)\mathrm{T}}\mathbf{A}\mathbf{d}^{(k-1)}. \tag{3.84}$$

The term $\mathbf{c}^{(k)\mathrm{T}}\mathbf{d}^{(k-1)}$ in (3.84) becomes zero by invoking the line search criteria and the term $\mathbf{d}^{(k)\mathrm{T}}\mathbf{A}\mathbf{d}^{(k-1)}$ becomes zero due to $\mathbf{A}$-conjugacy. Thus we can say that the term $\mathbf{c}^{(k+1)\mathrm{T}}\mathbf{c}^{(k)} = \beta_{k-1}\mathbf{c}^{(k+1)\mathrm{T}}\mathbf{d}^{(k-1)} = 0$ and therefore the Polak–Ribiere formula gives:

$$\beta_k = \frac{\mathbf{c}^{(k+1)\mathrm{T}}\mathbf{c}^{(k+1)}}{\mathbf{c}^{(k)\mathrm{T}}\mathbf{c}^{(k)}} = \frac{\|\mathbf{c}^{(k+1)}\|}{\|\mathbf{c}^{(k)}\|}. \tag{3.85}$$

This is the Fletcher–Reeves formula. The Fletcher–Reeves formula is the most compact and also the most popular conjugate-gradient formula but also requires an exact line search. In general, the Hestenes–Stiefel formula is best when we are not sure that the line search is exact.

Problems

1. Use the steepest-descent method to minimize the function

$$f(\mathbf{x}) = x^2 + e^{-x} + \sin(4x).$$

Start from $\mathbf{x}^{(0)} = 1$ and perform three iterations. Repeat the problem with $x^{(0)} = -1$. Comment on your results.

2. Consider the following function:

$$f(\mathbf{x}) = x_1^2 + 15x_2^2 - x_1x_2.$$

Start from $\mathbf{x}^{(0)} = (1, 1)$ and perform three iterations of the steepest-descent method. Can you scale the design variables to converge in a single iteration?

3. Consider the following function:

$$f(\mathbf{x}) = x_1^2 + 15x_2^2 - x_1x_2.$$

Start from $\mathbf{x}^{(0)} = (1, 1)$ and perform three iterations of the steepest-descent method. Use a constant step size.

4. Consider the following function:

$$f(\mathbf{x}) = x_1^2 + 15x_2^2 - x_1x_2.$$

Start from $\mathbf{x}^{(0)} = (1, 1)$ and perform two iterations of the Fletcher–Reeves, Hestenes–Stiefel and Polak–Ribiere methods.

5. Consider a quadratic function:

$$f(\mathbf{x}) = \frac{1}{2}\mathbf{x}^{\mathrm{T}}\mathbf{A}\mathbf{x}.$$

$$\mathbf{A} = \begin{bmatrix} 3 & 1 & 1 \\ 1 & 2 & 0 \\ 2 & 0 & 3 \end{bmatrix}.$$

A starting direction is known as $\mathbf{d}^{(0)} = (1, 0, 0)$. Find the conjugate directions, if possible.

6. Minimize the following function starting from $(0, 0)$:

$$f(\mathbf{x}) = x_1^2 - x_1x_2 + 2x_2^2 - 2x_1 + e^{x_1+x_2} + 10.$$

Use the steepest-descent method and the Fletcher–Reeves conjugate-gradient method with exact analytical line search. Perform two iterations. Repeat the problem starting from $(-1, 1)$. Comment on your results.

7. Find the rate of convergence and rate constant of the sequence:

(a) $1, 1/2, 1/3, 1/4, \ldots$

(b) $1, 3/2, 5/4, 9/8, \ldots$

(c) $1, 3/2, 4/9, 8/27, \ldots$

8. Minimize the following function starting from (2, 2):

$$f(\mathbf{x}) = \frac{1}{2}(x_1 - 2x_2)^2 + x_1^4 + 2.$$

Use the Fletcher–Reeves conjugate-gradient method and perform two iterations.

9. Write a computer program to implement the steepest-descent and three conjugate-gradient methods. Using this program and starting from different points in the design space, find the minimum of the function:

$$f(\mathbf{x}) = 2x_1^2 + x_2^2 - 2x_1x_2 + 2x_1^3 + x_1^4 + 5.$$

Use the golden-section program from the problems in the previous chapter for the 1D search. Use the convergence criterion: $\|\mathbf{c}\| < 10^{-5}$. How do the methods compare in terms of function evaluations?

10. Using your computer program, minimize the function:

$$f(\mathbf{x}) = \frac{1}{2}(x_1 - 2x_2)^2 + x_1^4 + 2.$$

Use the conjugate-gradient methods. Use a convergence criterion of $\|\mathbf{c}\| < 10^{-5}$. Start from (1, 1), (−1, 1), (1, −1), (−1, −1). Comment on your results.

11. Minimize the function:

$$f(\mathbf{x}) = x_1^2 + cx_2^2.$$

Perform the steepest-descent iterations with an exact line search for values of $c =$ 1, 10, 100, 1000, 10000. Use the convergence criterion: $\|\mathbf{c}\| < 10^{-5}$. What is the rate constant in each case and how do these values compare with the estimated upper bounds?

12. Minimize the function:

$$f(\mathbf{x}) = x_1^2 + cx_2^2.$$

Perform the conjugate-gradient iterations with an exact line search for values of $c =$ 1, 10, 100, 1000, 10000. Use the convergence criterion: $\|\mathbf{c}\| < 10^{-5}$ and the three methods covered in this chapter. What is the rate constant for each of these cases and how do these values compare with the steepest descent method obtained in Problem 11?

13. In Problems 11 and 12, what is the effect of using a diagonal preconditioner?

14. Find the minimum point of the Rosenbrock function:

$$f(\mathbf{x}) = 100(x_2 - x_1^2)^2 + (1 - x_1)^2.$$

Start from $\mathbf{x}^{(0)} = (-1, 1)$ and use the three conjugate-gradient methods. Compare them to the steepest-descent method. Use a convergence criterion of $\|\mathbf{c}\| < 10^{-5}$.

15. Use your computer program to minimize the function:

$$f(\mathbf{x}) = x_1^2 - x_1x_2 + 2x_2^2 - 2x_1 + e^{x_1+x_2} + 10.$$

Start from (0, 0) and use the three conjugate-gradient methods. Use a convergence criterion of $\|\mathbf{c}\| < 10^{-5}$.

16. Wood's function is given by:

$$f(\mathbf{x}) = 100(x_2 - x_1^2)^2 + (1 - x_1)^2 + 90(x_4 - x_3^2)^2 + (1 - x_3)^2$$
$$+ 10.1[(x_2 - 1)^2 + (x_4 - 1)^2] + 19.8(x_2 - 1)(x_4 - 1).$$

Use $\mathbf{x}^{(0)} = (-3, -1, -3, -1)$, and compare the three conjugate-gradient methods. Use the convergence criterion: $\|\mathbf{c}\| < 10^{-5}$.

17. Find the minimum point of the function:

$$f(\mathbf{x}) = (x_1 + 2x_2 - 7)^2 + (2x_1 + x_2 - 5)^2.$$

Start from $\mathbf{x}^{(0)} = (1, 1)$ and use the Hestenes–Stiefel method and an inexact line search based on Armijo's rule. Use a convergence criterion of $\|\mathbf{c}\| < 10^{-5}$. How do the results change when an exact line search based on the golden-section method is used?

18. Use the steepest-descent method with a small fixed step size to find the minimum point of the function:

$$f(\mathbf{x}) = (x_1 + 2x_2 - 7)^2 + (2x_1 + x_2 - 5)^2.$$

Start from $\mathbf{x}^{(0)} = (1, 1)$ and use the convergence criterion: $\|\mathbf{c}\| < 10^{-5}$. How do the results change when an exact line search based on the golden-section method is used?

19. Use the Fletcher–Reeves method to find the minimum point of Brown's function:

$$f(\mathbf{x}) = (x_1 - 10^6)^2 + (x_2 - 2.10^{-6})^2 + (x_1x_2 - 2)^2.$$

Use different starting designs. Use the convergence criterion: $\|\mathbf{c}\| < 10^{-5}$. Also, use a preconditioner to improve the convergence behaviour. Use any accurate 1D search method.

20. Consider the Freudenstein–Roth function:

$$f(\mathbf{x}) = (-13 + x_1 + ((5 - x_2)x_2 - 2)x_2)^2$$
$$+ (-29 + x_1 + ((x_2 + x_1)x_2 - 14)x_2)^2.$$

This function has some local minima and a global minimum. Use any method discussed in this chapter to find the minimum points. Use the convergence criterion: $\|\mathbf{c}\| < 10^{-5}$. Use starting designs of your choice. This problem shows the difficulty in coming up with good starting designs when using gradient-based methods.

21. Use the Polak–Ribiere method to find the minimum of Powell's quartic function:

$$f(\mathbf{x}) = (x_1 + 10x_2)^2 + 5(x_3 - x_4)^2 + (x_2 - 2x_3)^4 + 10(x_1 - x_4)^4.$$

Start from $\mathbf{x}^{(0)} = (3, -1, 0, 1)$. Use the convergence criterion: $\|\mathbf{c}\| < 10^{-5}$.

22. Some research suggests that the steepest-descent method works well when used with quadratic approximations of the function. Consider the function:

$$f(\mathbf{x}) = x_1^2 + 2x_2^2 + e^{-x_1 - x_2}.$$

Expand this function in a second-order Taylor series about point (1, 2). Apply the steepest-descent method to the approximated function and get a minimum point. Use this minimum point to construct another Taylor series approximation and again get the minimum point. How does the minimum point obtained compare with Example 3.2.

23. The conjugate-gradient methods are low-storage methods and probably the best methods for problems with a very large number of design variables. Consider the function:

$$f(\mathbf{x}) = x_1^2 + 2x_2^2 + 3x_3^2 + \cdots + nx_n^2 + e^{-x_1-x_2-x_3-\cdots-x_n}.$$

Find the minimum value of this function starting from $\mathbf{x}^{(0)} = (1, 1, 1, \ldots, 1)$ for the cases $n = 3, 10, 50, 100$ and 500. Use a convergence criterion of $\|\mathbf{c}\| < 10^{-5}$. Use the golden-section search and compare the results of the three conjugate-gradient formulas. Comment on your results.

4 Newtonian Methods

The steepest-descent method uses only first-order information. The conjugate-gradient method improves the estimation of the direction of steepest descent but is also limited to first-order information. Using only gradients leads to a linear local approximation of the function. If, instead we use the Hessian matrix or second-order information, it leads to a local quadratic approximation which is a more accurate local representation of nonlinear functions used in optimization problems. This idea is attributed to Newton and such methods using Hessian or approximations to it are discussed in this chapter. We call the class of methods discussed in this chapter as Newtonian methods.

4.1 Newton's Method

Newton's method uses the Hessian matrix and has a quadratic rate of convergence. For a positive definite quadratic function, the Newton's method converges in a single iteration. Consider a second-order Taylor series expansion of a function:

$$f(\mathbf{x}^{(k)} + \Delta\mathbf{x}) = f(\mathbf{x}^{(k)}) + \mathbf{c}^{\mathrm{T}}\Delta\mathbf{x} + \frac{1}{2}\Delta\mathbf{x}^{\mathrm{T}}\mathbf{H}\Delta\mathbf{x}. \tag{4.1}$$

From convex set theory, if $\mathbf{H}$ is positive semidefinite, there is a $\Delta\mathbf{x}$ which gives a global minimum for the function. If $\mathbf{H}$ is positive definite, the minimum is unique. Thus, the minimum point of f is obtained using the equation:[1]

$$\frac{\partial f}{\partial(\Delta\mathbf{x})} = 0 \Rightarrow \mathbf{c}^{(k)} + \mathbf{H}^{(k)}\Delta\mathbf{x}^{(k)} = 0, \tag{4.2}$$

$$\Delta\mathbf{x}^{(k)} = -\mathbf{H}^{(k)^{-1}}\mathbf{c}^{(k)} = \mathbf{d}^{(k)}. \tag{4.3}$$

Here we have assumed nonsingular $\mathbf{H}$. Consider the descent condition:

$$\mathbf{c}^{(k)\mathrm{T}}\mathbf{d}^{(k)} < 0 \quad \text{or} \quad -(\mathbf{H}^{(k)}\mathbf{d}^{(k)})^{\mathrm{T}}\mathbf{d}^{(k)} < 0 \quad \text{or} \quad \mathbf{d}^{(k)\mathrm{T}}\mathbf{H}^{(k)}\mathbf{d}^{(k)} > 0. \tag{4.4}$$

Unless $\mathbf{H}^{(k)}$ is positive definite, $\mathbf{d}^{(k)}$ will not be a descent direction. However, the Hessian matrix at the optimal point $\mathbf{x}^*$ is always positive semidefinite, and in fact, is usually positive definite. Thus, Newton's method generally works well in regions close to the optimal point, which is the source of the adage, 'Newton's method works well if you already know the answer'. In Newton's method, the nonlinear function $f(\mathbf{x})$ is approximated by a quadratic function at every iteration. The use of the search direction without using a step size leads to the classical Newton's method:

$$\mathbf{x}^{(k+1)} = \mathbf{x}^{(k)} - \mathbf{H}^{(k)^{-1}}\mathbf{c}^{(k)}. \tag{4.5}$$

If $\mathbf{H}$ is indefinite, the quadratic function does not have a clear minimum.

Example 4.1 Minimize the following function using the classical Newton's method:

$$f(\mathbf{x}) = x_1^2 + 2x_2^2 + e^{-x_1-x_2}.$$

Perform two iterations starting from the point (1, 2).

Solution: We first need to calculate the gradient and the Hessian matrix at the starting point.

$$\mathbf{c}^{(0)} = \begin{Bmatrix} 2x_1 - e^{-x_1-x_2} \\ 4x_2 - e^{-x_1-x_2} \end{Bmatrix} = \begin{Bmatrix} 1.9502 \\ 7.9502 \end{Bmatrix}.$$

$$\mathbf{H}^{(0)} = \begin{bmatrix} 2 + e^{-x_1-x_2} & e^{-x_1-x_2} \\ e^{-x_1-x_2} & 4 + e^{-x_1-x_2} \end{bmatrix} = \begin{bmatrix} 2.0497 & 0.0497 \\ 0.0497 & 4.0497 \end{bmatrix}.$$

We should check if the Hessian is positive definite. The eigenvalues of the Hessian are 2.045 and 4.055. Therefore, the Hessian is positive definite and Newton's method should give a descent direction. The search direction is obtained as follows:

$$\mathbf{d}^{(0)} = -\mathbf{H}^{(0)^{-1}}\mathbf{c}^{(0)} = \begin{bmatrix} 2.0497 & 0.0497 \\ 0.0497 & 4.0497 \end{bmatrix}^{-1} \begin{Bmatrix} 1.9502 \\ 7.9502 \end{Bmatrix} = \begin{Bmatrix} -0.9041 \\ -1.9520 \end{Bmatrix}.$$

The first design increment is then given by

$$\mathbf{x}^{(1)} = \mathbf{x}^{(0)} + \mathbf{d}^{(0)} = \begin{Bmatrix} 1 \\ 2 \end{Bmatrix} + \begin{Bmatrix} -0.9041 \\ -1.9520 \end{Bmatrix} = \begin{Bmatrix} 0.0959 \\ 0.0480 \end{Bmatrix}.$$

This ends the first iteration. To continue with the second iteration, we recalculate the gradient at the new design point.

$$\mathbf{c}^{(1)} = \begin{Bmatrix} -0.6743 \\ -0.6743 \end{Bmatrix}, \qquad \|\mathbf{c}^{(1)}\| = 0.9536.$$

The Hessian can then be calculated and it is given by:

$$\mathbf{H}^{(1)} = \begin{bmatrix} 2.866 & 0.866 \\ 0.866 & 4.866 \end{bmatrix}.$$

We should check for positive definiteness once again. The eigenvalues of the Hessian are now 2.5421 and 3.1888. Thus the Hessian is positive definite. The new search direction is calculated.

$$\mathbf{d}^{(1)} = -\mathbf{H}^{(1)^{-1}}\mathbf{c}^{(1)} = \begin{bmatrix} 2.866 & 0.866 \\ 0.866 & 4.866 \end{bmatrix}^{-1} \begin{Bmatrix} -0.6743 \\ -0.6643 \end{Bmatrix} = \begin{Bmatrix} 0.2044 \\ 0.1022 \end{Bmatrix}.$$

The new design point can be immediately obtained.

$$\mathbf{x}^{(2)} = \mathbf{x}^{(1)} + \mathbf{d}^{(1)} = \begin{Bmatrix} 0.0959 \\ 0.0479 \end{Bmatrix} + \begin{Bmatrix} 0.2044 \\ 0.1022 \end{Bmatrix} = \begin{Bmatrix} 0.3003 \\ 0.1501 \end{Bmatrix}.$$

The gradient at the point is the following:

$$\mathbf{c}^{(2)} = \begin{Bmatrix} -0.037 \\ -0.022 \end{Bmatrix}, \qquad \|\mathbf{c}^{(2)}\| = 0.05.$$

The fast convergence of Newton's method can be inferred from the rapid decrease in the norm of the gradient.

Example 4.2 Minimize the function $f(x) = x + e^{-x}$ using Newton's method. Perform three iterations starting from $x^{(0)} = 1$ and estimate the rate of convergence and the rate constant.

Solution: The derivatives of the function are $f'(x) = 1 - e^{-x}$, $f''(x) = e^{-x}$. Newton's method gives the following equation.

$$x^{(k+1)} = x^{(k)} - \frac{f'(x^{(k)})}{f''(x^{(k)})} = x^{(k)} - e^{x^{(k)}} + 1.$$

The iterations give

$$x^{(1)} = 1 - e + 1 = -0.7183.$$

$$x^{(2)} = -0.20587.$$

$$x^{(3)} = -0.0198.$$

$$x^{(4)} = -1.947.10^{-4}.$$

$$x^{(5)} = -1.896.10^{-8}.$$

The sequence of errors is $e_0 = x^{(1)} - x^* = 1 - 0 = 1$, $e_1 = -0.71828$, $e_2 = -0.0198$, $e_3 = -1.947.10^{-4}$, $e_5 = -1.896.10^{-8}$. We can calculate the rate constant assuming quadratic convergence. It is given by

$$\frac{\|e_2\|}{\|e_1\|^2} = 0.0384, \qquad \frac{\|e_3\|}{\|e_2\|^2} = 0.4966, \qquad \frac{\|e_4\|}{\|e_3\|^2} = 0.5.$$

Thus we see that Newton's method converges quadratically, with a rate constant of 0.5.

Near the minimum, the Hessian is usually positive definite and always positive semidefinite. A nonpositive definite Hessian mostly occurs far from the optimum point. A technique which can be used in such situations is to replace the Hessian by a positive definite matrix. If the Hessian is modified appropriately so that it remains positive definite, the algorithm will generally converge using a line search.

The modified positive definite Hessian can be found in a simple manner. Recall from Newton's method:

$$\mathbf{Hd} = -\mathbf{c}. \tag{4.6}$$

This is useful in finding the search direction. The linear system defined above is typically solved in place of $\mathbf{d} = -\mathbf{H}^{-1}\mathbf{c}$, which involves computationally expensive matrix inversion. If the Hessian is positive definite, then the factorization

$$\mathbf{H} = \mathbf{LDL}^{\mathrm{T}} \tag{4.7}$$

results in the diagonal matrix $\mathbf{D}$ with positive diagonal entries. If the Hessian is not positive definite at some iteration, this means that for some value of n, $d_{ii} < 0$. If this happens, the negative d_{ii} can be replaced by a positive entry, as for instance $|d_{ii}|$. Modifying the Hessian matrix in this manner is equivalent to modifying the Hessian, which leads to a new, modified Hessian matrix:[2]

$$\mathbf{H}^{(\mathrm{mod})} = \mathbf{H} + \Delta\mathbf{H}. \tag{4.8}$$

Here $\Delta\mathbf{H}$ is a diagonal matrix. There is considerable freedom in the selection of $\Delta\mathbf{H}$, so that the modified Hessian is positive definite. However, the modification should not lead to a singular Hessian. As a simple rule, $\Delta\mathbf{H}_{ii} = \max(2|d_{ii}|, 1)$ can be used to assure that the modified Hessian does not become singular. Then

$$\mathbf{H}^{(\mathrm{mod})}\mathbf{d} = -\mathbf{c}, \tag{4.9}$$

is used to calculate the search direction. Typically, the system $\mathbf{Hd} = -\mathbf{c}$ is solved using factorization or $\mathbf{LDL}^{\mathrm{T}}\mathbf{d} = -\mathbf{c}$ so that $\mathbf{D}$ is always available. Therefore, the modification to the Hessian can be easily made.

Returning to the classical Newtonian method, we see that the method uses a step size of one. This can be generalized by adding a variable step size:

$$\mathbf{x}^{(k+1)} = \mathbf{x}^{(k)} + \alpha_k \Delta\mathbf{x}^{(k)} = \mathbf{x}^{(k)} - \alpha_k \mathbf{H}^{(k)^{-1}}\mathbf{c}^{(k)}. \tag{4.10}$$

We see that when $\mathbf{H}^{(k)} = \mathbf{I}$, the modified Newtonian method coincides with the steepest-descent method. The Newtonian method can also be viewed as a modified steepest-descent method with the descent direction $\mathbf{d}^{(k)} = -\mathbf{c}^{(k)}$ being modified to $\mathbf{d}^{(k)} = -\mathbf{Gc}^{(k)}$, where $\mathbf{G}$ is a matrix which deflects the search direction to prevent the zigzag behaviour of the steepest-descent method.

The Newtonian method suffers from some shortcomings. The Hessian needs $n(n+1)/2$ second-order derivatives of $f(\mathbf{x})$ which can lead to a huge computational effort for realistic engineering optimization problems. The method also has no memory and does not use the past history or calculated gradient and Hessian information from previous iterations. In addition, the method has much larger storage and computer time requirements for problems with a large number of design variables when compared to the conjugate-gradient method because of the need to store the Hessian and solve the linear system with every iteration. However, on the positive side, Newton's method shows quadratic convergence. It is also the basis of the popular quasi-Newtonian methods which will be studied later in this chapter, and which have become the workhorse for optimization problems.

Example 4.3 Minimize the following function using the modified Newtonian method.

$$f(\mathbf{x}) = x_1^2 + 2x_2^2 + \mathrm{e}^{-x_1-x_2}.$$

Perform one iteration starting from the point (1, 2) and use line search.

Solution: The steps followed until the search direction calculations are the same as in Example 4.1.

$$\mathbf{d}^{(0)} = -\mathbf{H}^{(0)^{-1}}\mathbf{c}^{(0)} = \begin{bmatrix} 2.0497 & 0.0497 \\ 0.0497 & 4.0497 \end{bmatrix}^{-1} \begin{Bmatrix} 1.9502 \\ 7.9502 \end{Bmatrix} = \begin{Bmatrix} -0.9041 \\ -1.9520 \end{Bmatrix}.$$

The new design point is given by

$$\mathbf{x}^{(1)} = \mathbf{x}^{(0)} + \alpha\mathbf{d}^{(0)} = \begin{Bmatrix} 1 \\ 2 \end{Bmatrix} + \alpha \begin{Bmatrix} -0.9041 \\ -1.9520 \end{Bmatrix} = \begin{Bmatrix} 1 - 0.9041\alpha \\ 2 - 1.9520\alpha \end{Bmatrix}.$$

Putting this design in the function yields

$$f(\alpha) = (1 - 0.9041\alpha)^2 + 2(2 - 1.9520\alpha)^2 + \mathrm{e}^{-3+2.8543\alpha}.$$

This function can be minimized using a 1D method. Starting with $\delta = 0.25$, we bracket the minimum between 0.75 and 1.25. Further reducing the interval of uncertainty, we get $\alpha^* = 0.915$. Thus, the new design point is given by the following expression:

$$\mathbf{x}^{(1)} = \mathbf{x}^{(0)} + \mathbf{d}^{(0)} = \begin{Bmatrix} 1 \\ 2 \end{Bmatrix} + 0.915 \begin{Bmatrix} -0.9041 \\ -1.9520 \end{Bmatrix} = \begin{Bmatrix} 0.1727 \\ 0.2139 \end{Bmatrix}.$$

The gradient and its norm take the following values:

$$\mathbf{c}^{(1)} = \begin{Bmatrix} -0.3340 \\ 0.1762 \end{Bmatrix}, \qquad \|\mathbf{c}^{(1)}\| = 0.3630.$$

When we compare this with Example 4.1, we see that the step size selection using the 1D method has resulted in a better design for this problem. We can now state Newton's method as an algorithm.

4.1.1 Algorithm for Newton's method

1. Estimate $\mathbf{x}^{(0)}$. Set $k = 0$. Choose a value for ε.
2. Calculate the gradient, $\mathbf{c}^{(k)}$.

   If $\|\mathbf{c}^{(k)}\| < \varepsilon$, stop, otherwise continue.

3. Calculate the Hessian $\mathbf{H}^{(k)}$. Factorize the Hessian using $\mathbf{H}^{(k)} = \mathbf{LDL}^{\mathrm{T}}$. If any $d_{ii} < 0$, calculate $\mathbf{H}^{(\mathrm{mod})} = \mathbf{H}^{(k)} + \Delta\mathbf{H}$, where $\Delta\mathbf{H}_{ii} = \max(2|d_{ii}|, 1)$ for the i where $d_{ii} < 0$. Factorize $\mathbf{H}^{(\mathrm{mod})} = \mathbf{LDL}^{\mathrm{T}}$.
4. Calculate search direction.

   $$\mathbf{LDL}^{\mathrm{T}}\mathbf{d}^{(k)} = -\mathbf{c}^{(k)}.$$

5. Minimize $f(\mathbf{x}^{(k)} + \alpha_k \mathbf{d}^{(k)})$ and calculate α_k using 1D search.
6. Set $k = k + 1$. Go to step 2.

Example 4.4 Consider the Rosenbrock function:

$$f = 100(x_2 - x_1^2)^2 + (1 - x_1)^2.$$

Perform two iterations of Newton's method starting from (0, 0.005).

Solution: We need to evaluate the gradient and Hessian of the given function:

$$\mathbf{c} = \begin{Bmatrix} -400x_1(x_2 - x_1^2) - 2(1 - x_1) \\ 200(x_2 - x_1^2) \end{Bmatrix}.$$

$$\mathbf{H} = \begin{bmatrix} 400(3x_1^2 - x_2) + 2 & -400x_1 \\ -400x_1 & 200 \end{bmatrix}.$$

To perform the first iteration, we need to start from $\mathbf{x}^{(0)} = (0, 0.005)$. The function value at this point is 1.0025. The gradient and Hessian at this point take up the following expressions:

$$\mathbf{c}^{(0)} = \begin{Bmatrix} -2 \\ 1 \end{Bmatrix}, \qquad \mathbf{H}^{(0)} = \begin{bmatrix} 0 & 0 \\ 0 & 200 \end{bmatrix}.$$

We can see that the Hessian is singular as its eigenvalues are 0 and 200. For this matrix, the Hessian has to be repaired before using Newton's method. We can obtain the factorized matrix:

$$\mathbf{H}^{(0)} = \mathbf{LDL}^{\mathrm{T}} = \begin{bmatrix} 1 & 0 \\ 0 & 1 \end{bmatrix} \begin{bmatrix} 0 & 0 \\ 0 & 200 \end{bmatrix} \begin{bmatrix} 1 & 0 \\ 0 & 1 \end{bmatrix}.$$

The factorization here is simple as the Hessian is already diagonal. We can create the modified Hessian:

$$\mathbf{H}_{\mathrm{mod}}^{(0)} = \begin{bmatrix} 1 & 0 \\ 0 & 200 \end{bmatrix}.$$

Search direction can now be calculated using the equation:

$$\mathbf{H}_{\mathrm{mod}}^{(0)} \mathbf{d}^{(0)} = -\mathbf{c}^{(0)}.$$

$$\mathbf{d}^{(0)} = \begin{Bmatrix} 2 \\ -0.005 \end{Bmatrix}.$$

Now we find $\alpha = 0.0678$ using a 1D search such that $f(\mathbf{x}^{(0)} + \alpha \mathbf{d}^{(0)})$ is minimized. The next design is, therefore

$$\mathbf{x}^{(1)} = \mathbf{x}^{(0)} + \alpha \mathbf{d}^{(0)} = \begin{Bmatrix} 0.1356 \\ 0.0047 \end{Bmatrix}.$$

The function value at this point is 0.766, down from 1.0025 at the starting point. For iteration 2, we evaluate the gradient and Hessian about the new design point.

$$\mathbf{c}^{(1)} = \begin{Bmatrix} -0.9843 \\ -2.7453 \end{Bmatrix},$$

$$\mathbf{H}^{(1)} = \begin{bmatrix} 22.20 & -54.24 \\ -54.24 & 200 \end{bmatrix}.$$

The eigenvalues of the Hessian are 6.96 and 215.24. Therefore, the Hessian is positive definite. The search direction is now given by the expression:

$$\mathbf{H}^{(1)}\mathbf{d}^{(1)} = -\mathbf{c}^{(1)},$$

$$\mathbf{d}^{(1)} = \begin{Bmatrix} 0.2308 \\ 0.0763 \end{Bmatrix}.$$

Again, we find $\alpha = 0.6679$ to be the value that minimizes the function $f(\mathbf{x}^{(1)} + \alpha\mathbf{d}^{(1)})$. This leads to the new design:

$$\mathbf{x}^{(2)} = \mathbf{x}^{(1)} + \alpha\mathbf{d}^{(1)} = \begin{Bmatrix} 0.2898 \\ 0.0557 \end{Bmatrix}.$$

The function value at this point has again decreased to 0.5844.

Note that the Hessian modification in Example 4.4 has saved the problem from the pitfalls of a nonpositive and singular Hessian matrix. This also shows that the Hessian matrix is not sacrosanct and can be replaced by another positive definite and nonsingular matrix. This basic idea of modifying the Hessian as long as we preserve positive definiteness is used in quasi-Newton methods discussed later in this chapter.

Sometimes, there can be a situation where the Hessian is positive definite along the iteration path but not at the optimal point. In such cases, Newton's method converges slowly, as in the following example.

Example 4.5 Apply Newton's method to $f(x) = x^4 - 1$, starting from $x^{(0)} = 1$. What are the convergence rate and rate constant?

Solution: The Newtonian method for this problem gives the following equation:

$$x^{(k+1)} = x^{(k)} - \frac{f'(x^{(k)})}{f''(x^{(k)})} = x^{(k)} - \frac{4x^{(k)^3}}{12x^{(k)^2}} = x^{(k)} - \frac{x^{(k)}}{3} = \frac{2}{3}x^{(k)}.$$

The Newton iterates are $1, 2/3, 4/9, 8/27, 16/81 \ldots$. The optimal solution occurs at $x^* = 0$, $f(x^*) = -1$. The error term can be obtained:

$$e_k = x^{(k)} - x^* = \left(\frac{2}{3}\right)^k.$$

The convergence rate in this problem is linear and the rate constant is the following:

$$c = \frac{\|e_{k+1}\|}{\|e_k\|} = \frac{2}{3}.$$

The example shows that quadratic convergence is not possible for all cases. The rate constant being quite high, it will take many iterations to converge to the minimum with reasonable precision in this problem.

Example 4.6 Consider the function,

$$f(x) = x^2 + e^{-x} + \sin[4x].$$

Perform two iterations of Newton's method for the function at $x = -1$. Again perform two iterations of Newton's method at $x = 1$. Find the minimum points of the function analytically and compare with your results.

Solution:

Iterations from $x = -1$

Iteration $1(k = 0)$

We should first calculate the gradient and the Hessian matrix at the starting point $x = -1$.

$$f'^{(0)} = \{2x - e^{-x} + 4\cos[4x]\} = -7.333 \, f''^{(0)} = [2 + e^{-x} - 16\sin[4x]] = -7.391.$$

The search direction is obtained.

$$d^{(0)} = -f''^{(0)-1} f'^{(0)} = -\frac{f'^{(0)}}{f''^{(0)}} = -0.992.$$

The first design increment is the following:

$$x^{(1)} = x^{(0)} + d^{(0)} = -1.992.$$

Iteration $2(k = 1)$

Now, we recalculate the gradient and the Hessian matrix at the new design point.

$$f'^{(1)} = \{2x - e^{-x} + 4\cos[4x]\} = -11.769 \, f''^{(1)} = [2 + e^{-x} - 16\sin[4x]] = 25.226.$$

The new search direction is given below:

$$d^{(1)} = -f''^{(1)-1} f'^{(1)} = -\frac{f'^{(1)}}{f''^{(1)}} = 0.467.$$

New design point is calculated: $x^{(2)} = x^{(1)} + d^{(1)} = -1.525$. Further iterations show the iterates: $x^{(3)} = -0.517$, $x^{(4)} = -0.257$, $x^{(5)} = -0.2722$, $x^{(6)} = -0.2724$.

Iterations from $x = 1$

Iteration $1(k = 0)$

We now calculate the gradient and the Hessian matrix at the starting point $x = 1$.

$$f'^{(0)} = \{2x - e^{-x} + 4\cos[4x]\} = -0.982.$$
$$f''^{(0)} = [2 + e^{-x} - 16\sin[4x]] = 14.476.$$

Therefore, the Hessian is positive definite and the Newtonian method should give a descent direction. The search direction is obtained.

$$d^{(0)} = -f''^{(0)-1} f'^{(0)} = -\frac{f'^{(0)}}{f''^{(0)}} = 0.0678.$$

The first design increment is given by

$$x^{(1)} = x^{(0)} + d^{(0)} = 1.0678.$$

Iteration $2(k = 1)$

Now, we recalculate the gradient and the Hessian matrix at the new design point.

$$f'^{(1)} = \{2x - e^{-x} + 4\cos[4x]\} = 0.0837 f''^{(1)} = [2 + e^{-x} - 16\sin[4x]] = 16.812.$$

The new search direction is calculated.

$$d^{(1)} = -f''^{(1)-1} f'^{(1)} = -\frac{f'^{(1)}}{f''^{(1)}} = -0.00497.$$

New design point is calculated.

$$x^{(2)} = x^{(1)} + d^{(1)} = 1.06283.$$

The gradient and Hessian at the point take on the expressions and values given below:

$$f'^{(2)} = \{2x - e^{-x} + 4\cos[4x]\} = 0.00006 f''^{(2)}$$
$$= [2 + e^{-x} - 16\sin[4x]] = 16.674.$$

The search direction is obtained.

$$d^{(2)} = -f''^{(2)-1} f'^{(2)} = -0.0000035.$$

New design point is calculated.

$$x^{(3)} = x^{(2)} + d^{(2)} = 1.062826 \approx 1.06283.$$

Further iterations converge to the same design point, $x = 1.0628$. This is an example of a multimodal function, with more that one minimum point. The example illustrates a pitfall of the gradient-based methods which is their convergence to a local minimum. The example also shows that by starting from different points, the best minimum point can be found. This is the philosophy behind *multistart* methods. The function is shown in Figure 4.1. We can see the two minimum points found by Newton's method.

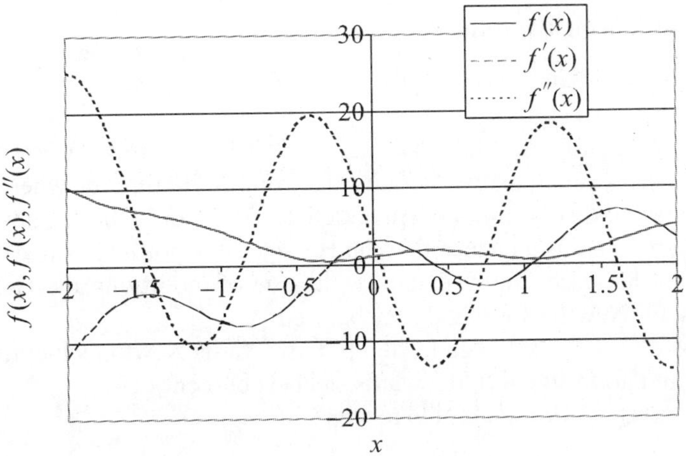

Figure 4.1 *Multimodal function*

4.2 Marquardt's Method

Near the optimal point, the Hessians are positive definite or at least positive semidefinite. Therefore, Newton's method works well near the optimal point. In contrast, the steepest-descent method provides rapid decrease in the objective function in the first few iterations and then *gets stuck* near the optimal point. Recall that the negative gradient represents the direction of maximum decrease of the function, so it is likely that the first few iterations will yield large reductions before the zigzag problem kicks in. Marquardt (1963) suggested a hybrid method which combines the good points of both these methods.[1]

$$\mathbf{d}^{(k)} = -(\mathbf{H} + \lambda\mathbf{I})^{-1}\mathbf{c}^{(k)}. \tag{4.11}$$

The search direction defined above can be controlled by using λ. Consider the two extreme cases of $\lambda \to \infty$ and $\lambda \to 0$. When $\lambda \to \infty$, $\mathbf{d}^{(k)} = -(\mathbf{H} + \lambda\mathbf{I})^{-1}\mathbf{c}^{(k)} = -(\lambda\mathbf{I})^{-1}\mathbf{c}^{(k)} = -(1/\lambda)\mathbf{c}^{(k)}$, which is the steepest-descent method with $\alpha_k = 1/\lambda$ as step size. Thus for large values of λ, this method becomes the steepest-descent method with a small step size. When $\lambda \to 0$, $\mathbf{d}^{(k)} = -(\mathbf{H} + \lambda\mathbf{I})^{-1}\mathbf{c}^{(k)} \approx -\mathbf{H}^{-1}\mathbf{c}^{(k)}$, which is the classical Newton's method with unit step size.

The main idea in Marquardt's method is to start with a large value of λ and reduce it as the algorithm progresses. This leads to the algorithm starting with the steepest-descent method with progressively increasing step sizes which then morphs into Newton's method in the limit as $\lambda \to 0$.

4.2.1 Marquardt algorithm

1. Select the starting design and parameters, $\mathbf{x}^{(0)}$, ε, $k = 0$, $\lambda_0 = 10000$ (large constant).
2. Calculate $\mathbf{c}^{(k)}$:

   If $\|\mathbf{c}^{(k)}\| < \varepsilon$, then stop. If not, continue the process.

3. Calculate $\mathbf{H}^{(k)}$.

4. Calculate $\mathbf{d}^{(k)}$, using the formula:

$$\mathbf{d}^{(k)} = -(\mathbf{H}^{(k)} + \lambda_k \mathbf{I})^{-1}\mathbf{c}^{(k)}.$$

Note that addition of the diagonal matrix with large terms ensures that the matrix $(\mathbf{H}^{(k)} + \lambda_k \mathbf{I})$ remains positive definite far from the optimum, where λ is large and where the possibility of a nonpositive definite Hessian is the greatest. Closer to the optimal there remains a chance that the Hessian may not be positive definite at some iteration. In that case, the safeguard technique of modifying the Hessian discussed previously for Newton's method may be used.

5. If $f(\mathbf{x}^{(k)} + \mathbf{d}^{(k)}) < f(\mathbf{x}^{(k)})$, go to step 6 (Go towards Newton's method). Else, define $\lambda_k = 2\lambda_k$ and go to step 4 (Go towards steepest descent).
6. $\lambda_{k+1} = (1/2)\lambda_k, \quad k = k+1$. Go to step 2.

Marquardt's modification is a typical hybrid method which combines two different methods. Other such hybrid methods can be created by combining two or more methods and evaluated based on numerical experiments on test functions.

Example 4.7 Minimize the following function using Marquardt's method.

$$f(\mathbf{x}) = x_1^2 + 2x_2^2 + e^{-x_1-x_2}.$$

Perform two iterations starting from the point (1, 2).

Solution: We calculate the gradient and the Hessian matrix at the starting point.

$$\mathbf{c}^{(0)} = \begin{Bmatrix} 2x_1 - e^{-x_1-x_2} \\ 4x_2 - e^{-x_1-x_2} \end{Bmatrix} = \begin{Bmatrix} 1.9502 \\ 7.9502 \end{Bmatrix}.$$

$$\mathbf{H}^{(0)} = \begin{bmatrix} 2 + e^{-x_1-x_2} & e^{-x_1-x_2} \\ e^{-x_1-x_2} & 4 + e^{-x_1-x_2} \end{bmatrix} = \begin{bmatrix} 2.0497 & 0.0497 \\ 0.0497 & 4.0497 \end{bmatrix}.$$

Let $\lambda_0 = 10000$. Then, the search direction is obtained as follows:

$$\mathbf{d}^{(0)} = -(\mathbf{H}^{(0)} + \lambda_0 \mathbf{I})^{-1}\mathbf{c}^{(0)} = \begin{Bmatrix} -0.195e-3 \\ -0.7947e-3 \end{Bmatrix}.$$

We check that $f(\mathbf{x}^{(0)} + \mathbf{d}^{(0)}) < f(\mathbf{x}^{(0)})$, therefore, set $\lambda_1 = \lambda_0/2 = 5000$.

The first design increment is then obtained as follows:

$$\mathbf{x}^{(1)} = \mathbf{x}^{(0)} + \mathbf{d}^{(0)} = \begin{Bmatrix} 0.9903 \\ 1.9604 \end{Bmatrix}.$$

This ends the first iteration. To continue with the second iteration, we recalculate the gradient at the new design point.

$$\mathbf{c}^{(1)} = \begin{Bmatrix} 1.9283 \\ 7.7893 \end{Bmatrix}, \qquad \|\mathbf{c}^{(1)}\| > 0.$$

The Hessian is calculated.

$$\mathbf{H}^{(1)} = \begin{bmatrix} 2.0523 & 0.0523 \\ 0.0523 & 4.0523 \end{bmatrix}.$$

We should check for positive definiteness. The eigenvalues of the Hessian are now 2.0509 and 4.0537. Thus, the Hessian is positive definite. The new search direction is calculated below:

$$\mathbf{d}^{(1)} = -(\mathbf{H}^{(1)} + \lambda_1 \mathbf{I})^{-1}\mathbf{c}^{(1)} = \begin{Bmatrix} -0.0004 \\ -0.0016 \end{Bmatrix}.$$

The new design point can be immediately obtained:

$$\mathbf{x}^{(2)} = \mathbf{x}^{(1)} + \mathbf{d}^{(1)} = \begin{Bmatrix} 0.9899 \\ 1.9588 \end{Bmatrix}.$$

Since $f(\mathbf{x}^{(1)} + \mathbf{d}^{(1)}) < f(\mathbf{x}^{(1)})$, set $\lambda_2 = \lambda_1/2 = 2500$, and continue with further iterations. We see that though the method does not need step size, the progress can be slow depending on the selection of λ_0. This is an obvious disadvantage of Marquardt's method.

4.3 Quasi-Newton Methods

Quasi-Newton methods are some of the most widely used optimization methods. They have been incorporated into many software libraries. The basic idea behind these methods is to calculate either the Hessian or its inverse by using some approximate formula which makes use of changes in the design and gradient vectors in the past iterations. The key issue in developing update formulas for the Hessian is the need to keep the approximate Hessian symmetric and positive definite. Positive definiteness is essential; otherwise the search direction is not guaranteed to be a descent direction.

The basic idea behind the quasi-Newton method can be grasped by considering the Newton and secant methods in 1D. Consider an expansion of the function $f(x)$ as a quadratic approximation:[2]

$$f(x + d) = f(x) + f'(x)d + \frac{1}{2}f''(x)d^2. \tag{4.12}$$

Here d is analogous to the design change $\Delta\mathbf{x}$ in Newton's method. The optimal design change is obtained when the following condition is satisfied:

$$\frac{df}{dd} = f'(x) + df''(x) = 0 \Rightarrow d = -\frac{f'(x)}{f''(x)}. \tag{4.13}$$

Newton's method in 1D can therefore be written in the following way:

$$x^{(k+1)} = x^{(k)} - \frac{f'(x^{(k)})}{f''(x^{(k)})}. \tag{4.14}$$

A simple way to replace the second derivative in the above equation is to use the backward finite-difference approximation:

$$f''(x^{(k)}) = \frac{f'(x^{(k)}) - f'(x^{(k-1)})}{x^{(k)} - x^{(k-1)}}. \tag{4.15}$$

This leads to the secant method for minimizing a 1D function

$$x^{(k+1)} = x^{(k)} - \frac{f'(x^{(k)})(x^{(k)} - x^{(k-1)})}{f'(x^{(k)}) - f'(x^{(k-1)})}. \tag{4.16}$$

It can be shown that while Newton's method converges quadratically, the secant method converges superlinearly with the rate of convergence being equal to the golden ratio, 1.618.

The secant formula in (4.15) can be written as follows:

$$f''(x^{(k)})(x^{(k)} - x^{(k-1)}) = f'(x^{(k)}) - f'(x^{(k-1)}). \tag{4.17}$$

Generalizing to multiple dimensions leads to the equation:

$$\mathbf{H}^{(k)}(\mathbf{x}^{(k)} - \mathbf{x}^{(k-1)}) = \mathbf{c}^{(k)} - \mathbf{c}^{(k-1)}. \tag{4.18}$$

It is required that the quasi-Newton approximation of the Hessian matrix, denoted by $\mathbf{B}^{(k)}$, satisfies the *secant condition*:

$$\mathbf{B}^{(k)}(\mathbf{x}^{(k)} - \mathbf{x}^{(k-1)}) = \mathbf{c}^{(k)} - \mathbf{c}^{(k-1)}. \tag{4.19}$$

Consider a quadratic form given by $f(\mathbf{x}) = (1/2)\mathbf{x}^{\mathrm{T}}\mathbf{A}\mathbf{x} - \mathbf{b}^{\mathrm{T}}\mathbf{x}$. Then,

$$\mathbf{A}(\mathbf{x}^{(k)} - \mathbf{x}^{(k-1)}) = (\mathbf{A}\mathbf{x}^{(k)} - \mathbf{b}) - (\mathbf{A}\mathbf{x}^{(k-1)} - \mathbf{b}) = \mathbf{c}^{(k)} - \mathbf{c}^{(k-1)}. \tag{4.20}$$

Therefore, **A** which is the Hessian of a quadratic form must satisfy the secant condition. For a general nonlinear function, this interpretation holds locally in an approximate manner. In general, quasi-Newton methods find the approximation $\mathbf{B}^{(k)}$ so as to approximate the behaviour of the Hessian matrix which gives the change in gradient when multiplied by the change in design according to the secant condition. Methods which try to approximate the Hessian are called direct-update methods.

4.4 Direct-Update Methods

In the direct-update methods, the Hessian is updated using a formula. Several such methods exist and are based on a similar logic. To understand the ideas behind the quasi-Newton method, consider the following two vectors related to the change in the design vector and change in the gradient vector which occur in update formulas.

$$\mathbf{s}^{(k)} = \mathbf{x}^{(k+1)} - \mathbf{x}^{(k)} = \alpha_k \mathbf{d}^{(k)} \tag{4.21}$$

$$\mathbf{y}^{(k)} = \mathbf{c}^{(k+1)} - \mathbf{c}^{(k)}. \tag{4.22}$$

The secant condition then becomes:

$$\mathbf{B}^{(k)}\mathbf{s}^{(k-1)} = \mathbf{y}^{(k-1)} \quad \text{or} \tag{4.23}$$

$$\mathbf{B}^{(k+1)}\mathbf{s}^{(k)} = \mathbf{y}^{(k)}. \tag{4.24}$$

The update formulas must satisfy the above equation. For example, consider a simple update formula:[2]

$$\mathbf{B}^{(k+1)} = \mathbf{B}^{(k)} + \frac{(\mathbf{y}^{(k)} - \mathbf{B}^{(k)}\mathbf{s}^{(k)})(\mathbf{y}^{(k)} - \mathbf{B}^{(k)}\mathbf{s}^{(k)})^{\mathrm{T}}}{(\mathbf{y}^{(k)} - \mathbf{B}^{(k)}\mathbf{s}^{(k)})^{\mathrm{T}}\mathbf{s}^{(k)}}. \tag{4.25}$$

This formula satisfies the secant condition:

$$\mathbf{B}^{(k+1)}\mathbf{s}^{(k)} = \mathbf{B}^{(k)}\mathbf{s}^{(k)} + \frac{(\mathbf{y}^{(k)} - \mathbf{B}^{(k)}\mathbf{s}^{(k)})(\mathbf{y}^{(k)} - \mathbf{B}^{(k)}\mathbf{s}^{(k)})^{\mathrm{T}}\mathbf{s}^{(k)}}{(\mathbf{y}^{(k)} - \mathbf{B}^{(k)}\mathbf{s}^{(k)})^{\mathrm{T}}\mathbf{s}^{(k)}} = \mathbf{y}^{(k)}. \tag{4.26}$$

The update formula shows that the approximate Hessian can be obtained by using only two sets of information: change in gradient and change in design. To start the method, the condition $\mathbf{B}^{(0)} = \mathbf{I}$ can be used. However, better performance may be obtained if a more realistic approximation can be obtained. For example, the Hessian could be calculated at the starting design and then used with a quasi-Newton method.

All direct quasi-Newton methods are based on the formula,

$$\mathbf{B}^{(k+1)} = \mathbf{B}^{(k)} + \Delta\mathbf{B}^{(k)}. \tag{4.27}$$

Here $\Delta\mathbf{B}^{(k)}$ is an update to $\mathbf{B}^{(k)}$. One of the most powerful direct-update methods is the Broyden–Fletcher–Goldfarb–Shanno (BFGS) method.

4.5 Broyden–Fletcher–Goldfarb–Shanno Method

The BFGS algorithm was proposed in 1970 and gives an update formula which is robust to lack of accuracy in the line search. This makes the BFGS method computationally efficient, as function calls can be saved by performing somewhat inaccurate line searches. The BFGS algorithm is summarized below.[1]

4.5.1 BFGS algorithm

1. Estimate $\mathbf{x}^{(0)}$. Choose a positive definite $\mathbf{B}^{(0)}$. If no information is available, select $\mathbf{B}^{(0)} = \mathbf{I}$. Choose ε. Set $k = 0$. Compute $\mathbf{c}^{(0)}$.
2. Check for optimal point:

   Calculate $\|\mathbf{c}^{(k)}\|$. If $\|\mathbf{c}^{(k)}\| < \varepsilon$ stop. If not, continue the process.

3. Find the search direction $\mathbf{d}^{(k)}$:

   $$\mathbf{B}^{(k)}\mathbf{d}^{(k)} = -\mathbf{c}^{(k)}.$$

4. Compute $\alpha_k = \alpha$ to minimize $f(\mathbf{x}^{(k)} + \alpha\mathbf{d}^{(k)})$.
5. Update design according to the following rule:

   $$\mathbf{x}^{(k+1)} = \mathbf{x}^{(k)} + \alpha_k\mathbf{d}^{(k)}.$$

6. Update the Hessian approximation as follows:

   $$\mathbf{s}^{(k)} = \alpha_k\mathbf{d}^{(k)}.$$

   $$\mathbf{y}^{(k)} = \mathbf{c}^{(k+1)} - \mathbf{c}^{(k)}.$$

$$\mathbf{B}^{(k+1)} = \mathbf{B}^{(k)} + \frac{\mathbf{y}^{(k)}\mathbf{y}^{(k)\mathrm{T}}}{\mathbf{y}^{(k)(\mathrm{T})}\mathbf{s}^{(k)}} + \frac{\mathbf{c}^{(k)}\mathbf{c}^{(k)\mathrm{T}}}{\mathbf{c}^{(k)(\mathrm{T})}\mathbf{d}^{(k)}}. \tag{4.28}$$

7. Set $k = k + 1$. Go to Step 2.

The BFGS update formulation keeps the Hessian approximately positive definite. In numerical calculations, difficulties may sometimes arise due to inexact line search and round-off and truncation errors, in which case the Hessian can become singular or indefinite. In such a situation, an approach similar to the one used for Newton's method can be used by making the updated Hessian positive definite to ensure that the search direction is a descent direction.

Example 4.8 Show that the BFGS update formula maintains symmetry and satisfies the secant condition.

Solution: The BFGS formula is given by the following equation:

$$\mathbf{B}^{(k+1)} = \mathbf{B}^{(k)} + \frac{\mathbf{y}^{(k)}\mathbf{y}^{(k)\mathrm{T}}}{\mathbf{y}^{(k)(\mathrm{T})}\mathbf{s}^{(k)}} + \frac{\mathbf{c}^{(k)}\mathbf{c}^{(k)\mathrm{T}}}{\mathbf{c}^{(k)(\mathrm{T})}\mathbf{d}^{(k)}}.$$

Taking the transpose of the matrices on both sides yields the result given below.

$$\mathbf{B}^{(k+1)\mathrm{T}} = \mathbf{B}^{(k)\mathrm{T}} + \frac{(\mathbf{y}^{(k)}\mathbf{y}^{(k)\mathrm{T}})^{\mathrm{T}}}{\mathbf{y}^{(k)\mathrm{T}}\mathbf{s}^{(k)}} + \frac{(\mathbf{c}^{(k)}\mathbf{c}^{(k)\mathrm{T}})}{\mathbf{c}^{(k)\mathrm{T}}\mathbf{d}^{(k)}},$$

where the fact has been used that the denominator terms on the right-hand side of the equation are scalar and so are unchanged by taking the transpose. Assuming $\mathbf{B}^{(k)}$ is symmetric, we get:

$$\mathbf{B}^{(k+1)\mathrm{T}} = \mathbf{B}^{(k)} + \frac{\mathbf{y}^{(k)\mathrm{T}^{\mathrm{T}}}\mathbf{y}^{(k)\mathrm{T}}}{\mathbf{y}^{(k)\mathrm{T}}\mathbf{s}^{(k)}} + \frac{\mathbf{c}^{(k)\mathrm{T}^{\mathrm{T}}}\mathbf{c}^{(k)\mathrm{T}}}{\mathbf{c}^{(k)\mathrm{T}}\mathbf{d}^{(k)}} = \mathbf{B}^{(k)} + \frac{\mathbf{y}^{(k)}\mathbf{y}^{(k)\mathrm{T}}}{\mathbf{y}^{(k)\mathrm{T}}\mathbf{s}^{(k)}} + \frac{\mathbf{c}^{(k)}\mathbf{c}^{(k)\mathrm{T}}}{\mathbf{c}^{(k)\mathrm{T}}\mathbf{d}^{(k)}}.$$

To put it in other words:

$$\mathbf{B}^{(k+1)\mathrm{T}} = \mathbf{B}^{(k+1)},$$

where we use the fact that for any matrix, in general, let us call it $\mathbf{A}$, the relationship $\mathbf{A}^{\mathrm{T}^{\mathrm{T}}} = \mathbf{A}$ holds true. Thus the BFGS formula maintains symmetry.

To see if the formula satisfies the secant condition, we multiply both sides by $\mathbf{s}^{(k)}$:

$$\mathbf{B}^{(k+1)}\mathbf{s}^{(k)} = \mathbf{B}^{(k)}\mathbf{s}^{(k)} + \frac{\mathbf{y}^{(k)}\mathbf{y}^{(k)\mathrm{T}}\mathbf{s}^{(k)}}{\mathbf{y}^{(k)\mathrm{T}}\mathbf{s}^{(k)}} + \frac{\mathbf{c}^{(k)}\mathbf{c}^{(k)\mathrm{T}}\mathbf{s}^{(k)}}{\mathbf{c}^{(k)\mathrm{T}}\mathbf{d}^{(k)}}.$$

The elements $\mathbf{c}$, $\mathbf{s}$, and $\mathbf{d}$ obey the relations given below:

$$\mathbf{c}^{(k)\mathrm{T}}\mathbf{s}^{(k)} = \mathbf{c}^{(k)\mathrm{T}}\mathbf{s}^{(k)} = \mathbf{c}^{(k)\mathrm{T}}\alpha_k\mathbf{d}^{(k)} = \alpha_k\mathbf{c}^{(k)\mathrm{T}}\mathbf{d}^{(k)}.$$

Therefore, the matrix equation may be simplified to read as shown below:

$$\mathbf{B}^{(k+1)}\mathbf{s}^{(k)} = \mathbf{B}^{(k)}\mathbf{s}^{(k)} + \mathbf{y}^{(k)} + \alpha_k\mathbf{c}^{(k)}.$$

Since, $\mathbf{B}^{(k)}\mathbf{s}^{(k)} = \mathbf{B}^{(k)}\alpha_k\mathbf{d}^{(k)} = -\alpha_k\mathbf{c}^{(k)}$, we get

$$\mathbf{B}^{(k+1)}\mathbf{s}^{(k)} = \mathbf{y}^{(k)},$$

and the secant condition is satisfied.

Example 4.9 Minimize the following function using the BFGS method.

$$f(\mathbf{x}) = x_1^2 + 2x_2^2 + \mathrm{e}^{-x_1-x_2}.$$

Perform two iterations starting from the point (1, 2).

Solution: In the BFGS method, we need to calculate the gradient. We assume an approximation for the matrix **B** to start the algorithm.

For the first iteration about point (1, 2),

$$\mathbf{c}^{(0)} = \begin{Bmatrix} 2x_1 - \mathrm{e}^{-x_1-x_2} \\ 4x_2 - \mathrm{e}^{-x_1-x_2} \end{Bmatrix} = \begin{Bmatrix} 1.9502 \\ 7.9502 \end{Bmatrix}, \qquad \mathbf{B}^{(0)} = \begin{bmatrix} 1 & 0 \\ 0 & 1 \end{bmatrix}.$$

The search direction is then obtained using the relation given below:

$$\mathbf{B}^{(0)}\mathbf{d}^{(0)} = -\mathbf{c}^{(0)}.$$

Solving the equation, we get an expression for **d**:

$$\mathbf{d}^{(0)} = \begin{Bmatrix} -1.9502 \\ -7.9502 \end{Bmatrix}.$$

We numerically find $\alpha = 0.23779$ to minimize $f(\mathbf{x}^{(0)} + \alpha\mathbf{d}^{(0)})$. The new design is then given below:

$$\mathbf{x}^{(1)} = \mathbf{x}^{(0)} + \alpha\mathbf{d}^{(0)} = \begin{Bmatrix} 0.5362 \\ 0.1095 \end{Bmatrix}.$$

We now need to update the Hessian approximation for the next iteration. We calculate the various vectors needed:

$$\mathbf{s}^{(0)} = \alpha\mathbf{d}^{(0)} = \begin{Bmatrix} -0.4637 \\ -1.8905 \end{Bmatrix},$$

$$\mathbf{y}^{(0)} = \mathbf{c}^{(1)} - \mathbf{c}^{(0)} = \begin{Bmatrix} 0.5481 \\ -0.0863 \end{Bmatrix} - \begin{Bmatrix} 1.9502 \\ 7.9502 \end{Bmatrix} = \begin{Bmatrix} -1.4021 \\ -8.0365 \end{Bmatrix}.$$

Then,

$$\mathbf{B}^{(1)} = \mathbf{B}^{(0)} + \frac{\mathbf{y}^{(0)}\mathbf{y}^{(0)\mathrm{T}}}{\mathbf{y}^{(0)\mathrm{T}}\mathbf{s}^{(0)}} + \frac{\mathbf{c}^{(0)}\mathbf{c}^{(0)\mathrm{T}}}{\mathbf{c}^{(0)\mathrm{T}}\mathbf{d}^{(0)}} = \begin{bmatrix} 1.0673 & 0.4798 \\ 0.4798 & 4.1332 \end{bmatrix}.$$

We can now proceed with the second iteration:

$$\mathbf{x}^{(1)} = \begin{Bmatrix} 0.5362 \\ 0.1095 \end{Bmatrix} \mathbf{c}^{(1)} = \begin{Bmatrix} 0.5481 \\ -0.0863 \end{Bmatrix}.$$

The search direction can be found using the following equation.

$$\mathbf{B}^{(1)}\mathbf{d}^{(1)} = -\mathbf{c}^{(1)}.$$

Solving this yields the result:

$$\mathbf{d}^{(1)} = \begin{Bmatrix} -0.5517 \\ 0.0849 \end{Bmatrix}.$$

We again find α using the 1D search. It comes to 0.40549. The new design point is as shown:

$$\mathbf{x}^{(2)} = \mathbf{x}^{(1)} + \alpha\mathbf{d}^{(1)} = \begin{Bmatrix} 0.3123 \\ 0.1440 \end{Bmatrix}.$$

At this point, the gradient has decreased to the following:

$$\mathbf{c}^{(2)} = \begin{Bmatrix} -0.009 \\ -0.056 \end{Bmatrix}.$$

We again need to update the Hessian approximation. We obtain the intermediate vector, given by:

$$\mathbf{s}^{(1)} = \alpha_1\mathbf{d}^{(1)} = \begin{Bmatrix} -0.2239 \\ 0.0345 \end{Bmatrix},$$

and

$$\mathbf{y}^{(1)} = \mathbf{c}^{(2)} - \mathbf{c}^{(1)} = \begin{Bmatrix} -0.5571 \\ 0.0303 \end{Bmatrix}.$$

The updated Hessian approximation can be written as shown below:

$$\mathbf{B}^{(2)} = \mathbf{B}^{(1)} + \frac{\mathbf{y}^{(1)}\mathbf{y}^{(1)\mathrm{T}}}{\mathbf{y}^{(1)\mathrm{T}}\mathbf{s}^{(1)}} + \frac{\mathbf{c}^{(1)}\mathbf{c}^{(1)\mathrm{T}}}{\mathbf{c}^{(1)\mathrm{T}}\mathbf{d}^{(1)}} = \begin{bmatrix} 2.5662 & 0.50619 \\ 0.50619 & 4.1157 \end{bmatrix}.$$

Out of curiosity, we check this with the actual Hessian:

$$\mathbf{H}^{(2)} = \begin{bmatrix} 2 + \mathrm{e}^{-x_1-x_2} & \mathrm{e}^{-x_1-x_2} \\ \mathrm{e}^{-x_1-x_2} & 4 + \mathrm{e}^{-x_1-x_2} \end{bmatrix} = \begin{bmatrix} 2.6336 & 0.6336 \\ 0.6336 & 4.6336 \end{bmatrix}.$$

It is clear that the BFGS method approximates the Hessian quite well in just two iterations, even when we started with the unit matrix as the first guess.

4.6 Davidson–Fletcher–Powell Method

The Davidson–Fletcher–Powell (DFP) method approximates the inverse of the Hessian and is one of the most powerful methods in unconstrained optimization.[1] It was developed by Davidson in 1959 and modified by Fletcher and Powell in 1963. By approximating the inverse of the Hessian, the method avoids the need for a solution of the linear system of equations while calculating the search direction. Instead, the search direction is obtained by a matrix-vector multiplication.

4.6.1 DFP algorithm

1. Estimate $\mathbf{x}^{(0)}$. Choose a symmetric, positive definite matrix $\mathbf{A}^{(0)}$ as an estimate for the inverse of the Hessian. A rough guess to start with is $\mathbf{A}^{(0)} = \mathbf{I}$. Select ε. Set $k = 0$. Compute the gradient, $\mathbf{c}^{(0)}$.
2. Compute $\|\mathbf{c}^{(k)}\|$. If $\|\mathbf{c}^{(k)}\| < \varepsilon$, stop the process, if not continue.
3. Determine the search direction.

$$\mathbf{d}^{(k)} = -\mathbf{A}^{(k)}\mathbf{c}^{(k)}.$$

4. Compute $\alpha_k = \alpha$ to minimize $f(\mathbf{x}^{(k)} + \alpha\mathbf{d}^{(k)})$.
5. Update the design in the following manner:

$$\mathbf{x}^{(k+1)} = \mathbf{x}^{(k)} + \alpha_k\mathbf{d}^{(k)}.$$

6. Update $\mathbf{A}^{(k)}$.
Find the change in design vector and gradient vectors.

$$\mathbf{s}^{(k)} = \alpha_k\mathbf{d}^{(k)},$$

$$\mathbf{y}^{(k)} = \mathbf{c}^{(k+1)} - \mathbf{c}^{(k)}$$

$$\mathbf{z}^{(k)} = \mathbf{A}^{(k)}\mathbf{y}^{(k)},$$

$$\mathbf{A}^{(k+1)} = \mathbf{A}^{(k)} + \frac{\mathbf{s}^{(k)}\mathbf{s}^{(k)\mathrm{T}}}{\mathbf{s}^{(k)\mathrm{T}}\mathbf{y}^{(k)}} - \frac{\mathbf{z}^{(k)}\mathbf{z}^{(k)\mathrm{T}}}{\mathbf{y}^{(k)\mathrm{T}}\mathbf{z}^{(k)}}. \tag{4.29}$$

This particular formula can be applied without storing the intermediate vectors $\mathbf{s}^{(k)}$, $\mathbf{y}^{(k)}$ and $\mathbf{z}^{(k)}$ so as to save storage.
7. Set $k = k + 1$. Go to Step 2.
It can be shown for the DFP method that the following two points hold true:

(1) The matrix $\mathbf{A}$ is positive definite for all k.
(2) When the method is applied to a positive definite quadratic form, $\mathbf{A}^{(k)}$ converges to the inverse of the Hessian of the quadratic form.

Example 4.10 Show that the DFP formula preserves the symmetry of the component matrices and satisfies the modified secant condition, $\mathbf{A}^{(k+1)}\mathbf{y}^{(k)} = \mathbf{s}^{(k)}$.

Solution:

$$\mathbf{A}^{(k+1)} = \mathbf{A}^{(k)} + \frac{\mathbf{s}^{(k)}\mathbf{s}^{(k)\mathrm{T}}}{\mathbf{s}^{(k)\mathrm{T}}\mathbf{y}^{(k)}} - \frac{\mathbf{z}^{(k)}\mathbf{z}^{(k)\mathrm{T}}}{\mathbf{y}^{(k)\mathrm{T}}\mathbf{z}^{(k)}}.$$

Taking the transpose yields,

$$\mathbf{A}^{(k+1)\mathrm{T}} = \mathbf{A}^{(k)\mathrm{T}} + \frac{(\mathbf{s}^{(k)}\mathbf{s}^{(k)\mathrm{T}})^{\mathrm{T}}}{\mathbf{s}^{(k)\mathrm{T}}\mathbf{y}^{(k)}} - \frac{(\mathbf{z}^{(k)}\mathbf{z}^{(k)\mathrm{T}})^{\mathrm{T}}}{\mathbf{y}^{(k)\mathrm{T}}\mathbf{z}^{(k)}}.$$

Here we have used the fact that the denominators of the second and third terms on the right-hand side are scalar products and so are unchanged by taking the transpose.

$$\mathbf{A}^{(k+1)\mathrm{T}} = \mathbf{A}^{(k)\mathrm{T}} + \frac{\mathbf{s}^{(k)\mathrm{T}^{\mathrm{T}}}\mathbf{s}^{(k)\mathrm{T}}}{\mathbf{s}^{(k)\mathrm{T}}\mathbf{y}^{(k)}} - \frac{\mathbf{z}^{(k)\mathrm{T}^{\mathrm{T}}}\mathbf{z}^{(k)\mathrm{T}}}{\mathbf{y}^{(k)\mathrm{T}}\mathbf{z}^{(k)}}.$$

$$\mathbf{A}^{(k+1)\mathrm{T}} = \mathbf{A}^{(k)} + \frac{\mathbf{s}^{(k)}\mathbf{s}^{(k)\mathrm{T}}}{\mathbf{s}^{(k)\mathrm{T}}\mathbf{y}^{(k)}} - \frac{\mathbf{z}^{(k)}\mathbf{z}^{(k)\mathrm{T}}}{\mathbf{y}^{(k)\mathrm{T}}\mathbf{z}^{(k)}} = \mathbf{A}^{(k+1)}.$$

Thus, if $\mathbf{A}^{(k)}$ is symmetric, the DFP update formula preserves the symmetry of $\mathbf{A}^{(k+1)}$. Consider the descent condition:

$$\mathbf{A}^{(k+1)}\mathbf{y}^{(k)} = \mathbf{A}^{(k)}\mathbf{y}^{(k)} + \frac{\mathbf{s}^{(k)}\mathbf{s}^{(k)\mathrm{T}}\mathbf{y}^{(k)}}{\mathbf{s}^{(k)\mathrm{T}}\mathbf{y}^{(k)}} - \frac{\mathbf{z}^{(k)}\mathbf{z}^{(k)\mathrm{T}}\mathbf{y}^{(k)}}{\mathbf{y}^{(k)\mathrm{T}}\mathbf{z}^{(k)}}.$$

Now, $\mathbf{z}^{(k)\mathrm{T}}\mathbf{y}^{(k)} = (\mathbf{A}^{(k)}\mathbf{y}^{(k)})\mathrm{T}\mathbf{y}^{(k)} = \mathbf{y}^{(k)\mathrm{T}}\mathbf{A}^{(k)}\mathbf{y}^{(k)}$ and $\mathbf{y}^{(k)\mathrm{T}}\mathbf{z}^{(k)} = \mathbf{y}^{(k)\mathrm{T}}\mathbf{A}^{(k)}\mathbf{y}^{(k)}$, so we get

$$\mathbf{A}^{(k+1)}\mathbf{y}^{(k)} = \mathbf{A}^{(k)}\mathbf{y}^{(k)} + \mathbf{s}^{(k)} - \mathbf{z}^{(k)}.$$

However, we have $\mathbf{z}^{(k)} = \mathbf{A}^{(k+1)}\mathbf{y}^{(k)}$. Thus, we get

$$\mathbf{A}^{(k+1)}\mathbf{y}^{(k)} = \mathbf{s}^{(k)}.$$

We see that the DFP formula satisfies the modified secant condition.

4.6.2 General comments on unconstrained minimization

We have covered several gradient-based optimization methods in Chapter 3 and in the current chapter. These methods have been studied extensively by researchers on a large variety of test problems, and considerable knowledge has been gained about their numerical performance. We now summarize some recommendations for handling these methods.[1–6]

1. The conjugate-gradient and DFP methods are good and efficient. They work well for most nonlinear optimization problems. The BFGS method uses Hessian updates and is an excellent method, besides having strong theoretical underpinnings. The BFGS method is robust to sloppy line searches, which can save considerable computer time. These three methods should be chosen for general nonlinear unconstrained optimization problems.
2. The steepest-descent and Newton's method are classical methods. They were discussed because they form the basis of many other methods. However, Newton's method has the theoretical advantage of quadratic convergence and is a benchmark for comparing new algorithms which typically deliver superlinear convergence. Marquardt's method and Newton's method require expensive Hessian calculations. These methods should not be used for practical problems.

3. Though the conjugate-gradient methods are less efficient and less robust compared with quasi-Newton methods, they have low storage requirements. For problems exceeding 100 design variables, the conjugate-gradient methods become indispensable, since the size of the Hessian approximations in quasi-Newton methods becomes too large.

4.7 Numerical Derivatives

Gradient-based methods depend completely on accurate calculations of gradients for a search direction. For simple functions, it is possible to analytically differentiate the objective function and obtain the gradient and Hessian matrices. However, most optimization problems involve the use of a computer program for calculating the objective function and constraints, as shown in Figure 4.2. The use of numerical derivatives is thus necessary for most practical problems and it is worth spending some time studying these.

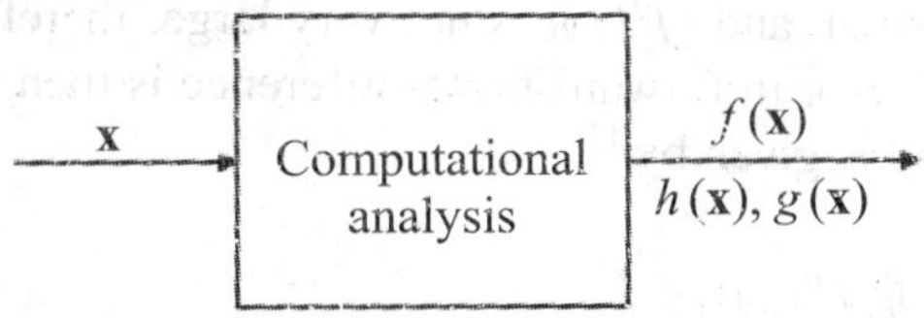

Figure 4.2 *Typical computer model for calculation of objective function and constraints from design variables*

The definition of a derivative as used in calculus is the ratio given below:

$$f'(x) = \lim_{h \to 0} \frac{f(x+h) - f(x)}{h}. \tag{4.30}$$

By choosing an *appropriately small* value of h, the derivative can be approximated in terms of the forward-difference formula as follows:

$$f'(x) \approx \frac{f(x+h) - f(x)}{h}. \tag{4.31}$$

Unfortunately, the problem of finding an *approximately small* value of h on a computer is nontrivial. Errors that can occur in this derivative calculation fall into two categories: truncation errors and roundoff errors. The origin of truncation errors can be seen while expanding $f(x)$ in a Taylor series as follows:

$$f(x+h) = f(x) + hf'(x) + \frac{1}{2}h^2 f''(x) + \frac{1}{6}h^3 f'''(x) + \cdots$$

$$\Rightarrow \frac{f(x+h) - f(x)}{h} = f'(x) + \frac{1}{2}hf'' + \frac{1}{6}h^2 f''' + \cdots \tag{4.32}$$

In the above case, the truncation error results from omission of the higher-order terms of the Taylor series expansion, and the total error can be written as

$$\varepsilon_t = \frac{1}{2}hf'' + \frac{1}{6}h^2 f''' + \cdots \tag{4.33}$$

Obviously, this truncation error tends to zero as $h \to 0$. So, we understand that truncation error has its origin in the mathematical approximation of retaining a limited number of terms in the Taylor series. Also, it can be made arbitrary small by reducing h to a desired small value. On the other hand, the roundoff error has a different origin. It occurs due to finite-precision computer arithmetic, and the extent of roundoff error sets a limit below which it is not advantageous to reduce h. Roundoff error occurs in the computer because $f(x+h) - f(x) \to 0$ as $h \to 0$ due to finite-precision arithmetic. To put it simply, a large value of h leads to high truncation error; while a very small value of h leads to roundoff error, since two nearly equal quantities are subtracted.

Assume ε_p is the precision of the computer arithmetic. The roundoff error is then given by:

$$\varepsilon_r \approx \frac{|f(x)|\varepsilon_p}{h} + |f'(x)|\varepsilon_p \approx \frac{|f(x)|\varepsilon_p}{h}. \tag{4.34}$$

In most situations, h is small and $|f'(x)|$ is not very large; therefore, the first term is the dominant one. The total error in forward finite-difference is then the sum of the roundoff and truncation errors, and is given by:[2]

$$\varepsilon \approx \frac{|f(x)|\varepsilon_p}{h} + \frac{1}{2}h|f''(x)|. \tag{4.35}$$

To find the value of h which gives minimum error, we can minimize the error term with h as the design variable.

$$-\frac{|f(x)|\varepsilon_p}{h}^2 + \frac{1}{2}|f''(x)| = 0$$

$$\Rightarrow h = \sqrt{\frac{2|f(x)|\varepsilon_p}{|f''(x)|}}. \tag{4.36}$$

In cases where $|f(x)|$ and $|f''(x)|$ are neither too large nor too small, the following approximate formula can be used to determine the step size.

$$h = \sqrt{\varepsilon_p}. \tag{4.37}$$

For example, for single-precision arithmetic, $\varepsilon_p = 10^{-8}$, $h = 10^{-4}$. Another practical guideline is to use a perturbation of 1% if the function is not too nonlinear ($h = 0.01|x|$). Thus, we see that there are several practical recommendations for the choice of h. However, there is no universal rule that will be valid for all types of functions. In general, as h is decreased, the truncation error decreases and as it becomes very low, the roundoff error increases. Roundoff error can be decreased by using double-precision arithmetic, $\varepsilon_p = 10^{-16}$, which is common for most numerical computations. A further increase in precision to quadruple it is possible on some computers.

Truncation error can be reduced by choosing the central-difference formula:

$$f'(x) = \frac{f(x+h) - f(x-h)}{2h}. \tag{4.38}$$

To obtain this formula, consider the following Taylor series expansions of the function $f(x)$ in both forward and backward directions:

$$f(x+h) = f(x) + hf'(x) + \frac{1}{2}h^2 f''(x) + \frac{1}{6}h^3 f'''(x) + \cdots$$
$$f(x-h) = f(x) - hf'(x) + \frac{1}{2}h^2 f''(x) - \frac{1}{6}h^3 f'''(x) + \cdots \quad (4.39)$$

Subtracting the second expression from the first yields the following.

$$f(x+h) - f(x-h) = 2hf'(x) + \frac{1}{3}h^3 f'''(x) + \cdots \quad (4.40)$$

The central-difference formula can then be obtained.

$$\frac{f(x+h) - f(x-h)}{2h} = f'(x) + \frac{2}{3}h^2 f'''(x) + \cdots \quad (4.41)$$

The truncation error is now $\varepsilon_t = (2/3)h^2 f'''(x)$. The price one pays for the lower error in the central-difference method is the additional function evaluation as compared to the forward-difference method.

4.7.1 Gradient and Hessian matrices

Typically, the forward-difference method is used to calculate gradients and Hessian matrices, since it needs fewer function evaluations. Using forward difference, the ith partial derivative of $f(\mathbf{x})$ can be calculated using the expression:

$$\frac{\partial f}{\partial x_i} \approx \frac{f(x_1^0, x_2^0, \ldots, x_i^0 + h, \ldots, x_n^0) - f(\mathbf{x}^{(0)})}{h}. \quad (4.42)$$

Each variable is perturbed one by one and the value of $f(\mathbf{x})$ is evaluated. The calculation of the gradient vector therefore needs $n + 1$ function calls. If the objective function is evaluated using some finite-element code or CFD analysis, the time taken to evaluate gradients becomes very high. To get an idea of how much more time is needed, consider a finite-element code which takes 5 minutes to calculate a function and an optimization problem with 20 design variables. Then the gradient calculation takes (20 + 1)*6 = 105 minutes, or 1 hour 45 minutes. One way to reduce this computer time is to calculate the derivatives analytically as part of the simulation program. Recall that gradient calculations need to be made many times during optimization, so the gradient calculations become very important. If one considers more computationally expensive function evaluations which increasingly occur in engineering analysis, the computer time required becomes much larger and can limit the use of gradient-based optimization methods.

To calculate the partial derivative for the Hessian, the forward-difference formula can be used.

$$\frac{\partial}{\partial x_j}\left(\frac{\partial f}{\partial x_i}\right) \approx \frac{1}{h}\left[\begin{array}{c} \frac{f(x_1^0, x_2^0, \ldots, x_i^0 + h, \ldots, x_j^0 + h, \ldots) - f(x_1^0, x_2^0, \ldots, x_i^0, \ldots, x_j^0 + h, \ldots)}{h} \\ -\frac{f(x_1^0, x_2^0, \ldots, x_i^0 + h, \ldots, x_j^0, \ldots) - f(\mathbf{x})}{h} \end{array}\right]. \quad (4.43)$$

Each $\mathbf{H}_{ij}$ needs three function calls. Since the Hessian is symmetric, it has $(n^2+n)/2$ terms. Including the baseline term, the Hessian needs $(n^2+n)/2+1$ function evaluations. Since the number of terms is proportional to n^2, the computational expense increases dramatically as the number of design variables increase. For an optimization problem with 20 design variables, if each code run takes 5 minutes of computer time, the Hessian calculation takes 211 function evaluations and therefore, 1055 minutes or 17 hours, 35 minutes.

Since the Hessian evaluation is very time consuming, practical optimization algorithms never use the Hessian approach. However, approximations to the Hessian based on first-derivative information are used in the so-called quasi-Newton methods which we have discussed earlier in this chapter.

Example 4.11 Find the gradient and Hessian matrix at $x=(0,0)$ for the function,

$$f = x_1^2 + e^{-x_1-x_2} + \sin[4x_1] + 2x_2^2,$$

using the forward finite-difference method. Use $h=10^{-4}$ and $h=0.1$ and compare the results with the analytical gradient and Hessian.

Solution:

A. Analytical method

Gradient at $\mathbf{x}=(0,0)$ is given by $\mathbf{c}=\begin{Bmatrix} 2x_1-e^{-x_1-x_2}+4\cos[4x_1] \\ -e^{-x_1-x_2}+4x_2 \end{Bmatrix}=\begin{Bmatrix} 3 \\ -1 \end{Bmatrix}$.

Hessian at $\mathbf{x}=(0,0)$ is $\mathbf{H}=\begin{bmatrix} 2+e^{-x_1-x_2}-16\sin[4x_1] & e^{-x_1-x_2} \\ e^{-x_1-x_2} & e^{-x_1-x_2}+4 \end{bmatrix}=\begin{bmatrix} 3 & 1 \\ 1 & 5 \end{bmatrix}$.

B. Forward finite-difference method with $h=10^{-4}$

Consider the case of gradients at $\mathbf{x}=(0,0)$ and $h=10^{-4}$. The forward-difference formula gives:

$$\frac{\partial f}{\partial x_1}=\frac{f(x_1+h,x_2)-f(\mathbf{x}^{(0)})}{h}=\frac{1.000300015-1}{10^{-4}}=3.00015.$$

Similarly,

$$\frac{\partial f}{\partial x_2}=\frac{f(x_1,x_2+h)-f(\mathbf{x}^{(0)})}{h}=\frac{0.999900025-1}{10^{-4}}=-0.99975.$$

Hence, the gradients are given by the following expression:

$$\mathbf{c}=\begin{Bmatrix} 3.00015 \\ -0.99975 \end{Bmatrix}.$$

We see that the gradient is very close to the analytical value.

To calculate the Hessian matrix, the forward-difference formulas can be derived as follows:

$$\frac{\partial}{\partial x_1}\left(\frac{\partial f}{\partial x_1}\right) = \frac{\partial}{\partial x_1}\left(\frac{f(x_1+h,x_2)-f(x_1,x_2)}{h}\right)$$
$$= \frac{1}{h}\left[\frac{f(x_1+2h,x_2)-f(x_1+h,x_2)}{h} - \frac{f(x_1+h,x_2)-f(x_1,x_2)}{h}\right]$$
$$= \frac{1}{10^{-4}}\left[\frac{1.00060006 - 1.000300015}{10^{-4}} - \frac{1.000300015 - 1}{10^{-4}}\right] = 3.$$

Similarly, the following equation may be written.

$$\frac{\partial}{\partial x_2}\left(\frac{\partial f}{\partial x_2}\right) = \frac{\partial}{\partial x_2}\left(\frac{f(x_1,x_2+h)-f(x_1,x_2)}{h}\right)$$
$$= \frac{1}{h}\left[\frac{f(x_1,x_2+2h)-f(x_1,x_2+h)}{h} - \frac{f(x_1,x_2+h)-f(x_1,x_2)}{h}\right]$$
$$= \frac{1}{10^{-4}}\left[\frac{0.9998001 - 0.999900025}{10^{-4}} - \frac{0.999900025 - 1}{10^{-4}}\right] = 5.$$

Similarly, with respect to the other variable.

$$\frac{\partial}{\partial x_2}\left(\frac{\partial f}{\partial x_1}\right)$$
$$= \frac{\partial}{\partial x_2}\left(\frac{f(x_1+h,x_2)-f(x_1,x_2)}{h}\right)$$
$$= \frac{1}{h}\left[\frac{\partial f}{\partial x_2}(x_1+h,x_2) - \frac{\partial f}{\partial x_2}(x_1,x_2)\right]$$
$$= \frac{1}{h}\left[\frac{f(x_1+h,x_2+h)-f(x_1+h,x_2)}{h} - \frac{f(x_1,x_2+h)-f(x_1,x_2)}{h}\right]$$
$$= \frac{1}{10^{-4}}\left[\frac{1.00020005 - 1.000300015}{10^{-4}} - \frac{0.999900025 - 1}{10^{-4}}\right] = 1.$$

Hence,

$$\frac{\partial}{\partial x_2}\left(\frac{\partial f}{\partial x_1}\right) = \frac{\partial}{\partial x_1}\left(\frac{\partial f}{\partial x_2}\right) = 1.$$

Hence, the Hessian matrix is obtained.

$$\mathbf{H} = \begin{bmatrix} 3 & 1 \\ 1 & 5 \end{bmatrix}.$$

The Hessian matches the exact analytical values.

C. Forward finite-difference method with $h = 0.1$

The gradient can be obtained from the equation:

$$\frac{\partial f}{\partial x_1} = \frac{f(x_1 + h, x_2) - f(\mathbf{x}^{(0)})}{h} = \frac{1.30425576 - 1}{0.1} = 3.04255.$$

Similarly,

$$\frac{\partial f}{\partial x_2} = \frac{f(x_1, x_2 + h) - f(\mathbf{x}^{(0)})}{h} = \frac{0.924837418 - 1}{0.1} = -0.75163.$$

Hence, the gradient is given by the following matrix:

$$\mathbf{c} = \begin{Bmatrix} 3.04255 \\ -0.75163 \end{Bmatrix}.$$

We see that the gradient is not very accurate. To calculate the Hessian matrix, the forward-difference formula gives:

$$\frac{\partial}{\partial x_1}\left(\frac{\partial f}{\partial x_1}\right) = \frac{1}{0.1}\left[\frac{1.576086844 - 1.30425576}{0.1} - \frac{1.30425576 - 1}{0.1}\right]$$

$$= -3.24246.$$

Similarly,

$$\frac{\partial}{\partial x_2}\left(\frac{\partial f}{\partial x_2}\right) = \frac{1}{0.1}\left[\frac{0.898730753 - 0.924837418}{0.1} - \frac{0.924837418 - 1}{0.1}\right]$$

$$= 4.9055917,$$

and

$$\frac{\partial}{\partial x_2}\left(\frac{\partial f}{\partial x_1}\right) = \frac{1}{0.1}\left[\frac{1.238149095 - 1.30425576}{0.1} - \frac{0.924837418 - 1}{0.1}\right]$$

$$= 0.905592.$$

Hence,

$$\frac{\partial}{\partial x_2}\left(\frac{\partial f}{\partial x_1}\right) = \frac{\partial}{\partial x_1}\left(\frac{\partial f}{\partial x_2}\right) = 0.905592.$$

Hence, the Hessian matrix is the following:

$$\mathbf{H} = \begin{bmatrix} -3.242 & 0.905 \\ 0.905 & 4.905 \end{bmatrix}.$$

Note that this matrix is close but not very accurate. We see that the finite-difference based derivatives are always prone to error due to step-size selection. Therefore, efforts to obtain high-quality gradients are an important part of optimization research.

4.8 Automatic Differentiation

Automatic differentiation (AD) involves differentiation of the statements in computer programs to evaluate derivatives. Since most computational analysis problems involve computation of objective functions and constraints through computer programs, this approach is useful for getting high-quality gradients. The problems associated with finite-difference derivatives can also be avoided by using automatic differentiation.

The automatic differentiation (AD) software takes a program which typically calculates the values of a function $f(\mathbf{x})$ and creates another program which calculates the values of the function $f(\mathbf{x})$ and its gradient $\mathbf{c}$. The basic mathematical concept in AD involves the use of chain-rule differentiation. The function evaluation process is expressed in terms of a sequence of simple calculations which involve, at most, two variables. In general, intermediate variables need to be defined to express a function in this form. For example, calculations such as $x_1 + x_2$, x_1x_2, x_1^2, $\sin(x_1)$ and e^{x_1} are permitted. However, the AD software performs this step of expressing the function in a simple form and the user does not have to write the code in this manner. The procedure behind AD can be understood by creating an evaluation graph for a given function.[2]

Example 4.12 Create an evaluation graph for the function:

$$f(\mathbf{x}) = x_1x_2 + \sin(x_1).$$

Use this graph to calculate the gradient.

Solution: The evaluation graph can be drawn as shown below.

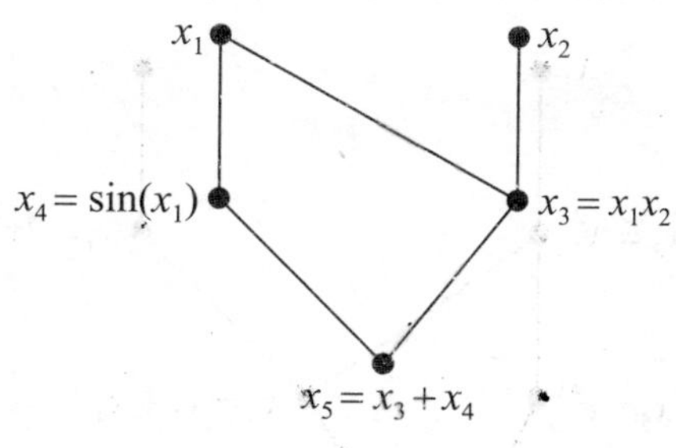

We start from the bottom of the graph and proceed upwards. We immediately see that

$$f(\mathbf{x}) = x_5 = x_4 + x_3.$$

Then, we get, using chain-rule differentiation:

$$\frac{\partial f}{\partial x_5} = 1.$$

$$\frac{\partial f}{\partial x_3} = \frac{\partial f}{\partial x_5}\frac{\partial x_5}{\partial x_3} = 1.1 = 1.$$

$$\frac{\partial f}{\partial x_4} = \frac{\partial f}{\partial x_5}\frac{\partial x_5}{\partial x_4} = 1.1 = 1.$$

$$\frac{\partial f}{\partial x_2} = \frac{\partial f}{\partial x_3}\frac{\partial x_3}{\partial x_2} = 1.x_1 = x_1.$$

$$\frac{\partial f}{\partial x_1} = \frac{\partial f}{\partial x_3}\frac{\partial x_3}{\partial x_1} + \frac{\partial f}{\partial x_4}\frac{\partial x_4}{\partial x_1} = 1.x_2 + 1.\cos(x_1) = x_2 + \cos(x_1).$$

We see that the gradient has been obtained using the evaluation graph. We see that the graph indicates the relationship between the different variables and determines the chain-rule application. In the above example, only node x_1 has a connection to two nodes x_3 and x_4, which effects the chain-rule terms. The efficiency of AD comes from the evaluation of gradients starting from the bottom of the graph.

Example 4.13 Create an evaluation graph for the following function and find the gradient at (0,0):

$$f(\mathbf{x}) = x_1^2 + 2x_2^2 + e^{x_1^2}.$$

Solution: We can write the function calculation in terms of the following steps:

$$x_3 = x_1^2,$$

$$x_4 = 2x_2^2,$$

$$x_5 = e^{x_3},$$

$$x_6 = x_3 + x_4,$$

$$x_7 = x_5 + x_6.$$

The evaluation graph can be drawn as shown below:

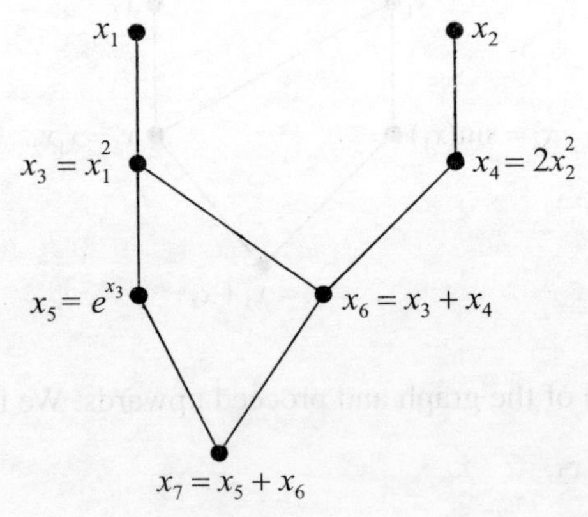

This evaluation graph can be used to perform the chain-rule differentiation:

$$f(\mathbf{x}) = x_7 = x_5 + x_6.$$

$$\frac{\partial f}{\partial x_7} = 1,$$

$$\frac{\partial f}{\partial x_6} = \frac{\partial f}{\partial x_7}\frac{\partial x_7}{\partial x_6} = 1,$$

$$\frac{\partial f}{\partial x_5} = \frac{\partial f}{\partial x_5}\frac{\partial x_5}{\partial x_6} = 1,$$

$$\frac{\partial f}{\partial x_4} = \frac{\partial f}{\partial x_6}\frac{\partial x_6}{\partial x_4} = 1,$$

$$\frac{\partial f}{\partial x_3} = \frac{\partial f}{\partial x_5}\frac{\partial x_5}{\partial x_3} + \frac{\partial f}{\partial x_6}\frac{\partial x_6}{\partial x_3} = 1 + \mathrm{e}^{x_3},$$

$$\frac{\partial f}{\partial x_2} = \frac{\partial f}{\partial x_4}\frac{\partial x_4}{\partial x_2} = 4x_2,$$

$$\frac{\partial f}{\partial x_1} = \frac{\partial f}{\partial x_3}\frac{\partial x_3}{\partial x_1} = 2x_1(1 + \mathrm{e}^{x_1^2}).$$

At point (0, 0), the gradient is (0, 0).

Easy-to-use AD software which can be downloaded for free are available on the Internet. One such software is TAPENADE, developed at INRIA Sophia-Antipolis, France. Currently, TAPENADE works with Fortran programs, though extensions to other languages are possible in the future. To understand how AD works on code, consider the line of code given by $x_1 = x_2^* t(10) + x_3$. Here x_1, x_2 and x_3 are design variables, and in general, the vector t could be a function of the design variables. The differentiated program executes the operations which should lead to $dx_1 = dx_2^* t(10) + x_2^* dt(10) + dx_3$. Of course, for most programs, control-flow issues need to be addressed and the AD softwares do a lot of complicated calculations. TAPENADE as well as supporting information and a tutorial can be found at http://www-sop.inria.fr/tropics/tapenade.html.

4.9 Analytical Gradients for Computational Problems

For some engineering problems, it is possible to efficiently calculate the gradients as a part of the solution process by analytically differentiating the underlying vectors and matrices with respect to the design variables. These calculations are illustrated for static and dynamic finite-element calculations. However, the basic theme behind these analytical gradients can be applied to any other problem.[6]

4.9.1 Static finite-element analysis

Consider a finite-element analysis based calculation of displacement of the structure subject to an applied loading. The problem may involve design of a structure for minimum weight subject to constraints on strength and displacement. To evaluate the stresses, we need to find the displacements. The derivatives of stress-related constraints have derivatives of the displacements. These can be calculated as follows. The standard finite-element equations after assembly and application of boundary conditions can be written as

$$\mathbf{Kq} = \mathbf{F}. \tag{4.44}$$

Here the design variables typically affect the stiffness matrix **K** and displacement vector **q** and may also affect the load vector **F**. Typically, we want to find the displacements of the structures when given the load vector and the stiffness matrix through the solution of the linear system. However, the stresses and strains in the structure depend on displacements and these derivatives are needed for many optimization problems. Also, one may have displacement constraints on the structure. Differentiating (4.44) with respect to design variables x_i, we obtain the following equation.

$$\frac{d\mathbf{K}}{dx_i}\mathbf{q} + \mathbf{K}\frac{d\mathbf{q}}{dx_i} = \frac{d\mathbf{F}}{dx_i}. \tag{4.45}$$

This leads to the derivatives of the displacements with respect to the design variables.

$$\frac{d\mathbf{q}}{dx_i} = \mathbf{K}^{-1}\frac{d\mathbf{F}}{dx_i} - \mathbf{K}^{-1}\frac{d\mathbf{K}}{dx_i}\mathbf{K}^{-1}\mathbf{F} = \mathbf{K}^{-1}\frac{d\mathbf{F}}{dx_i} - \mathbf{K}^{-1}\frac{d\mathbf{K}}{dx_i}\mathbf{q}. \tag{4.46}$$

These derivatives can then be used to calculate the derivatives of strain using the strain–displacement relationships. Derivatives of stresses can be calculated using the stress–strain relationship.

In many structural problems, loads do not depend on typical design variables such as stiffness, cross-section dimensions or mass. In such cases, $d\mathbf{F}/dx_i = 0$. Furthermore, the global stiffness matrix is obtained by assembling the element stiffness matrices:

$$\frac{\partial \mathbf{K}}{\partial x_i} = \sum_{j=1}^{Ne} \frac{\partial \mathbf{k}_j}{\partial x_i}. \tag{4.47}$$

Here $\mathbf{k}_j$ are the element stiffness matrices and Ne is the number of finite-elements used in the discretization process. If the expressions for the stiffness matrix are known in closed form, the derivatives of the element stiffness matrix can be obtained and assembled to obtain the gradients of the displacements with respect to the design variables. If the stiffness is obtained numerically, finite-difference methods can be used to obtain the derivatives of the stiffness matrix. It is generally a good idea to obtain analytical derivatives as a part of developing the computer program as they can then be used for optimization.

4.9.2 Dynamic finite-element analysis

Frequencies of a structure can be calculated by solving the following eigenvalue problem:

$$\mathbf{K}\Phi = \omega^2\mathbf{M}\Phi, \tag{4.48}$$

where $\mathbf{K}$ is the global stiffness matrix, $\mathbf{M}$ is the global mass matrix, Φ are the eigenvectors representing the mode shapes of the structure and ω are the natural frequencies which can be calculated by taking the square root of the eigenvalues. Differentiating the eigenvalue problem in (4.48) yields the equation,

$$\mathbf{K}\frac{\partial \Phi}{\partial x_i} + \frac{\partial \mathbf{K}}{\partial x_i}\Phi = 2\omega\frac{\partial \omega}{\partial x_i}\mathbf{M}\Phi + \omega^2\mathbf{M}\frac{\partial \Phi}{\partial x_i} + \omega^2\frac{\partial \mathbf{M}}{\partial x_i}\Phi. \tag{4.49}$$

or

$$\left(\frac{\partial \mathbf{K}}{\partial x_i} - \omega^2\frac{\partial \mathbf{M}}{\partial x_i}\right)\Phi = 2\omega\frac{\partial \omega}{\partial x_i}\mathbf{M}\Phi + (\omega^2\mathbf{M} - \mathbf{K})\frac{\partial \Phi}{\partial x_i}. \tag{4.50}$$

Premultiplying (4.50) by Φ^{T} yields the following expression:

$$\Phi^{\mathrm{T}}\left(\frac{\partial \mathbf{K}}{\partial x_i}-\omega^2\frac{\partial \mathbf{M}}{\partial x_i}\right)\Phi = 2\omega\frac{\partial \omega}{\partial x_i}\Phi^{\mathrm{T}}\mathbf{M}\Phi + \Phi^{\mathrm{T}}(\omega^2\mathbf{M}-\mathbf{K})\frac{\partial \Phi}{\partial x_i}. \tag{4.51}$$

The second term on the right-hand side of (4.51) vanishes. To see this, consider the transpose of the eigenvalue problem:

$$(\mathbf{K}\Phi)^{\mathrm{T}} = (\omega^2\mathbf{M}\Phi)^{\mathrm{T}} \Rightarrow \Phi^{\mathrm{T}}\mathbf{K}^{\mathrm{T}} = \omega^2\Phi^{\mathrm{T}}\mathbf{M}^{\mathrm{T}}. \tag{4.52}$$

Since the mass and stiffness matrices are symmetric:

$$\Phi^{\mathrm{T}}\mathbf{K} = \omega^2\Phi^{\mathrm{T}}\mathbf{M} \Rightarrow \Phi^{\mathrm{T}}(\omega^2\mathbf{M}-\mathbf{K}) = 0. \tag{4.53}$$

Therefore, we obtain the equation:

$$\Phi^{\mathrm{T}}\left(\frac{\partial \mathbf{K}}{\partial x_i}-\omega^2\frac{\partial \mathbf{M}}{\partial x_i}\right)\Phi = 2\omega\frac{\partial \omega}{\partial x_i}\Phi^{\mathrm{T}}\mathbf{M}\Phi. \tag{4.54}$$

The above equation can be used to solve for frequency derivatives. The derivative of the stiffness and mass matrices with respect to the design variables can be obtained from the equation:

$$\frac{\partial \mathbf{K}}{\partial x_i} = \sum_{j=1}^{Ne}\frac{\partial \mathbf{k}_j}{\partial x_i},$$

$$\frac{\partial \mathbf{M}}{\partial x_i} = \sum_{j=1}^{Ne}\frac{\partial \mathbf{m}_j}{\partial x_i}. \tag{4.55}$$

The gradient calculation uses the frequency and eigenvector information and can therefore be coded immediately after the frequency calculation to yield the frequency derivatives. If the stiffness matrices are analytically differentiated from closed-form expressions, the derivatives are called analytical derivatives. However, it is also possible to differentiate the stiffness matrices using finite-differences and then use the above formulation to calculate the frequency derivatives. This is also advantageous as it does not require the frequencies to be calculated many times when the finite-difference loop is over the eigenvalue problem. Such derivatives are called semi-analytical derivatives.

The possibility of using analytical derivatives exists in almost all engineering optimization problems. However, analytical derivatives require one to make changes inside the computer code which requires considerable domain knowledge, and this is not possible for commercial software. In addition, any changes to the code require an appropriate change in the calculation of the gradients which must be carefully updated. The advantages of having a code with built-in analytical derivative calculations are, however, immense for computationally expensive problems and should be attempted wherever possible.

Problems

1. Minimize the following function starting from (0, 0):

$$f(\mathbf{x}) = x_1^2 - x_1x_2 + 2x_2^2 - 2x_1 + e^{x_1+x_2} + 10.$$

Use the classical Newton's method and Newton's method with exact analytical line search. Perform three iterations. Repeat the problem starting from (−1, 1). Comment on your results.

2. Minimize the following function using Newton's method

$$f(\mathbf{x}) = x_1^2 + 2x_2^2 + e^{-x_1-x_2}.$$

Perform two iterations starting from the point (10, 10). Repeat the problem using $\mathbf{H} = \mathbf{I}$. Comment on your results.

3. Minimize the following function starting from (2, 2):

$$f(\mathbf{x}) = \frac{1}{2}(x_1 - 2x_2)^2 + x_1^4 + 2.$$

Use the classical Newton's method and Marquardt modification. Perform three iterations. Does the Hessian remain positive definite at each iteration of Newton's method? Comment on your results.

4. Consider the function $f(\mathbf{x}) = x_1^2 + 15x_2^2 - x_1x_2$. Perform three iterations of the classical Newton's method (unit step size) starting from (1, 1) to minimize this function. Repeat the problem with a one-dimensional minimization. Comment on your results.
5. Consider the function $f(\mathbf{x}) = x_1^2 + 15x_2^2 - x_1x_2$. Perform two iterations of Marquardt's method starting from (1, 1) to minimize this function. Choose $\lambda_0 = 10$.
6. Consider the function $f(\mathbf{x}) = x_1^2 + 15x_2^2 - x_1x_2$. Perform two iterations of the DFP starting from (1, 1) to minimize this function. Compare the Hessian inverse with the actual value. Comment on your results.
7. Consider the function $f(\mathbf{x}) = x_1^2 + 15x_2^2 - x_1x_2$. Perform two iterations of the BFGS starting from (1, 1) to minimize this function. Compare the Hessian with the actual value. Comment on your results.
8. Minimize the following function using Marquardt's method.

$$f(\mathbf{x}) = x_1^2 + 2x_2^2 + e^{-x_1-x_2}.$$

Perform two iterations starting from the point (1, 2). Start with $\lambda_0 = 1$ and compare the result with Example 4.3.

9. Minimize the following function using the DFP method

$$f(\mathbf{x}) = x_1^2 + 2x_2^2 + e^{-x_1-x_2}$$

Perform two iterations starting from the point (1, 2). Compare the inverse of the Hessian at the end of two iterations with the actual value.

10. Minimize the following function using the BFGS method:

$$f(\mathbf{x}) = x_1^2 + 2x_2^2 + e^{-x_1 - x_2}.$$

Perform two iterations starting from the point (0, 0). Compare the Hessian at the end of two iterations with the actual value.

11. Consider the function:

$$f(x) = x^2 + e^{-x}.$$

Find the derivative of this function at $x = 1$ using the forward finite-difference method. Numerically experiment with different step sizes on a computer and find a suitable h where the approximations are closest to the analytical derivative.

12. Consider the function:

$$f(x) = x^2 + e^{-x}.$$

Find the derivative of this function at $x = 1$ using the central finite-difference method. Numerically experiment with different step sizes and find a suitable h where the approximations are closest to the analytical derivative. Compare your result with the previous problem.

13. Consider the function:

$$f(\mathbf{x}) = x_1^2 + 2x_2^2 + e^{-x_1 - x_2}.$$

Find the gradient and Hessian of this function at (1, 2) using the forward finite-difference method. Numerically experiment with different step sizes and find a suitable h where the approximations are closest to the actual gradient and Hessian in terms of norms.

14. Consider the function:

$$f(\mathbf{x}) = x_1^2 + 2x_2^2 + e^{-x_1 - x_2}.$$

Find the gradient and Hessian of this function at (1, 2) using the central finite-difference method. Numerically experiment with different step sizes and find a suitable h where the approximations are closest to the actual gradient and Hessian in terms of norms. Compare your result with the previous problem.

15. Consider the function:

$$f(x) = \sin(100x) + e^{10x^3}.$$

Use the forward-difference and central-difference approach to estimate the derivative at (−1, 1) with different values of h. What value of h produces the best estimate of the derivative? How does this value compare with the theoretically suggested values in this chapter?

16. Create an evaluation graph for the function:

$$f(\mathbf{x}) = \frac{1}{2}(x_1 - 2x_2)^2 + x_1^4 + 2.$$

Use this graph to calculate the gradient of the function.

17. Write a computer program to implement Newton's method, modified Newton's method, BFGS method and DFP method. Using this program and starting from different points in the design space, find the minimum of the function

$$f(\mathbf{x}) = 2x_1^2 + x_2^2 - 2x_1x_2 + 2x_1^3 + x_1^4 + 5.$$

Use the golden-section program from the problems in the previous chapter for the 1D search. Continue until an accuracy of five decimal places is reached. Comment on your results.

18. Use your program for Newton's method, modified Newton's method, BFGS method and DFP method, and starting from different points in the design space, find the minimum of the function

$$f(\mathbf{x}) = 2x_1^2 + x_2^2 - 2x_1x_2 + 2x_1^3 + x_1^4 + 5.$$

Use the golden-section program from the problems in the previous chapter for the 1D search. Continue until an accuracy of five decimal places is reached. Calculate the gradient and Hessian using forward finite-differences. Use $h = 0.1, 0.01, 0.001$ and 0.0001. Compare your convergence results in terms of function values and number of evaluations needed with the case in the last problem where analytical derivatives were used. Comment on your results.

19. Consider the function:

$$f(\mathbf{x}) = x_1^2 + 2x_2^2 + e^{-x_1-x_2}.$$

Find the gradient and Hessian of this function at (1, 2) using the central finite-difference method with $h = 0.1, 0.01, 0.001$ and 0.0001. Perform steepest-descent, conjugate-gradient and Newton's method iterations using the finite-difference gradients. Compare the results with those obtained using analytical gradients. Also track the function evaluations needed for each approach to converge to an accuracy of five decimal places.

20. Using your computer program, minimize the function:

$$f(\mathbf{x}) = \frac{1}{2}(x_1 - 2x_2)^2 + x_1^4 + 2.$$

Use the BFGS and DFP method. Start from $(1, 1), (-1, 1), (1, -1), (-1, -1)$ and continue until an accuracy of five decimal places is reached. Comment on your results.

21. Use your computer program to minimize the following equation:

$$f(\mathbf{x}) = x_1^2 - x_1x_2 + 2x_2^2 - 2x_1 + e^{x_1+x_2} + 10.$$

Start from (0, 0) and use the BFGS and DFP method. Continue until an accuracy of five decimal places is reached. Comment on your results.

22. Use your computer program to minimize the equation:

$$f(\mathbf{x}) = x_1^2 - x_1x_2 + 2x_2^2 - 2x_1 + e^{x_1+x_2} + 10.$$

Start from (0, 0) and use the BFGS and DFP method. Continue until an accuracy of five decimal places is reached. Calculate the gradient and Hessian using forward finite-differences. Comment on your results.

23. Minimize the function:

$$f(\mathbf{x}) = x_1^2 + cx_2^2.$$

Perform the modified Newton's iterations with an exact line search for values of $c = 1, 10, 100, 1000, 10000$. Use a convergence criterion of $\|\mathbf{c}\| < 10^{-5}$. What is the rate constant for each of these cases and how do these values compare with the estimated upper bounds? How do these results compare with the steepest-descent results obtained in the problems in Chapter 3.

24. Wood's function is given by the following equation:

$$f(\mathbf{x}) = 100(x_2 - x_1^2) + (1 - x_1)^2 + 90(x_4 - x_3^2)^2 + (1 - x_3)^2$$
$$+ 10.1[(x_2 - 1)^2 + (x_4 - 1)^2] + 19.8(x_2 - 1)(x_4 - 1).$$

Use $\mathbf{x}^{(0)} = (-3, -1, -3, -1)$, and compare the modified Newton's method, DFP and BFGS methods. Use a convergence criterion of $\|\mathbf{c}\| < 10^{-5}$.

25. Find the minimum point of the equation:

$$f(\mathbf{x}) = (x_1 + 2x_2 - 7)^2 + (2x_1 + x_2 - 5)^2.$$

Start from $\mathbf{x}^{(0)} = (1, 1)$ and use the modified Newton's method, DFP and BFGS methods and an inexact line search based on Armijo's rule. Use a convergence criterion of $\|\mathbf{c}\| < 10^{-5}$. How do the results change when an exact line search based on the golden-section method is used?

26. Use Newton's method with a unit step size to find the minimum point of

$$f(\mathbf{x}) = (x_1 + 2x_2 - 7)^2 + (2x_1 + x_2 - 5)^2.$$

Start from $\mathbf{x}^{(0)} = (1, 1)$ and use a convergence criterion of $\|\mathbf{c}\| < 10^{-5}$. How do the results change when an exact line search based on the golden-section method is used?

27. Use the modified Newton's method, DFP and BFGS method to find the minimum point of Brown's function:

$$f(\mathbf{x}) = (x_1 - 10^6)^2 + (x_2 - 2.10^{-6})^2 + (x_1x_2 - 2)^2.$$

Use different starting designs. Use a convergence criterion of $\|\mathbf{c}\| < 10^{-5}$. Use any accurate 1D search method.

28. Consider the Freudenstein–Roth function:

$$f(\mathbf{x}) = (-13 + x_1 + ((5 - x_2)x_2 - 2)x_2)^2$$
$$+ (-29 + x_1 + ((x_2 + x_1)x_2 - 14)x_2)^2.$$

This function has some local minima and a global minimum. Use any method discussed in this chapter to find the minimum points. Use a convergence criterion of $\|\mathbf{c}\| < 10^{-5}$. Use any starting design. This problem shows the problem of coming up with good starting designs when using gradient-based methods.

29. Use the BFGS method to find the minimum of Powell's quartic function:

$$f(\mathbf{x}) = (x_1 + 10x_2)^2 + 5(x_3 - x_4)^2 + (x_2 - 2x_3)^4 + 10(x_1 - x_4)^4.$$

Start from $\mathbf{x}^{(0)} = (3, -1, 0, 1)$. Use a convergence criterion of $\|\mathbf{c}\| < 10^{-5}$.

30. Consider the function:

$$f(\mathbf{x}) = x_1^2 + 2x_2^2 + \mathrm{e}^{-x_1 - x_2}.$$

Expand this function in a second-order Taylor series about (1, 2). Apply the DFP method to the approximated function and get a minimum point. Use this minimum point to construct another Taylor series approximation and again get the minimum point.

31. Consider the function:

$$f(\mathbf{x}) = x_1^2 + 2x_2^2 + 3x_3^2 + \cdots + nx_n^2 + \mathrm{e}^{-x_1 - x_2 - x_3 - \cdots - x_n}.$$

Find the minimum value of this function starting from $\mathbf{x}^{(0)} = (1, 1, 1, \ldots 1)$ for the cases $n = 3, 10, 50, 100$ and 500. Use a convergence criterion of $\|\mathbf{c}\| < 10^{-5}$. Use the golden-section search and compare the results of the three conjugate-gradient formulas with Newton's method, DFP method and BFGS method. Do you encounter any problems with quasi-Newton methods when n becomes large? Comment on your results.

5 Constrained Optimization Methods

We studied optimality criteria for problems of constrained optimization in Chapter 1. However, in practice, constrained optimization problems mostly require a direct numerical approach. In this chapter, we study the numerical approaches to linear and nonlinear constrained optimization problems.

5.1 Linear Programming

Linear programs arise in diverse areas such as water resources engineering; systems engineering; traffic-flow control; management of resources; transportation problems and electrical engineering.[1] Linear programs are a key aspect of the study of the closely related field of operations research. In aerospace, automotive, structural or mechanical system design, most problems are not linear. Nevertheless, knowledge of linear programming (LP) is important for a complete study of optimization. There are also methods such as sequential linear programming where nonlinear optimization problems are transformed into a *sequence of linear programming problems*. Quadratic programming problems can also be solved using a modified simplex method which is developed for linear programs. LP can also be used to solve optimization problems with linear response surface approximations which we shall discuss in Chapter 6.

All general optimization approaches can be used for LP problems. However, numerical methods to solve LP problems are available. They are more elegant and far more efficient and exploit their linearity. Linear programming problems have somewhat different definitions and nomenclature compared to nonlinear programming problems. This is partly due to the difference in their evolution which does not utilize the calculus-based approach widely used in nonlinear programming. We define various terms involved in linear programming and the standard form of the LP problem.

5.1.1 Constraints

The ith linear inequality or equality constraint involving k design variables y_j, $j = 1, 2, \ldots, k$ can be written as

$$a_{i1}y_1 + a_{i2}y_2 + a_{i3}y_3 + \cdots + a_{ik}y_k \begin{matrix} \leq \\ = \\ \geq \end{matrix} b_i, \tag{5.1}$$

where a_{ij}, b_i are known constants. The right-hand side of (5.1) contains the resource limits b_i which must be nonnegative or $b_i \geq 0$. Due to this $b_i \geq 0$ requirement, we cannot put all inequalities in the $\leq$ form as was done for nonlinear programs, where we used $g(\mathbf{x}) \leq 0$ as the inequality constraint and converted the $\geq$ form to the $\leq$ form by simply multiplying both sides by -1. For example, consider the following inequality:

$$3y_1 + 2y_2 \geq 5. \tag{5.2}$$

We multiply both sides of (5.2) by -1 to convert it into the $\leq$ form, as shown below:

$$-3y_1 - 2y_2 \leq -5. \tag{5.3}$$

Here, converting the $\geq$ form to the $\leq$ form leads to $b_i \leq 0$ which is not permitted. Also, consider the inequality:

$$\begin{aligned} &3y_1 + 2y_2 \leq -7 \\ &\Rightarrow -3y - 2y_2 \geq 7. \end{aligned} \tag{5.4}$$

Here we have a $\geq$ form if we want $b_i \geq 0$. Thus, all $\leq$, $\geq$ and $=$ constraints must be addressed in the LP solution.

In standard LP, all constraints are expressed as equality constraints. Since both $\geq$ and $\leq$ inequality constraints are possible, slack and surplus variables are used. For the $\leq$ constraints, we add a slack variable s_i.

$$a_{i1}y_1 + a_{i2}y_2 + \cdots + a_{ik}y_k + s_i = b_i. \tag{5.5}$$

For the $\geq$ constraint s, we subtract a surplus variable s_i.

$$a_{i1}y_1 + a_{i2}y_2 + \cdots + a_{ik}y_k - s_i = b_i. \tag{5.6}$$

The slack and surplus variables are additional unknowns that must be derived as part of the solution. Note that in nonlinear programming, we use s_i^2 as a slack variable to ensure that $s_i^2 \geq 0$ is automatically satisfied. However, for linear programming, addition of s_i^2 would make the problem nonlinear. Therefore, $s_i \geq 0$ is imposed as a constraint for both the slack and surplus variables we have defined.

For the standard LP, all design variables need to be nonnegative, that is:

$$y_i \geq 0, \qquad i = 1 \quad \text{to} \quad k. \tag{5.7}$$

However, in many practical problems, some design variables can be unrestricted or free in sign. Fortunately, there is a mathematical way to ensure that if a design variable is unrestricted in sign, it can be written as the difference of two nonnegative variables,

$$y_j = y_j^+ - y_j^- \tag{5.8}$$

$$y_j^+ \geq 0, \quad y_j^- \geq 0 \tag{5.9}$$

Equations (5.8) and (5.9) are substituted in the LP problem and the LP problem is solved. At the optimum, if $y_j^+ \geq y_j^-$, then y_j is nonnegative and if $y_j^+ \leq y_j^-$, then y_j is nonpositive. Each free variable increases the number of design variables by one. We can now add the objective function to the constraints and define the standard LP problem.

5.1.2 Standard LP

Let **x** be a vector of size n with k original design variables and $n-k$ slack, surplus or other variables. The standard LP problem is defined as follows. Find **x** to minimize the objective function given below:

$$f(\mathbf{x}) = c_1x_1 + c_2x_2 + c_3x_3 + \cdots + c_nx_n. \tag{5.10}$$

It is subject to m equality constraints:

$$\begin{aligned} a_{11}x_1 + a_{12}x_2 + \cdots + a_{1n}x_n &= b_1 \\ a_{21}x_1 + a_{22}x_2 + \cdots + a_{2n}x_n &= b_2 \\ &\vdots \\ a_{m1}x_1 + a_{m2}x_2 + \cdots + a_{mn}x_n &= b_m, \end{aligned} \tag{5.11}$$

and nonnegativity constraints on the design variables:

$$x_j \geq 0 \qquad j = 1, 2, \ldots, n. \tag{5.12}$$

The quantities $b_i \geq 0$, c_j and $a_{ij}(i = 1, 2, \ldots, m;\ j = 1, 2, \ldots, n)$ are known constants and m and n are positive integers. We will discuss a different approach for handling problems with $b_i < 0$ later in this chapter.

The LP may be written in matrix form:
Minimize

$$f(\mathbf{x}) = \mathbf{C}^{\mathrm{T}}\mathbf{x}, \tag{5.13}$$

subject to

$$\begin{aligned} \mathbf{Ax} &= \mathbf{b} \\ \mathbf{x} &\geq 0 \end{aligned} \tag{5.14}$$

Here **A** is an $m \times n$ matrix, **C** and **x** are $n \times 1$ vectors and **b** is an $m \times 1$ vector. Converting a maximization problem to a minimization problem is quite simple.

Saying maximize

$$z = d_1x_1 + d_2x_2 + \cdots + d_nx_n \tag{5.15}$$

is equivalent to saying:
Minimize,

$$f = -(d_1x_1 + d_2x_2 + \cdots + d_nx_n) \tag{5.16}$$

Example 5.1 Write the following problem as a standard LP:
Maximize

$$z = 2y_1 + 7y_2$$

subject to conditions

$$3y_1 + 4y_2 \le 13$$
$$2y_1 + 5y_2 \ge 4.$$

Here, $y_1 \ge 0$ and y_2 is unrestricted in sign. Also, put the LP problem in matrix form.

Solution: We first replace the unrestricted sign variable with two nonnegative variables:

$$y_2 = y_2^+ - y_2^-, \qquad y_2^+ \ge 0, \qquad y_2^- \ge 0.$$

The problem now becomes:
Maximize

$$z = 2y_1 + 7(y_2^+ - y_2^-)$$

subject to,

$$3y_1 + 4(y_2^+ - y_2^-) \le 13$$
$$2y_1 + 5(y_2^+ - y_2^-) \ge 4$$
$$y_1, y_2^+, y_2^- \ge 0.$$

We next convert the objective function to a minimization problem by changing the sign and the constraints to equalities by adding a slack variable and subtracting a surplus variable. Thus, we get:
Minimize

$$f = -2y_1 - 7(y_2^+ - y_2^-)$$

subject to,

$$3y_1 + 4(y_2^+ - y_2^-) + s_1 = 13$$
$$2y_1 + 5(y_2^+ - y_2^-) - s_2 = 4$$
$$y_1, y_2^+, y_2^-, s_1, s_2 \ge 0$$

For notational convenience, it is best to redefine the solution variables:

$$x_1 = y_1, \qquad x_2 = y_2^+, \qquad x_3 = y_2^-, \qquad x_4 = s_1, \qquad x_5 = s_2,$$

and rewrite the problem in standard form as follows.
Minimize

$$f = -2x_1 - 7x_2 + 7x_3,$$

subject to

$$3x_1 + 4x_2 - 4x_3 + x_4 = 13$$

$$2x_1 + 5x_2 - 5x_3 - x_5 = 4$$

$$x_i \geq 0, \qquad i = 1, 5.$$

It is instructive to convert the problem to matrix form. We have two constraints and five design variables, so $m = 2, n = 5$. We then get,

$$\mathbf{x} = [x_1,\ x_2,\ x_3,\ x_4,\ x_5]^{\mathrm{T}}$$

$$\mathbf{C} = \begin{bmatrix}-2, & -7, & 7, & 0, & 0\end{bmatrix}^{\mathrm{T}}.$$

Note that $\mathbf{C}$ contains the gradient of $f(\mathbf{x})$:

$$\mathbf{b} = [13, 4]^{\mathrm{T}},$$

$$\mathbf{A} = \begin{bmatrix} 3 & 4 & -4 & 1 & 0 \\ 2 & 5 & -5 & 0 & -1 \end{bmatrix}.$$

Note that $\mathbf{A}$ contains the gradient information about the constraints.

Since all constraint functions are linear in an LP problem, the feasible region is convex. The cost function is convex because it is linear. The LP problem is convex and if an optimum solution exists, it is global. To see this mathematically, note that the points in the feasible region must satisfy the constraint equations:[2]

$$\mathbf{Ax} = \mathbf{b}, \qquad x_i \geq 0, i = 1, \ldots, n. \tag{5.17}$$

Let $\mathbf{y}$ and $\mathbf{z}$ be two other points in the feasible region which satisfy the constraints. Then, we can write,

$$\mathbf{Ay} = \mathbf{b}, \qquad y_i \geq 0, i = 1, \ldots, n, \tag{5.18}$$

$$\mathbf{Az} = \mathbf{b}, \qquad z_i \geq 0, i = 1, \ldots, n. \tag{5.19}$$

If we can show that any point that lies on a line connecting $\mathbf{y}$ and $\mathbf{z}$ also lies in the feasible region, then we can show that the LP feasible region forms a convex set. A point on the general line segment connecting $\mathbf{y}$ and $\mathbf{z}$ is given as $\alpha\mathbf{y} + (1 - \alpha)\mathbf{z}$. Using this definition of the point in (5.17) yields the following:

$$\mathbf{A}(\alpha\mathbf{y} + (1 - \alpha)\mathbf{z}) = \alpha\mathbf{Ay} + (1 - \alpha)\mathbf{Az} = \alpha\mathbf{b} + (1 - \alpha)\mathbf{b} = \mathbf{b}. \tag{5.20}$$

Here $0 < \alpha < 1$. Thus, the point $\alpha\mathbf{y} + (1 - \alpha)\mathbf{z}$ satisfies the constraint equation and lies in the feasible region. The point also satisfies the nonnegativity constraint. Noting that $0 < \alpha < 1 \Rightarrow 0 < 1 - \alpha < 1$, we get the inequality

$$\alpha\mathbf{y} + (1 - \alpha)\mathbf{z} \geq 0, \tag{5.21}$$

since $\mathbf{y}$ and $\mathbf{z}$ are nonnegative. Thus the point satisfies all the requirements of being in the feasible region and the feasible region is a convex set.

Another important concept for LP problems is that the solution to the LP problem, if it exists, lies on the boundary of the feasible region. To check this, consider the objective function:

$$f(\mathbf{x}) = c_1x_1 + c_2x_2 + \cdots + c_nx_n = \mathbf{C}^{\mathrm{T}}\mathbf{x}. \tag{5.22}$$

For an unconstrained minimum:

$$\nabla f(\mathbf{x}) = \mathbf{C} = 0, \tag{5.23}$$

$$\Rightarrow c_1 = c_2 = \cdots = c_n = 0. \tag{5.24}$$

If equations (5.24) are true, then the objective function defined by (5.22) does not exist. So there is no unconstrained minimum point for a linear function. An LP problem must have constraints to have a useful solution.

Another important fact about LPs is that the solution of a constrained LP problem must lie at the boundary of the feasible region. This can be seen geometrically from Figure 5.1, where the dotted lines represent the different values of the objective function and the solid line represents constraints. A line has no minimum unless it is bounded by some constraints which are other lines in a well-posed LP problem. In the problem in Figure 5.1, there is a well-formed feasible region with two constraints and nonnegativity conditions on the design variables.

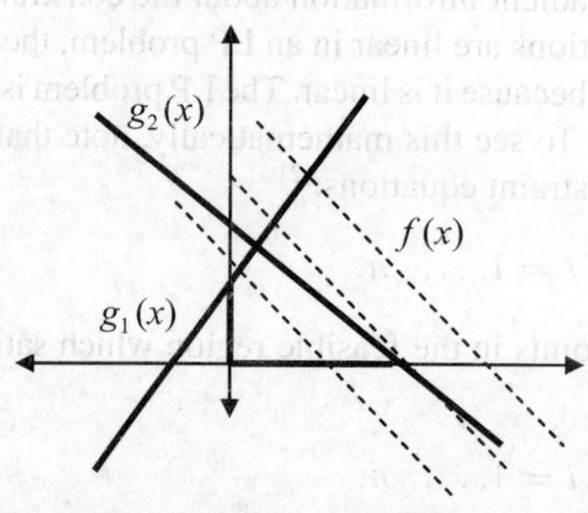

Figure 5.1 *A line has a bounded minimum point only in the presence of constraints*

The optimum solution must satisfy the equality constraints:

$$\mathbf{Ax} = \mathbf{b}. \tag{5.25}$$

Here **A** has a full row rank, which means that the rows of **A** are linearly independent. In case **A** does not have full row rank, the constraints may be inconsistent or redundant. For inconsistent constraints, the problem has no solution. The feasible region in such cases is empty and there is no extreme or vertex point. Redundant constraints can be removed from the problem without changing the solution.

There are three possible cases, depending on the values of m and n. Let us assume that the m equality constraints are linearly independent. Then,

1. If $m = n$, we can solve for the design variables and the objective function does not matter. In such cases, the feasible region is obtained by solving $\mathbf{Ax} = \mathbf{b}$ and will contain one point if $x_i \geq 0, i = 1, \ldots, n$ or be empty of any $x_i < 0$.

2. If $m > n$, there may be no solution in most cases.
3. The only case where the objective function comes into play is where $m < n$, which leads to multiple possible solutions and a well-defined feasible region.

Thus, the number of linearly independent equality constraints must be less than the number of design variables. This means there are no redundant equations but the number of constraints is less than the number of design variables. We seek a feasible solution that minimizes the cost function.

5.1.3 Important LP definitions

Some terms will be routinely used in the study of LP. These are formally defined below.[1–2]

5.1.3.1 Vertex point

This refers to a point on a set that does not lie on a line segment joining two other points on the set. It is also sometimes known as an extreme point. For example, as shown in Figure 5.2, the points at the vertices of the polygon are vertex points. However, for a circle, all points lying on the circumference are vertex points. A vertex point is related to the definition of a convex set. Consider a point $\mathbf{x} \in S$ which is a vertex point of a convex set S. Then, the point $\mathbf{x}$ cannot be written as a linear combination of two feasible points $\mathbf{y}$ and $\mathbf{z}$ which are different from $\mathbf{x}$:

$$\mathbf{x} \neq \alpha \mathbf{y} + (1 - \alpha)\mathbf{z}, \tag{5.26}$$

Here, $\mathbf{x}, \mathbf{y}, \mathbf{z} \in S$, $0 < \alpha < 1$ and $\mathbf{y}, \mathbf{z} \neq \mathbf{x}$.

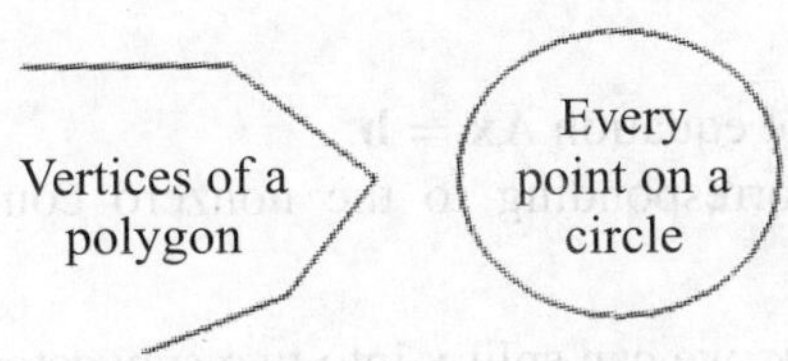

Figure 5.2 *Vertex points*

5.1.3.2 Feasible solution

Any solution of the m constraint equations $\mathbf{Ax} = \mathbf{b}$ satisfying $x_i \geq 0$, $i = 1, n$ is a feasible solution.

5.1.3.3 Basic solution

The solution of the constraint equation, $\mathbf{Ax} = \mathbf{b}$, obtained by setting the *redundant* $(n - m)$ variables equal to zero and solving the equations for the remaining variables is called the basic solution. The $(n - m)$ variables that have been set equal to zero are called nonbasic. The m remaining variables are called basic.

5.1.3.4 Basic feasible solution

A basic solution satisfying $x_i \geq 0, i = 1, n$ is called a basic feasible solution.

5.1.3.5 Degenerate basic variable

If a basic variable has zero value, it is called a degenerate basic variable. This leads to a degenerate LP. Such situations arise when there is a redundant constraint.

5.1.3.6 Optimum solution

A feasible solution point minimizing the cost function is called an optimum solution.

5.1.3.7 Convex polyhedron

If the feasible region (constraint set) for an LP problem is bounded, it is called a convex polyhedron.

5.1.3.8 Basis

The columns of the coefficient matrix **A** of the constraint equation corresponding to the basic variables are said to form a basis for the m-dimensional vector space.

5.1.4 Basic solutions

The concept of a basic solution is very important in linear programming. Consider an LP expressed in standard form. A point **x** is a basic solution if the following conditions are satisfied:

1. The point **x** satisfies the equation $\mathbf{Ax} = \mathbf{b}$.
2. The columns of **A** corresponding to the nonzero components of **x** are linearly independent

Since **A** has full row rank, we can split **x** into two subvectors called the basic variables $\mathbf{x}_B$ and the nonbasic variables $\mathbf{x}_N$. The nonbasic variables must be zero (a way to remember this is **n**onbasic = **n**il). Given that the number of basic variables is m, then there are $(n - m)$ nonbasic variables.

If **x** is a basic feasible solution, we can write after reordering the variables:

$$\mathbf{x} = \begin{Bmatrix} \mathbf{x}_B \\ \mathbf{x}_N \end{Bmatrix}. \tag{5.27}$$

We can also split the matrix **A** into two submatrices:

$$\mathbf{A} = (\mathbf{B}\ \ \mathbf{N}). \tag{5.28}$$

Thus, we get:

$$\mathbf{Ax} = \mathbf{b} \Rightarrow (\mathbf{B}\ \ \mathbf{N}) \begin{Bmatrix} \mathbf{x}_B \\ \mathbf{x}_N \end{Bmatrix} = \mathbf{Bx}_B + \mathbf{Nx}_N = \mathbf{b}. \tag{5.29}$$

Since the nonbasic variables are all zero, $\mathbf{x}_N = 0$, we get,

$$\mathbf{B}\mathbf{x}_B = \mathbf{b}. \tag{5.30}$$

This equation can be used to get the basic variables. We call the matrix **B** as the basis and the columns of **B** are called the basic columns. For a problem with n design variables and m constraints, there are at most $n!/m!(n-m)!$ basic solutions. However, some of these points will not satisfy $x_i \geq 0, i = 1, n$ and so will not be feasible basic solutions.

Example 5.2 Minimize

$$f = -x_2,$$

subject to the following constraints,

$$x_1 + x_2 \leq 16$$
$$x_1 + 2x_2 \leq 28$$
$$x_1, x_2, \geq 0.$$

Solution: We first write the problem in standard form:
Minimize

$$f = -x_2$$

subject to the following constraints,

$$x_1 + x_2 + x_3 = 16$$
$$x_1 + 2x_2 + x_4 = 28$$
$$x_i \geq 0, \qquad i = 1, 4.$$

where x_3, x_4 are slack variables.

The above two constraint equations are linearly independent. Also, $n > m$ since $4 > 2$, therefore a unique solution cannot exist for $\mathbf{Ax} = \mathbf{b}$. The two constraint equations can be written as shown below:

$$x_3 = 16 - x_1 - x_2$$
$$x_4 = 28 - x_1 - 2x_2$$

Here x_1 and x_2 are independent variables and x_3, x_4 are dependent variables. Different values of x_1 and x_2 generate different values of x_3, x_4. A solution obtained by setting $p = n - m$ variables to zero is called a basic solution. In this case, $p = 4 - 2 = 2$. For example, set $x_1 = 0, x_2 = 0$ which gives $x_3 = 16, x_4 = 28$. Setting $x_1 = 0, x_3 = 0$ leads to $x_2 = 16, x_4 = -4$. Proceeding in this manner and setting two variables to zero at a time leads to the set of six basic solutions given below. For the function, $f = -x_2$, location D in Figure 5.3 corresponds to the minimum point.

5.1.5 Six basic solutions

No.	x_1	x_2	x_3	x_4	f	Location	f_1	f_2	f_3
1	0	0	16	28	0	A	0	0	0
2	0	16	0	−4	~	Infeasible	~	~	~
3	0	14	2	0	$\underline{-14}$	D	−42	0	42
4	16	0	0	12	0	B	−32	$\underline{-16}$	$\underline{16}$
5	28	0	−12	0	~	Infeasible	~	~	~
6	4	12	0	0	−12	C	$\underline{-44}$	−4	40

Interestingly, the basic solutions do not change if we change the cost function. This is because the basic solution depends only on the constraints. Consider the functions:

$$f_1 = -2x_1 - 3x_2,$$

$$f_2 = -x_1,$$

$$f_3 = x_1 + 3x_2.$$

For these minimization problems, the function values are also given in the above table. The optimal values are underlined in the table. We can see that the optimal point changes with the function but always lies at one of the vertex points in Figure 5.3.

Several important issues can be observed by carefully studying the feasible region for the problem in Figure 5.3 and comparing the results with the six basic solutions.

1. For a problem of n variables and m constraints, there are at most $n!/m!(n-m)!$ basic solutions. For the given problem, this condition translates into $4!/2!2! = 6$, hence there are six basic solutions.
2. Of the six solutions, exactly four correspond to the vertices of the polygon given by points A, B, C and D. The two remaining solutions violate nonnegativity restrictions

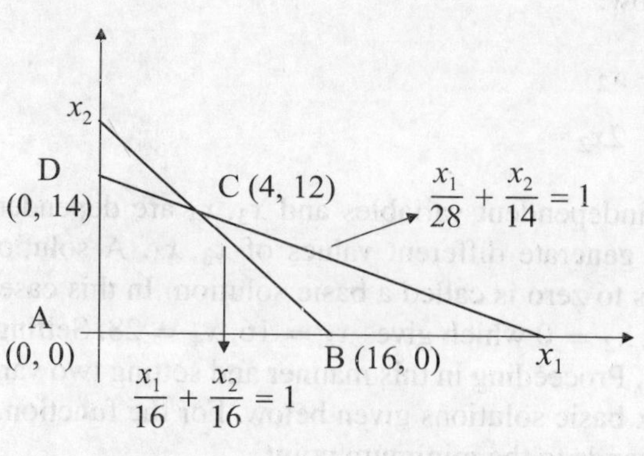

Figure 5.3 *Feasible region for profit maximization problem*

on the design variables, that is, $x_i < 0$ in these cases. Only four of the six basic solutions are therefore feasible. All the basic feasible solutions correspond to vertex points of the feasible region.

3. The optimum solution depends on the cost function and is a basic feasible solution. It is at one of the vertices of the constraint polygon. This is an important and general property of any LP problem. If an LP problem has a solution, it lies at one of the vertices of the feasible region. An exception occurs when the cost function is parallel to a constraint, in which case, the feasible solution also lies on the constraint line.

The intuitive observations made until now can be formalized into the following theorem:[1]

The collection of feasible solutions for an LP problem contains a convex set whose vertex points correspond to basic feasible solutions. Let the $m \times n$ coefficient matrix **A** *of constraint equations have full row rank i.e.,* **rank (A)** $= m$. [1]

Then,

1. If a feasible solution exists, then a basic feasible solution also exists.
2. If there is any feasible solution to the LP problem, there must be at least one extreme point or vertex of the convex feasible region.
3. If an optimum feasible solution exists, then an optimum basic feasible solution also exists.
4. If the LP problem has a solution, then it lies on one of the vertices of the converse polyhedron representing feasible solution.

For a problem of n variables and m constraints there are at most $n!/m!(n-m)!$ basic solutions. If we systematically locate these solutions and compare them, we can get the optimum. However, for large-size problems, this procedure is inefficient and better methods such as the *simplex method* can be used.

5.2 The Simplex Method

The simplex method proceeds from one solution to another in a way so as to progressively decrease the cost function until a minimum is reached. It is based on a geometrical object called the simplex. In a two-dimensional (2D) space, the simplex is a structure made up of any three points that do not lie on a straight line. In 3D space, it is formed by four points that do not lie in the same plane. For example, a triangle and a pyramid represent simplexes in 2D and 3D space, respectively. A simplex in n-dimensional space is a convex hull of any set of $(n+1)$ points that do not lie on one hyper-plane.[1] A convex hull of $(n+1)$ points is the smallest convex set containing all the points. Thus, a simplex represents a convex set.

A canonical form of the equations is used in the simplex method. An $m \times n$ system of simultaneous equations $\mathbf{Ax} = \mathbf{b}$ with rank $(\mathbf{A}) = m$ is said to be in the canonical form if each equation has a variable with unit coefficient that does not appear in any other equation. Thus, a canonical form can be written as shown below:

[1]The rank of an $m \times n$ matrix is the order of the largest nonsingular square submatrix of a given matrix.

$$x_1 + a_{1,m+1}x_{m+1} + a_{1,m+2}x_{m+2} + \cdots + a_{1,n}x_n = b_1$$
$$x_2 + a_{2,m+1}x_{m+1} + a_{2,m+2}x_{m+2} + \cdots + a_{2,n}x_n = b_2$$
$$\vdots$$
$$x_m + a_{n,m+1}x_{m+1} + a_{m,m+2}x_{m+2} + \cdots + a_{m,n}x_n = b_m \tag{5.31}$$

Here x_1 appears in the first equation, x_2 in the second equation and so on until x_m appears in the mth equation. In matrix form, we can write the canonical form as follows:

$$\mathbf{I}\mathbf{x}_m + \mathbf{Q}\mathbf{x}_{n-m} = \mathbf{b}. \tag{5.32}$$

Here,

$$\mathbf{I} = m \times m \quad \text{identity matrix}$$
$$\mathbf{x}_m = [x_1, x_2, x_3, \ldots, x_m]^{\mathrm{T}}; \qquad m \times 1 \quad \text{vector}$$
$$\mathbf{x}_{n-m} = [x_{m+1}, x_{m+2}, \ldots, x_n]^{\mathrm{T}}; \qquad (n-m) \times 1 \quad \text{vector}$$

Further, $\mathbf{Q} = m \times (n - m)$, which is the matrix made up of the coefficients of variables x_{m+1} to x_n and $\mathbf{b} = [b_1, b_2, \ldots, b_m]^{\mathrm{T}}$ is an $m \times 1$ vector.

The procedure of Gauss–Jordan elimination can be used to convert a given system of equations into the canonical form. The canonical form makes the evaluation of basic solutions quite simple. If we set the nonbasic variables $\mathbf{x}_{n-m} = 0$, then $\mathbf{x}_m = \mathbf{b}$ gives the basic solution. The canonical form can be represented in a tableau which allows a systematic determination of the basic solutions. The tableau is a useful tool for illustrating the simplex method. In practice, the simplex method is easily coded and written as a computer program. However, the tableau can be used to solve simple problems by hand to gain insights into the method. A typical tableau is shown below:

Basic	x_1	x_2	$\cdots$	x_m	x_{m+1}	x_{m+2}	$\cdots$	x_n	**RHS**
x_1	1	0	$\cdots$	0	$a_{1,m+1}$	$a_{1,m+2}$	$\cdots$	$a_{1,n}$	b_1
x_2	0	1	$\cdots$	0	$a_{2,m+1}$	$a_{2,m+2}$	$\cdots$	$a_{2,n}$	b_2
x_3	0	0	$\cdots$	0	$a_{3,m+1}$	$a_{3,m+2}$	$\cdots$	$a_{3,n}$	b_3
$\vdots$	$\vdots$	$\vdots$	$\vdots$	$\vdots$	$\vdots$	$\vdots$	$\cdots$	$\vdots$	$\vdots$
x_m	0	0	$\cdots$	1	$a_{m,m+1}$	$a_{m,m+2}$	$\cdots$	$a_{m,n}$	b_m

In general, one could find all the basic feasible solutions and compare them to find the best point. We used this approach in Example 5.2. Unfortunately, most general LP problems are very large in size and so investigating all the basic feasible solutions can be very computationally expensive. A more efficient approach is to use the simplex method. Here one starts with the basic feasible solution at one of the vertices of the convex polyhedron. Then we move to another point only if there is greatest possible decrease in the objective function. The simplex method is much more efficient than searching all the basic feasible solutions.

The simplex method starts from an initial basic feasible solution and addresses two key issues. Firstly, the simplex method indicates which current nonbasic variable should be made basic. Secondly, the simplex method also points out which current basic variable should become nonbasic.

To automate the change from basic to nonbasic and vice versa, the Gauss–Jordan elimination method is used. A key ingredient of this method is called the *pivot step*. The pivot step is used to replace a current basic variable with a nonbasic variable to search for the best basic feasible solution. The step involves the selection of a basic variable $x_p (1 \leq p \leq m)$ to replace a nonbasic variable $x_q ((n-m) \leq q \leq n)$. This requires that the pth basic column be interchanged with the qth nonbasic column. This is only possible when the pivot element $a_{pq} \neq 0$ as we need to divide by a_{pq}. Following the pivot step, x_q will become basic if it is eliminated from all equations except the pth equation. This can be done by performing a Gauss–Jordan elimination step on the qth column of the tableau using the pth row for elimination. This gives $a_{pq} = 1$ and zeros elsewhere in the qth column.

The row used for the elimination process (pth row) is called the *pivot row*. The column on which the elimination is performed (qth column) is called the *pivot column*. The process of interchanging a basic variable with a nonbasic variable is called the pivot step. Let a'_{ij} denote the new coefficients that have been introduced into the matrix in the canonical form, after the pivot step. Then, the pivot step is described by the following arithmetic operations:[1]

$$a'_{pj} = \frac{a_{pj}}{a_{pq}}; \qquad j = 1, n,$$

$$b'_p = \frac{b_p}{a_{pq}},$$

$$a'_{ij} = a_{ij} - \left(\frac{a_{pj}}{a_{pq}}\right) a_{iq}; \qquad i \neq p,\ i = 1, m\ j = 1, n,$$

$$b'_i = b_i - \left(\frac{b_p}{a_{pq}}\right) a_{iq}; \qquad i \neq p,\ i = 1 \text{ to } m. \tag{5.33}$$

We now derive the logic which is used by the simplex method in interchanging basic and nonbasic variables. Let us first consider the case of a *basic variable to be made nonbasic*. Let x_r be a nonbasic variable which is tapped to become basic. Then the rth nonbasic column should replace some other column which is currently basic. We transfer all terms associated with x_r to the right-hand side, in the canonical form given by (5.31).

$$x_1 + a_{1,m+1}x_{m+1} + \cdots + a_{1,n}x_n = b_1 - a_{1,r}x_r,$$

$$x_2 + a_{2,m+1}x_{m+1} + \cdots + a_{2,n}x_n = b_2 - a_{2,r}x_r,$$

$$\vdots$$

$$x_m + a_{m,m+1}x_{m+1} + \cdots + a_{m,n}x_n = b_n - a_{m,r}x_r. \tag{5.34}$$

Since x_r is to become a basic variable, its value must become nonnegative. If x_r becomes too large, some of the right-hand side parameters, $b_i - a_{i,r}x_r$, shall become negative. Since the right-hand side parameters are the new values of the basic variables, this will violate the nonnegative constraints and the new basic solution will not be feasible. Thus, the following equations may be written:

$$b_i - a_{i,r}x_r \geq 0, \qquad i = 1 \text{ to } m. \tag{5.35}$$

Two cases are possible from (5.35). For $a_{i,r} \leq 0$, $a_{i,r}x_r \leq 0$ since $x_r \geq 0$. Hence, (5.35) is satisfied. For $a_{i,r} > 0$, x_r can be increased from 0 until one of the inequalities (say s) becomes active, which implies the following:

$$b_s - a_{s,r}x_r = 0. \tag{5.36}$$

Further increase in x_r violates the nonnegativity considerations. Thus, the maximum value of x_r can be calculated from (5.36):

$$\frac{b_s}{a_{s,r}} = \min_i \left\{ \frac{b_i}{a_{i,r}}, a_{i,r} > 0, i = 1, m \right\}. \tag{5.37}$$

In simple language, (5.37) tells us to take the ratio of b_i with positive $a_{i,r}$ and select the row index s with the least ratio. If all $a_{i,r} \leq 0$, then x_r can be increased indefinitely. In such a case, the LP problem is unbounded, and the problem formulation needs to be examined. In case two variables are equal, any one of the indexes can be selected as s. The resulting feasible solution may be degenerate, which means that a basic variable is zero.

The second key issue in the simplex method involves the selection of a *nonbasic variable which should become basic*. We want to bring a nonbasic variable into the basic set to reduce the current value of the cost function. We need to write the cost function in terms of only the nonbasic variables, by using the canonical form, as given below:[1]

$$x_i = b_i - \sum_{j=m+1}^{n} a_{ij}x_j, \qquad i = 1 \text{ to } m. \tag{5.38}$$

The cost function is written down:

$$f = \sum_{i=1}^{n} c_i x_i, \qquad i = 1, n. \tag{5.39}$$

$$f = f_o + \sum_{j=m+1}^{n} c'_j x_j, \tag{5.40}$$

where

$$f_o = \sum_{i=1}^{m} b_i c_i. \tag{5.41}$$

$$c'_j = c_j - \sum_{i=1}^{m} a_{ij} c_i, \qquad j = (m+1) \text{ to } n. \tag{5.42}$$

Here c'_j is the cost function of the nonbasic variables and is called the reduced cost function. In general, c'_j may be positive, negative or zero. Let one of the c'_j be negative. Then, from (5.40), we can see that the cost function will decrease, since $x_j > 0$ and therefore:

$$c'_j x_j < 0. \tag{5.43}$$

For maximum decrease of the cost function, the negative c'_j with the largest absolute value should be selected.

Thus, if any c'_j; $m + 1 \leq j \leq n$ (nonbasic variables) is negative, then it is possible to find a new basic feasible solution that will further reduce the cost function. However, if any $c'_j = 0$, then the associated nonbasic variable can be made basic without affecting the cost function. An alternative minimum can also exist. Also, if $c'_j > 0$; $m + 1 \leq j \leq n$, it is not possible to reduce f any further. The current solution is the optimum.

We can now state the simplex algorithm.

5.2.1 Simplex algorithm

This consists of the following steps:

1. Start with an initial basic feasible solution obtained using the canonical form.
2. Express the cost function in terms of the nonbasic variables only.
3. If all the reduced cost coefficients c'_j for the nonbasic variables are nonnegative, we have the optimal solution. In any reduced cost coefficient, c'_j is negative; identify the pivot column in this case.
4. If all elements in the pivot column are negative, the problem is unbounded. If there are positive elements in the pivot column, take the ratio of the right-hand side with positive elements in the pivot column, and identify a row with the smallest ratio.
5. Complete the pivot step using the Gauss–Jordan elimination procedure (5.33).
6. Identify basic and nonbasic variables and their values using the new canonical form. Calculate cost function and go to step 3.

Example 5.3 Use the simplex method to solve the LP problem given below:
Minimize

$$f = -2x_1 - 3x_2$$

subject to the constraints:

$$x_1 + x_2 \leq 16,$$

$$x_1 + 2x_2 \leq 28,$$

$$x_1, x_2 \geq 0.$$

Solution: First, we transform the problem into the standard form:
Minimize

$$f = -2x_1 - 3x_2,$$

subject to the constraints:

$$x_1 + x_2 + x_3 = 16,$$

$$x_1 + 2x_2 + x_4 = 28,$$

$$x_1, x_2 \geq 0.$$

Thus, $n = 4$, $m = 2$, $p = 2$. There are two basic variables, x_3 and x_4, and two nonbasic variables. We form a tableau as follows:

Basic	x_1	x_2	x_3	x_4	b	b/a
x_3	1	1	1	0	16	$16/1 = 16$
x_4	1	2	0	1	28	$28/2 = 14$
Cost	−2	−3	0	0	$f - 0$	

The cost is lowest for the column corresponding to the variable x_2. We calculate b_i/a_{i2} for each row and find that the row corresponding to x_4 has the lowest value for this. The pivot element is 2. The new tableau after pivot operations is performed is given below:

Basic	x_1	x_2	x_3	x_4	b	b/a
x_3	0.5	0	1	−0.5	2	4
x_2	0.5	1	0	0.5	14	28
Cost	−0.5	0	0	1.5	$f + 42$	

We see that the column corresponding to x_1 is the most negative. We calculate b_i/a_{i1} for each row and find that the row corresponding to x_3 is the least. The pivot element is 0.5. Again, we form a tableau to yield:

Basic	x_1	x_2	x_3	x_4	b	b/a
x_1	1	0	2	−1	4	4
x_2	0	1	−1	1	12	12
Cost	0	0	1	1	$f + 44$	

The cost row is now nonnegative which means that we have found the optimal point. The solution is $x_1 = 4$, $x_2 = 12$, $x_3 = 0$, $x_4 = 0$, which gives the cost function as $f = -44$. The solution corresponds to the point C in Figure 5.3 in Example 5.2.

5.3 Two-Phase Simplex Method

Recall the standard LP problem:

Minimize

$$f = \mathbf{C}^{\mathrm{T}}\mathbf{x} \tag{5.44}$$

subject to the constraint:

$$\begin{aligned} &\mathbf{Ax} = \mathbf{b} \\ &b_i \geq 0 \qquad i = 1, m \\ &x_j \geq 0 \qquad j = 1, n. \end{aligned} \tag{5.45}$$

If the problem consists of inequalities, $\leq$ type constraints, with nonnegative right-hand side parameters, then addition of slack variables yields the canonical form. The initial basic solution can be obtained immediately by setting all the original design variables to zero. Note that all the examples studied until now had $\leq$ constraints and the canonical form yielded an initial basic solution.

Many LP problems have $\geq$ or $=$ constraints. For such constraints, the initial basic feasible solution is not readily available. To obtain such a solution, new nonnegative variables are added to each $\geq$ type or equality constraint. These are called *artificial variables* and are different from slack or surplus variables. They are numerical constructs that allow us to obtain a basic feasible solution to start the simplex method. Their addition yields an initial basic feasible solution by treating them as basic. This leads to the two-phase simplex method for LP which is needed for $\geq$ or $=$ constraints.

In Phase I of the simplex method, we create an artificial cost function w using the m artificial variables x_{n+i}:[1]

$$w = x_{n+1} + x_{n+2} + \cdots + x_{n+m} = \sum_{i=1}^{m} x_{n+i}, \tag{5.46}$$

subject to

$$\begin{aligned} a_{11}x_1 + a_{12}x_2 + \cdots + a_n x_n + x_{n+1} &= b_1, \\ a_{21}x_1 + a_{22}x_2 + \cdots + a_{2n}x_n + x_{n+2} &= b_2, \\ &\vdots \\ a_{m1}x_1 + a_{m2}x_2 + \cdots + a_{mn}x_n + x_{n+m} &= b_m, \end{aligned} \tag{5.47}$$

$$x_i \geq 0, \qquad i = 1, n + m, \tag{5.48}$$

where x_{n+j}; $j = 1, m$ are artificial variables. In summation form, the constraints in (5.47) can be written as follows:

$$\sum_{j=1}^{n} a_{ij}x_j + x_{n+i} = b_i \qquad i = 1, m, \tag{5.49}$$

$$\Rightarrow x_{n+i} = b_i - \sum_{j=1}^{n} a_{ij}x_j \qquad i = 1, m. \tag{5.50}$$

Next, we eliminate the artificial variables from the artificial cost function given by (5.46)

$$w = \sum_{i=1}^{m} x_{n+i} = \sum_{i=1}^{m} b_i - \sum_{j=1}^{n}\sum_{i=1}^{m} a_{ij}x_j = f_0 + \sum_{j=1}^{n} c'_j x'_j. \tag{5.51}$$

From the above discussion, it emerges that (5.51) contains the *reduced cost coefficients*,

$$c'_j = -\sum_{i=1}^{m} a_{ij}. \tag{5.52}$$

The artificial cost function has the form $w = \mathbf{C}^{\mathrm{T}}\mathbf{x}$ since f_0 is a constant, and the standard simplex method can now be used to minimize the artificial cost function. In the second phase, the original cost function is treated as a constraint. The two-phase simplex method is now stated as an algorithm.

5.3.1 Phase I of the simplex algorithm

Phase I of the simplex algorithm consists of the following steps:

1. Introduce slack and surplus variables in the constraints and express them in the standard form. All $b_i \geq 0$. If jth design variable y_j is unrestricted in sign, substitute $y_j = y_j^+ - y_j^-$.
2. Define artificial variables for the $\geq$ type constraints. These gives a canonical form for Phase I. Define the cost function of artificial variables w and express the artificial cost function in terms of nonbasic variables only.
3. Write a simplex tableau for the problem. The artificial cost function is written in the last row and the original cost function in the second-last row.
4. Scan the last row of the tableau and note the most-negative coefficient. Let its index be r. This implies that x_r should become a basic variable.
5. Calculate the ratios of the right-hand side parameters with the positive coefficients in the rth column and select a row index s. This implies that x_s should become nonbasic. If there is no pivot element, the problem is unbounded.
6. Perform the pivot step on the rows of the tableau with a_{sr} as the pivot element and the sth row as the pivot row.
7. If there are negative entries in the last row, go to step 4, otherwise go to step 8.
8. If all the entries in the last row are nonnegative and w is zero, Phase I of the simplex algorithm is complete and an initial basic feasible solution is obtained for the original problem. If all elements in the last row are non-negative and $w \neq 0$, the problem is infeasible.

5.3.2 Phase II of the simplex algorithm

In the final tableau from Phase I, the last row is replaced by the actual cost function equation. The basic variables, however, should not appear in the cost function. Thus, pivot steps need to be performed on the cost function equations to eliminate the basic variables from it. A convenient way of accomplishing this is to treat the cost function as one of the equations in the Phase I tableau, say the second equation from the bottom. Elimination is performed on this equation along with others. In this way, the cost function will be in the correct form to continue with Phase II.

1. Same as Step 4 of Phase I
2. Same as Step 5 of Phase I
3. Same as Step 6 of Phase I
4. If there are negative entries in the last row, go to Step 1, otherwise last tableau yields the optimum solution for the problem.

Example 5.4 Maximize $z = 3x_1 + 2x_2$, subject to:

$$x_1 - x_2 \geq 0,$$

$$x_1 + x_2 \geq 2,$$

$$2x_1 + x_2 \leq 6,$$

$$x_1, x_2 \geq 0.$$

Use the simplex method.

Solution: The standard LP form can be written as follows:
Minimize

$$f = -3x_1 - 2x_2.$$

The first constraint can also be written as $-x_1 + x_2 \leq 0$. Now, rewriting the constraints along with slack/surplus variables and artificial variables, we get

$$-x_1 + x_2 + x_3 = 0,$$

$$x_1 + x_2 - x_4 + x_6 = 2,$$

$$2x_1 + x_2 + x_5 = 6.$$

Here, x_3, x_4, x_5 are slack/surplus variables and x_6 is the artificial variable. We need to use the two-phase simplex method for this problem. The artificial cost function is given by $w = x_6 = 2 - x_1 - x_2 + x_4$.

The first tableau is given below:

Variable	x_1	x_2	x_3	x_4	x_5	x_6	b
x_3	−1	1	1	0	0	0	0
x_6	**1**	1	0	−1	0	1	2
x_5	2	1	0	0	1	0	6
Cost	−3	−2	0	0	0	0	$f - 0$
Artificial cost	**−1**	−1	0	1	0	0	$w - 2$

The pivot element is a_{21}. Therefore, x_6 goes out of the basic variable set and x_1 comes in as a basic variable. The next tableau takes the form given below:

Basic variable	x_1	x_2	x_3	x_4	x_5	x_6	**b**
x_3	0	2	1	−1	0	1	2
x_1	1	1	0	−1	0	1	2
x_5	0	−1	0	**2**	1	−2	2
Cost	0	1	0	−3	0	3	$f+6$
Artificial cost	0	0	0	0	0	1	$w-0$

The new pivot element is a_{34}. Thus, x_5 goes out and x_4 comes in as the basic variable. Since the artificial cost coefficients are all zero, Phase 1 of the simplex method is over. The first tableau corresponding to Phase 2 is given below:

x_3	**0**	**3/2**	**1**	**0**	**1/2**	**0**	**3**
x_1	1	1/2	0	0	1/2	0	3
x_4	0	−1/2	0	1	1/2	0	1
Cost	0	**−1/2**	0	0	3/2	0	$f+9$

The pivot element is a_{12}. x_3 goes out and x_2 comes in. Then, the second Phase 2 tableau is obtained:

x_2	**0**	**1**	**2/3**	**0**	**1/3**	**0**	**2**
x_1	1	0	1/3	0	1/3	0	2
x_4	0	0	1/3	1	2/3	−1	2
Cost	0	0	1/3	0	5/3	0	$f+10$

The final tableau gives the following results:

Basic variables: x_1, x_2, $x_4 = 2$; nonbasic variables: x_3, x_5, $x_6 = 0$; optimum cost function: $f = -10$, or $z = 10$. The feasible region is shown in Figure 5.4. The optimal point corresponds to (2, 2).

5.4 Penalty and Barrier Methods

We now address nonlinear constrained optimization problems. Some of the conceptually simplest approaches to solving such problems are the penalty and barrier methods. These

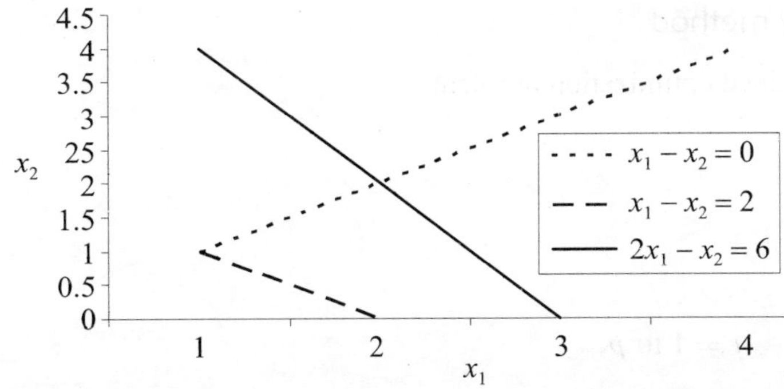

Figure 5.4 *Feasible region for the discussion in Example 5.4*

methods convert a constrained optimization problem into an unconstrained optimization problem. The penalty method imposes a penalty for violating a constraint. The barrier method imposes a penalty for reaching the boundary of an inequality constraint. To understand the philosophy behind these methods, consider a constrained optimization problem of the form shown below:[5]
Minimize

$$f(\mathbf{x}) \tag{5.53}$$

within the feasible region $\mathbf{x} \in S$. The feasible region includes all points which satisfy the constraints. Define the function:

$$\sigma(\mathbf{x}) = \begin{cases} 0, \mathbf{x} \in S \\ +\infty, \mathbf{x} \notin S \end{cases} \tag{5.54}$$

The function $\sigma(\mathbf{x})$ imposes an infinite penalty for violating feasibility. The constrained optimization problem can then be transformed to the following unconstrained problem:
Minimize

$$f(\mathbf{x}) + \sigma(\mathbf{x}). \tag{5.55}$$

Unfortunately, it is not practical to solve this problem because $\sigma(\mathbf{x})$ is not defined outside the feasible region. Even if $\sigma(\mathbf{x})$ is replaced by a large positive number, the unconstrained optimization problem is very complicated due to e presence of discontinuities. Barrier and penalty methods avoid this problem by solving a *sequence* of unconstrained subproblems. The penalty $\sigma(\mathbf{x})$ is replaced by a continuous function which sequentially approaches $\sigma(\mathbf{x})$.

In barrier methods, a *barrier function* is used which approaches $\sigma(\mathbf{x})$ from the *interior* of the feasible region. Therefore, barrier methods are also called *interior-point methods*. Barrier methods create a barrier or wall around the feasible region that prevents the design variables from reaching the boundary. In penalty methods, the *penalty function* approaches $\sigma(\mathbf{x})$ from the *exterior* of the feasible region. Therefore, penalty methods are also called *exterior-point methods*. The penalty function acts as a penalty for the point being infeasible. The barrier and penalty methods are also known as sequential unconstrained minimization techniques (SUMT). In the following sections, we discuss the penalty method in detail followed by the barrier meth d.

5.4.1 Penalty method

Recall the constrained optimization problem:
Minimize,

$$f(\mathbf{x}), \tag{5.56}$$

subject to

$$h_i(\mathbf{x}) = 0 \qquad i = 1 \text{ to } p,$$
$$g_j(\mathbf{x}) \le 0 \qquad j = 1 \text{ to } m. \tag{5.57}$$

A transformation function can be defined for solving this:[1]

$$\phi(\mathbf{x}, r) = f(\mathbf{x}) + P(\mathbf{h}(\mathbf{x}), \mathbf{g}(\mathbf{x}), r). \tag{5.58}$$

Here $P(\mathbf{h}(\mathbf{x}), \mathbf{g}(\mathbf{x}), r)$ is a penalty function, and r is a scalar penalty parameter. The penalty function $P(\mathbf{x})$ should be nonnegative, that is, $P(\mathbf{x}) \ge 0$. In addition, $P(\mathbf{x}) = 0$, if and only if $\mathbf{x} \in S$. That is, the design point lies in the feasible region. One popular choice of penalty function is the following:

$$P(\mathbf{h}(\mathbf{x}), \mathbf{g}(\mathbf{x}), r) = r\left\{\sum_{i=1}^{p}(h_i(\mathbf{x}))^2 + \sum_{j=1}^{m}(g_i^+(\mathbf{x}))^2\right\}. \tag{5.59}$$

Here,

$$g_i^+(\mathbf{x}) = \max\,(0, g_i(\mathbf{x})). \tag{5.60}$$

Note that (5.60) indicates that

$$g_i^+(\mathbf{x}) \ge 0. \tag{5.61}$$

There are two possible cases from (5.61):

(1) $g_i^+(\mathbf{x}) = 0$ for inactive $(g_j(\mathbf{x}) < 0)$ or active inequality $(g_j(\mathbf{x}) = 0)$
(2) $g_i^+(\mathbf{x}) > 0$ if inequality is violated.

Therefore, if equality is not satisfied or inequality is violated, then $P(\mathbf{x})$ has a positive value. So the unconstrained minimization of $f(\mathbf{x}) + P(\mathbf{x})$ can be used to solve the constrained optimization problem in (5.56–58). The starting design for the methods can be arbitrary. An arbitrary starting point is likely to be infeasible and thus, the method iterates through the infeasible region. Therefore, these methods are called exterior-point methods.

In general, penalty methods are more suited to equality constrained problems. Though it is possible to apply penalty methods to inequality constrained problems, the second derivatives can be discontinuous at points where some $g_i(\mathbf{x}) = 0$. One cannot use Newton's method safely with such problems since the Hessian can become ill-conditioned. The gradients of the penalty function can be obtained as follows:

$$\frac{\partial P(\mathbf{h}(\mathbf{x}),\mathbf{g}(\mathbf{x}),r)}{\partial x_l} = 2r\left\{\sum_{i=1}^{p}(h_i(\mathbf{x}))\frac{\partial h_i(\mathbf{x})}{\partial x_l} + \sum_{j=1}^{m}(g_i^+(x))\frac{\partial g_j^+(\mathbf{x})}{\partial x_l}\right\}. \tag{5.62}$$

$$\frac{\partial g_i^+(\mathbf{x})}{\partial x_l} = \max \quad (0, g_i(\mathbf{x}))\frac{\partial g_i(\mathbf{x})}{\partial x_l}. \tag{5.63}$$

There are some other problems with the penalty method. Since the method iterates through the infeasible region, if the method terminates prematurely, the intermediate iterations cannot be used for design as they are infeasible. Furthermore, infeasible designs may not be calculable for some engineering problems due to physical reasons. Many times, constraints are imposed on physical variables, for example, slenderness of beams or structural deflections, to also ensure that the model remains valid in the feasible region. For example, the mathematical model of a structure based on linear theory may not be valid if the deflections become large.

Example 5.5 Consider the problem:
Minimize

$$f(x) = 10 + x^2 - 8x,$$

subject to

$$x = 6.$$

Use the penalty method to find the optimal solution starting from $x = 0$ and increasing values of the penalty parameter $r = 0, 1, 10, 100, 1000$.

Solution: The transformation function can be written as follows:

$$\phi(x,r) = f(x) + P(h(x)) = 10 + x^2 - 8x + r(x-6)^2.$$

The local minimum occurs when

$$\frac{\partial \phi}{\partial x} = 2x - 8 + 2r(x-6) = 0.$$

$$\frac{\partial^2 \phi}{\partial x^2} = 2 + 2r > 0.$$

The necessary condition gives the expression:

$$x = \frac{12r + 8}{2 + 2r}.$$

The sufficiency condition yields the expression:

$$r > -1.$$

This is satisfied for the values of the penalty parameters considered here. We then get the following as the solutions for the problem:

r	x^*
0	4
1	5
10	5.8181
100	5.9802
1000	5.998002

We clearly see that the optimal solution approaches the exact solution $x = 6$.

There is a class of penalty functions called *exact penalty functions*. For such functions, we do not need to repeat the problem for various values of the penalty parameter r. While for the penalty method discussed earlier, a sequence of unconstrained optimization points approach the solution of the constrained problem, they can never reach it exactly. Exact penalty methods seek to solve the constrained optimization problem exactly. An example of an exact penalty function is given by the expression:

$$P_1(\mathbf{h}(\mathbf{x}), \mathbf{g}(\mathbf{x}), r) = r \left\{ \sum_{i=1}^{p} |h_i(\mathbf{x})| + \sum_{j=1}^{m} |g_i^+(\mathbf{x})| \right\}. \tag{5.64}$$

Here, the penalty term is expressed in terms of an absolute value rather than a square term. Thus, we are using the L_1 norm here, rather than the L_2 norm which was used in the earlier definition of the penalty term. If we choose a large value of r, minimizing the function P_1 will also solve the constrained optimization problem. Thus the need to solve a series of unconstrained optimization problems can be avoided. We can see that the function P_1 is continuous but is not differentiable at all points. It turns out that exact penalty functions are nondifferentiable, restricting the use of many gradient-based methods. However, they can be effective with zero-order methods such as the genetic algorithm which will be discussed in Chapter 7.[7–9]

Example 5.6 Consider the problem:
Minimize

$$f(x) = 10 + x^2 - 8x,$$

subject to

$$x = 6.$$

Use the exact penalty method to find the optimal solution starting from $x = 0$ and penalty parameter $r = 10$.

Solution: The transformation function can be written as

$$\phi(x, r) = 10 + x^2 - 8x + r|(x - 6)|.$$

This function is plotted in Figure 5.5 using function values ranging from $x = 0$ to $x = 8$. We clearly see that the optimal solution matches the exact solution $x = 6$.

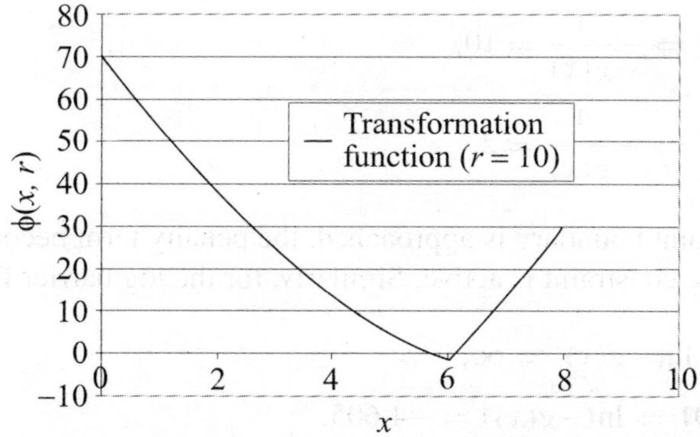

Figure 5.5 *Transformation function for exact penalty method*

5.4.2 Barrier methods

Barrier function methods are applicable only to inequality constrained problems. However, note that the equality constraint $h(\mathbf{x}) = 0$ can be expressed as inequalities. For example, two inequality constraints can be used:

$$h(\mathbf{x}) = 0 \Rightarrow h(\mathbf{x}) \leq 0, \qquad h(\mathbf{x}) \geq 0. \tag{5.65}$$

Another alternative is to use

$$\|h(\mathbf{x})\| \leq 0. \tag{5.66}$$

The transformation function is defined as[1]

$$\phi(\mathbf{x}, r) = f(\mathbf{x}) + B(\mathbf{g}(\mathbf{x}), r), \tag{5.67}$$

where $B(\mathbf{x})$ is the barrier function and r is the penalty parameter. The barrier function must be continuous, $B(\mathbf{x}) \geq 0$ and $B(\mathbf{x}) \to \infty$ as $\mathbf{x}$ approaches the boundaries of the feasible region. Popular barrier functions are the following:

A. Inverse barrier function:

$$B(\mathbf{g}(\mathbf{x}), r) = \frac{1}{r} \sum_{i=1}^{m} \left(-\frac{1}{g_i(\mathbf{x})} \right). \tag{5.68}$$

B. Log barrier function:

$$B(\mathbf{g}(\mathbf{x}), r) = \frac{-1}{r} \sum_{i=1}^{m} \ln(-g_i(\mathbf{x})). \tag{5.69}$$

Note that the barrier method must start from inside the feasible region where $g_i(\mathbf{x}) \leq 0$. For the inverse barrier function, we can see that

$$g(x) = 0 \Rightarrow -\frac{1}{g(x)} = \infty,$$

$$g(x) = -0.01 \Rightarrow -\frac{1}{g(x)} = 100,$$

$$g(x) = -0.1 \Rightarrow -\frac{1}{g(x)} = 10,$$

$$g(x) = -0.5 \Rightarrow -\frac{1}{g(x)} = 2. \tag{5.70}$$

Thus as the constraint boundary is approached, the penalty term becomes larger and goes to infinity when the constraint is active. Similarly, for the log barrier function

$$g(x) = 0 \Rightarrow \ln(-g(x)) = \infty,$$

$$g(x) = -0.01 \Rightarrow \ln(-g(x)) = -4.605,$$

$$g(x) = -0.1 \Rightarrow \ln(-g(x)) = -2.302,$$

$$g(x) = -0.5 \Rightarrow \ln(-g(x)) = -0.693,$$

$$g(x) = -1 \Rightarrow \ln(-g(x)) = 0. \tag{5.71}$$

For $g(x) < -1$, the log function again starts going up, so we can define $\ln(-g(x)) = 0$, $g(x) < -1$. This type of constraint is a very inactive inequality, provided we scale the constraints. For example, a constraint such as $g(x) = x - 1000 \leq 0$ should be written as $g(x) = x/1000 - 1 \leq 0$ and can be expressed as $g(y) = y - 1 \leq 0$ using the scaled variable $y = x/1000$. Such scaling is a recommended practice in optimization even for equality constraints. Thus, $h(x) = x - 1000 = 0$ should be written as $h(x) = x/1000 - 1 = 0$ or $h(y) = y - 1 = 0$, where $y = x/1000$.

Function $B(\mathbf{x})$ becomes infinite if any of the inequalities become active. A large barrier or wall is constructed around the feasible region similar to a fort surrounding a castle. Since the iterative process is started from a feasible point, it cannot go into the infeasible region, because the iterative process cannot cross the huge barrier. Note that as $r \to \infty$, $\mathbf{x}(r) \to \mathbf{x}^*$, where $\mathbf{x}(r)$ is the minimum of the transformed function $\phi(\mathbf{x}, r)$ and $\mathbf{x}^*$ is the solution of the original optimization problem.

There are some features of the barrier methods which limit their use. The method is not suitable for equality constraints, despite the possibility of converting equality constraints into inequality constraints shown in (5.65) and (5.66). Recall that the method needs the feasible region to be nonempty. It is also not easy to find a feasible starting design for nonlinear equality constraints since one must find a solution for one or more nonlinear equations which comprise the constraints.

However, an advantage of the method is that it iterates through the feasible region. Therefore, if it terminates prematurely, the design is feasible and hence usable. Furthermore, the problem of designs being in the infeasible region which may occur for penalty methods is avoided.

Finally, we should observe that both the penalty and barrier methods share some problems. Penalty and barrier methods tend to be ill-behaved near the boundary of the feasible region where the optimum points usually lie. It is difficult to properly select $r^{(k)}$, though the general requirement is that it must start from a small number and increase progressively. The solutions of the past iterations with small $r^{(k)}$ are used as the starting designs for the next iterations. Therefore, as $r^{(k)}$ increases, the penalty function and barrier functions approach $\sigma(\mathbf{x})$ in the limit as $r^{(k)} \to \infty$.

However, the Hessian matrix of the function $\phi(\mathbf{x}, r)$ becomes ill-conditioned as $r^{(k)} \to \infty$. In addition, as r increases, the function becomes highly nonlinear and gradients become difficult to calculate especially using finite-difference methods. These problems can be avoided by using the penalty and barrier methods with gradient-free optimization algorithms such as genetic algorithms (GA). For GA, one can use a large value of r, such as 1000, because the issues of discontinuity and problems with derivative calculations are not important. The increasing popularity of GA has lead to a resurrection in the use of penalty methods in recent years.

5.4.3 Algorithm for penalty and barrier methods

1. Select a small number ε. For some $r_1 > 0$, find the unconstrained local minimum of $\phi(\mathbf{x}, r_1)$. Solution is $\mathbf{x}(r_1)$. A typical choice is $r_1 = 1$.
2. Choose $r_2 > r_1$ and use $\mathbf{x}(r_1)$ as the starting guess. A typical choice is $r_2 = 10r_1$. Minimize $\phi(\mathbf{x}, r_2)$. Solution is $\mathbf{x}(r_2)$.
3. Proceed in this fashion, minimizing $\phi(\mathbf{x}, r)$ for a strictly monotonically increasing sequence $r = 1, 10, 100, 1000, 10000, \ldots$, until two values of $\mathbf{x}(r)$ are almost identical or $\|\mathbf{x}(r_{k+1}) - \mathbf{x}(r_k)\| < \varepsilon$.

Example 5.7 Using the penalty method to minimize

$$f = -x_1 x_2,$$

subject to

$$g_1 = x_1 + x_2^2 - 1 \le 0,$$

$$g_2 = -x_1 - x_2 \le 0.$$

Solution: Form the composite function and calculate the gradients:

$$\phi(\mathbf{x}, r) = -x_1 x_2 + r\{\max(0, x_1 + x_2^2 - 1)\}^2 + r\{\max(0, -x_1 - x_2)\}^2,$$

$$\frac{\partial \phi}{\partial x_1}(\mathbf{x}, r) = -x_2 + 2r\{\max(0, x_1 + x_2^2 - 1)\} - 2r\{\max(0, -x_1 - x_2)\}$$

$$\frac{\partial \phi}{\partial x_2}(\mathbf{x}, r) = -x_1 + 4r x_2\{\max(0, x_1 + x_2^2 - 1)\} - 2r\{\max(0, -x_1 - x_2)\}$$

We can use a method such as the Davidson–Fletcher–Powell (DFP) method to solve this problem with a sequence of increasing values of penalty parameters r.

Iteration	$x^{(0)}$	r	x^*
0	(1, 5)	1	(−0.212, 1.163)
1	(−0.212, 1.163)	10	(0.686, 0.586)
2	(0.686, 0.586)	100	(0.669, 0.578)
3	(0.669, 0.578)	1000	(0.667, 0.577)

Example 5.8 Using the barrier method, minimize the function $f = -x_1x_2$ subject to

$$g_1 = x_1 + x_2^2 - 1 \leq 0,$$
$$g_2 = -x_1 - x_2 \leq 0.$$

Solution: The problem can be rewritten using a log barrier function.

$$\phi(x, r) = -x_1x_2 - \frac{1}{r}[\log(-x_1 - x_2^2 + 1) + \log(-(-x_1 - x_2))].$$

$$\phi(x, r) = -x_1x_2 - \frac{1}{r}[\log(1 - x_1 - x_2^2) + \log(x_1 + x_2)].$$

Now, we will calculate the Karusch–Kuhn–Tucker (KKT) condition to find the optimal point,

$$\frac{\partial\phi}{\partial x_1} = -x_2 - \frac{1}{r}\left[\frac{1}{x_1 + x_2^2 - 1} + \frac{1}{x_1 + x_2}\right] = 0.$$

$$\frac{\partial\phi}{\partial x_2} = -x_1 - \frac{1}{r}\left[\frac{2x_2}{x_1 + x_2^2 - 1} + \frac{1}{x_1 + x_2}\right] = 0.$$

We have two equations and three unknowns and can solve the above equation for different values of r.

r	x_1^*	x_2^*
1	0.97095	0.43217
10	0.56063	0.52709
100	0.6556	0.52709
1000	0.66555	0.57681
10000	0.66655	0.577296

We know that as $r \to \infty$, we get x_1^*, x_2^* as the optimal value of the given problem. Since there is no change in the value of x after $r = 10000$, we can stop the iteration with the final solution.

$$x_1^* = 0.66655, \qquad x_2^* = 0.57729,$$
$$f = -0.38479.$$

Example 5.9 Using the penalty method, minimize

$$f = -x_1x_2$$

subject to

$$g_1 = x_1 + x_2^2 - 1 \leq 0,$$

$$g_2 = -x_1 - x_2 \leq 0.$$

Use Monte Carlo simulations in the region (0, 1) to get an approximate minimum point.

Solution: In a Monte Carlo simulation, we use random numbers for the design variables, x_1 and x_2 and calculate the function values at various points on the design space. In this given problem, we calculate the penalty function at 100 randomly generated points (x_1, x_2). These points are calculated using the *rand()* function which gives uniformly random numbers. Figure 5.6 shows the penalty function values for these 100 points. We use a value of $r = 1000$, which results in infeasible points in the domain becoming very large. The approximate minimum is found by taking the lowest function value which for this simulation comes out to -0.37105 and for which the design point is (0.617, 0.601). We can see that this point is not too far from the actual minimum point where the function value is -0.38479. The constraints are both satisfied at this point.

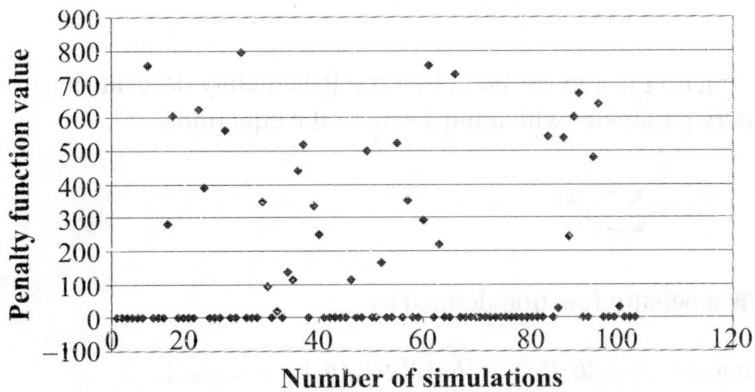

Figure 5.6 *Monte Carlo simulations with penalty functions*

Given the enormous and rising power of modern computers, such an approach can be used for more and more problems in optimization, especially for finding good starting designs for gradient search. This is the basic idea behind the stochastic optimization methods that we will discuss in later chapters.

5.5 Important Definitions

Some mathematical concepts required for the development of other constrained optimization methods in this chapter are now introduced.

5.5.1 Descent function

In unconstrained optimization, the cost function is used to monitor the progress of the optimization algorithm towards the minimum point. For a constrained optimization problem, a descent function is created by adding a penalty to the value of the cost function based on constraint violations. The descent function's value at the optimum should be the same as the cost function, since the constraints are satisfied at the optimum. To construct a descent function, consider the Lagrange function given by[1]

$$L(\mathbf{x}) = f(\mathbf{x}) + \sum_{i=1}^{p} v_i h_i(\mathbf{x}) + \sum_{i=1}^{n} u_i g_i(\mathbf{x}). \tag{5.72}$$

Here, the Lagrange multipliers for the equality constraints v_i are free in sign and that for the inequality constraints $u_i \geq 0$. Using absolute values of $|v_i h_i|$, we can derive a descent function $\Phi(\mathbf{x})$ as shown below:

$$L(\mathbf{x}) \leq f(\mathbf{x}) + \sum_{i=1}^{p} |v_i h_i| + \sum_{i=1}^{m} u_i g_i, \tag{5.73}$$

$$L(\mathbf{x}) \leq f(\mathbf{x}) + \left(\sum_{i=1}^{p} |v_i| + \sum_{i=1}^{m} u_i \right) V(\mathbf{x}), \tag{5.74}$$

$$L(\mathbf{x}) \leq f(\mathbf{x}) + RV(\mathbf{x}) = \Phi(\mathbf{x}). \tag{5.75}$$

The Lagrange function is a lower bound on the Pshenichny descent function $\Phi(\mathbf{x})$. Here, $R > 0$ is a penalty parameter which must satisfy the equations:

$$R \geq \sum_{i=1}^{p} |v_i^{(k)}| + \sum_{i=1}^{m} u_i^{(k)}, \tag{5.76}$$

and $V(\mathbf{x}) \geq 0$ is a penalty function defined as

$$V(\mathbf{x}) = \max\{0; |h_1|, |h_2|, \ldots, |h_p|; |g_1|, |g_2|, \ldots, |g_m|\}. \tag{5.77}$$

At iteration k and point $\mathbf{x}^{(k)}$, the descent function becomes

$$\Phi(\mathbf{x}^{(k)}) = f(\mathbf{x}^{(k)}) + RV(\mathbf{x}^{(k)}). \tag{5.78}$$

Here $R > 0$ is the current value of the penalty parameter.

5.5.2 ε-active constraint

Besides the descent function, another important concept in constrained optimization is the ε-active constraint. An inequality $g_i(\mathbf{x}) < 0$ is ε-active at a point $\mathbf{x}^{(k)}$ if

$$g_i(\mathbf{x}^{(k)}) + \varepsilon \geq 0, \tag{5.79}$$

and

$$g_i(\mathbf{x}^{(k)}) < 0. \tag{5.80}$$

Here $\varepsilon > 0$ is a small number. Geometrically, (5.79) and (5.80) mean that a point is close to the constraint boundary.

5.6 Sequential Linear Programming

A simple idea for solving nonlinear constrained optimization problems is to linearize the problem about a given point and then solve it using well-developed tools of linear programming. By doing this sequentially, a better design may be obtained. We will introduce this concept which leads to an algorithm called sequential linear programming (SLP) in this section.

5.6.1 Linearization

Most constrained optimization methods solve an approximate linear sub-problem at every iteration. This sub-problem is obtained by writing linear Taylor series expansions of the cost and constraint functions. The linear problem may be written as[1]
Minimize

$$f(\mathbf{x}^{(k)} + \Delta\mathbf{x}^{(k)}) \approx f(\mathbf{x}^{(k)}) + \nabla f^{\mathrm{T}}(\mathbf{x}^{(k)})\Delta\mathbf{x}^{(k)}, \tag{5.81}$$

subject to

$$h_j(\mathbf{x}^{(k)} + \Delta\mathbf{x}^{(k)}) \approx h_j(\mathbf{x}^{(k)}) + \nabla h_j^{\mathrm{T}}(\mathbf{x}^{(k)})\Delta\mathbf{x}^{(k)} = 0, \qquad j = 1, p \tag{5.82}$$

and

$$g_j(\mathbf{x}^{(k)} + \Delta\mathbf{x}^{(k)}) \approx g_j(\mathbf{x}^{(k)}) + \nabla g_j^{\mathrm{T}}(\mathbf{x}^{(k)})\Delta\mathbf{x}^{(k)} \le 0, \qquad j = 1, m. \tag{5.83}$$

Here ∇f is the gradient of the cost function, ∇h_j is the gradient of the jth equality constraint and ∇g_j is the gradient of the jth inequality constraint. Let us define some compact notations,

$$f_k = f(\mathbf{x}^{(k)}), \qquad \mathrm{e}_j = -h_j(\mathbf{x}^{(k)}), \qquad b_j = -g_j(\mathbf{x}^{(k)}),$$

$$c_i = \frac{\partial f(\mathbf{x}^{(k)})}{\partial x_i}, \qquad n_{ij} = \frac{\partial h_j(\mathbf{x}^{(k)})}{\partial x_i}, \qquad a_{ij} = \frac{\partial g_j(\mathbf{x}^{(k)})}{\partial x_i},$$

$$d_i = \Delta x_i^{(k)}. \tag{5.84}$$

Since linearization is done at design iteration k, henceforth, we can drop the superscript k. Now that $f(\mathbf{x}^{(k)})$ is known at iteration k, we can proceed to rewrite (5.81–84) as shown below:
Minimize

$$\bar{f} = \mathbf{c}^{\mathrm{T}}\mathbf{d}, \tag{5.85}$$

subject to the constraints:

$$\mathbf{N}^{\mathrm{T}}\mathbf{d} = \mathbf{e}, \tag{5.86}$$

$$\mathbf{A}^{\mathrm{T}}\mathbf{d} \le \mathbf{b}. \tag{5.87}$$

Here, $\mathbf{N}$ is an $n \times p$ matrix whose columns contain the gradients of the equality constraints. $\mathbf{A}$ is an $n \times m$ matrix whose columns are the gradients of the inequality constraints. The jth column of $\mathbf{N}$ and $\mathbf{A}$ can be written as follows:

$$\mathbf{n}^{(j)} = \left(\frac{\partial h_j}{\partial x_1}, \frac{\partial h_j}{\partial x_2}, \ldots, \frac{\partial h_j}{\partial x_n}\right), \tag{5.88}$$

$$\mathbf{a}^{(j)} = \left(\frac{\partial g_j}{\partial x_1}, \frac{\partial g_j}{\partial x_2}, \ldots, \frac{\partial g_j}{\partial x_n}\right). \tag{5.89}$$

Then, $\mathbf{N} = [\mathbf{n}^{(j)}]_{n\times p}$ and $\mathbf{A} = [\mathbf{a}^{(j)}]_{n\times m}$.

After linearization of the equations, the objective and constraints are linear in d_i. So we can use linear programming to solve the problem defined by (5.85–87). To solve this problem using the standard simplex method, we require that e_j and b_j on the right-hand side must be nonnegative, that is, $e_j \geq 0, b_j \geq 0$. If b_j is negative, we can multiply it by -1 and reverse the equation to a $\geq$ inequality.

We know that a linear Taylor series approximation of a nonlinear function is likely to be valid only in a small neighbourhood of the design point. So we must apply move limits to restrict the design space. The changes allowed in the ith variable at the kth iteration are then given below:

$$-\Delta_{il}^{(k)} \leq d_i \leq \Delta_{iu}^{(k)}, \qquad k = 1, \ldots, n. \tag{5.90}$$

Here $\Delta_{il}^{(k)}$ are the lower bounds and $\Delta_{iu}^{(k)}$ are the upper bounds placed for the design variable.

A proper selection of move limits is critical to the performance of the SLP algorithm. One should select move limits as a fraction of the current design variables (from 1% to 100%). Since we are using linear Taylor series approximations, small move limits are more appropriate. The variable d_i in the SLP can be positive or negative and the new design point is given by:

$$\mathbf{x}^{(k+1)} = \mathbf{x}^{(k)} + \mathbf{d}. \tag{5.91}$$

So d_i are free to have any sign, positive or negative. Thus each d_i should be replaced by two variables, $d_i = d_i^+ - d_i^-$. The SLP does not have well-defined stopping criteria based on descent conditions. Some popular stopping criteria are the following:

1. All constraints must be satisfied, that is, $g_i \leq \varepsilon_1 i = 1, n$; $|h_i| \leq \varepsilon_1 i = 1, p$. Here $\varepsilon_1 > 0$ is a small tolerance for constraint violation (recall the ε-active constraints).
2. Change in design should be almost zero, or $\|\mathbf{d}\| \leq \varepsilon_2$, $\varepsilon_2 > 0$.

We can now state a simple SLP algorithm.

5.6.2 A simple SLP algorithm

1. Estimate the starting design $\mathbf{x}^{(0)}$. Set $k = 0$, specify ε_1 and ε_2 as two small numbers.
2. Evaluate the cost and constraint functions at $\mathbf{x}^{(k)}$. Calculate $f(\mathbf{x}^{(k)})$, **b**, **e**.
3. Calculate gradients at $\mathbf{x}^{(k)}$: **c**, **N**, **A**
4. Select the move limits, $\Delta_{il}^{(k)}, \Delta_{iu}^{(k)}$.
5. Define the LP sub-problem.
6. Convert the LP sub-problem to a simplex form. Solve for $\mathbf{d}^{(k)}$.
7. Check for convergence. If $g_i \leq \varepsilon_1$; $i = 1$ to m; $|h_i| \leq \varepsilon_1$; $i = 1$, to p; $\|\mathbf{d}^{(k)}\| \leq \varepsilon_2$, then stop the process. If not, continue.
8. Update the design as follows: $\mathbf{x}^{(k+1)} = \mathbf{x}^{(k)} + \mathbf{d}^{(k)}$, then set $k = k+1$, and go to step 2.

The main challenge in performing the SLP lies in appropriate selection of the move limits. If the move limits are too restrictive, there may be no solution for the LP sub-problem. Also, the rate of convergence may be very slow, and it may depend on appropriate selection of the move limits. The absolute value or exact value penalty function can be used as a descent function to monitor the progress of the method. We can decide to reject a new design point if the exact penalty function value increases.

Example 5.10 Perform an iteration of the SLP for the following problem. Use $\mathbf{x}^{(0)} = (1, 0.5)$ as the starting point and 100% move limits.
Minimize

$$f(\mathbf{x}) = x_1^2 + x_2^2 - 2x_1 - 2x_2,$$

subject to

$$x_1^2 + x_2^2 \leq 16,$$

$$2 - x_1 \leq 0,$$

$$-x_1, -x_2 \leq 0.$$

Solution: The starting design point is $\mathbf{x}^{(0)} = (1, 0.5)$, $f(\mathbf{x}^{(0)}) = -1.75$. Let $\varepsilon_1 = \varepsilon_2 = 0.001$ and choose move limits such that 100% design change is permissible. Now, the linearized sub-problem with appropriate move limits on design changes d_1 and d_2 is obtained as follows:
Minimize

$$\bar{f} = -d_2,$$

subject to the constraints:

$$2d_1 + d_2 \leq 14.75,$$

$$-d_1 \leq -1 \Rightarrow d_1 \geq 1,$$

$$-1 \leq d_1 \leq 1,$$

$$-0.5 \leq d_2 \leq 0.5.$$

To solve this problem using the simplex method, we must define new variables A, B, C and D such that $d_1 = A - B$, $d_2 = C - D$ and A, B, C and $D \geq 0$. Now, substituting these new variables into the linearized sub-problem, we can rewrite the LP in a standard form as shown below:
Minimize

$$\bar{f} = -C + D,$$

subject to

$$2A - 2B + C - D \leq 14.75,$$

$$-A + B \leq -1 \Rightarrow A - B \geq 1,$$

$$C - D \leq 0.5,$$

$$A - B \leq 1,$$
$$B - A \leq 1,$$
$$D - C \leq 0.5.$$

The solution for the above LP problem with the simplex method is $A = 0$, $B = 0$, $C = 0.5$, $D = 0$. Now,

$$d_1 = 0,$$
$$d_2 = 0.5.$$

Updating the design we get,

$$\mathbf{x}^{(1)} = \mathbf{x}^{(0)} + \mathbf{d}^{(0)} = (1, 1),$$
$$f(\mathbf{x}^{(1)}) = -2.$$

In this iteration, the cost function value has decreased for the new design compared to starting design, but the new design point still violates the second constraint.

The concept of an SLP was introduced by Griffith and Stewart in 1961. This is now widely used in the oil and chemical industry. If the optimal point lies at the vertex of the linearized feasible region, then fast convergence of the method can be obtained. The SLP algorithm is suitable for highly constrained nonlinear optimization problems that have as many linearly independent active constraints as variables. For example, practical refinery model problems are of this type.

The implementation of the SLP given until now is very simple and not robust. There have been many attempts to improve the SLP algorithms since efficient LP solvers are widely available. There are several approaches to improving SLP. For example, the exact penalty function can be actively used to find the search direction. Another approach known as the *method of centres* involves fitting the largest circle (or hypersphere) in the linearized design space and using the centre of this circle to guide the design. Recent research also shows the possibility of combining the SLP approach with the trust region approach. This kind of trust region framework will be discussed later in this chapter. However, despite these developments, the use of SLP remains limited in practical design optimization.

5.7 Quadratic Programming

Quadratic programming (QP) is an extension of linear programming to a problem with a quadratic cost function and linear constraints. Quadratic approximations are much more accurate than linear ones for typical nonlinear optimization problems. Therefore, quadratic programming algorithms are often used at some stage in many constrained optimization algorithms. The QP problem can be formally defined as given below:[1]
Minimize

$$\bar{f} = \mathbf{c}^{\mathrm{T}}\mathbf{d} + 0.5\mathbf{d}^{\mathrm{T}}\mathbf{d}, \tag{5.92}$$

subject to the constraints:

$$\mathbf{N}^{\mathrm{T}}\mathbf{d} = \mathbf{e}, \tag{5.93}$$

$$\mathbf{A}^{\mathrm{T}}\mathbf{d} \leq \mathbf{b}. \tag{5.94}$$

Comparing this with the problem defined in (5.85–87), we can see that only the objective function has been changed for the QP problem. The QP problem defined above is convex and the solution to the QP problem is unique. We can also express the QP in terms of the original design variable $\mathbf{x}$ by taking a Taylor series with gradient and Hessian as follows: Minimize

$$q(\mathbf{x}) = \mathbf{c}^{\mathrm{T}}\mathbf{x} + \frac{1}{2}\mathbf{x}^{\mathrm{T}}\mathbf{H}\mathbf{x}, \tag{5.95}$$

subject to the constraints:

$$\mathbf{A}^{\mathrm{T}}\mathbf{x} \leq \mathbf{b}, \tag{5.96}$$

$$\mathbf{N}^{\mathrm{T}}\mathbf{x} = \mathbf{e},$$

$$\mathbf{x} \geq 0. \tag{5.97}$$

Here, $\mathbf{x}$ and $\mathbf{c}$ are $n \times 1$ vectors, $\mathbf{b}$ is an $m \times 1$ vector, $\mathbf{e}$ is a $p \times 1$ vector, $\mathbf{A}$ is an $n \times m$ matrix, $\mathbf{H}$ is an $n \times n$ matrix and $\mathbf{N}$ is an $n \times p$ matrix. If $\mathbf{H}$ is positive semidefinite, then the QP is convex. If $\mathbf{H}$ is positive definite, the QP is strictly convex. We assume that $\mathbf{H}$ is at least positive semidefinite. Most applications satisfy this requirement.

An efficient approach for solving QP problems involves the use of KKT conditions. Introduce slack variables into (5.96),

$$\mathbf{A}^{\mathrm{T}}\mathbf{x} + \mathbf{s} = \mathbf{b}, \quad \mathbf{s} \geq 0 \tag{5.98}$$

or

$$\mathbf{s} = \mathbf{b} - \mathbf{A}^{\mathrm{T}}\mathbf{x}. \tag{5.99}$$

The inequality $-\mathbf{x} \leq 0$ does not need slack variables since $x_i \geq 0$ is itself a slack variable. The Lagrange function can then be formed from the equations (5.95–98).

$$L = \mathbf{c}^{\mathrm{T}}\mathbf{x} + \frac{1}{2}\mathbf{x}^{\mathrm{T}}\mathbf{H}\mathbf{x} + \mathbf{u}^{\mathrm{T}}(\mathbf{A}^{\mathrm{T}}\mathbf{x} + \mathbf{s} - \mathbf{b}) - \xi^{\mathrm{T}}\mathbf{x} + \mathbf{v}^{\mathrm{T}}(\mathbf{N}^{\mathrm{T}}\mathbf{x} - \mathbf{e}). \tag{5.100}$$

Here $\mathbf{u}$, $\mathbf{v}$, $\boldsymbol{\xi}$ are vectors containing the Lagrange multipliers. The KKT conditions are given:[1]

$$\frac{\partial L}{\partial \mathbf{x}} = \mathbf{c} + \mathbf{H}\mathbf{x} - \xi + \mathbf{N}\mathbf{v} = 0,$$

$$\mathbf{A}^{\mathrm{T}}\mathbf{x} + \mathbf{s} - \mathbf{b} = 0,$$

$$\mathbf{N}^{\mathrm{T}}\mathbf{x} - \mathbf{e} = 0,$$

$$u_i s_i = 0, \qquad i = 1, m,$$

$$\xi_i x_i = 0, \qquad i = 1, n,$$

$$s_i \geq 0, \qquad u_i \geq 0 \quad i = 1, m,$$

$$\xi_i \geq 0, \qquad i = 1, n. \tag{5.101}$$

Lagrange multipliers for equality constraints are free in sign. We can decompose them:

$$\mathbf{v} = \mathbf{y} - \mathbf{z}, \qquad \mathbf{y}, \mathbf{z} \geq 0. \tag{5.102}$$

We write the objective and the two main constraints as one matrix equation:

$$\begin{bmatrix} \mathbf{H} & \mathbf{A} & -\mathbf{I}_n & \mathbf{0}_{n\times m} & \mathbf{N} & -\mathbf{N} \\ \mathbf{A}^{\mathrm{T}} & \mathbf{0}_{m\times m} & \mathbf{0}_{m\times n} & \mathbf{I}_m & \mathbf{0}_{m\times p} & \mathbf{0}_{n\times p} \\ \mathbf{N}^{\mathrm{T}} & \mathbf{0}_{p\times m} & \mathbf{0}_{p\times n} & \mathbf{0}_{p\times m} & \mathbf{0}_{p\times p} & \mathbf{0}_{p\times p} \end{bmatrix} \begin{Bmatrix} \mathbf{x} \\ \mathbf{u} \\ \xi \\ \mathbf{s} \\ \mathbf{y} \\ \mathbf{z} \end{Bmatrix} = \begin{bmatrix} -\mathbf{c} \\ \mathbf{b} \\ \mathbf{e} \end{bmatrix}, \tag{5.103}$$

where $\mathbf{I}_n$ and $\mathbf{I}_m$ are $n\times n$ and $m\times m$ identity matrices, respectively, and the entries labelled $\mathbf{0}$ are zero matrices of the indicated order. We can rewrite (5.103) in compact notation as $\mathbf{BX} = \mathbf{D}$, where $\mathbf{B}$ is an $[(n+m+p)\times(2n+2m+2p)]$ matrix, $\mathbf{X}$ is a $(2n+2m+2p)\times 1$ vector and $\mathbf{D}$ is an $(n+m+p)\times 1$ vector. The KKT conditions now involve solving (5.103) subject to the switching constraints and ≥ 0 constraints. Thus the KKT conditions can be written: Solve for $\mathbf{X}$,

$$\mathbf{BX} = \mathbf{D} \tag{5.104}$$

subject to the constraints:

$$u_i s_i = 0, \qquad i = 1, m, \tag{5.105}$$

$$\xi_i x_i = 0, \qquad i = 1, n, \tag{5.106}$$

$$s_i, u_i \geq 0, \qquad i = 1, m, \tag{5.107}$$

$$\xi_i \geq 0, \qquad i = 1, n, \tag{5.108}$$

$$y_i \geq 0, \qquad z_i \geq 0, \qquad i = 1, p. \tag{5.109}$$

Now, the switching conditions (5.105) and (5.106) can be written as follows:

$$X_i X_{n+m+i} = 0, \qquad i = 1 \text{ to } n+m, \tag{5.110}$$

and (5.107) and (5.108) become:

$$X_i \geq 0, \qquad i = 1, (2n+2m+2p). \tag{5.111}$$

Hence, the final solution of the QP

$$\mathbf{BX} = \mathbf{D} \tag{5.112}$$

subject to constraints:

$$X_i X_{n+m+i} = 0, \qquad i = 1, n+m,$$

$$X_i \geq 0, \qquad i = 1, 2n+2m+2p. \tag{5.113}$$

Note that the slackness conditions are nonlinear constraints.

5.7.1 Simplex method for solving QP problem

Though the problem posed using equations (5.112) and (5.113) is nonlinear, there is a way to solve this problem using the two-phase simplex method, provided **H** is positive definite.

Introduce artificial variables:[1]

$$\mathbf{BX} + \mathbf{Y} = \mathbf{D} \qquad \mathbf{Y} \rightarrow (n + m + p) \times 1. \tag{5.114}$$

Here, X_i is non-basic, Y_j is basic and $D_i \geq 0$. We define the artificial cost function:

$$w = \sum_{i=1}^{n+m+p} Y_i. \tag{5.115}$$

Next, we express artificial variables is terms of nonbasic variables:

$$w = \sum_{i=1}^{n+m+p} D_i - \sum_{j=1}^{2(n+m+p)} \sum_{i=1}^{n+m+p} B_{ij} X_j, \tag{5.116}$$

$$w = w_0 + \sum_{j=1}^{2(n+m+p)} c_j X_j, \tag{5.117}$$

where,

$$c_j = - \sum_{i=1}^{n+m+p} B_{ij} \quad \text{and} \quad w_0 = \sum_{i=1}^{n+m+p} D_i.$$

Here w_0 is the initial value of the artificial cost function, and c_j is the initial relative cost coefficient obtained by adding the elements of the jth column of the matrix **B** and changing its sign. The slackness condition can be expressed as

$$X_i X_{n+m+i} = 0. \tag{5.118}$$

The above equation (5.118), states that X_i and X_{n+m+i} are not simultaneously basic. This approach to solving QP problem is summarized next.

5.7.2 Procedure for solving QP problems

1. Define matrix **B**.
2. Define vector **D**, check all $D_i \geq 0$.
3. Calculate current value of the artificial cost function and relative cost coefficients.
4. Complete Phase I of the simplex method. If the artificial cost is nonzero and all relative cost coefficients are nonnegative, or no pivot element can be determined, then the original QP problem is infeasible.
5. If a feasible solution is found, use the definition of vector **X** to rename the values of QP variables **x**, Lagrange multipliers **u**, **v**, ξ and slack variables **s**.

Example 5.11 Minimize the function $f(\mathbf{x}) = x_1^2 + x_2^2 - 2x_1 - 2x_2$ subject to the constraints:

$$x_1 + x_2 - 4 \le 0,$$

$$2 - x_1 \le 0,$$

$$x_1, x_2 \ge 0.$$

Use quadratic programming.

Solution: We express the cost function in a generalized QP form:

$$q(\mathbf{x}) = [-2 \quad -2]\begin{bmatrix} x_1 \\ x_2 \end{bmatrix} + 0.5[x_1 \quad x_2]\begin{bmatrix} 2 & 0 \\ 0 & 2 \end{bmatrix}\begin{bmatrix} x_1 \\ x_2 \end{bmatrix}.$$

We can identify the following quantities:

$$\mathbf{c} = \begin{bmatrix} -2 \\ -2 \end{bmatrix}; \qquad \mathbf{H} = \begin{bmatrix} 2 & 0 \\ 0 & 2 \end{bmatrix};$$

$$\mathbf{A} = \begin{bmatrix} 1 & -1 \\ 1 & 0 \end{bmatrix}; \qquad \mathbf{b} = \begin{bmatrix} 4 \\ -2 \end{bmatrix}.$$

Using these quantities, matrix **B** and vectors **D** and **X** are identified:

$$\mathbf{B} = \begin{bmatrix} 2 & 0 & 1 & -1 & -1 & 0 & 0 & 0 \\ 0 & 2 & 1 & 0 & 0 & -1 & 0 & 0 \\ 1 & 1 & 0 & 0 & 0 & 0 & 1 & 0 \\ -1 & 0 & 0 & 0 & 0 & 0 & 0 & 1 \end{bmatrix},$$

$$\mathbf{D} = [2 \quad 2 \mid 4 \mid -2], \quad \mathbf{X} = [x_1 \quad x_2 \mid u_1 \quad u_2 \mid \zeta_1 \quad \zeta_2 \mid s_1 \quad s_2].$$

But all elements of vector **D** must be nonnegative. Hence, we change the sign and multiply by -1 the corresponding row of matrix **B**.

$$\text{New } \mathbf{B} = \begin{bmatrix} 2 & 0 & 1 & -1 & -1 & 0 & 0 & 0 \\ 0 & 2 & 1 & 0 & 0 & -1 & 0 & 0 \\ 1 & 1 & 0 & 0 & 0 & 0 & 1 & 0 \\ 1 & 0 & 0 & 0 & 0 & 0 & 0 & -1 \end{bmatrix},$$

$$\text{New } \mathbf{D} = [2 \quad 2 \mid 4 \mid 2].$$

The optimum solution for the original QP problem is: $x_1 = 2, x_2 = 1, u_1 = 0, u_2 = 2$ and at this point, $f(2, 1) = -1$.

5.8 Constrained Steepest-Descent Method

This method uses a steepest-descent direction which is modified to include the effect of constraints. The method can handle both equality and inequality constraints. The solution

Simplex solution procedure for QP problem shown in Example 5.11

Basic variable	x_1	x_2	x_3	x_4	x_5	x_6	x_7	x_8	y_1	y_2	y_3	y_4	D
y_1	2	0	1	−1	−1	0	0	0	1	0	0	0	2
y_2	0	2	1	0	0	−1	0	0	0	1	0	0	2
y_3	1	1	0	0	0	0	1	0	0	0	1	0	4
y_4	1	1	0	0	0	0	0	−1	0	0	0	1	2
	<u>−4</u>	−3	−2	1	1	1	−1	1	0	0	0	0	$w - 10$
x_1	1	0	1/2	−1/2	−1/2	0	0	0	1/2	0	0	0	1
y_2	0	2	1	0	0	−1	0	0	0	1	0	0	2
y_3	0	1	−1/2	1/2	1/2	0	1	0	−1/2	0	1	0	3
y_4	0	0	−1/2	1/2	1/2	0	0	−1	−1/2	0	0	1	1
	0	<u>−3</u>	0	−1	−1	1	−1	1	2	0	0	0	$w - 6$
x_1	1	0	1/2	−1/2	−1/2	0	0	0	1/2	0	0	0	1
x_2	0	1	1/2	0	0	−1/2	0	0	0	1/2	0	0	1
y_3	0	0	−1	1/2	1/2	1/2	1	0	−1/2	−1/2	1	0	2
y_4	0	0	−1/2	1/2	1/2	0	0	−1	−1/2	0	0	1	1
	0	0	3/2	−1	−1	−1/2	<u>−1</u>	1	2	3/2	0	0	$w - 3$

Continued on the next page

Table continued.

Basic variable	x_1	x_2	x_3	x_4	x_5	x_6	x_7	x_8	y_1	y_2	y_3	y_4	D
x_1	1	0	1/2	−1/2	−1/2	0	0	0	1/2	0	0	0	1
x_2	0	1	1/2	0	0	−1/2	0	0	0	1/2	0	0	1
x_7	0	0	−1	1/2	1/2	1/2	1	0	−1/2	−1/2	1	0	2
y_4	0	0	−1/2	1/2	1/2	0	0	−1	−1/2	0	0	1	1
	0	0	1/2	**−1/2**	−1/2	0	0	1	3/2	1	1	0	$w - 1$
x_1	1	0	0	0	0	0	0	−1	0	0	0	1	2
x_2	0	1	1/2	0	0	−1/2	0	0	0	1/2	0	0	1
x_7	0	0	−1/2	0	0	1/2	1	1	0	−1/2	1	−2	1
x_4	0	0	−1	1	1	0	0	−2	−1	0	0	2	2
	0	0	0	0	0	0	0	0	1	1	1	1	$w - 0$

point of the sequence $\mathbf{x}^{(k)}$ generated by the algorithm is a KKT point. It uses only active and violated constraints for determination of the QP sub-problem. Consider the problem: Minimize[1]

$$\bar{f} = \mathbf{c}^{\mathrm{T}}\mathbf{d} + \frac{1}{2}\mathbf{d}^{\mathrm{T}}\mathbf{d}. \tag{5.119}$$

The necessary condition for minimization is:

$$\frac{d\bar{f}}{dd} = \mathbf{c} + \mathbf{d} = 0 \Rightarrow \mathbf{d} = -\mathbf{c}. \tag{5.120}$$

This is the steepest descent method. In the CSD method, we use the solution of the QP sub-problem at a given point $\mathbf{x}^{(k)}$ to determine the search direction. To monitor the convergence of the method, consider the descent function:

$$\Phi(\mathbf{x}) = f(\mathbf{x}) + RV(\mathbf{x}). \tag{5.121}$$

Here, $R > 0$ is a positive number initially specified by the user and later adjusted using Lagrange multipliers. Also, $V(\mathbf{x}) \geq 0$ is either the maximum constraint violation or zero.

The step-size determination problem is to calculate α_k so as to minimize the descent function $\Phi(\mathbf{x}^{(k)} + \alpha_k \mathbf{d}^{(k)})$. Practical implementations of the method show that the inexact line search works quite well with this method and efficiency can be increased by avoiding exact methods such as the golden-section search. The CSD approach can be stated as an algorithm.

5.8.1 Algorithm for the constrained steepest-descent (CSD) method

1. Set $k = 0$, select $\mathbf{x}^{(0)}$, R_0. A good choice is $R_0 = 1$. Also select constraint parameter ε_1 and convergence parameter ε_2.
2. Calculate $f(\mathbf{x}), h(\mathbf{x}), g(\mathbf{x})$ and their gradients. Calculate maximum constraint violation V_k.
3. Define QP sub-problem about $\mathbf{x}^{(0)}$ and solve to get search direction $\mathbf{d}^{(k)}$ and Lagrange multiplier vectors $\mathbf{v}^{(k)}$ and $\mathbf{u}^{(k)}$.
4. If $\|\mathbf{d}\| \leq \varepsilon_2$ and $V_k \leq \varepsilon_1$, then stop. If not, continue.
5. Calculate r_k using the Lagrange multipliers. Set $R = \max(R_k, r_k)$.
6. Use one-dimensional inexact line search to find α_k such that $\Phi(\mathbf{x}^{(k)} + \alpha_k \mathbf{d}^{(k)}) < \Phi(\mathbf{x}^{(k)})$.
7. Put $R_{k+1} = R$. Set $k = k + 1$. Go to step 2.

Example 5.12 Solve the following problem using the CSD method.
Minimize,

$$f(x_1, x_2) = x_1^2 + x_2^2 - 2x_1 - 2x_2$$

subject to

$$x_1^2 + x_2^2 \leq 16,$$

$$2 - x_1 \leq 0,$$

$$-x_1, -x_2 \leq 0.$$

Assume $\mathbf{x}^{(0)} = (2, 2)$; $R_0 = 2$; $\gamma = 0.5 (0 < \gamma < 1)$; $\varepsilon_1 = \varepsilon_2 = 0.001$.

Solution: *Iteration 1* ($k = 0$)

Step 1: The initial data are specified:

$$\mathbf{x}^{(0)} = (2, 2); \qquad R_0 = 2; \qquad \gamma = 0.5(0 < \gamma < 1); \qquad \varepsilon_1 = \varepsilon_2 = 0.001.$$

Step 2: To form the QP sub-problem, the cost and the constraint functions and their gradients must be evaluated at the initial design point.

$$f(2, 2) = 0.$$

Now

$$g_1 = -8 < 0 \text{ (inactive)}, \qquad g_2 = 0 \text{ (active)},$$

$$g_3 = -2 < 0 \text{ (inactive)}, \qquad g_4 = -2 < 0 \text{ (inactive)}.$$

Therefore, maximum constraint violation is

$$V_o = \max\{0; -8, 0, -2, -2\} = 0,$$

$$\nabla f(2, 2) = (2, 2).$$

Now

$$\nabla g_1 = (4, 4), \qquad \nabla g_2 = (-1, 0).$$
$$\nabla g_3 = (-1, 0), \qquad \nabla g_4 = (0, -1).$$

Step 3: Using the preceding values, the QP sub-problem at (2, 2) is given by Minimize

$$\bar{f} = (2d_1 + 2d_2) + 0.5(d_1^2 + d_2^2),$$

subject to the constraints:

$$4d_1 + 4d_2 \leq 8,$$
$$-d_1 \leq 0,$$
$$-d_1 \leq 2, \qquad -d_2 \leq 2.$$

Solving the above QP sub-problem using KKT conditions, we get the following equations:

$$\mathbf{d}^0 = (0, -2), \qquad \mathbf{u}^0 = (0, 2, 0, 0), \qquad \bar{f} = -2.$$

Step 4: $\|\mathbf{d}^{(0)}\| = 2 > \varepsilon_2$, the convergence criterion is not satisfied.

Step 5:

$$r_0 = \Sigma u_i = 2,$$

$$R = \max\{R_0, r_0\} = 2.$$

Step 6: For step size determination, we use inexact line search.
The current descent function is evaluated:

$$\Phi_0 = f_0 + RV_0 = 0,$$

$$\beta_0 = \gamma \|\mathbf{d}^{(0)}\|^2 = 2.$$

Trial step size ($t_0 = 1$)

The trial design point is calculated.

$$\mathbf{x}^{(1,0)} = \mathbf{x}^{(0)} + t_0\mathbf{d}^{(0)} = (2, 0).$$

At this trial design point, the cost and constraint functions are evaluated.

$$f_{1,0} = f(2, 0) = 0.$$

Now

$$g_1 = -12 < 0 \text{ (inactive)}, \qquad g_2 = 0 \text{ (active)},$$

$$g_3 = -2 < 0 \text{ (inactive)}, \qquad g_4 = 0 \text{ (active)}.$$

The maximum constraint violation:

$$V_{1,0} = \max\{0; -12, 0, -2, 0\} = 0,$$

$$\Phi_{1,0} = f_{1,0} + RV_{1,0} = 0.$$

For the descent condition:

$$\Phi_{k+1,j} + t_j\beta_k \le \Phi_k.$$

For this iteration:

$$\Phi_{1,0} + t_0\beta_0 \le \Phi_0.$$

LHS = 2, RHS = 0.
Hence, the descent condition of inequality is not satisfied.
Let us bisect the trail step size to $t_1 = 0.5$.

$$\mathbf{x}^{(1,1)} = \mathbf{x}^{(0)} + t_1\mathbf{d}^{(0)} = (2, 1),$$

$$f_{(1,1)} = f(2, 1) = -1,$$

$$V_{(1,1)} = \max\{0; -11, 0, -2, -1\} = 0,$$

$$\Phi_{1,1} = f_{1,1} + RV_{1,1} = -1,$$

$$\Phi_{1,1} + t_1\beta_0 = 0,$$

$$\Phi_0 = 0.$$

Hence, the descent condition of inequality, ($\Phi_{1,1} + t_1\beta_0 \le \Phi_0$) is satisfied. Also, the optimum solution is obtained as $\mathbf{x}^* = (2, 1)$, $f = -1$.

5.9 Trust Region Methods

These are also called restricted step methods and they try to find a search step within a *trust region* around the current point $\mathbf{x}^{(k)}$. They are methods for unconstrained optimization but are discussed in this chapter since they rely on QP techniques and the region of trust is treated using a constraint.

Newton's method, based on a quadratic approximate of $f(\mathbf{x})$, breaks down when $\mathbf{H}$ is not positive definite or when the function is highly nonlinear. These problems arise from trying to minimize the quadratic approximation $q(\mathbf{x}) \approx f(\mathbf{x})$ in a region which is outside the validity of the quadratic approximation. We can overcome the difficulties if we attempt to minimize $q(\mathbf{x})$ within a region around $\mathbf{x}^{(k)}$ whenever the second-order Taylor series approximation is valid. Thus, we define a region of trust:[6]

$$\Omega_k = \{\mathbf{x} : \|\mathbf{x} - \mathbf{x}^{(k)}\| \leq h^{(k)}\}. \tag{5.122}$$

Here $h^{(k)}$ is the size of the trust region which is dynamically adjusted and the quadratic approximation $q(\mathbf{x})$ is minimized within Ω.
Minimize,

$$q(\Delta\mathbf{x}) = f(\mathbf{x}^{(k)}) + \mathbf{c}^{\mathrm{T}}\Delta\mathbf{x} + \frac{1}{2}\Delta\mathbf{x}^{\mathrm{T}}\mathbf{H}^{(k)}\Delta\mathbf{x}$$

subject to

$$-h^{(k)} \leq \Delta x_i \leq h^{(k)}, \qquad i = 1, \ldots, n. \tag{5.123}$$

Here we have a quadratic objective function and linear constraint typical of a quadratic programming problem. We need to solve for $\Delta\mathbf{x}$.

If we solve for $\Delta\mathbf{x}^{(k)}$, we obtain the actual change in the objective function,

$$\Delta f = f(\mathbf{x}^{(k)}) - f(\mathbf{x}^{(k)} + \Delta\mathbf{x}^{(k)}), \tag{5.124}$$

and the predicted change in the objective function is given below:

$$\Delta q = f(\mathbf{x}^{(k)}) - q(\Delta\mathbf{x}). \tag{5.125}$$

Define the reliability index:

$$r_k = \frac{\Delta f}{\Delta q}. \tag{5.126}$$

The closer r_k is to unity (1), the more accurately $q(\Delta\mathbf{x})$ approximates $f(\mathbf{x}^{(k)} + \Delta\mathbf{x}^{(k)})$. Consider the following possibilities:

1. If r_k is small (say $r_k < r^{\mathrm{low}}$), then the approximation is not good and the trust region needs to be decreased.
2. If r_k is large (say $r_k > r^{\mathrm{high}}$), then the approximation is quite good and the trust region can be increased.
3. If $r_k < 0$, then the search direction can result in an increase in the objective function. This is not a good choice, and the trust region needs to be decreased.

Here r^{low} is a number which is closer to zero than one and r^{high} is a number which is closer to one. For example, $r^{\mathrm{low}} = 0.25$ and $r^{\mathrm{high}} = 0.75$ can be selected. These observations are used to create the trust region algorithm.

5.9.1 Trust region algorithm

1. Estimate $\mathbf{x}^{(0)}$ and $h^{(0)}$ (set $h^{(0)} = 1$); Choose small number ε.
2. Calculate $\mathbf{c}$ and $\mathbf{H}$. If $\|\mathbf{c}\| < \varepsilon$, stop.
3. Solve the quadratic programming problem to get $\Delta\mathbf{x}^{(k)}$.
4. Evaluate $f(\mathbf{x}^{(k)} + \Delta\mathbf{x}^{(k)})$ and hence r_k.
5. Update trust region size.
   If,

$$r_k < 0.25, \qquad \text{set } h_{k+1} = \frac{\|\Delta\mathbf{x}^{(k)}\|}{4},$$

$$r_k > 0.75, \qquad \text{set } h_k = \|\Delta\mathbf{x}^{(k)}\|, \qquad h_{k+1} = 2h_k.$$

   Else, set $h_{k+1} = h_k$.
6. Determine new point:

$$\text{If } r_k \leq 0, \qquad \text{set } \mathbf{x}^{(k+1)} = \mathbf{x}^{(k)}, \qquad \text{set } k = k+1. \text{ Return to step 3}$$

$$\Rightarrow f(\mathbf{x}^{(k)} + \Delta\mathbf{x}^{(k)}) > f(\mathbf{x}^{(k)}).$$

   Else update:

$$\mathbf{x}^{(k+1)} = \mathbf{x}^{(k)} + \Delta\mathbf{x}^{(k)}, \qquad \text{set } k = k+1. \text{ Return to step 2.}$$

Trust region algorithms are very robust and not sensitive to scaling, and this is their great advantage.

Problems

1. Solve by finding all the basic feasible solutions.
   Minimize

$$f = 2x_1 - x_2,$$

   subject to the constraints:

$$-x_1 + 2x_2 \leq 10,$$
$$3x_1 + 2x_2 \leq 17,$$
$$x_1, x_2 \geq 0.$$

   Verify the result graphically.
2. Solve by finding all the basic feasible solutions.
   Minimize

$$f = 5x_1 + 4x_2 - x_3,$$

   subject to the constraints:

$$x_1 + 2x_2 - x_3 \geq 1,$$
$$2x_1 + x_2 + x_3 \geq 3.$$

   Here $x_1, x_2 \geq 0$ and x_3 is unrestricted in sign.

3. Solve using the simplex method.
Minimize

$$f = -x_1 - 2x_2,$$

subject to the constraints:

$$-2x_1 + x_2 \leq 2,$$
$$-x_1 + 2x_2 \leq 9,$$
$$x_1 \leq 3,$$
$$x_1, x_2 \geq 0.$$

4. Minimize using the simplex method

$$f = 3x_1 - 9x_2 + 5x_3 - 6x_4,$$

subject to the constraints:

$$4x_1 + 3x_2 + 5x_3 + 8x_4 \geq 25,$$
$$2x_1 - 7x_2 - 4x_3 - 6x_4 \geq 18,$$
$$x_1, x_2, x_3, x_4 \geq 0.$$

5. Maximize using the simplex method

$$f = 3x_1 - 9x_2 + 5x_3 - 6x_4,$$

subject to the constraints:

$$4x_1 + 3x_2 - 8x_3 + 7x_4 = 11,$$
$$3x_1 + 2x_2 + 7x_3 + 6x_4 \geq 24,$$
$$7x_1 + 4x_2 + 3x_3 + 2x_4 \leq 13,$$
$$x_1, x_2 \geq 0, x_3 \leq 0, \quad x_4 \text{ unrestricted.}$$

6. A refinery uses two different types of crude oil. The light crude costs Rs. 2500 per barrel and the heavy crude costs Rs. 1500 per barrel. The refinery produces petrol, diesel, jet fuel and lubricant oil. The yield per barrel of each type of petroleum product is given below:

	Petrol	**Diesel**	**Jet Fuel**	**Lubricant**
Light crude oil	0.4	0.25	0.22	0.11
Heavy crude oil	0.3	0.35	0.17	0.04

The demand is found to be 10 million barrels of petrol, 8 million barrels of diesel, 4 million barrels of jet fuel and 1 million barrels of lubricant. How much light crude and heavy crude should be purchased by the refinery?

7. A farmer has the choice of producing different vegetables on his 20-acre farm. The yield per acre of different crops, labour man days required and expenses on seed, fertilizers and pesticides are given below:

	Yield/ acre (Rs.)	**Labour man days/ acre**	**Seed cost/ acre (Rs.)**	**Fertilizer cost/ acre (Rs.)**	**Pesticide cost/ area (Rs.)**	**Irrigation cost/ area (Rs.)**
Tomato	20,000	6	300	30	80	100
Capsicum	14,400	7	500	50	400	150
Cucumber	16,000	5	200	15	240	200
Cauliflower	24,000	8	250	40	325	125
Potato	7,000	4	185	7	35	80

A total of 750 man days of labour is available. Assuming there are no other expenses, find the optimal crop combination to maximize profit.

8. Minimize

$$f(\mathbf{x}) = x_1^2 + 15x_2^2 - x_1x_2,$$

subject to the constraint:

$$x_1 + x_2 - 4 = 0.$$

Use the penalty method starting from (1, 1).

9. Minimize

$$f(\mathbf{x}) = x_1^2 + 15x_2^2 - x_1x_2,$$

subject to the constraint:

$$x_1 + x_2 - 4 = 0.$$

Use the exact penalty method starting from (1, 1). Use only function evaluations using the Monte Carlo method to get the optimal point.

10. Minimize

$$f(\mathbf{x}) = x_1^2 + 15x_2^2 - x_1x_2,$$

subject to the constraint:

$$x_1 + x_2 - 4 \geq 0.$$

Use the barrier method starting from (2, 3).

11. Minimize

$$f = e^{3x_1+4x_2},$$

subject to the constraint:

$$h = x_1^2 + x_2^2 - 1 = 0.$$

Use the penalty or barrier methods. Use starting point of $(-1, -1)$.

12. Minimize

$$f(\mathbf{x}) = x_1^2 + (x_2+3)^2,$$

subject to the constraint:

$$x_2 \geq e^{2x_1}.$$

Select any starting point and do two iterations of the barrier method.

13. Solve using SLP.
Minimize

$$f = (x_1 - 3)^2 + (x_2 - 3)^2,$$

subject to the constraints:

$$x_1 + x_2 \leq 6,$$
$$x_1, x_2 \geq 0.$$

14. Solve using SLP.
Minimize

$$f = 2x_1 - x_2^{1.5},$$

subject to the constraints:

$$-x_1 + 2x_2 \leq 10,$$
$$3x_1 + 2x_2 \leq 17,$$
$$x_1, x_2 \geq 0.$$

15. Solve using QP.
Minimize

$$f = (x_1 - 1)^2 + (x_2 - 1)^2,$$

subject to the constraints:

$$x_1 + x_4 - 5 \leq 0,$$
$$x_1 - x_2 - 2 \geq 0.$$

16. Solve using QP.
Minimize

$$f = x_1^2 + x_2^2 - 2x_1 - 2x_2,$$

subject to the constraints:

$$x_1 + x_4 - 5 \leq 0,$$
$$2 - x_1 \leq 0,$$
$$x_1, x_2 \geq 0.$$

17. Minimize

$$f(\mathbf{x}) = x_1^2 + (x_2 + 3)^2,$$

subject to the constraint:

$$x_2 \geq e^{2x_1}.$$

Start from (0, 0) and perform two iterations of the CSD method.

18. Minimize the Rosenbrock function using the trust region method:

$$f(\mathbf{x}) = 100(x_2 - x_1^2)^2 + (1 - x_1^2)^2.$$

Start from (3, 2) and perform two iterations.

19. Minimize the following function using the trust region method:

$$f(\mathbf{x}) = x_1^2 + 2x_2^2 + 3x_3^2 + e^{-x_1 - x_2 - x_3}.$$

Perform two iterations starting from (0, 0, 0).

20. Using the trust region method, minimize the function f:

$$f(\mathbf{x}) = (x_1 - 2)^4 + (x_2 - 1)^2.$$

Start from (1, 0) and perform two iterations.

21. Write a computer program to implement the QP algorithm. Using this program, minimize f:

$$f(\mathbf{x}) = (x_1 - 1)^2 + (x_2 + 2)^2 + (x_3 - 2)^2,$$

subject to the constraints:

$$2x_1 + 3x_2 - 1 = 0,$$
$$x_1 + x_2 + 2x_3 - 4 = 0.$$

22. Write a program for the CSD method. Using this program, minimize f:

$$f(\mathbf{x}) = 3x_1^2 - 2x_1x_2 + 5x_2^2 + 8x_2 + 10,$$

subject to

$$x_1^2 - x_2^2 + 8x_2 \leq 16.$$

23. Write a computer program to implement the trust region method. Using this program, minimize

$$f(\mathbf{x}) = (3x_1^2 + 12x_2^2 + 10x_1)^2 + (24x_1x_2 + 4x_2^2 + 3)^2.$$

Start from $(-1, 1)$.

24. Solve the following problem using your CSD program; minimize f:

$$f(\mathbf{x}) = (x_1 - 28)^2 + x_2^2,$$

subject to the constraints:

$$x_1 + x_2 \leq 16,$$

$$x_1 + 2x_2 \leq 28,$$

$$x_1, x_2 \geq 0.$$

Start from $(0, 0)$.

6 Response Surface Method

With the increasing power of computers and advances in computational sciences, simulation codes for physical phenomenon have become very large and complex. It is a difficult and cumbersome task to link optimization algorithms to these codes. Furthermore, today, much of the work of analysis is done using commercial or proprietary software which are even more difficult to link with optimization software. Some researchers have advocated creation of approximate models of the computer codes which can then be used easily with optimization algorithms. Such a process decouples the analysis problem and the optimization problem and is becoming popular for the application of optimization in industry.

6.1 Response Surfaces

One approach to simplify an optimization problem is to create a *metamodel*. A metamodel is a model of a model. The metamodel therefore replaces the typical computational analysis by multidimensional functional approximations of the objective functions and constraints, as shown in Figure 6.1. The computational analyses are typically physics-based models which solve the governing partial differential equations of the problem with appropriate initial and boundary conditions. The metamodel, on the other hand, is a mathematical approximation of the computational analysis. Typically, various mathematical functions can be used for these approximations such as polynomials, sigmoid functions and radial basis functions. The response surface approximations consist of polynomial approximations of the computational analysis and are the most widely used metamodels in optimization.

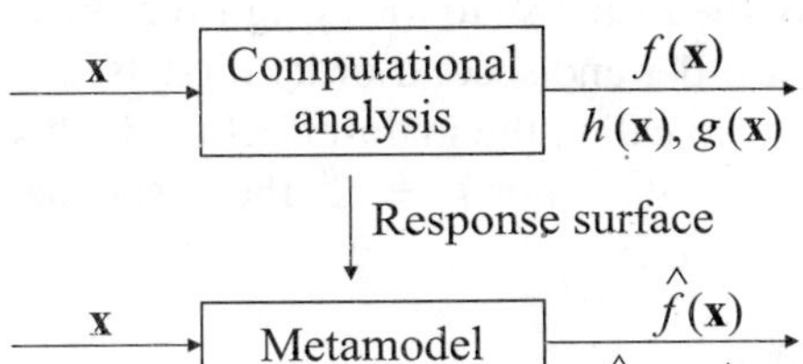

Figure 6.1 *The metamodel of a computational analysis for optimization applications*

A good metamodel provides reasonably accurate estimates, $\hat{f}(\mathbf{x})$, $\hat{h}(\mathbf{x})$ and $\hat{g}(\mathbf{x})$, of the objective functions and constraints.

Response surface methods (RSM) are a collection of statistical and mathematical techniques which were originally created for developing, improving and optimizing products and processes.[10] These methods are used extensively in the industry, particularly where several input variables influence some performance measure or quality characteristic. The performance measure or quality characteristic is called the *response*. The response is thus a function of the inputs and the relationship is typically influenced by tests or experiments. That is the reason why some of the methods we will study are also called *design of experiments* or DOE methods.

An RSM is also closely linked to quality control, since quality metrics can be used as a response. In this work, we are interested in the use of RSM for optimization. However, a general introduction to RSM is useful for motivating the application to optimization.

When a graph of the response is plotted against the inputs, we obtain a response surface. Use of such response surfaces either graphically (for 2–3 inputs) or analytically (for more than 3 inputs) for performing product or process improvement or optimization is called the response surface method. The response surface seeks to find a functional relationship between an output variable and a set of input variables:

$$y = f(\xi_1, \xi_2, \xi_3, \ldots, \xi_k) + \varepsilon. \tag{6.1}$$

Here f is an unknown function. The term ε represents the error in the approximation. In an RSM, the error, ε, is treated as a statistical error, with a normal distribution, zero mean and variance σ^2. For optimization problems, $\xi_1, \xi_2, \ldots, \xi_k$ represent natural design variables as they are expressed in units of measurement such as metres. *In this chapter, we use the notation k* **for the number of design variables in place of *n* which we had used in the earlier chapters**. This is because k is widely used in response surface literature and allows the reader to understand the nomenclature regarding the factorial designs we will discuss later in this chapter. In RSM work, natural variables are converted into coded variables, $x_1, x_2, \ldots, x_k$, using a linear transformation. The coded variables are a normalized form of natural variables where each variable has a range from $(-1, 1)$ for its low and high values.

Thus $\boldsymbol{\eta} = f(x_1, x_2, \ldots, x_k)$ is the function we seek to approximate. The true form of the response function f is unknown. Therefore, an approximation needs to be made about its nature. A natural choice is to use low-order polynomials to approximate the function. These low-order models capture the basic slopes and curvature of the function and provide an idea about the sensitivity of the response to the design variables. The simplest polynomial approximations are the first-order and second-order models.

The first-order model is also called the main-effect model because it captures the slope of the function and its mean value. For $k = 2$, the first-order model is defined by the following equation:

$$\eta = \beta_0 + \beta_1 x_1 + \beta_2 x_2. \tag{6.2}$$

The second-order model captures the curvature and interaction effects along with the slopes. For $k = 2$, the second-order model is given below:

$$\eta = \beta_0 + \beta_1 x_1 + \beta_2 x_2 + \beta_{12} x_1 x_2 + \beta_{11}^2 x_1^2 + \beta_{22}^2 x_2^2. \tag{6.3}$$

Recall that most nonlinear functions can be approximated by a quadratic approximation in a small neighbourhood. The second-order model is widely used in RSM.

In general, a first-order response surface can be written as follows:

$$\eta = \beta_0 + \beta_1 x_1 + \beta_2 x_2 + \cdots + \beta_k x_k \tag{6.4}$$

and a second-order response surface can be written as shown below:

$$\eta = \beta_0 + \sum_{j=1}^{k} \beta_j x_j + \sum_{j=1}^{k} \beta_{jj} x_j^2 + \sum_{i<j}\sum \beta_{ij} x_i x_j. \tag{6.5}$$

There is a close connection between RSM and linear regression analysis. Consider the first-order response surface:

$$y = \beta_0 + \beta_1 x_1 + \beta_2 x_2 + \cdots + \beta_k x_k + \varepsilon. \tag{6.6}$$

Here the βs are unknown parameters. We must collect data linking y and $\mathbf{x}$ at several points for the system we are studying. Regression analysis is a branch of statistical model building that uses these data to estimate the βs. The model $y = \beta_0 + \beta_1 x_1 + \beta_2 x_2 + \cdots + \beta_k x_k + \varepsilon$ is also called a *multiple linear regression model* with k regression variables (x_j). The parameters β_j, $j = 0, 1, 2, \ldots, k$ are called *regression coefficients*. The model is a hyper-plane in k-dimensional space of the regression variables (x_j).

More complex models can still be analysed by multiple linear regression techniques. Consider the second-order response surface:

$$y = \beta_0 + \beta_1 x_1 + \beta_2 x_2 + \beta_{11} x_1^2 + \beta_{22} x_2^2 + \beta_{12} x_1 x_2 + \varepsilon. \tag{6.7}$$

We define variables $x_3 = x_1^2$, $x_4 = x_2^2$, $x_5 = x_1 x_2$ in (6.7). Since the regression variables x_1 and x_2 are known at a given point, x_3, x_4 and x_5 can be easily calculated. Then (6.7) can be written as follows:

$$y = \beta_0 + \beta_1 x_1 + \beta_2 x_2 + \beta_{11} x_3 + \beta_{22} x_4 + \beta_{12} x_5 + \varepsilon. \tag{6.8}$$

In general, any regression model that is linear in *parameters* β is a linear regression model, regardless of the shape of the response surface it generates.

6.2 The Least-Squares Method

The method of *least squares* is typically used to estimate the regression coefficients in a multiple linear regression model. If we have n different sets of points where the response can be obtained, the data can be put in the following form:

$$\begin{array}{ccccc} y & x_1 & x_2 & \cdots & x_k \\ y_1 & x_{11} & x_{12} & \cdots & x_{1k} \\ y_2 & x_{21} & x_{22} & \cdots & x_{2k} \\ \vdots & & & & \\ y_n & x_{n1} & x_{n2} & \cdots & x_{nk} \end{array} \tag{6.9}$$

To fit a first-order RSM through this data, one equation can be obtained for each i and the output can be written as given below:

$$\begin{aligned} y_i &= \beta_0 + \beta_1 x_{i1} + \beta_2 x_{i2} + \cdots + \beta_k x_{ik} + \varepsilon_i \\ &= \beta_0 + \sum_{j=1}^{k} \beta_j x_{ij} + \varepsilon_i, \qquad i = 1, 2, \ldots, n. \end{aligned} \tag{6.10}$$

There are n equations and k unknown regression coefficients. The least-square error is given by the equation

$$L = \sum_{i=1}^{n} \varepsilon_i^2 = \sum_{i=1}^{n} \left(y_i - \beta_0 - \sum_{j=1}^{k} \beta_j x_{ij} \right)^2. \tag{6.11}$$

To find the βs, the function L must be minimized with respect to the βs. Differentiating (6.11) with respect to β_0 yields the following equations:

$$\left.\frac{\partial L}{\partial \beta_0}\right|_{b_0 b_1, \ldots, b_k} = -2 \sum_{i=1}^{n} \left(y_i - b_0 - \sum_{j=1}^{k} b_j x_{ij} \right) = 0, \qquad j = 1, 2, \ldots, k. \tag{6.12}$$

Here $b_0, b_1, \ldots, b_k$ are called the least square estimators. Again, differentiating (6.11) with respect to β_j yields the following:

$$\left.\frac{\partial L}{\partial \beta_j}\right|_{b_0 b_1, \ldots, b_k} = -2 \sum_{i=1}^{n} \left(y_i - b_0 - \sum_{j=1}^{k} b_j x_{ij} \right) x_{ij} = 0, \qquad j = 1, 2, \ldots, k. \tag{6.13}$$

Solving (6.12) and (6.13), we get $b_0, b_1, b_2, \ldots, b_k$. The fitted model is then:

$$\hat{y} = b_0 + b_1 x_1 + b_2 x_2 + \cdots + b_k x_k. \tag{6.14}$$

The least-squares procedure can also be expressed in a compact matrix form. This is described in the next section.

6.2.1 Matrix form

In matrix form, (6.10) can be written as

$$\mathbf{y} = \boldsymbol{X\beta} + \boldsymbol{\varepsilon}, \tag{6.15}$$

where the underlying vectors are given as

$$\begin{aligned} \mathbf{y} &= (y_1, y_2, \ldots, y_n)^{\mathrm{T}}, \\ \boldsymbol{\beta} &= (\beta_0, \beta_1, \ldots, \beta_k)^{\mathrm{T}}, \\ \boldsymbol{\varepsilon} &= (\varepsilon_1, \varepsilon_2, \ldots, \varepsilon_n)^{\mathrm{T}}, \end{aligned} \tag{6.16}$$

and,

$$\mathbf{X} = \begin{bmatrix} 1 & x_{11} & x_{12} & \cdots & x_{1k} \\ 1 & x_{21} & x_{22} & \cdots & x_{2k} \\ \vdots & & & & \\ 1 & x_{n1} & x_{n2} & & x_{nk} \end{bmatrix}. \tag{6.17}$$

The least-squares error is obtained from the following equation:

$$L = \sum_{i=1}^{n} \varepsilon_i^2 = \boldsymbol{\varepsilon}^{\mathrm{T}}\boldsymbol{\varepsilon} = (\mathbf{y} - \boldsymbol{X\beta})^{\mathrm{T}}(\mathbf{y} - \boldsymbol{X\beta}) = (\mathbf{y}^{\mathrm{T}} - \boldsymbol{\beta}^{\mathrm{T}}\mathbf{X}^{\mathrm{T}})(\mathbf{y} - \boldsymbol{X\beta}). \tag{6.18}$$

Expanding (6.18) yields

$$L = \mathbf{y}^{\mathrm{T}}\mathbf{y} - \mathbf{y}^{\mathrm{T}}\mathbf{X}\boldsymbol{\beta} - \boldsymbol{\beta}^{\mathrm{T}}\mathbf{X}^{\mathrm{T}}\mathbf{y} + \boldsymbol{\beta}^{\mathrm{T}}\mathbf{X}^{\mathrm{T}}\mathbf{X}\boldsymbol{\beta}. \tag{6.19}$$

Now, the third term on the right-hand side of (6.19) can be written as

$$(\boldsymbol{\beta}^{\mathrm{T}}\mathbf{X}^{\mathrm{T}}\mathbf{y})^{\mathrm{T}} = (\mathbf{X}^{\mathrm{T}}\mathbf{y})^{\mathrm{T}}\boldsymbol{\beta}^{\mathrm{T}^{\mathrm{T}}} = \mathbf{y}^{\mathrm{T}}\mathbf{X}\boldsymbol{\beta} = \text{scalar}.$$

Here we have used the fact that all terms in (6.19) are scalars and that taking the transpose of a scalar does not change it. Equation (6.19) can therefore be written as given below:

$$L = \mathbf{y}^{\mathrm{T}}\mathbf{y} - 2\boldsymbol{\beta}^{\mathrm{T}}\mathbf{X}^{\mathrm{T}}\mathbf{y} + \boldsymbol{\beta}^{\mathrm{T}}\mathbf{X}^{\mathrm{T}}\mathbf{X}\boldsymbol{\beta}. \tag{6.20}$$

To find the optimal value of the regression coefficients $\boldsymbol{\beta}$, set

$$\left.\frac{\partial L}{\partial \boldsymbol{\beta}}\right|_b = -2\mathbf{X}^{\mathrm{T}}\mathbf{y} + 2\mathbf{X}^{\mathrm{T}}\mathbf{X}\mathbf{b} = 0. \tag{6.21}$$

Solving (6.21) yields:

$$\mathbf{X}^{\mathrm{T}}\mathbf{X}\mathbf{b} = \mathbf{X}^{\mathrm{T}}\mathbf{y}, \tag{6.22}$$

$$\mathbf{b} = (\mathbf{X}^{\mathrm{T}}\mathbf{X})^{-1}\mathbf{X}^{\mathrm{T}}\mathbf{y}. \tag{6.23}$$

Equation (6.23) can be easily evaluated numerically. The fitted regression model is the following:

$$\hat{\mathbf{y}} = \mathbf{X}\mathbf{b}, \tag{6.24}$$

and the residual is

$$\boldsymbol{\varepsilon} = \mathbf{y} - \hat{\mathbf{y}}. \tag{6.25}$$

It is a good idea to study the fitted RSM to ensure that it provides an adequate approximation to the objective function. For some simple problems with two or three design variables and a fast simulation code, we can plot the actual function values and the response surface to see the accuracy of fit. For most real problems, such a comparison is not possible. In those cases, analysis of residuals provides important information to check model adequacy. In particular, they should approximately satisfy the requirement of a normal distribution.

Example 6.1 An equation of the form $y = a + (b/x)$ is used to provide a best fit, in the sense of least squares, for the following points:

$$(x, y) = (1, 6), (3, 10) \text{ and } (6, 2).$$

Determine a and b.

Solution: Minimize

$$f = \sum_{i=1}^{3}\left(\left(a + \frac{b}{x_i}\right) - y_i\right)^2$$

$$= \left(\left(a + \frac{b}{1}\right) - 6\right)^2 + \left(\left(a + \frac{b}{3}\right) - 10\right)^2 + \left(\left(a + \frac{b}{6}\right) - 2\right)^2$$

$$= 3a^2 + \frac{41}{36}b^2 + 3ab - \frac{58}{3}b - 36a + 140.$$

To minimize f,

$$\frac{\partial f}{\partial a} = 6a + 3b - 36 = 0, \qquad \frac{\partial f}{\partial b} = \frac{41}{18}b + 3a - \frac{58}{3} = 0.$$

or $\quad a^* = 5.1428, \qquad b^* = 1.7143, \qquad f^* = 30.86.$

This yields $y(x) = 5.1428 + (1.7143/x)$, which is the desired least-squares fit through the three points.

6.3 Two-Level Factorial Designs

A very important issue in the design of experiments is the appropriate selection of points (values of design variables) where the experiment should be conducted so that a good approximate model can be developed. For a *main-effect model,* a fewer number of experiments need to be conducted than for a second-order model. The two-level factorial designs are useful for developing the main-effect models.[10]

If there are k factors of interest, each is evaluated at two levels (low and high). Thus, each such design has 2^k experimental trials or rows. These are called 2^k factorial designs. Consider the case with two design variables: x_1 and x_2. Such a design is called a 2^2 factorial design and is shown in Figure 6.2. The design has four points represented by the corners of the square in Figure 6.2. For example, *low* can represent a 15 percent reduction in the design variable and *high* can represent a 15 percent increase in the design variable. We can intuitively see that if we wanted to obtain a basic idea of the system behaviour by performing experiments, it would be better to perform them at these four points than at some randomly selected four points shown by the empty circles in Figure 6.2. The DOE approach therefore provides a systematic way of selecting points where experiments need to be run or simulations need to be performed.

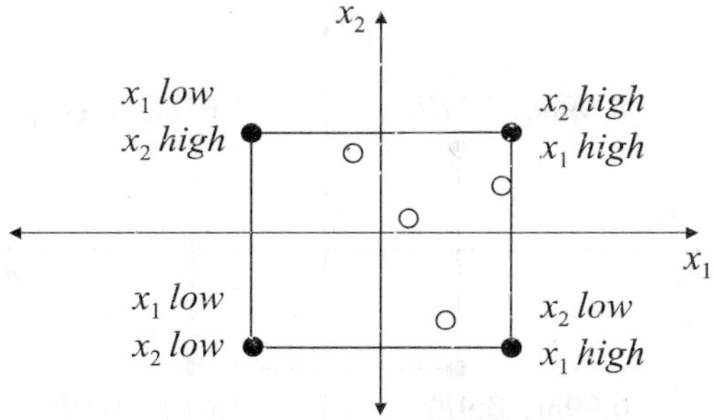

Figure 6.2 *Two-level factorial design for two-dimensional space (shaded circles) versus randomly selected points (empty circles)*

Example 6.2 To understand the application to a physical system, consider the problem of finding the natural frequency of a uniform cantilever beam shown in Figure 6.3. The beam frequencies can be solved using the governing partial differential equation:

$$EI\frac{\partial^4 w}{\partial x^4} + m\frac{\partial^2 w}{\partial^2 t} = 0,$$

with the given boundary conditions, using $w(x, t) = W(x)e^{i\omega t}$.

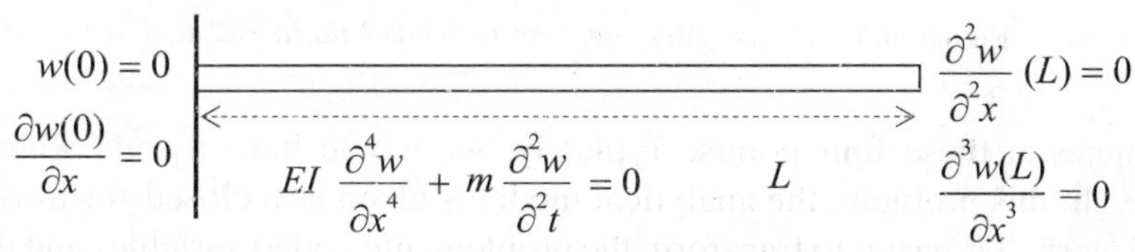

Figure 6.3 *Mathematical model for calculating the frequency of a cantilever beam*

Here EI is the flexural stiffness of the beam and m is the mass per unit length. The two variables (EI, m) are the design variables for the beam, and we wish to find a *metamodel* by performing an experiment or running a code which gives us the first natural frequency of the beam. It is given that the beam's fundamental natural frequency can be obtained using

$$\omega = 3.516\sqrt{\frac{EI}{mL^4}}.$$

Fit a main effects model using the 2^k design. Select perturbations of $\pm 10\%$ for EI and $\pm 1\%$ for m about a baseline design ($EI_0 = 400\,\text{Nm}^2$, $m_0 = 1.8816\,\text{kg/m}$). The length L of the beam is 1.504 m. Compare the predicted values at the 2^k points and at the centre point.

Solution: To find a 2^k design, we need four points. Choosing perturbations of 10 per cent for EI and 1 per cent for m about a baseline design (EI_0, m_0), we get the following natural variables: $(1.10EI_0, 1.01m)$, $(1.10EI_0, 0.99m)$, $(0.90EI_0, 1.01m)$ and $(0.90EI_0, 0.99m_0)$. These designs correspond to the points *(high, high), (high, low), (low, high)* and *(low, low)* in Figure 6.2, respectively, and are shown in Figure 6.4.

We have two possibilities: we could make four different beams and measure the frequencies, or we could write a code or develop an analytical model to predict

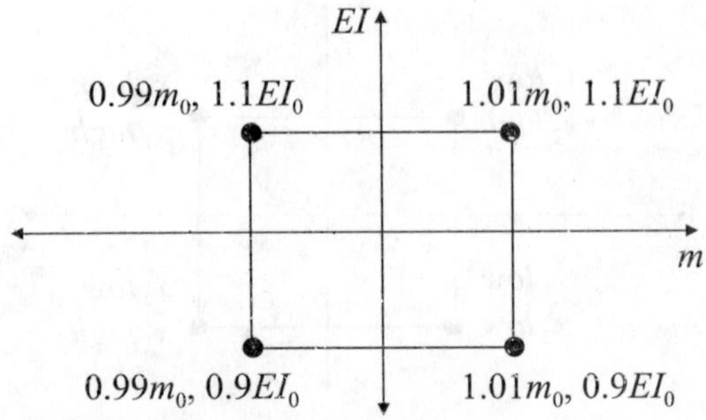

Figure 6.4 *Physical variables for the two-level factorial design and beam frequency problem*

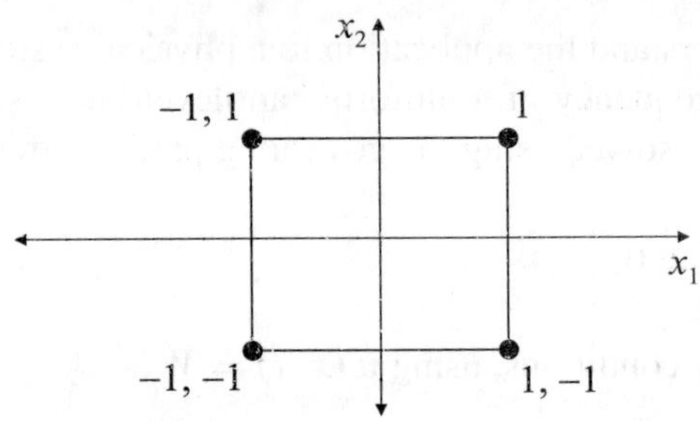

Figure 6.5 *Coded variables for two-level factorial design*

the frequencies at these four points. Typically, we would have a code which gives the frequencies. In this problem, the analytical model is given as a closed-form solution.

In RSM work, it is easier to transform the problem into coded variables and then solve it. The coded variables for the two-level factorial design for two design variables are shown in Figure 6.5. We want to transform the physical variables to coded variables such that

$$x_1 = am + b,$$

$$x_2 = cEI + d.$$

Here, a, b, c and d are constants which we need to find. Comparing the factorial points in Figures 6.4 and 6.5, we can write four equations:

$$1 = 1.01am_0 + b,$$

$$-1 = 0.99am_0 + b,$$

$$1 = 1.1cEI_0 + d,$$

$$-1 = 0.9cEI_0 + d.$$

Solving these four equations for the four constants, yields the relations between the physical variables and coded variables:

$$x_1 = \frac{100}{m_0}m - 100,$$

$$x_2 = \frac{10}{EI_0}EI - 10.$$

We next find the value of the frequency ω at all the factorial points. These are calculated and shown in the table.

Number	Physical points	Coded points	Frequency ω
1	$(1.01m_0, 1.1EI_0)$	(1, 1)	$3.516\sqrt{\frac{1.1EI_0}{1.01m_0L^4}} = 23.6515$
2	$(1.01m_0, 0.9EI_0)$	(1, −1)	$3.516\sqrt{\frac{0.9EI_0}{1.01m_0L^4}} = 21.3935$
3	$(0.99m_0, 0.9EI_0)$	(−1, −1)	$3.516\sqrt{\frac{0.9EI_0}{0.99m_0L^4}} = 21.6086$
4	$(0.99m_0, 1.1EI_0)$	(−1, 1)	$3.516\sqrt{\frac{1.1EI_0}{0.99m_0L^4}} = 23.888$

Now, we want to fit a main-effect model using these data:

$$\hat{\omega} = b_0 + b_1x_1 + b_2x_2.$$

This can be written in matrix form as follows:

$$\boldsymbol{\omega} = \mathbf{Xb}.$$

The form of the above matrices can be written out explicitly:

$$\boldsymbol{\omega} = \begin{Bmatrix} 23.6515 \\ 21.3935 \\ 21.6086 \\ 23.888 \end{Bmatrix}, \qquad \mathbf{X} = \begin{bmatrix} 1 & 1 & 1 \\ 1 & 1 & -1 \\ 1 & -1 & -1 \\ 1 & -1 & 1 \end{bmatrix}, \qquad \mathbf{b} = \begin{Bmatrix} b_0 \\ b_1 \\ b_2 \end{Bmatrix}.$$

We can then find the regression coefficients **b** using:

$$\mathbf{b} = (\mathbf{X}^{\mathrm{T}}\mathbf{X})^{-1}\mathbf{X}^{\mathrm{T}}\boldsymbol{\omega}.$$

These matrix manipulations can be easily performed in Matlab, to yield the following solution for **b**:

$$\mathbf{b} = \begin{Bmatrix} 22.6354 \\ -0.1129 \\ 1.1344 \end{Bmatrix}.$$

The main-effects model is thus:

$$\hat{\omega} = 22.6354 - 0.1129x_1 + 1.1344x_2.$$

In terms of physical variables, we can write

$$\hat{\omega} = 22.5814 - 6.0002m + 0.0284EI.$$

The beauty of the response surface method is the ability to reduce relationships between input and output variables into a simple polynomial form.

Let us compare the predictions of the main-effects model at the factorial points and at the centre point. Also, the error in prediction is obtained as follows:

$$\varepsilon = \omega - \hat{\omega}.$$

These calculations are shown below.

Number	Coded points	ω	$\hat{\omega}$	$\varepsilon = \omega - \hat{\omega}$
1	(1, 1)	23.6515	23.6569	−0.0054
2	(1, −1)	21.3935	21.3881	0.0054
3	(−1, −1)	21.6086	21.6125	−0.0039
4	(−1, 1)	23.888	23.8827	0.0053
5	(0, 0)	22.6633	22.6354	0.0279

We see that the error is very much lower at the factorial points used to generate the model and also quite a bit lower at the centre point.

Factorial designs are widely used in experiments involving several factors where it is necessary to investigate the joint effects of the factors on a response variable. The total number of points in such a design in $2 \times 2 \times 2 \cdots \times 2 = 2^k$ and it is therefore called a 2^k design.

For an optimization problem, the experiments are replaced by function evaluations which can be considered to be numerical experiments. The 2^k design is useful at the start of a response surface study where screening experiments should be performed to identify the important design variable. The 2^k design is a basic building block used to create other response surface designs, as we will see later in this chapter. An example is used to demonstrate the basic concepts behind the 2^k design (adapted from Montgomery and Myers 1995).

Example 6.3 Consider the viscosity of a fluid which depends on two design variables, (1) reactant concentration and (2) the feed rate. Let the reactant concentration be design variable A, and let the two levels of interest be 15 per cent and 20 per cent. The feed rate is design variable B, with the low level being 20 kg/h and the high level being 30 kg/h. We want to generate a main-effect model experimentally.

Solution: The four points where the experiments are conducted can be represented schematically as shown in Figure 6.6. By conducting the experiments, the following data are obtained.

In a real experiment, it is normal to make multiple measurements to remove the effects of noise. This approach is also valid for probabilistic simulations where the material or other physical properties of the system are assumed to be random variables. Response surface approximations can therefore account for uncertainty in the system through a process of smoothing, the way least-squares fits do to data with random scatter. The response surfaces, therefore, lead to more robust designs if performed with probabilistic simulations.

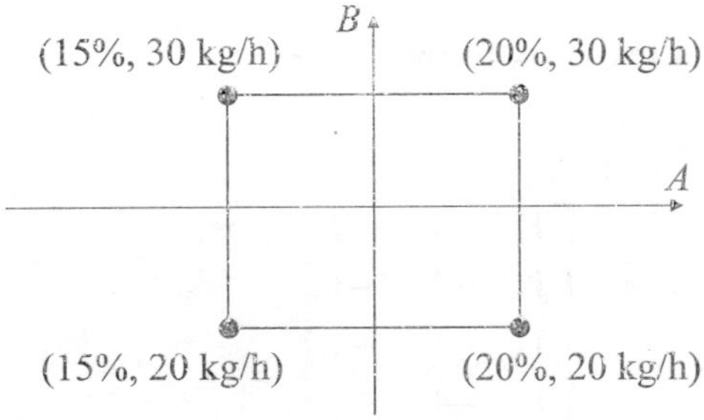

Figure 6.6 *Two-level factorial points with physical variables*

Design variables	Viscosity measurement 1	Viscosity measurement 2	Viscosity measurement 3	Viscosity measurement 4
A low, B low	144.56	147.86	143.87	146.23
A high, B low	156.74	154.23	155.71	156.12
A low, B high	136.21	139.78	142.03	137.36
A high, B high	149.82	153.04	147.43	151.21

Note that at this point physical variables are used in Figure 6.6 and they have different units with different magnitudes. Therefore, the physical variables are typically converted into coded variables. The coded variables are given in Figure 6.5 and form the cornerstone of RSM work. The coded variables are a linear transformation from the physical variables into the $(-1, 1)$ set of numbers. For example, the physical variables are related to the coded variables as follows:

$$A = mx_1 + c, \qquad B = m'x_2 + c'.$$

Comparing Figures 6.5 and 6.6, we can write down the following equations:

$$20 = m(1) + c, \qquad 30 = m'1 + c',$$

$$15 = m(-1) + c, \qquad 20 = m'(-1) + c'.$$

Solving these equations yields the relation between the physical and coded variables.

$$A = 2.5x_1 + 17.5, \qquad B = 5x_2 + 25.$$

Returning to the main problem, let y = viscosity. We want to find a main-effect model relating viscosity to the two design variables. Let us try to fit a first-order model:

$$y = \beta_0 + \beta_1 x_1 + \beta_2 x_2 + \varepsilon.$$

The data points can be put in matrix form:

$$\mathbf{y} = \mathbf{X}\boldsymbol{\beta} + \boldsymbol{\varepsilon}.$$

$$\mathbf{y} = \begin{bmatrix} 144.56 \\ 147.86 \\ 143.87 \\ 146.23 \\ \hline 156.74 \\ 154.23 \\ 155.71 \\ 156.12 \\ \hline 136.21 \\ 139.78 \\ 142.03 \\ 137.36 \\ \hline 149.82 \\ 153.04 \\ 147.43 \\ 151.21 \end{bmatrix}_{16\times 1} \quad \mathbf{X} = \begin{bmatrix} 1 & -1 & -1 \\ 1 & -1 & -1 \\ 1 & -1 & -1 \\ 1 & -1 & -1 \\ \hline 1 & 1 & -1 \\ 1 & 1 & -1 \\ 1 & 1 & -1 \\ 1 & 1 & -1 \\ \hline 1 & -1 & 1 \\ 1 & -1 & 1 \\ 1 & -1 & 1 \\ 1 & -1 & 1 \\ 1 & 1 & 1 \\ 1 & 1 & 1 \\ 1 & 1 & 1 \\ 1 & 1 & 1 \end{bmatrix}_{16\times 3} \quad b = \begin{Bmatrix} b_0 \\ b_1 \\ b_2 \end{Bmatrix}_{3\times 1} \quad \boldsymbol{\varepsilon} = \begin{bmatrix} \varepsilon_1 \\ \varepsilon_2 \\ \varepsilon_3 \\ \varepsilon_4 \\ \varepsilon_5 \\ \varepsilon_6 \\ \varepsilon_7 \\ \varepsilon_8 \\ \varepsilon_9 \\ \varepsilon_{10} \\ \varepsilon_{11} \\ \varepsilon_{12} \\ \varepsilon_{13} \\ \varepsilon_{14} \\ \varepsilon_{15} \\ \varepsilon_{16} \end{bmatrix}_{16\times 1}$$

The least square estimates of β_0, β_1 and β_2 are found from $\mathbf{b} = (\mathbf{X}^{\mathrm{T}}\mathbf{X})^{-1}\mathbf{X}^{\mathrm{T}}\mathbf{y}$. Doing the necessary matrix algebra in Matlab yields:

$$\begin{Bmatrix} b_0 \\ b_1 \\ b_2 \end{Bmatrix} = \begin{Bmatrix} 147.6375 \\ 5.4000 \\ -3.0275 \end{Bmatrix}.$$

The fitted regression model:

$$\hat{y} = 147.6375 + 5.4x_1 - 3.0275x_2.$$

Plotting this yields the response surface in Figure 6.7 which graphically shows the main effects of the design variables on the system response, which is viscosity for this problem. The main-effect model immediately tells us that viscosity increases as reactant concentration increases and feed rate decreases. A fitted surface such as this can be used to determine the direction of potential improvement for an objective function. The main-effect model clearly shows that the best way to minimize viscosity is to decrease reactant concentration and increase the feed rate. Also note that the RSM approach has accounted for the noise and randomness in the data in the response surface.

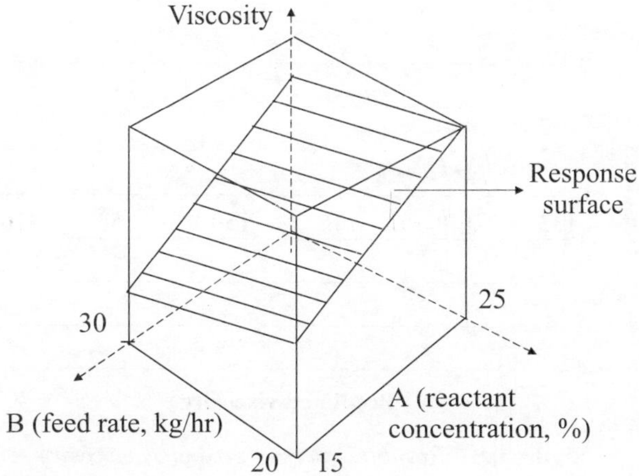

Figure 6.7 *Main-effects model or first-order response surface*

6.3.1 Residual analysis

Once a response surface is obtained, it is important to check how well the function approximates the underlying data. The errors given by ε provide a way to further investigate the response surface using *residual analysis*. The response surface model can be used to generate data at each of the sixteen points considered in the previous example, and then the error at these points between the response surface predictions and the actual data can be found. For example, when reactant concentration is at the low level ($x_1 = -1$) and feed rate is also at the low level ($x_2 = -1$), the predicted viscosity is given by:

$$\hat{y} = 147.6375 + 5.4(-1) - 3.0275(-1) = 145.265.$$

From y_1, y_2, y_3, y_4, the first four observations can be used to set the following residuals:

$$\varepsilon_1 = 144.56 - 145.265 = 0.705,$$

$$\varepsilon_2 = 147.86 - 145.265 = 2.595,$$

$$\varepsilon_3 = 143.87 - 145.265 = -1.395,$$

$$\varepsilon_4 = 146.23 - 145.265 = 0.965.$$

Similarly, other residuals can be obtained:

$$\varepsilon_5 = 0.675, \quad \varepsilon_6 = -1.835, \quad \varepsilon_7 = -0.355,$$

$$\varepsilon_8 = -055, \quad \varepsilon_9 = -3.000, \quad \varepsilon_{10} = 0.57,$$

$$\varepsilon_{11} = 2.82, \quad \varepsilon_{12} = -1.85, \quad \varepsilon_{13} = -0.19,$$

$$\varepsilon_{14} = 3.03, \quad \varepsilon_{15} = -2.58, \quad \varepsilon_{16} = 1.2.$$

A simple check on the residuals is obtained by plotting them with respect to the predicted system response, as shown in Figure 6.8. If the residuals show no particular patterns and are randomly scattered, the residual analysis is satisfactory and the response surface shows no unusual problems. The random scatter suggests that the variance of the original observations

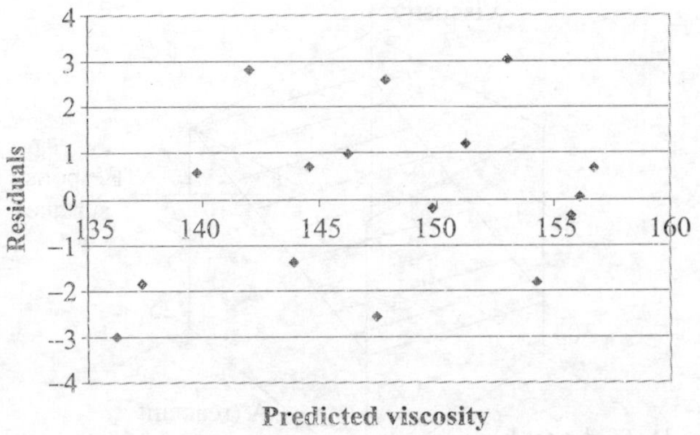

Figure 6.8 *Residuals versus predicted viscosity*

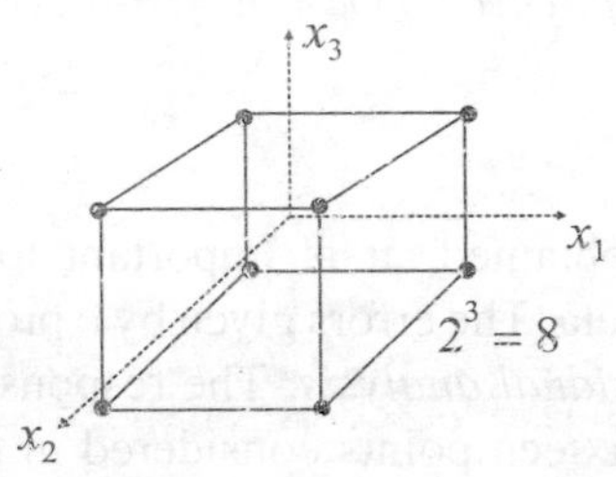

Figure 6.9 *Two-level factorial points in three-dimensional space*

is constant for all values of y. If a distinct pattern is seen, there is a need to transform the response variable y.

In Example 6.3, we looked at a two-dimensional response surface using the 2^2 design. A natural extension of this situation is when we have three design variables, which leads to the 2^3 design. Here the points where the runs need to be performed lie on the corners of a cube (three dimensions) instead of a square as in two dimensions. In general, the 2^k design lies at the corners of a hypercube in k dimensions. Each corner of the cube corresponds to a coded variable where +1 implies *high* and −1 implies *low* in the two-level factorial designs, as shown in Figure 6.9. The eight runs needed for the design in terms of coded variables are given below:

Run	x_1	x_2	x_3
1	−1	−1	−1
2	+1	−1	−1
3	−1	+1	−1
4	+1	+1	−1
5	−1	−1	+1
6	+1	−1	+1
7	−1	+1	+1
8	+1	+1	+1

6.3.2 Single replicate of two-level design

For even a moderate number of design variables k, the total number of runs in a 2^k factorial design is large. This can be observed from:

$$2^1 \rightarrow 2, \quad 2^3 \rightarrow 8, \quad 2^3 \rightarrow 8, \quad 2^4 \rightarrow 16, \quad 2^5 \rightarrow 32, \quad 2^6 \rightarrow 64, \quad 2^7 \rightarrow 128,$$

$$2^8 \rightarrow 256, \quad 2^9 \rightarrow 512, \quad 2^{10} \rightarrow 1024.$$

With ten variables, we need data at 1024 points. Since experimental resources are limited, typically single replicate is often used. For numerical optimization applications of response surfaces, single replicates are sufficient since most engineering problems involve deterministic simulations where different runs of the computer experiment (code) give the same results. However, in some engineering problems, stochastic simulations are used to account for uncertainty in the design variables. The use of response surfaces with multiple replicates is reasonable in such cases to smooth out the randomness in the data and create a more robust design.

6.4 Addition of Centre Points

Two-level factorial designs are useful in the case of a primarily linear relationship with respect to the design variables. The 2^k design can work quite well even when the linearity assumption holds very approximately, because it gives the main effects and sensitivity. By adding centre points to the 2^k design, however, we can get some curvature effects.[10] These points consist of n_c replicates at the centre point ($x_i = 0, i = 1, 2, \ldots, k$) and result in $2^k + n_c$ points where experiments or simulations are needed. For a two-dimensional problem, this can be shown in Figure 6.10.

Also, when we add centre points, we can consider fitting a second-order response surface. Of course, only one centre run is sufficient for deterministic simulations. A first-order model of the form,

$$y = \beta_0 + \beta_1 x_1 + \beta_2 x_2 + \cdots + \beta_k x_k + \varepsilon,$$

has $k + 1$ regression coefficients which need to be determined. To determine them to a good level of accuracy, we should have more number of points where the experiment is run

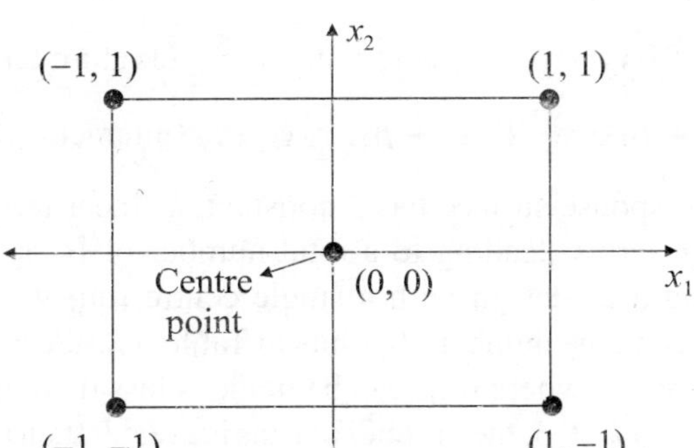

Figure 6.10 *Addition of centre point(s) to the 2^k design*

Table 6.1 *Calculation of first-order response surface in 2^k factorial design*

k	Number of regression coefficients	Number of runs
2	3	4
3	4	8
4	5	16
5	6	32
6	7	64
7	8	128
8	9	256
9	10	512
10	11	1024

compared to the number of regression coefficients. These are shown for different values of k in Table 6.1 for the two-level factorial design.

It can be seen that the 2^k design provides enough points to overfit the first-order response surface for values of k equal to and greater than two.

As we have seen, nonlinear objective functions can often be better approximated by quadratic functions in a small neighbourhood. In fact, such approximations based on the Taylor series form the basis of Newtonian methods. It is also possible to get second-order approximations using response surfaces, which tend to be more *global* that the *local* approximations made using the Taylor series. The general second-order response surface can be written as shown below:

$$y = \beta_0 + \sum_{j=1}^{k} \beta_j x_j + \sum_{j=1}^{k} \beta_{jj} x_j^2 + \sum_{i<j}\sum \beta_{ij} x_i x_j, \tag{6.26}$$

and in an expanded form, as follows:

$$\begin{aligned} y = {} & \beta_0 \text{ (constant)} + \beta_1 x_1 + \beta_2 x_2 + \cdots + \beta_k x_k \text{ (linear terms)} \\ & + \beta_{11} x_1^2 + \beta_{22} x_2^2 + \cdots + \beta_{kk} x_k^2 \text{ (square or curvature terms)} \\ & + \beta_{12} x_1 x_2 + \beta_{13} x_1 x_3 + \cdots + \beta_{k-1,k} x_{k-1} x_k \text{ (interaction terms)} + \varepsilon. \end{aligned} \tag{6.27}$$

The second-order response surface has 1 constant, k linear terms, k square terms, and $(k^2 - k)/2$ interaction terms, leading to a total number of $(k+1)(k+2)/2$ regression coefficients. Assuming a 2^k design with a single centre run, we can see the number of regression coefficients and the number of points in Table 6.2. We can see that for $k = 2$ and $k = 3$, the number of points where runs can be made is less than the number of regression coefficients. However, for $k > 3$, the number of runs is greater than the number of regression coefficients and we can overfit the response surfaces. The 2^k design with an added centre point is an efficient approach which captures the basic curvatures in the design space.

Table 6.2 *Calculation of second-order response surface in 2^k factorial design with one centre run*

k	Number of regression coefficients	Number of runs
2	6	4
3	10	9
4	15	17
5	21	33
6	28	65
7	36	129
8	45	257
9	55	513
10	66	1025

6.5 Central Composite Design (CCD)

For most engineering optimization problems, the nonlinearity in functions is so high that some more points are needed beyond the two-level factorial enhanced with a centre run to accurately estimate the curvature. The central composite design is widely used in optimization applications. The CCD design includes the 2^k factorial points, n_c centre runs and $2k$ additional points called the axial points which are shown by the black points in Figure 6.11.[10] The name *axial point* is given because these points lie on the axis. Only one variable (x_1 or x_2) varies at the axial point. Therefore, they do not help in obtaining the interaction terms such as x_1x_2. However, they help in accurate and efficient estimation of the quadratic terms such as x_1^2 and x_2^2, which are very important to get a good second-order

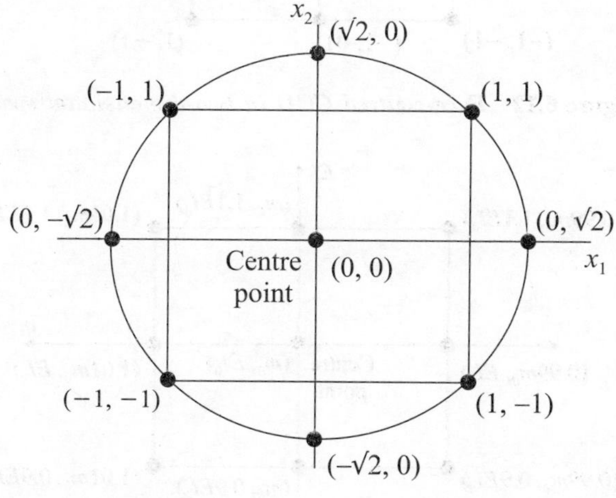

Figure 6.11 *Central composite design (CCD) in two-dimensional space*

surface for optimization applications. The CCD has a total of $2^k + 2k + n_c$ points, which becomes $2^k + 2k + 1$ for the single centre run typical of deterministic simulations.

The centre run provides information about the existence of curvature in the system. The axial terms allow efficient estimation of the quadratic or square terms. The value of the axial distance can be selected ranging from 1 to $\sqrt{k}$. For the 2D problem, $k = 2$ and therefore, $\sqrt{2}$ is selected as the axial distance. The axial points lie on a circle of radius 2 for the two-dimensional problem as shown in Figure 6.11. For a 3D problem, the axial points lie on a sphere of radius 3. In a problem with k design variables, the axial points lie in a hypersphere of radius k.

In some applications of RSM, it is preferable to use the face-centred CCD where the axial distance is 1 and the axial points lie on the surface of the square for the 2D design. The face-centred CCD is shown in Figure 6.12 where the axial points lie on the face of the square (or cube for the case with three design variables). For many optimal design problems, the design variables have move limits which can be converted to the bounds for the FCD design. Moreover, in some physical problems, it may not be possible to run the simulation outside the move limits.

Example 6.4 For the beam frequency problem in Example 6.2, fit a second-order response surface for the fundamental frequency using an FCD. Repeat the problem using CCD.

Solution: The face-centred design involves addition of new axial points as shown in Figure 6.13.

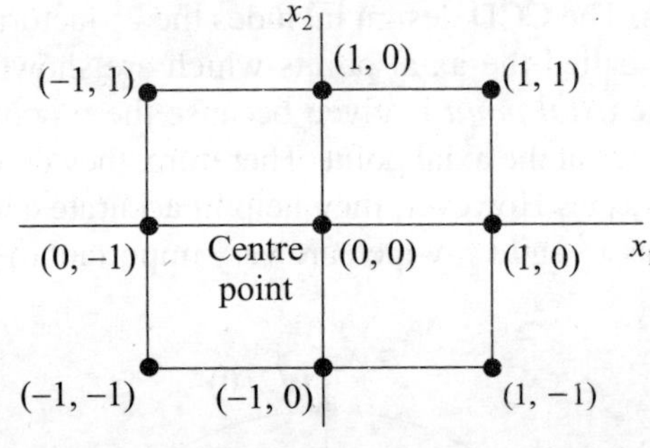

Figure 6.12 *Face-centred CCD in two-dimensional space*

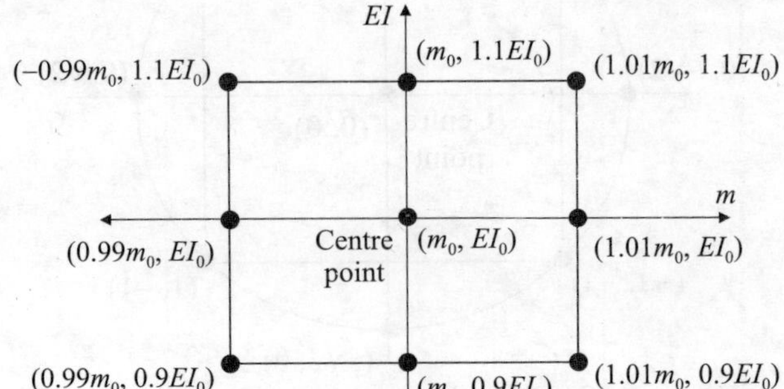

Figure 6.13 *Face-centred design for beam frequency problem*

We need to calculate the values for the frequency at the nine FCD points. These points and the corresponding values for the output are shown below.

Number	Physical points	Coded points	Frequency ω
1	$(1.01m_0, 1.1EI_0)$	$(1, 1)$	$3.516\sqrt{\frac{1.1EI_0}{1.01m_0L^4}} = 23.6515$
2	$(1.01m_0, 0.9EI_0)$	$(1, -1)$	$3.516\sqrt{\frac{0.9EI_0}{1.01m_0L^4}} = 21.3935$
3	$(0.99m_0, 0.9EI_0)$	$(-1, -1)$	$3.516\sqrt{\frac{0.9EI_0}{0.99m_0L^4}} = 21.6086$
4	$(0.99m_0, 1.1EI_0)$	$(-1, 1)$	$3.516\sqrt{\frac{1.1EI_0}{0.99m_0L^4}} = 23.8889$
5	(m_0, EI_0)	$(0, 0)$	$3.516\sqrt{\frac{EI_0}{m_0L^4}} = 22.6633$
6	$(m_0, 1.1EI_0)$	$(0, 1)$	$3.516\sqrt{\frac{1.1EI_0}{m_0L^4}} = 23.7695$
7	$(1.01m_0, EI_0)$	$(1, 0)$	$3.516\sqrt{\frac{EI_0}{1.01m_0L^4}} = 22.5508$
8	$(0.99m_0, EI_0)$	$(-1, 0)$	$3.516\sqrt{\frac{EI_0}{0.99m_0L^4}} = 22.7775$
9	$(m_0, 0.9EI_0)$	$(0, -1)$	$3.516\sqrt{\frac{0.9EI_0}{m_0L^4}} = 21.5003$

Once these data have been obtained, we can fit a second-order response surface through the data. Such a model can be written as shown below:

$$\omega = \beta_0 + \beta_1 x_1 + \beta_2 x_2 + \beta_{11} x_1^2 + \beta_{22} x_2^2 + \beta_{12} x_1 x_2 + \varepsilon.$$

We create the vectors and matrices needed for solving the least-squares problem using the data generated for the FCD points.

$$\boldsymbol{\omega} = \begin{Bmatrix} 23.6515 \\ 21.3935 \\ 21.6086 \\ 23.8889 \\ 22.6633 \\ 23.7695 \\ 22.5508 \\ 22.7775 \\ 21.5003 \end{Bmatrix} \quad \mathbf{X} = \begin{bmatrix} & x_1 & x_2 & x_1^2 & x_2^2 & x_1x_2 \\ 1 & 1 & 1 & 1 & 1 & 1 \\ 1 & 1 & -1 & 1 & 1 & -1 \\ 1 & -1 & -1 & 1 & 1 & 1 \\ 1 & -1 & 1 & 1 & 1 & -1 \\ 1 & 0 & 0 & 0 & 0 & 0 \\ 1 & 0 & 1 & 0 & 1 & 0 \\ 1 & 1 & 0 & 1 & 0 & 0 \\ 1 & -1 & 0 & 1 & 0 & 0 \\ 1 & 0 & -1 & 0 & 1 & 0 \end{bmatrix} \quad \boldsymbol{\beta} = \begin{Bmatrix} \beta_0 \\ \beta_1 \\ \beta_2 \\ \beta_{11} \\ \beta_{22} \\ \beta_{12} \end{Bmatrix}.$$

We solve for the regression coefficients using $\mathbf{b} = (\mathbf{X}^T\mathbf{X})^{-1}\mathbf{X}^T\boldsymbol{\omega}$. The response surface is thus obtained as follows:

$$\hat{\omega} = 22.6634 - 0.1132x_1 + 1.1346x_2 + 0.008x_1^2 - 0.0285x_2^2 - 0.0056x_1x_2.$$

We see that the main effect model derived in Example 6.2,

$$(\hat{\omega} = 22.6354 - 0.1129x_1 + 1.1344x_2),$$

is close to the second-order estimate for the first three terms. However, the presence of the second-order and interaction terms makes the second-order estimate more accurate, especially since the relationship between frequencies and the two design variables considered here is nonlinear.

We next repeat this problem using the CCD. The required data is calculated at the CCD points shown in Figure 6.14. We need to calculate the values for the frequency at the nine CCD points. These points and the corresponding values are shown below.

Number	**Physical points**	**Coded points**	**Frequency** $\boldsymbol{\omega}$
1	$(1.01m_0, 1.1EI_0)$	$(1, 1)$	$3.516\sqrt{\frac{1.1EI_0}{1.01m_0L^4}} = 23.6515$
2	$(1.01m_0, 0.9EI_0)$	$(1, -1)$	$3.516\sqrt{\frac{0.9EI_0}{1.01m_0L^4}} = 21.3935$
3	$(0.99m_0, 0.9EI_0)$	$(-1, -1)$	$3.516\sqrt{\frac{0.9EI_0}{0.99m_0L^4}} = 21.6086$
4	$(0.99m_0, 1.1EI_0)$	$(-1, 1)$	$3.516\sqrt{\frac{1.1EI_0}{0.99m_0L^4}} = 23.8889$
5	(m_0, EI_0)	$(0, 0)$	$3.516\sqrt{\frac{EI_0}{m_0L^4}} = 22.6633$
6	$(m_0, 1.1414EI_0)$	$(0, 1.414)$	$3.516\sqrt{\frac{1.1414EI_0}{m_0L^4}} = 24.2126$
7	$(1.01414m_0, EI_0)$	$(1.414, 0)$	$3.516\sqrt{\frac{EI_0}{1.01414m_0L^4}} = 22.5047$
8	$(0.98586m_0, EI_0)$	$(-1.414, 0)$	$3.516\sqrt{\frac{EI_0}{0.98586m_0L^4}} = 22.8252$
9	$(m_0, 0.8586EI_0)$	$(0, -1.414)$	$3.516\sqrt{\frac{0.8586EI_0}{m_0L^4}} = 21.0000$

Note that only the axial points change for the CCD when compared to the FCD. The CCD permits larger change in the design variables relative to the centre point. We can now fit a second-order response surface through the data. We create the vectors and matrices needed for solving the least-squares problem using the data generated for the CCD points.

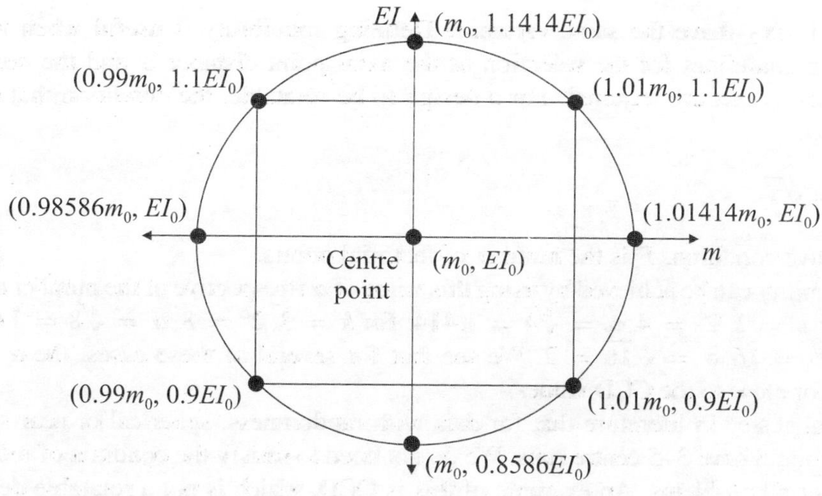

Figure 6.14 *Central composite design for beam frequency problem*

$$
\boldsymbol{\omega} = \begin{Bmatrix} 23.6515 \\ 21.3935 \\ 21.6086 \\ 23.8889 \\ 22.6633 \\ 24.2126 \\ 22.5047 \\ 22.8252 \\ 21.0000 \end{Bmatrix} \quad
\mathbf{X} = \begin{bmatrix} & x_1 & x_2 & x_1^2 & x_2^2 & x_1x_2 \\ 1 & 1 & 1 & 1 & 1 & 1 \\ 1 & 1 & -1 & 1 & 1 & -1 \\ 1 & -1 & -1 & 1 & 1 & 1 \\ 1 & -1 & 1 & 1 & 1 & -1 \\ 1 & 0 & 0 & 0 & 0 & 0 \\ 1 & 0 & 1.414 & 0 & 2 & 0 \\ 1 & 1.414 & 0 & 2 & 0 & 0 \\ 1 & -1.414 & 0 & 2 & 0 & 0 \\ 1 & 0 & -1.414 & 0 & 2 & 0 \end{bmatrix} \quad
\boldsymbol{\beta} = \begin{Bmatrix} \beta_0 \\ \beta_1 \\ \beta_2 \\ \beta_{11} \\ \beta_{22} \\ \beta_{12} \end{Bmatrix}
$$

We solve for the regression coefficients using the equation given below:

$$\mathbf{b} = (\mathbf{X}^{\mathrm{T}}\mathbf{X})^{-1}\mathbf{X}^{\mathrm{T}}\boldsymbol{\omega}.$$

The response surface is obtained:

$$\hat{\omega} = 22.6633 - 0.1132x_1 + 1.1353x_2 + 0.0008x_1^2 - 0.0285x_2^2 - 0.0056x_1x_2.$$

It is relevant to ask at this point if the FCD design or the CCD design is better. To answer this we need to introduce a new concept called rotatability. The *rotatability of the design* establishes that CCD is a better design.

6.5.1 Rotatable design

Rotatability is a quality which ensures that for two points in the design space, $\mathbf{x}_1$ and $\mathbf{x}_2$, which are equidistant from the origin, $\left(\sqrt{\mathbf{x}_1^{\mathrm{T}}\mathbf{x}_1} = \sqrt{\mathbf{x}_2^{\mathrm{T}}\mathbf{x}_2}\right)$, the predicted values

$\hat{y}(\mathbf{x}_1)$ and $\hat{y}(\mathbf{x}_2)$ have the same variance. Defining rotatibility is useful when it comes to making guidelines for the selection of the axial point distance α and the number of centre runs n_c that are required. For a design to be rotatable, the condition that must be satisfied is:

$$\alpha = \sqrt[4]{F}.$$

In the above condition, F is the number of factorial points.

Rotatability can be achieved by using this value of α irrespective of the number of centre runs. For $k = 2$, $2^k = 4, \alpha = \sqrt[4]{4} = 1.414$; for $k = 3$, $2^k = 8, \alpha = \sqrt[4]{8} = 1.682$; for $k = 4$, $2^k = 16, \alpha = \sqrt[4]{16} = 2$. We see that for several of these cases, the α value is identical or close to the CCD values.

It is suggested in literature that for data with randomness, spherical or near-spherical designs should have 3–5 centre runs. We do not need to satisfy the conditon of rotatability exactly for all problems. An example of this is CCD, which is not a rotatable design but comes quite close. Another example, the FCD is not rotatable but is the practical design for many problems. Numerical experiments can be used to determine which designs are best for different functions and design spaces.

Next, the choice of a cube or sphere for the design has to be made by the user. We have seen that spherical designs have the advantage of being rotatable or close to rotatable. In such cases, a cube design can be converted to a sphere by discarding some space, as shown in Figure 6.15. Thereby moving from a square to a circle, the space contained by the shaded grey areas is discarded in order to achieve better rotatability.

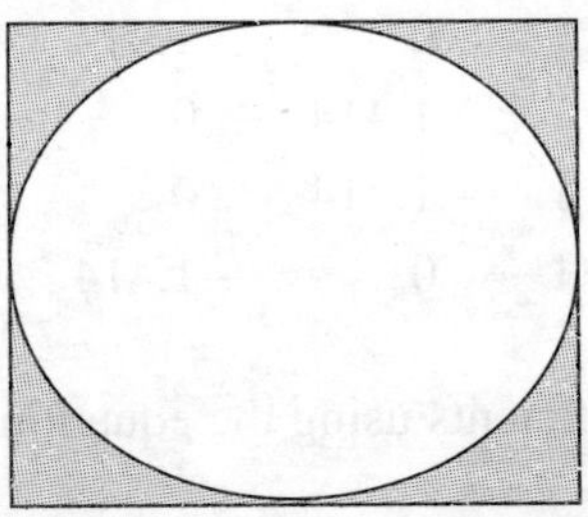

Figure 6.15 *Converting a cube design to a spherical design*

Example 6.5 Consider the beam frequency approximation problem in Examples 6.2 and 6.4. Expand the problem to consider the beam length L as a design variable. Let the *low* and *high* levels be 10 percent from the baseline design. Fit a second-order response surface using CCD points for the design variables EI, m and L.

Solution: For a 10 percent perturbation in L, the corresponding coded variable x_3 can be expressed using a similar equation to that used for EI.

$$x_3 = \frac{10}{L_0}L - 10.$$

The axial points for CCD correspond to $\alpha = 1.732$. The physical variables at these points can be obtained using the linear transformations between the coded and physical variables. The CCD points and the frequency values at these points are shown below.

Number	Physical points	Coded points	Frequency ω
1	$(1.01m_0, 1.1EI_0, 1.1L_0)$	$(1, 1, 1)$	$3.516\sqrt{\frac{1.1EI_0}{1.01m_0(1.1L_0)^4}} = 19.5467$
2	$(1.01m_0, 1.1EI_0, 0.9L_0)$	$(1, 1, -1)$	$3.516\sqrt{\frac{1.1EI_0}{1.01m_0(0.9L_0)^4}} = 29.1994$
3	$(0.99m_0, 1.1EI_0, 1.1L_0)$	$(-1, 1, 1)$	$3.516\sqrt{\frac{1.1EI_0}{0.99m_0(1.1L_0)^4}} = 19.7431$
4	$(0.99m_0, 0.9EI_0, 1.1L_0)$	$(-1, -1, 1)$	$3.516\sqrt{\frac{0.9EI_0}{0.99m_0(1.1L_0)^4}} = 17.8583$
5	$(0.99m_0, 0.9EI_0, 0.9L_0)$	$(-1, -1, -1)$	$3.516\sqrt{\frac{0.9EI_0}{0.99m_0(0.9L_0)^4}} = 26.6773$
6	$(0.99m_0, 1.1EI_0, 0.9L_0)$	$(-1, 1, -1)$	$3.516\sqrt{\frac{1.1EI_0}{0.99m_0(0.9L_0)^4}} = 29.4728$
7	$(1.01m_0, 0.9EI_0, 0.9L_0)$	$(1, -1, -1)$	$3.516\sqrt{\frac{0.9EI_0}{1.01m_0(0.9L_0)^4}} = 26.4118$
8	$(1.01m_0, 0.9EI_0, 1.1L_0)$	$(1, -1, 1)$	$3.516\sqrt{\frac{0.9EI_0}{1.01m_0(1.1L_0)^4}} = 17.6806$
9	(m_0, EI_0, L_0)	$(0, 0, 0)$	$3.516\sqrt{\frac{EI_0}{m_0(L_0)^4}} = 22.6633$
10	$(1.01732m_0, EI_0, L_0)$	$(1.732, 0, 0)$	$3.516\sqrt{\frac{EI_0}{1.01732m_0(L_0)^4}} = 22.4695$
11	$(m_0, 1.1732EI_0, L_0)$	$(0, 1.732, 0)$	$3.516\sqrt{\frac{1.1732EI_0}{m_0(L_0)^4}} = 24.5476$
12	$(m_0, EI_0, 1.1732L_0)$	$(0, 0, 1.732)$	$3.516\sqrt{\frac{EI_0}{m_0(1.1732L_0)^4}} = 16.4656$
13	$(0.98268m_0, EI_0, L_0)$	$(-1.732, 0, 0)$	$3.516\sqrt{\frac{EI_0}{0.98268m_0(L_0)^4}} = 22.8621$
14	$(m_0, 0.8268EI_0, L_0)$	$(0, -1.732, 0)$	$3.516\sqrt{\frac{0.8268EI_0}{m_0(L_0)^4}} = 20.6074$
15	$(m_0, EI_0, 0.8268L_0)$	$(0, 0, -1.732)$	$3.516\sqrt{\frac{EI_0}{m_0(0.8268L_0)^4}} = 33.1529$

The next step is to construct the vectors and matrices needed to get the least-squares estimates.

$$
\boldsymbol{\omega} = \begin{Bmatrix} 19.5467 \\ 29.1994 \\ 19.7431 \\ 17.8583 \\ 26.6773 \\ 29.4728 \\ 26.4118 \\ 17.6806 \\ 22.6633 \\ 22.4695 \\ 24.5476 \\ 16.4656 \\ 22.8621 \\ 20.6074 \\ 33.1529 \end{Bmatrix}
\quad
\mathbf{X} = \begin{array}{c} \begin{array}{cccccccccc} & x_1 & x_2 & x_3 & x_1^2 & x_2^2 & x_3^2 & x_1x_2 & x_2x_3 & x_1x_3 \end{array} \\ \begin{bmatrix}
1 & 1 & 1 & 1 & 1 & 1 & 1 & 1 & 1 & 1 \\
1 & 1 & 1 & -1 & 1 & 1 & 1 & 1 & -1 & -1 \\
1 & -1 & 1 & 1 & 1 & 1 & 1 & -1 & 1 & -1 \\
1 & -1 & -1 & 1 & 1 & 1 & 1 & 1 & -1 & -1 \\
1 & -1 & -1 & -1 & 1 & 1 & 1 & 1 & 1 & 1 \\
1 & -1 & 1 & -1 & 1 & 1 & 1 & -1 & -1 & 1 \\
1 & 1 & -1 & -1 & 1 & 1 & 1 & -1 & 1 & -1 \\
1 & 1 & -1 & 1 & 1 & 1 & 1 & -1 & -1 & 1 \\
1 & 0 & 0 & 0 & 0 & 0 & 0 & 0 & 0 & 0 \\
1 & 1.732 & 0 & 0 & 3 & 0 & 0 & 0 & 0 & 0 \\
1 & 0 & 1.732 & 0 & 0 & 3 & 0 & 0 & 0 & 0 \\
1 & 0 & 0 & 1.732 & 0 & 0 & 3 & 0 & 0 & 0 \\
1 & -1.732 & 0 & 0 & 3 & 0 & 0 & 0 & 0 & 0 \\
1 & 0 & -1.732 & 0 & 0 & 3 & 0 & 0 & 0 & 0 \\
1 & 0 & 0 & -1.732 & 0 & 0 & 3 & 0 & 0 & 0
\end{bmatrix} \end{array}
$$

$$
\boldsymbol{\beta} = \begin{Bmatrix} \beta_0 \\ \beta_1 \\ \beta_2 \\ \beta_3 \\ \beta_{11} \\ \beta_{22} \\ \beta_{33} \\ \beta_{12} \\ \beta_{23} \\ \beta_{13} \end{Bmatrix}
$$

We solve for the regression coefficients using $\mathbf{b} = (\mathbf{X}^{\mathrm{T}}\mathbf{X})^{-1}\mathbf{X}^{\mathrm{T}}\boldsymbol{\omega}$. The response surface is thus obtained:

$$
\hat{\omega} = 22.6633 - 0.0948x_1 + 1.1732x_2 - 4.6837x_3 - 0.0106x_1^2 - 0.0401x_2^2 + 0.7038x_3^2 - 0.0365x_1x_2 - 0.2622x_2x_3 - 0.0126x_1x_3.
$$

6.6 Sequential Nature of RSM

In RSM terminology, the region where the response surface is valid is called the *region of operability* R and the full design space is called the *region of interest* O, as shown in Figure 6.16.[10] Typically, R ⊂ O, but it is difficult to define how large R is with respect to O. Consider for example two RSMs created about two different centre points, x and x', in the design space O. Assuming x' is the optimal point, one would need a sequence of RSMs

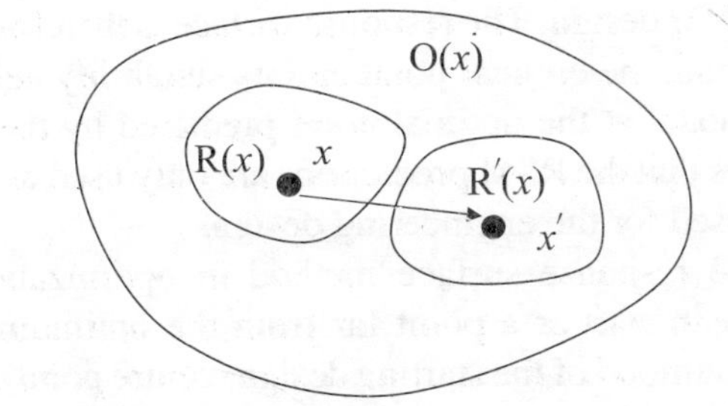

Figure 6.16 *Regions of interest and operability*

to move from point x to point x'. This is why a sequential application of RSM is needed for optimization problems.

One could use either the hypercube or hypersphere as a *trust region* where the response surface is valid and use *move limits* or constraints to search for the optimal point along the response surface only within this space. In some applications, it is advantageous to have a simple, linear move limit based on the face-centred CCD rather than the spherical constraint. However, the hypersphere allows for a larger design space. For example, the problem of minimizing the objective function with respect to the constraint that the optimal points lay within the hypersphere can be written as shown below.
Minimize

$$y = f(\mathbf{x}) = \beta_0 + \sum_{j=1}^{k} \beta_j x_j + \sum_{j=1}^{k} \beta_{jj} x_j^2 + \sum_{i<j}\sum \beta_{ij} x_i x_j, \tag{6.28}$$

subject to the constraints:

$$x_1^2 + x_2^2 + x_3^2 + \cdots + x_k^2 \leq k^2,$$
$$\Rightarrow g(\mathbf{x}) = x_1^2 + x_2^2 + x_3^2 + \cdots + x_k^2 - k^2 \leq 0. \tag{6.29}$$

For the face-centred CCD, we would have different expressions for the constraints, namely:
Minimize

$$y = f(\mathbf{x}) = \beta_0 + \sum_{j=1}^{k} \beta_j x_j + \sum_{j=1}^{k} \beta_{jj} x_j^2 + \sum_{i<j}\sum \beta_{ij} x_i x_j, \tag{6.30}$$

subject to the constraints:

$$-1 \leq x_i \leq 1, \qquad i = 1, k. \tag{6.31}$$

The RSM must be checked for a stationary point which can be easily obtained by setting the gradient of the RSM to zero and solving the resulting equations. The stationary point can be a minimum, maximum or saddle point. The minimum point in the trust region can also lie on the boundary of the region where the constraint is active. It should be noted that the optimal point of the fitted model need not be the optimal point of the actual computational model. *Therefore, one needs to run the simulation code at the optimal point predicted by the response surface to get the final optimal design.* In general, if this is an improved design, then the point can be used for design. The response surface is therefore used only as a guide and any final decisions about the optimal point and its suitability need to be confirmed by running the simulation model at the optimal point predicted by the RSM. This is a very important step and ensures that the RSM predictions are only used as a guide and the actual analysis predictions are used for the engineering design.

The application of the response surface method in optimization is best done in a sequential manner. One can start at a point far from the optimum and develop a CCD which is valid in a neighbourhood of the starting design (centre point). Typical optimization methods (numerical as well as those based on the KKT conditions) can then be used to find the minima using the CCD design. This new design can then be used as the starting design (centre point) to move further in the design space. The RSM therefore moves in the design space using quadratic approximations. It is a good idea to reduce the perturbations (high, low) as the response surfaces progress towards the optimal one. In contrast to the Taylor series approximation, quite large jumps in the design space are possible using RSM. The intermediate designs are all useful and even if one performs only a few RSM iterations, it is possible to get a better design than the starting design. RSM based optimization can therefore be used as an interactive procedure.

Another advantage of RSM is in their computational efficiency which makes it possible to use methods such as genetic algorithms for optimization. However, GA and RSM should be used together only in cases of discrete or integer design variables. In aircraft wing and helicopter rotor design with composite ply-angle design variables, such RSM–GA combinations have been used in research literature.

Example 6.6 Minimize the function $f(\mathbf{x}) = x_1^2 + 2x_2^2 + e^{-x_1-x_2}$ using the second-order response surface method. Use a face-centred design with a centre point at (0.5, 0.5) and ± 100 per cent perturbation on the design variables. Compare the minimum point of the response surface with that of the function.

Solution: The physical variables (x_1, x_2) for the FCD design can be shown as follows:

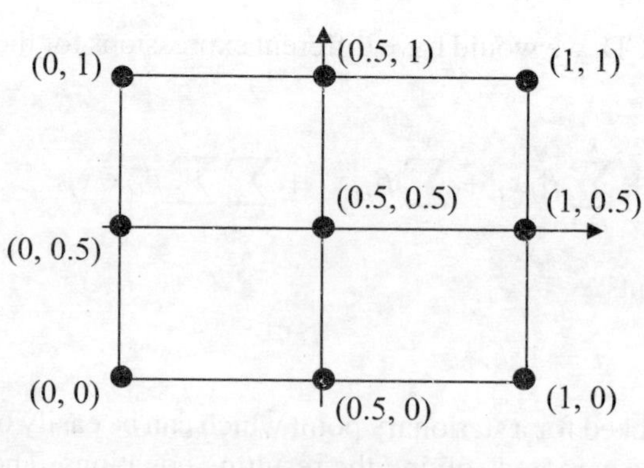

The physical variables are related to the coded variables as $x = m\xi + C$. Then, we can write $1 = m(1) + C$ and $0 = m(-1) + C$. Solving these equations yields the relation between the physical and the coded variables as $x = 0.5\xi + 0.5$. We need to calculate the value of the function at the FCD points. The points and the corresponding values are as given below.

Physical points	Coded points	f
(1, 1)	(1, 1)	3.1353
(1, 0)	(1, −1)	1.3679
(0, 0)	(−1, −1)	1
(0, 1)	(−1, 1)	2.3679
(0.5, 0.5)	(0, 0)	1.1179
(0.5, 1)	(0, 1)	2.4731
(1, 0.5)	(1, 0)	1.7231
(0.5, 0)	(0, −1)	0.8565
(0, 0.5)	(−1, 0)	1.1065

We can fit a second-order response surface through the data obtained. Such a model can be written as $f = \beta_0 + \beta_1\xi_1 + \beta_2\xi_2 + \beta_{11}\xi_1^2 + \beta_{22}\xi_2^2 + \beta_{12}\xi_1\xi_2$. We create the vectors and the matrices needed for solving the problem using the data generated for the FCD points.

$$\mathbf{y} = \begin{Bmatrix} 3.1353 \\ 1.3679 \\ 1 \\ 2.3679 \\ 1.1179 \\ 2.4731 \\ 1.7231 \\ 0.8565 \\ 1.1065 \end{Bmatrix} \quad \mathbf{X} = \begin{bmatrix} 1 & 1 & 1 & 1 & 1 & 1 \\ 1 & 1 & -1 & 1 & 1 & -1 \\ 1 & -1 & -1 & 1 & 1 & 1 \\ 1 & -1 & 1 & 1 & 1 & -1 \\ 1 & 0 & 0 & 0 & 0 & 0 \\ 1 & 0 & 1 & 0 & 1 & 0 \\ 1 & 1 & 0 & 1 & 0 & 0 \\ 1 & -1 & 0 & 1 & 0 & 0 \\ 1 & 0 & -1 & 0 & 1 & 0 \end{bmatrix} \quad \boldsymbol{\beta} = \begin{Bmatrix} \beta_0 \\ \beta_1 \\ \beta_2 \\ \beta_{11} \\ \beta_{22} \\ \beta_{12} \end{Bmatrix}.$$

We solve for the regression coefficients using $\boldsymbol{\beta} = (\mathbf{X}^{\mathrm{T}}\mathbf{X})^{-1}\mathbf{X}^{\mathrm{T}}\mathbf{y}$. The response surface thus obtained is:

$$\hat{f} = 1.1152 + 0.2920\xi_1 + 0.7920\xi_2 + 0.3009\xi_1^2 + 0.5509\xi_2^2 + 0.0999\xi_1\xi_2$$

and the minimum points are at $\xi_1 = -0.37$ and $\xi_2 = -0.68$. Substituting these values of ξ in $x = 0.5\xi + 0.5$, we get the physical variables $x_1 = 0.315$ and $x_2 = 0.16$, which are almost equal to the minimum points of the original function. Thus we can say that the RSM provides an adequate approximation to the objective function and results in the optimum in just a single iteration.

Example 6.7 Minimize the function $f(\mathbf{x}) = x_1^2 + 2x_2^2 + \mathrm{e}^{-x_1-x_2}$ using the second-order response surface method. Use a FCD with a centre point at (0, 0). Compare the minimum point of the response surface with that of the function. Perform sequential approximation with ±100 per cent perturbation on the design variables and see if you can reach the minimum.

Solution: In this problem, the physical and coded points are identical for the FCD.

Physical points	Coded points	f
(1, 1)	(1, 1)	3.1353
(1, −1)	(1, −1)	4.0
(−1, −1)	(−1, −1)	10.38
(−1, 1)	(−1, 1)	4.0
(0, 0)	(0, 0)	1.0
(0, 1)	(0, 1)	2.3679
(1, 0)	(1, 0)	1.3679
(0, −1)	(0, −1)	4.7183
(−1, 0)	(−1, 0)	3.7183

We can fit a second-order response surface using the model:

$$f = \beta_0 + \beta_1 x_1 + \beta_2 x_2 + \beta_{11} x_1^2 + \beta_{22} x_2^2 + \beta_{12} x_1 x_2.$$

The vectors and the matrices needed are as given below.

$$\mathbf{y} = \begin{Bmatrix} 3.1353 \\ 4 \\ 10.38 \\ 4 \\ 1 \\ 2.3679 \\ 1.3679 \\ 4.7183 \\ 3.7183 \end{Bmatrix} \quad \mathbf{X} = \begin{bmatrix} 1 & 1 & 1 & 1 & 1 & 1 \\ 1 & 1 & -1 & 1 & 1 & -1 \\ 1 & -1 & -1 & 1 & 1 & 1 \\ 1 & -1 & 1 & 1 & 1 & -1 \\ 1 & 0 & 0 & 0 & 0 & 0 \\ 1 & 0 & 1 & 0 & 1 & 0 \\ 1 & 1 & 0 & 1 & 0 & 0 \\ 1 & -1 & 0 & 1 & 0 & 0 \\ 1 & 0 & -1 & 0 & 1 & 0 \end{bmatrix} \quad \boldsymbol{\beta} = \begin{Bmatrix} \beta_0 \\ \beta_1 \\ \beta_2 \\ \beta_{11} \\ \beta_{22} \\ \beta_{12} \end{Bmatrix}.$$

We solve for the regression coefficients using $\boldsymbol{\beta} = (\mathbf{X}^T\mathbf{X})^{-1}\mathbf{X}^T\mathbf{y}$. The response surface thus obtained is the following:

$$\hat{f} = 0.8699 - 1.5992x_1 - 1.5992x_2 + 1.7382x_1^2 + 2.7382x_2^2 + 1.3788x_1x_2.$$

The minimum points of the response surface are at $x_1 = 0.31$ and $x_2 = 0.37$. When we compare these values of the minimum with that of the actual function, we see that x_2 does not match. Hence we perform sequential approximation using the design (0.31, 0.37) as the centre point and a reduced region for the FCD, and see if we can reach the minimum points. For the FCD with centre point at (0.31, 0.37) and using 100 per cent perturbation, the points obtained are as shown in the figure below.

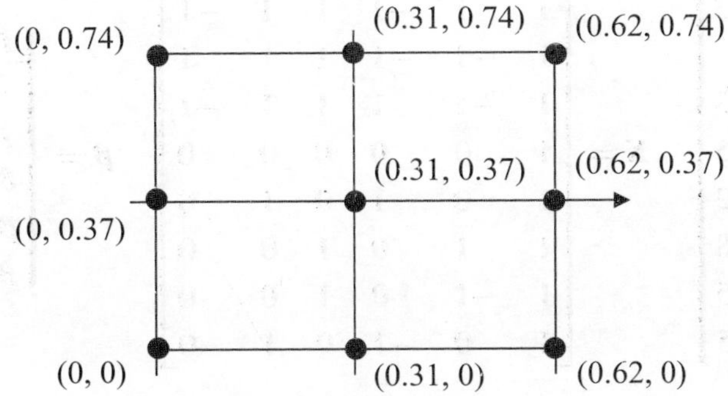

The relation between the physical and the coded points are determined as follows:

$$A = mx_1 + C, \qquad B = mx_1 + C.$$

We then get

$$0.62 = m(1) + C, \qquad 0.74 = m(1) + C,$$
$$0 = m(-1) + C, \qquad 0 = m(-1) + C.$$

Solving these equations yields the relation between the physical and coded variables as shown below:

$$A = 0.31x_1 + 0.31, \qquad B = 0.37x_2 + 0.37.$$

The values of the function at the FCD points are as follows.

Physical points	**Coded points**	f
(0.62, 0.74)	(1, 1)	1.7363
(0.62, 0)	(1, −1)	0.9223
(0, 0)	(−1, −1)	1.0
(0, 0.74)	(−1, 1)	1.5723
(0.31, 0.37)	(0, 0)	0.8765
(0.31, 0.74)	(0, 1)	1.5412
(0.62, 0.37)	(1, 0)	1.0298
(0.31, 0)	(0, −1)	0.8295
(0, 0.37)	(−1, 0)	0.9645

We can again fit a second-order response surface. The vectors and the matrices needed are as given below.

$$\mathbf{y} = \begin{Bmatrix} 1.7353 \\ 0.9223 \\ 1 \\ 1.5723 \\ 0.8765 \\ 1.5412 \\ 1.0298 \\ 0.8295 \\ 0.9645 \end{Bmatrix} \quad \mathbf{X} = \begin{bmatrix} 1 & 1 & 1 & 1 & 1 & 1 \\ 1 & 1 & -1 & 1 & 1 & -1 \\ 1 & -1 & -1 & 1 & 1 & 1 \\ 1 & -1 & 1 & 1 & 1 & -1 \\ 1 & 0 & 0 & 0 & 0 & 0 \\ 1 & 0 & 1 & 0 & 1 & 0 \\ 1 & 1 & 0 & 1 & 0 & 0 \\ 1 & -1 & 0 & 1 & 0 & 0 \\ 1 & 0 & -1 & 0 & 1 & 0 \end{bmatrix} \quad \boldsymbol{\beta} = \begin{Bmatrix} \beta_0 \\ \beta_1 \\ \beta_2 \\ \beta_{11} \\ \beta_{22} \\ \beta_{12} \end{Bmatrix}.$$

We solve for the regression coefficients using $\boldsymbol{\beta} = (\mathbf{X}^{\mathrm{T}}\mathbf{X})^{-1}\mathbf{X}^{\mathrm{T}}\mathbf{y}$. The response surface thus obtained is the following:

$$\hat{f} = 0.8758 + 0.0253x_1 + 0.3497x_2 + 0.1218x_1^2 + 0.3100x_2^2 + 0.0604x_1x_2.$$

The minimum points are at $x_1 = 0.036$ and $x_2 = -0.56$. Substituting these values of x_1 and x_2 in the equations, we get $A = 0.32$ and $B = 0.16$, which are almost equal to the minimum points of the original function. In this example, two iterations of response surface were needed as the starting FCD was quite large and the approximation was crude.

6.7 Limitations of RSM

The major limitation of the RSM is that the number of runs becomes very large as the number of design variables increase. This can be observed in Tables 6.1 and 6.2 for the 2^k and $2^k + n_c$ designs. Table 6.3 gives the number of regression coefficients needed for the second-order fit and the number of runs needed for the CCD design. In CCD, the number of design runs is always greater than the number of regression coefficients, which leads to *overfitting* the second-order RSM. Overfitting the response surface is always a good idea as it leads to more accurate approximations. Note that most of the number of runs come from the 2^k points for all two-level based designs.

The major limitation of the use of RSM in optimization is the rapid increase in the number of runs which occurs as the number of design variables k increases. In general, the use of RSM is difficult and cumbersome for design variables greater than 15. However, for optimization problems involving a few design variables (up to 10), *RSM is a good way to decouple the analysis problem and the optimization problem.* This is especially important for engineering optimization where the routine use of large computer codes means that it is difficult to make changes in the codes and to integrate the computer codes with optimization codes. In the industry where different groups work on different analysis problems (such as structures and fluid mechanics), it is possible for each group to create an RSM of a specific objective function with respect to the design variables which can then be integrated to perform multidisciplinary design optimization (MDO).

The RSM allows formulation of the optimization problem in terms of polynomials, thus allowing use of many optimization algorithms and even analytical solutions. Both objectives

Table 6.3 *Calculation of second-order response surface in CCD factorial design*

k	Number of regression coefficients	Number of runs
2	6	9
3	10	15
4	15	25
5	21	43
6	28	77
7	36	143
8	45	273
9	55	531
10	66	1045

and constraints can be expressed as response surfaces. It is important to keep the RSM to within a reasonably small region of the baseline design, and it is best to use sequential CCD approximations. These guidelines depend to some extent on the nature of the function considered. However, in some situations, it may be possible to use the two-level factorial enhanced by a centre point to get second-order RSMs at first, to start moving along the path of improvement before switching to the CCD near the optimum.

Example 6.8 Minimize $f(\mathbf{x}) = x_1^2+2x_2^2+e^{-x_1-x_2}$ subject to $g(\mathbf{x}) = 0.1-\sin(x_1x_2) \le 0$ using KKT conditions. Then form a FCD-based second-order response surface about (0, 0) with move limits of $0 \le x_i \le 0.5$ for the design variables for both the objective function $f(\mathbf{x})$ and constraint $g(\mathbf{x})$. Using these response surfaces, find the optimal solutions using the KKT conditions. Compare the result with the exact solution.

Solution:

A. To solve the constrained optimization problem using KKT conditions:

We form the Lagrange function

$$L = x_1^2 + 2x_2^2 + e^{-x_1-x_2} + u(0.1 - \sin(x_1x_2) + s^2).$$

Next, we set the gradient of the Lagrange function to zero

$$\frac{\partial L}{\partial x_1} = 2x_1 - e^{-x_1-x_2} - ux_2\cos(x_1x_2) = 0,$$

$$\frac{\partial L}{\partial x_2} = 4x_2 - e^{-x_1-x_2} - ux_1\cos(x_1x_2) = 0,$$

$$\frac{\partial L}{\partial u} = 0.1 - \sin(x_1 x_2) + s^2 = 0,$$

$$\frac{\partial L}{\partial s} = 2us = 0.$$

Now, we consider various possibilities created by the switching condition $us = 0$

Case 1

$$\begin{aligned} u = 0 \Rightarrow us &= 0, \\ 2x_1 - e^{-x_1 - x_2} &= 0, \\ 4x_2 - e^{-x_1 - x_2} &= 0, \\ 0.1 - \sin(x_1 x_2) + s^2 &= 0. \end{aligned}$$

Solving these equations, yields $x_1 = 0.3128$, $x_2 = 0.1564$, $s = \pm 0.24i$. However, $s = \pm 0.24i$ is not possible. Thus, this is not a valid solution.

Case 2

$$\begin{aligned} u = 0, s = 0 \Rightarrow us &= 0, \\ 2x_1 - e^{-x_1 - x_2} &= 0, \\ 4x_2 - e^{-x_1 - x_2} &= 0, \\ 0.1 - \sin(x_1 x_2) &= 0. \end{aligned}$$

Here the first two equations yields $x_1 = 0.3128$, $x_2 = 0.1564$. However, this does not satisfy the third equation. Therefore, this is not a valid solution.

Case 3

$$\begin{aligned} s = 0 \Rightarrow us &= 0, \\ 2x_1 - e^{-x_1 - x_2} - ux_2 \cos(x_1 x_2) &= 0, \\ 4x_2 - e^{-x_1 - x_2} - ux_1 \cos(x_1 x_2) &= 0, \\ 0.1 - \sin(x_1 x_2) &= 0. \end{aligned}$$

Solving these equations yields $x_1 = -0.3442$, $x_2 = -0.2905$, $u = 8.908$. This solution corresponds to a case where the inequality is active and is a valid solution. At this point, $f = 2.0893$, $g = 1.764\text{e} - 4$.

B. To solve this problem using the response surface method:

The second-order response surfaces obtained after solving for the regression coefficients are the ones below:

$$\hat{f} = 0.9928 - 0.5654y_1 - 0.5654y_2 + 0.3885y_1^2 + 0.6385y_2^2 + 0.2715y_1 y_2,$$

$$\hat{g} = 0.1 - 0.2474y_1 y_2.$$

We form the Lagrange function:

$$L = 0.9928 - 0.5654y_1 - 0.5654y_2 + 0.3885y_1^2 + 0.6385y_2^2 + 0.2715y_1y_2 + u(0.1 - 0.2474y_1y_2 + s^2).$$

Next, we set the gradient of the Lagrange function to zero:

$$\frac{\partial L}{\partial y_1} = -0.5654 + 0.777y_1 + 0.2715y_2 - 0.2474uy_2 = 0,$$

$$\frac{\partial L}{\partial y_2} = -0.5654 + 0.2715y_1 + 1.277y_2 - 0.2474uy_1 = 0,$$

$$\frac{\partial L}{\partial u} = 0.1 - 0.2474y_1y_2 + s^2 = 0,$$

$$\frac{\partial L}{\partial s} = 2su = 0.$$

Now, we consider various possibilities created by the switching condition $su = 0$.

Case 1

$$u = 0 \Rightarrow us = 0,$$

$$-0.5654 + 0.777y_1 + 0.2715y_2 = 0,$$

$$-0.5654 + 0.2715y_1 + 1.277y_2 = 0,$$

$$0.1 - 0.2474y_1y_2 + s^2 = 0.$$

Solving these equations, yields $y_1 = 0.6189$, $y_2 = 0.3111$, $s = \pm 0.22i$. This is not a valid solution.

Case 2

$$u = 0, s = 0 \Rightarrow us = 0,$$

$$-0.5654 + 0.777y_1 + 0.2715y_2 = 0,$$

$$-0.5654 + 0.2715y_1 + 1.277y_2 = 0,$$

$$0.1 - 0.2474y_1y_2 = 0.$$

Solving the first two equations, yields $y_1 = 0.6189$, $y_2 = 0.3111$. However, this does not satisfy the third equation $0.1 - 0.2474y_1y_2 = 0$. Thus, this is not a valid solution.

Case 3

$$s = 0 \Rightarrow us = 0,$$

$$-0.5654 + 0.777y_1 + 0.2715y_2 - 0.2474uy_2 = 0,$$

$$-0.5654 + 0.2715y_1 + 1.277y_2 - 0.2474uy_1 = 0,$$

$$0.1 - 0.2474y_1y_2 = 0.$$

Solving these equations yields two solutions and corresponds to a case where the inequality is active. The set of equations $y_1 = 0.795$, $y_2 = 0.509$ and $u = 1.519$ corresponds to the actual variables $x_1 = 0.3975$ and $x_2 = 0.254$. The other solution being $y_1 = -0.692$, $y_2 = -0.583$ and $u = 8.743$ which corresponds to the actual variables $x_1 = -0.3460$ and $x_2 = -0.2915$.

Hence, we see that case 3 is a valid solution. One of the solutions is close to the optimal point obtained for the exact problem. Putting these solutions in the original formula, we see that $f(0.3975, 0.254) = 0.8083$, $g(0.3975, 0.254) = -7.935\text{e} - 4$ and $f(-0.3460, -0.2915) = 2.818$, $g(-0.3460, -0.2915) = -6.88\text{e} - 4$.

Example 6.9 Minimize $f(\mathbf{x}) = \text{e}^{3x_1+4x_2}$ subjected to $h(\mathbf{x}) = x_1^2 + x_2^2 - 1 = 0$ using KKT conditions. Then form a FCD-based second-order response surface about (0, 0) with move limits of $-1 \le x_i \le 1$ for the design variables for both the objective function $f(\mathbf{x})$ and constraints $g(\mathbf{x})$. Using these response surfaces, find the optimal solutions using the KKT conditions.

Solution: We form the Lagrange function:

$$L = \text{e}^{3x_1+4x_2} + v(x_1^2 + x_2^2 - 1) = 0,$$

$$\frac{\partial L}{\partial x_1} = 3\text{e}^{3x_1+4x_2} + 2vx_1 = 0,$$

$$\frac{\partial L}{\partial x_2} = 4\text{e}^{3x_1+4x_2} + 2vx_2 = 0,$$

$$\frac{\partial L}{\partial v} = x_1^2 + x_2^2 - 1 = 0.$$

Solving the above equations, yields $x_1 = -0.6$ and $x_2 = -0.8$. At this point, $f = 6.738\text{e} - 3$ and $h = 0$. The second-order response surfaces obtained after solving for the regression coefficient are the following:

$$\hat{f} = -105.02 + 185.71x_1 + 192.26x_2 + 168.10x_1^2 + 185.34x_2^2 + 273.38x_1x_2,$$

$$\hat{h} = -1 + x_1^2 + x_2^2.$$

Next, we form the Langrange function and set the gradient of the Langrange function equal to zero.

$$L = -105.02 + 185.71x_1 + 192.26x_2 + 168.10x_1^2 + 185.34x_2^2 \\ + 273.38x_1x_2 + v(-1 + x_1^2 + x_2^2) = 0,$$

$$\frac{\partial L}{\partial x_1} = 185.71 + 336.2x_1 + 273.38x_2 + 2vx_1 = 0,$$

$$\frac{\partial L}{\partial x_2} = 192.26 + 273.38x_1 + 370.68x_2 + 2vx_2 = 0,$$

$$\frac{\partial L}{\partial v} = x_1^2 + x_2^2 - 1 = 0.$$

Solving the above equations yields multiple solutions for (v, x_1, x_2) and these are $(-447.32, 0.6878, 0.7258)$, $(-180.03, -0.6745, -0.7381)$, $(-41.93, 0.2981, -0.9545)$, and $(-37.59, -0.9692, 0.2460)$, respectively. The equality constraint is satisfied at all these points but the function value is minimum at $(-0.6745, -0.7381)$. Hence this point is considered as the valid point and is quite close to the exact solution. At this point, $f = 6.902e-3$ and $h = -2.58e-4$.

6.8 Other Experimental Designs

Until now, we have studied selected experimental designs such as the CCD which are widely used in response surface applications in optimization. Another approach which is sometimes used, is 3^k designs.[10] There are other ways to develop designs with a more intense sampling of the design space compared to CCD and 3^k. We shall discuss four such approaches next.

6.8.1 Three-level factorial designs

The 3^k design is an extension of the 2^k design to three levels: low, medium and high. Here the *medium* is the addition to the 2^k design. As in the 2^k design, the *low* and *high points* are represented by coded variables -1 and 1, respectively. The medium point is represented by coded variable 0. For a 2D problem, the 3^k design is shown in Figure 6.17.

The 3^k design requires a very large number of points at higher values of k as shown in Table 6.4. However, they are sometimes used to form cubic or even higher-order response surfaces. In literature, even fourth- and fifth-order response surfaces have been used. Just as in the Taylor series expansions, higher-order polynomials can lead to better fits in a more global sense. A third-order response surface in 2D space is described by the following equation:

$$\eta = \beta_0+\beta_1 x_1 + \beta_2 x_2 + \beta_3 x_1 x_2+\beta_4 x_1^2 + \beta_5 x_2^2+\underbrace{\beta_6 x_1 x_2^2 + \beta_7 x_1^2 x_2 + \beta_8 x_1^3 + \beta_9 x_2^3}_{\text{third-order terms}}. \tag{6.32}$$

Such a higher-order response surface makes it necessary to use a large number of points to accurately estimate the regression coefficients and it may require a 3^k design. Other designs such as 5^k are sometimes used and have five levels. More such designs can easily be constructed.

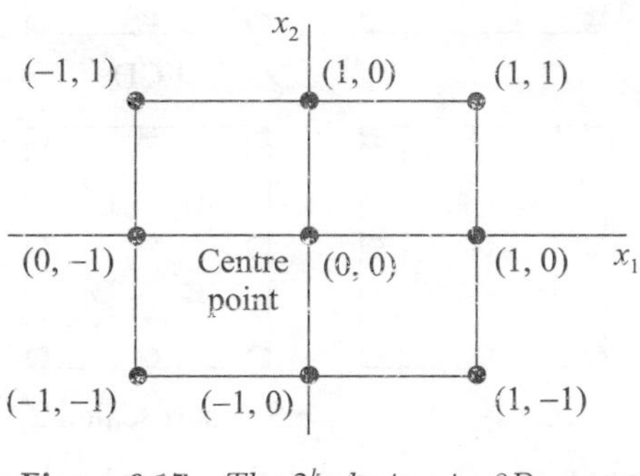

Figure 6.17 *The 3^k design in 2D space*

Table 6.4 *Calculation of second-order response surface in 3^k factorial design*

k	Number of regression coefficients	Number of runs
2	6	9
3	10	27
4	15	81
5	21	243
6	28	729
7	36	2187
8	45	6561
9	55	19683
10	66	59049

6.8.2 Progressive lattice sampling (PLS) method

In this approach, the number of points in the design space is upgraded while retaining the points in the previous design. A 2D PLS sequence is shown in Figure 6.18. Starting from a 2^k design, $2^2 = 4$ points, a face-centred CCD is constructed by adding the axial points and a centre point: $2^2 + 2 \times 2 + 1 = 9$ points. A 3^k design is generated from this by adding the midpoints of the edges. The CCD and 3^k designs are identical for two variables. Proceeding from the 3^k design, a sub-scale 2^k is formed within the design space with half the perturbation of the full-scale design, and thus the number of points increase to $3^2 + 2^2 = 13$ points. We can see that the advantage of the PLS method is that one can

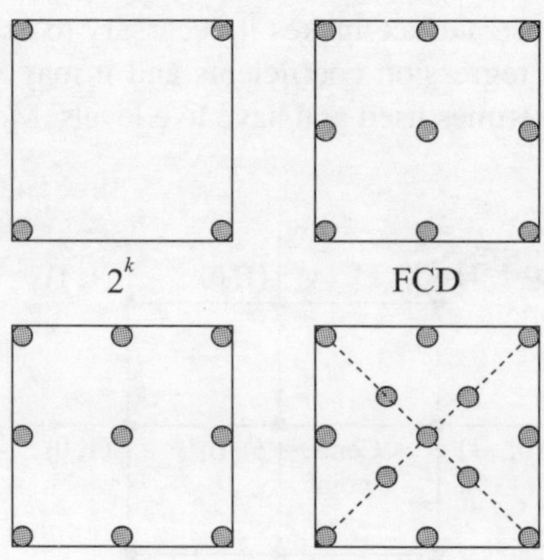

Figure 6.18 *Progressive lattice sampling method*

start with a CCD and then add more points to evaluate if a better response surface can be obtained. The points obtained earlier are used with each enhanced design and therefore the approach is computationally efficient. The addition of such new points also permits the use of higher-order response surfaces such as cubic polynomials.

6.8.3 Probabilistic enhancement

There is also the possibility of probabilistic enhancement of the design space. Random points can be generated in the design space which can then be used to create the response surface. If a computer code is developed for this random enhanced design, then repeated runs of the computer code can be used to develop different response surface and the best response surface can be selected for optimization. Thus, some of the strengths of stochastic methods can be introduced into the RSM approach. As an illustration of the concept, Figure 6.19 shows a 2^k design which is used to get four different enhanced designs with randomly added points. Note that the random points can sample the design space in different areas in different runs.

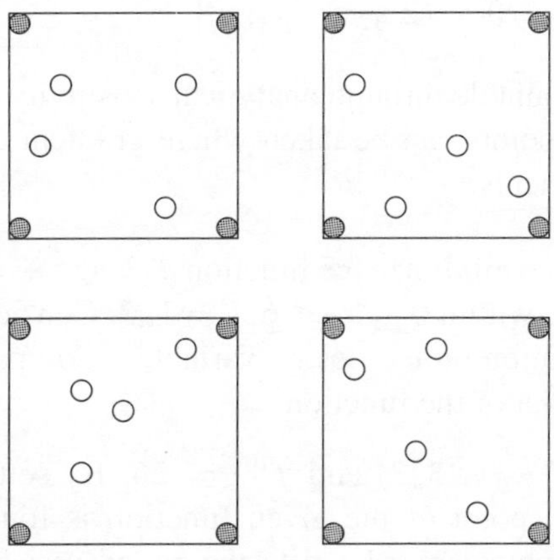

Figure 6.19 *Probabilistically enhanced 2^k designs*

6.8.4 Use of gradient information

Gradients can be used to increase the accuracy of response surfaces. The gradient of the function is evaluated with respect to the design variables, and the values are used in construction of the response surfaces. This process is computationally expensive for many problems and therefore the number of points where the gradients are evaluated is kept to a minimum. Two cases of gradient-enhanced design are considered. In the first case, the gradient is evaluated at the centre point. In the second case, the gradient is evaluated at the point at which the objective function value is lowest. These are two sample cases and the gradient evaluation can also be done at any other or more than at one point if desired.

In the case of the gradient-enhanced response surface method, the regression parameters are calculated:

$$\hat{\boldsymbol{\beta}} = (\mathbf{X}^{\mathrm{T}}\mathbf{X})^{-1}\mathbf{X}^{\mathrm{T}}\mathbf{y}. \tag{6.33}$$

Variables y and $\mathbf{X}$ for a two-design variable problem of quadratic response surface are defined below:

$$y = \{y_1, y_2, \ldots, y_n, g_{11}, g_{12}\}. \tag{6.34}$$

Here $\{y_1, y_2, \ldots, y_n\}$ are the values of the response at the design points, n being the number of design points depending on the experimental design used. Also, g_{11} and g_{12} are the gradients of the response at points 1 with respect to the design variables 1 and 2, respectively. The augmented $\mathbf{X}$ is then given below:

$$\mathbf{X} = \begin{bmatrix} 1 & x_{12} & x_{12} & x_{11}^2 & x_{12}^2 & x_{11}x_{12} \\ 1 & x_{21} & x_{22} & x_{21}^2 & x_{22}^2 & x_{21}x_{22} \\ \cdot & \cdot & \cdot & \cdot & \cdot & \cdot \\ \cdot & \cdot & \cdot & \cdot & \cdot & \cdot \\ 1 & x_{n1} & x_{n2} & x_{n1}^2 & x_{n2}^2 & x_{n1}x_{n2} \\ 0 & 1 & 0 & 2x_{11} & 0 & x_{12} \\ 0 & 0 & 1 & 0 & 2x_{12} & x_{11} \end{bmatrix}.$$

If cheap gradients are available through analytical sensitivity derivatives and automatic differentiation, then more points can be taken where gradient of the response surface is used with the function gradients.

Example 6.10 Use RSM to minimize the function $f = (x_1^2 + x_2 - 11)^2 + (x_1 + x_2^2 - 7)^2$. A minimum is known to lie within $0 \le x_i \le 6$, $i = 1, 2$. Consider a centre point at (3, 3) and ± 100 per cent perturbation on the design variables. Compare the minimum point of the response surface with that of the function.

Solution: We see that $x^{(0)} = (3, 3)$ and $f^{(0)} = 26$. By setting the gradient equal to zero, one of the minimum point of the given function is found to be at $x_1 = 3$ and $x_2 = 2$. The physical variables are related to the coded variables as $x = 3y + 3$. The second-order response surface thus obtained after solving for the regression coefficients is $\hat{f} = 26 + 426y_1 + 546y_2 + 432y_1^2 + 504y_2^2 + 216y_1y_2$ and the minimum point is at $y_1 = -0.37$ and $y_2 = -0.46$. Substituting these values of y, we get $x_1 = 1.89$ and $x_2 = 1.62$. However, at this point, the function value $f = 39.90$, which is higher than the starting point value of $f = 26$.

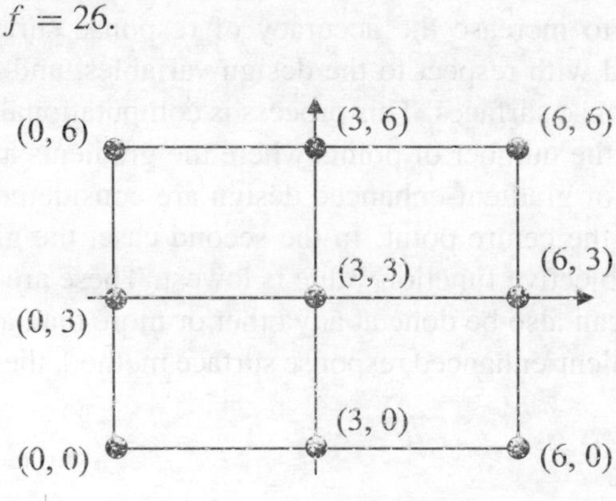

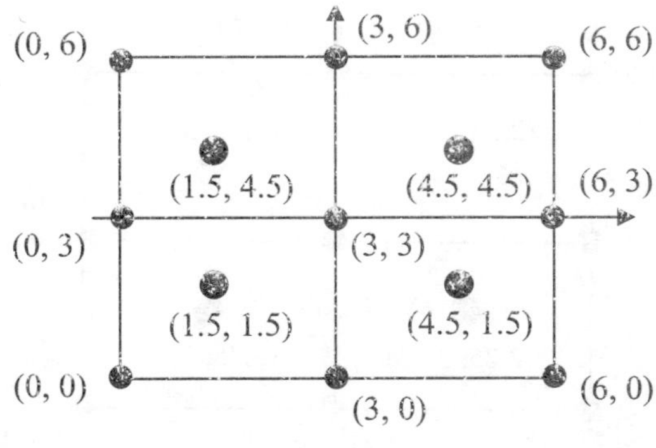

The function is more complex and therefore using the progressive lattice sampling approach, the number of points in the design space is upgraded retaining the points in the previous design. A subscale 2^k is formed within the design with half the perturbation of the full-scale design, and thus the number of points increase to 13 points.

The second-order response surface obtained after using this approach is $\hat{f} = 3.094 + 388.07y_1 + 508.07y_2 + 443.83y_1^2 + 515.83y_2^2 + 216y_1y_2$ and the minimum point is at $y_1 = -0.33$ and $y_2 = -0.42$. Substituting these values of y in $x = 3y + 3$, we get $x_1 = 2.01$ and $x_2 = 1.74$. The advantage of the PLS method is that one can add more points to evaluate if a better response can be obtained. However, the function value comes to $f = 32.36$ at this point. Though better than the previous point, this is still higher than the starting point. It is likely that the function is more nonlinear and therefore we use higher-order response surfaces such as the cubic polynomials to evaluate a better fit.

Using the data generated for the PLS method, the third-order response surface obtained is given by the equation:

$$f = 3.09 + 66y_1 + 186y_2 + 443.83y_1^2 + 515.83y_2^2 + 216y_1y_2 + 54y_1y_2^2 + 54y_1^2y_2 + 324y_1^3 + 324y_2^3.$$

Finding the minimum for the cubic function yields multiple possible solutions which are $(-0.90, -0.92)$, $(-0.83, -0.04)$, $(-0.02, -0.22)$, $(0.08, -0.81)$. As we know that a positive definite Hessian matrix is the sufficient condition for a local minimum, we calculate the Hessian at these stationary points and find $(-0.90, -0.92)$ is a maximum point; the points $(-0.83, -0.04)$ and $(0.08, -0.81)$ are the points of inflection and $(-0.02, -0.22)$ is found to be the minimum point. At $y_1 = -0.02$ and $y_2 = -0.22$ from equation ($x = 3y+3$) we get, $x_1 = 2.94$ and $x_2 = 2.34$ which is near to $(3, 2)$ of the actual function. At this point, $f = 2.00$ which is much less than the starting design. Thus we have obtained a better fit using a cubic polynomial which provides an adequate approximation to the objective function. For most practical optimization problems, the reduction in function value from $f = 26$ to $f = 2$ is a very good result.

However, we form another cubic response surface using the sub-scaled design since we now know that the minimum must be close to (2.94, 2.34).

The third-order response surface obtained is given below:

$$f = 24.6 + 33y_1 + 93y_2 + 93.55y_1^2 + 111.55y_2^2 + 54y_1y_2 + 6.75y_1y_2^2 + 6.75y_1^2y_2 + 40.5y_1^3 + 40.5y_2^3.$$

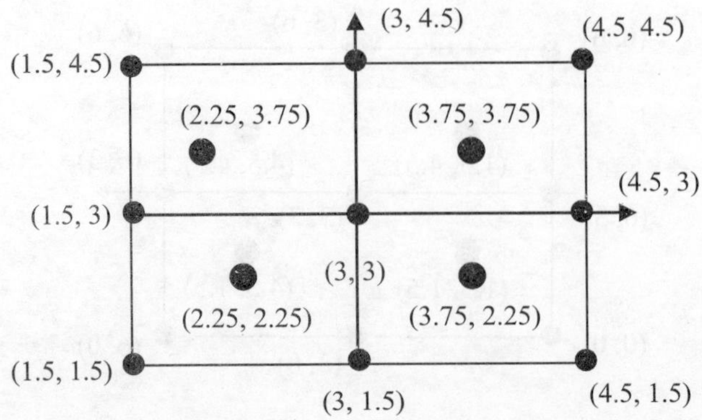

Finding the minimum for the cubic function yields multiple possible solutions which are $(-1.54, -1.52)$, $(-1.37, -0.17)$, $(-0.008, -0.63)$, $(0.10, -1.12)$. We calculated the Hessian at these stationary points and found $(-1.54, -1.52)$ is a maximum point; the points $(-1.37, -0.17)$ and $(0.10, -1.12)$ are the points of inflection and $(-0.008, -0.63)$ is the minimum point. At $y_1 = -0.008$ and $y_2 = -0.63$, we get $x_1 = 2.98$ and $x_2 = 2.05$. At this point $f = 0.03$, which is very much less than the starting design and very close to the actual minimum point.

6.9 Taguchi Orthogonal Arrays

The limitations of time and computation costs preclude the use of CCD or even 2^k designs for large k. The 3^k design is even more computationally expensive. Therefore, to efficiently and economically investigate the design space, *fractional factorial experimental designs* are sometime used. A fractional factorial experimental design (FFE) uses only a fraction of the total number of possible combinations to estimate the main effects and some of the interactions. Taguchi has developed a family of FFEs known as *Taguchi orthogonal arrays*, which can be used in various situations. Orthogonality here implies that the factors can be evaluated independently of one another.[11] Orthogonal arrays (OA) provide an ordered approach to conduct numerical experiments with a fraction of the designs required for the factorial design. Some low-dimensional OAs are the L_4, L_9 and L_{18} which are shown in Tables 6.5, 6.6 and 6.7, respectively. Table 6.5 shows the L_4 OA which can be used with three design variables and two levels.

Table 6.5 L_4 *orthogonal array*

	Design Variables		
Point	x_1	x_2	x_3
1	−1	−1	−1
2	−1	1	1
3	1	−1	1
4	1	1	−1

Table 6.6 *L_9 orthogonal array*

	Design variables		
Point	x_1	x_2	x_3
1	−1	−1	−1
2	−1	0	0
3	−1	1	1
4	0	−1	0
5	0	0	1
6	0	1	−1
7	1	−1	1
8	1	0	−1
9	1	1	0

Table 6.7 *L_{18} orthogonal array*

	Design variables					
Point	x_1	x_2	x_3	x_4	x_5	x_6
1	−1	−1	−1	−1	−1	−1
2	−1	0	0	0	0	0
3	−1	1	1	1	1	1
4	0	−1	−1	0	0	1
5	0	0	0	1	1	−1
6	0	1	1	−1	−1	0
7	1	−1	0	−1	−1	0
8	1	0	1	0	−1	−1
9	1	1	−1	1	0	0
10	−1	−1	1	1	0	−1
11	−1	0	−1	−1	1	0
12	−1	1	0	0	−1	1
13	0	−1	0	1	−1	0
14	0	0	1	−1	0	1
15	0	1	−1	0	1	−1
16	1	−1	1	0	1	0
17	1	0	−1	1	−1	1
18	1	1	0	−1	0	−1

Note that the columns corresponding to the design variables in Table 6.5 are orthogonal. In general, for an orthogonal array $A = (x_1, x_2, \ldots, x_k)$:

$$\mathbf{x}_i^{\mathrm{T}}\mathbf{x}_j = 0, \qquad i \neq j.$$

Thus,

$$(-1, -1, 1, 1) \cdot (-1, 1, -1, 1) = 0,$$

$$(-1, -1, 1, 1) \cdot (-1, 1, 1, -1) = 0,$$

and

$$(-1, 1, -1, 1) \cdot (-1, 1, 1, -1) = 0.$$

Since any two columns are independent, the levels of the two corresponding variables are linearly independent and their effect on the response is evaluated independently of each other. Note that the OA in Table 6.5 samples a three-variable problem in only 4 points compared to the 8 points needed by the 2^k design.

Table 6.6 shows an array which can be used for three design variables sampled at three levels. Again, it can be noted that the three columns corresponding to the three design variables are orthogonal to each other. Again, compared with the three-level factorial design which takes 27 points to sample the design space, the L_9 OA takes only 9 points. This advantage becomes particularly striking as the number of design variables increase. Thus a three-level design for six design variables is shown by the L_{18} OA in Table 6.7. For such a case, the three-level factorial design would require 729 points.

Example 6.11 Use an L_9 orthogonal array to fit a first-order response surface for the beam frequency problem in (6.4) using three design variables.

Solution: The L_9 OA points and the frequency values at these points are shown below.

Number	Physical points	Coded points	Frequency ω
1	$(0.99m_0, 0.9EI_0, 0.9L_0)$	$(-1, -1, -1)$	$3.516\sqrt{\frac{0.9EI_0}{0.99m_0(0.9L_0)^4}} = 26.6773$
2	$(0.99m_0, EI_0, L_0)$	$(-1, 0, 0)$	$3.516\sqrt{\frac{EI_0}{0.99m_0(L_0)^4}} = 22.7775$
3	$(0.99m_0, 1.1EI_0, 1.1L_0)$	$(-1, 1, 1)$	$3.516\sqrt{\frac{1.1EI_0}{0.99m_0(1.1L_0)^4}} = 19.7431$
4	$(m_0, 0.9EI_0, L_0)$	$(0, -1, 0)$	$3.516\sqrt{\frac{0.9EI_0}{m_0(L_0)^4}} = 21.5003$
5	$(m_0, EI_0, 1.1L_0)$	$(0, 0, 1)$	$3.516\sqrt{\frac{EI_0}{m_0(1.1L_0)^4}} = 18.73$
6	$(m_0, 1.1EI_0, 0.9L_0)$	$(0, 1, -1)$	$3.516\sqrt{\frac{1.1EI_0}{m_0(0.9L_0)^4}} = 29.3450$
7	$(1.01m_0, 0.9EI_0, 1.1L_0)$	$(1, -1, 1)$	$3.516\sqrt{\frac{0.9EI_0}{1.01m_0(1.1L_0)^4}} = 17.6806$
8	$(1.01m_0, EI_0, 0.9L_0)$	$(1, 0, -1)$	$3.516\sqrt{\frac{EI_0}{1.01m_0(0.9L_0)^4}} = 27.8405$
9	$(1.01m_0, 1.1EI_0, L_0)$	$(1, 1, 0)$	$3.516\sqrt{\frac{1.1EI_0}{1.01m_0(L_0)^4}} = 23.6515$

The next step is to construct the vectors and matrices needed to get the least-squares estimates.

$$\boldsymbol{\omega} = \begin{Bmatrix} 26.6773 \\ 22.7775 \\ 19.7431 \\ 21.5003 \\ 18.73 \\ 29.3450 \\ 17.6806 \\ 27.8405 \\ 23.6515 \end{Bmatrix} \quad \mathbf{X} = \begin{bmatrix} 1 & -1 & -1 & -1 \\ 1 & -1 & 0 & 0 \\ 1 & -1 & 1 & 1 \\ 1 & 0 & -1 & 0 \\ 1 & 0 & 0 & 1 \\ 1 & 0 & 1 & -1 \\ 1 & 1 & -1 & 1 \\ 1 & 1 & 0 & -1 \\ 1 & 1 & 1 & 0 \end{bmatrix} \quad \boldsymbol{\beta} = \begin{Bmatrix} \beta_0 \\ \beta_1 \\ \beta_2 \\ \beta_3 \\ \beta_{11} \\ \beta_{22} \\ \beta_{33} \\ \beta_{12} \\ \beta_{23} \\ \beta_{13} \end{Bmatrix}$$

We solve for the regression coefficients using the equation:

$$\mathbf{b} = (\mathbf{X}^{\mathrm{T}}\mathbf{X})^{-1}\mathbf{X}^{\mathrm{T}}\boldsymbol{\omega}.$$

The response surface is thus obtained:

$$\hat{\omega} = 23.1051 - 0.0042x_1 + 1.1469x_2 - 4.6182x_3.$$

Comparing with the response surface in Example 6.4, we see that the main effects are captured quite well with fewer design points.

It should be clear that the sparse sampling done by OAs may not result in high-quality response surfaces. However, they can provide an idea of the main effects using very few samples. Furthermore, in cases where *a better design* is needed quickly, one can use an OA based sampling of the design space to obtain a better design than the baseline design. Some researchers have used OA to develop *underfitted RSMs* and have shown reasonable performance in optimization problems. However, these results tend to be dependant on the function and design space and need to be investigated for different problems. No general guidelines about the use of OAs can be given for RSMs.

We should use any response surfaces generated using OAs with care. The OAs are better suited for rapid exploration of the design space. They could also be used to generate an initial population of points from which gradient based algorithms can be started to search the design space. Orthogonal arrays can also be utilized to enhance a starting population of genetic algorithms or for starting points for gradient-based algorithms for multimodal problems.

Example 6.12 Find a good starting point for gradient-based methods using the orthogonal arrays for the function given below:

$$f(\mathbf{x}) = x_1^2 + 2x_2^2 + 3x_3^2 + \mathrm{e}^{-x_1-x_2-x_3},$$

$$-1 \le x_i, \le 1, \qquad i = 1, 3.$$

Solution: We can use the L_9 OA to scan the design space within the given move limits. In this problem, the physical and coded variables are the same for the factorial points. We can calculate the function values at the L_9 OA points as given below

Number	Point (x)	$f(\mathbf{x})$
1	$-1, -1, -1$	26.08
2	$-1, 0, 0$	3.72
3	$-1, 1, 1$	6.37
4	$0, -1, 0$	4.72
5	$0, 0, 1$	3.37
6	$0, -1, -1$	6.00
7	$1, -1, 1$	6.37
8	$1, 0, -1$	5.00
9	$1, 1, 0$	3.13

The lowest value of $f(\mathbf{x})$ occurs at (1, 1, 0). This value can be used as a starting point for a gradient-based method. It could also be used as a satisfactory design point if optimization algorithms are not available. For instance, it is certainly much better than $(-1, -1, -1)$.

Problems

1. Fit a first-order and second-order response surface for the following function using the two-level factorial design and the CCD design, respectively. Use (0, 0) as the centre point and -5 and 5 as the lower and upper values corresponding to the factorial points.

$$f(\mathbf{x}) = x_1^2 - x_1x_2 + 2x_2^2 - 2x_1 + e^{x_1+x_2} + 10.$$

By plotting the curves, see how the approximations compare with the actual functions?

2. Minimize the following function starting from (2, 2)

$$f(\mathbf{x}) = \frac{1}{2}(x_1 - 2x_2)^2 + x_1^4 + 2.$$

Use second-order response surface approximations and FCD with moves of 100 per cent? Perform two sequential approximations and see if you can reach the minimum.

3. Fit a cubic response surface for the following function using the three-level factorial design.

$$f(x) = 2x_1^2 + x_2^2 - 2x_1x_2 + 2x_1^3 + x_1^4 + 5.$$

Use (0, 0) and the centre point and −5 and 5 foı the lower and upper factorial point coordinates, respectively. Compare the function and the approximation graphically and analyse the residuals.

4. Fit a second-order response surface using CCD for the function

$$f(\mathbf{x}) = x_1^2 + 2x_2^2 + e^{-x_1-x_2}.$$

Use (0.5, 0.5) as the centre point and −0.5 and +0.5 as the minimum and maximum moves for the factorial points. What is the minimum point of the response surface?

5. Fit a second-order response surface using CCD for the function

$$f(\mathbf{x}) = x_1^2 + 3x_2^2 + e^{-x_1-x_2}.$$

Use (0.5, 0.5) as the centre point and −0.5 and +0.5 as the minimum and maximum moves for the factorial points. What is the minimum point of the response surface?

6. Using FCD design, find the minimum point of the following problem in the first quadrant:

Minimize

$$f(\mathbf{x}) = x_1^2 + 3x_2^2 + e^{-x_1-x_2},$$

subject to the conditions:

$$x_1 + x_2 \geq 4,$$

$$0 \leq x_1, \qquad x_2 \leq 1.$$

Use KKT conditions along with the response surfaces.

7. Using FCD design, find the minimum point of the following problem:

Minimize

$$f(\mathbf{x}) = x_1^2 + 2x_2^2 + e^{-x_1-x_2},$$

subject to the conditions:

$$x_1 + x_2 \leq 4,$$

$$0 \leq x_1, \qquad x_2 \leq 1.$$

8. Fit a second-order response surface using CCD for the function

$$f(\mathbf{x}) = 10 - x_1 + x_1x_2 + x_2^2.$$

Take (0, 0) as the centre point and moves of −1 and +1 for the factorial points. Does the RSM match the quadratic function?

9. Use response surfaces based on PLS to find the minimum of

$$f(\mathbf{x}) = x_1^2 + 3x_2^2 + e^{-x_1-x_2}$$

$$-1 \leq x_1, \qquad x_2 \leq 1$$

Use the FCD to start the process and a sub-scaled FCD at 75 per cent, 50 per cent and 25 per cent of the FCD square. Try second-order and cubic response surfaces. Do not use a sequence of response surfaces but refine within the given move limits. Comment on your results.

10. Consider the function

$$f(\mathbf{x}) = x_1^2 + 2x_2^2 + 3x_3^2 + e^{-x_1-x_2-x_3},$$
$$-1 \le x_i \le 1, \qquad i = 1, 3.$$

Find a good starting point for gradient-search optimization using a 3^k design?

11. Consider the function

$$f(\mathbf{x}) = x_1^2 + 2x_2^2 + 3x_3^2 + 4x_4^2 + 5x_5^2 + 6x_6^2 + e^{-x_1-x_2-x_3-x_4-x_5-x_6},$$
$$-1 \le x_i \le 1, \qquad i = 1, 6.$$

Find a good starting point for gradient-search optimization using the L_{18} orthogonal array?

12. Find a second-order FCD response surface about the centre point $(2, -1, 0, 1)$ for the following function:

$$f(\mathbf{x}) = (x_1 + 2x_2 - 1)^2 + 5(x_3 - x_4)^2 + (x_2 - 3x_3)^4 + 10(x_1 - x_4)^4.$$

The design variables have the following move limits: $0 \le x_1 \le 4$, $-2 \le x_2, x_3, x_4 \le 2$. How does the approximation compare with the actual function at the FCD points? Plot and compare the two functions. How do the minimum points compare?

13. Find a third-order response surface about the centre point $(2, -1, 0, 1)$ for the following function:

$$f(\mathbf{x}) = (x_1 + 2x_2 - 1)^2 + 5(x_3 - x_4)^2 + (x_2 - 3x_3)^4 + 10(x_1 - x_4)^4.$$

Use a three-level factorial design. The design variables have the following move limits: $0 \le x_1 \le 4$, $-2 \le x_2, x_3, x_4 \le 2$. How does the approximation compare with the actual function at the 3^k points? Plot and compare the two functions. How do the minimum points compare?

14. Find a fourth-order response surface about the centre point $(2, -1, 0, 1)$ for the following function:

$$f(\mathbf{x}) = (x_1 + 2x_2 - 1)^2 + 5(x_3 - x_4)^2 + (x_2 - 3x_3)^4 + 10(x_1 - x_4)^4.$$

Use a three-level factorial design. The design variables have the following move limits: $0 \le x_1 \le 4$, $-2 \le x_2, x_3, x_4 \le 2$. How does the approximation compare with the actual function at the 3^k points? Plot and compare the two functions. How do the minimum points compare? Experiment with added random points to improve the response surface.

7 Genetic Algorithm

The genetic algorithm (GA) is based on Darwin's theory of natural selection. It was developed by John Holland in the mid-1960s. Genetic algorithms use the *survival of the fittest* strategy to find the optimal starting point from a population of candidate points. They are inspired by models from biology and simulate the process of evolution which leads to the selection of some species over others through generations.

Unlike gradient-based methods which require a starting point and are likely to settle into a local minimum, genetic algorithms have the ability to locate the global minimum by using a starting population. Functions with more than one local minimum are called multimodal functions and are better addressed by GA. In addition, genetic algorithms require only function evaluations and the problems associated with gradient calculations are avoided. In other words, gradient-based methods require differentiability of the objective function and constraints; whereas, GA is a zero-order method. However, genetic algorithms require a very large number of iterations and function evaluations because they work simultaneously on a population of points. Therefore, GA can be time-consuming for problems where the function evaluations are computationally expensive. Nevertheless, they are a good choice if there is a possibility of multiple minimum points in the feasible region, or when the design variables are integers or consist of discrete values.

7.1 Optimization Problems

Due to historical reasons, GA operates by means of maximization of a function. The objective function is called the *fitness function* and the goal of the program is to maximize *fitness*. The unconstrained optimization problem solved using GA should be expressed as follows:[7]

Maximize

$$f(\mathbf{x}), \tag{7.1}$$

subject to move limits

$$x_i^L \leq x_i \leq x_i^U, \qquad i = 1 \text{ to } n. \tag{7.2}$$

In GA, we want to keep the function $f(\mathbf{x}) > 0$ to enable us to apply various operators which are based on probability calculations. This is easily accomplished by adding a large positive constant to the objective function. Addition of such a constant does not change the optimal point. Another thing that is done in order to convert a minimization problem to a maximization problem, is to make the following transformation. Consider the problem of maximizing

$$F(\mathbf{x}) = \frac{1}{1 + f(\mathbf{x})}. \tag{7.3}$$

As can be seen, this is equivalent to the problem of minimizing the other function in the equation, namely, $f(\mathbf{x})$.

The constrained optimization problem can be converted to an unconstrained optimization problem using the penalty method discussed in Chapter 5.

$$\Phi(\mathbf{x}) = f(\mathbf{x}) + r\sum_{j=1}^{m} \max(0, g_j(\mathbf{x}))^2 + r\sum_{k=1}^{p} h_k(\mathbf{x})^2. \tag{7.4}$$

Here r is a penalty parameter which is usually kept constant through the GA simulation. Penalty functions show large nonlinearity near the constraint boundary and therefore create problems for many gradient-based methods when the value of r is increased. However, GAs can easily handle nonlinearity as they do not require gradient information and therefore, a large penalty r can be used in GAs. Exact penalty functions are also suitable for use in GAs as they do not need to be differentiated.

Another simple approach to handling constraints in GA is to use the so-called *death penalty*. In this approach, any design variable point that lies outside the feasible region is removed from the population.

There are two popular GA types: binary GA and real GA, which are discussed in the following sections.

7.2 Binary GA

As the name suggests, binary GA operates with a binary representation of the design variables. Since many practical optimization problems involve continuous design variables, these need to be expressed in terms of binary values through a transformation. The basic GA algorithm involves the following steps, which will be explained in detail later in the chapter.

7.2.1 Binary genetic algorithm summary

1. Binary GA begins with a population of random binary strings. Encoding and decoding is needed for the program to move between the binary numbers and continuous numbers for continuous design variables.
2. Each string is evaluated and the *objective function* corresponding to the string value called the *fitness value* is determined.
3. The population is then operated upon by three genetic operators: reproduction, crossover and mutation to create a new population of strings.
4. The new population is evaluated and tested for termination criteria.

5. If a termination criterion is not met, the population is operated upon by the three genetic operators and evaluated.
6. The generations are continued until the termination criteria are met.

In the following sections, we discuss these steps in detail and illustrate them using examples.

7.2.2 Coding and decoding of variables

In binary GA, we express the real design variables x_i as a binary string of m bits.[8] Typically, the length m of the string is determined by the desired solution accuracy. For example, two bits 0 and 1 can lead to (00), (01), (10) and (11) or four substrings. In general, m bits lead to 2^m unique substrings. In some combinatorial optimization problems, we need to select between several possible cases, and we also have to deal with discrete variables. In such cases, we can simply define each case using a substring. For example, if we have four material possibilities, we could define:

$$\begin{aligned}
(00) &\rightarrow \text{Steel}\\
(01) &\rightarrow \text{Aluminium}\\
(11) &\rightarrow \text{Graphite–epoxy composite}\\
(10) &\rightarrow \text{Titanium}
\end{aligned} \tag{7.5}$$

In such a problem, there is no need to move between the *real* and *binary* domains and so encoding–decoding is not needed. However, many optimization problems involve real-number design variables, and therefore, we need to factor in how to achieve encoding and decoding.

Consider two variables, x_1 and x_2. Let us use four bits to code each variable. Then (0000) represents the smallest value of the design variables and (1111) represents the highest value. Thus we have,

$$\begin{aligned}
(x_1^L, x_2^L) &= (0000, 0000) = (00000000)\\
(x_1^U, x_2^U) &= (1111, 1111) = (11111111)
\end{aligned} \tag{7.6}$$

Therefore, each of the two design variables can be written as an eight-bit string. Consider a string $s = (s_{m-1}, s_{m-2}, s_{m-3}, \ldots, s_2, s_1, s_0)$ composed of bits $s_i \in (0, 1)$. The decoded value of the string s can be expressed as shown below:

$$Dv(s) = \sum_{i=0}^{m-1} 2^i s_i. \tag{7.7}$$

For example, the string (0111) has a decoded value as given here:

$$\sum_{i=0}^{4-1} 2^i s_i = 2^0 s_0 + 2^1 s_1 + 2^2 s_2 + 2^3 s_3 = 2^0.1 + 2^1.1 + 2^2.1 + 2^3.0 = 7. \tag{7.8}$$

To see how the design space is represented by the binary strings, let $(x_1^L, x_2^L) = (0, 0)$ and $(x_1^U, x_2^U) = (10, 10)$. The point in the design space represented by a substring s_i can then be found using the following equation:

$$x_i = x_i^L + \frac{x_i^U - x_i^L}{2^m - 1} Dv(s_i). \tag{7.9}$$

Then,

$$x_1 = 0 + \frac{10}{2^4 - 1} Dv(s_i) = \frac{2}{3} Dv(s_i),$$
$$x_2 = 0 + \frac{10}{2^4 - 1} Dv(s_i) = \frac{2}{3} Dv(s_i). \tag{7.10}$$

For (0000) we have, $Dv(s_i) = 2^0.0 + 2^1.0 + 2^2.0 + 2^3.0 = 0$. For (1111) we have, $Dv(s_i) = 2^0.1 + 2^1.1 + 2^2.1 + 2^3.1 = 15$. Note that for a four-bit string, only $2^4 = 16$ distinct substrings are possible. We can get back the design variables from the strings for the lower and upper bounds as follows:

$$x_1^L = \frac{2}{3} Dv(s_i) = \frac{2}{3} \cdot 0 = 0 = x_2^L,$$
$$x_1^U = \frac{2}{3} Dv(s_i) = \frac{2}{3} \cdot 15 = 10 = x_2^U. \tag{7.11}$$

Now consider a generic string (0111) for which $Dv(s_i) = 7$. This gives

$$x_i = \frac{2}{3} Dv(s_i) = \frac{2}{3} \cdot 7 = 4.67. \tag{7.12}$$

Table 7.1 shows the various decoded values for the sixteen possible strings and their mapped values into the design space. It is clear that the 16 possible strings only provide a rough sampling of the design space in increments of 0.67. The sampling accuracy can be increased by adding more bits to each string. Thus, when we use a five-bit string, it results in thirty-two substrings which provide a denser sampling of the design space. It is also possible to code different design variables with different substring lengths, depending on the desired accuracy. In general, we can say: for a variable coded using *m* bits, the accuracy is given by $(x_i^U - x_i^L)/2^m$, approximately.

In binary GA, the number of bits used to represent a design variable is important for the accuracy of solution and the number of generations required for the GA to converge. In most cases, users tend to use too many bits to represent continuous design variables as they are misguided by the machine precision of the computer. However, long strings slow down the process of convergence of binary GA and also increase storage requirements. A better idea is to study each design variable using physical reasoning to identify the level of quantization needed. For example, design specifications, manufacturing limitations etc. contribute to the required numerical accuracy. *One advantage of binary GA is that when the problem is properly constructed, it explores the design space only to the desired level of accuracy.*

In some texts, strings are referred to as *chromosomes* in tune with the biological analogy. The continuous design variables are therefore expressed as chromosomes consisting of bits.

Table 7.1 *Binary, decoded and actual values for four-bit substrings*

	Four-bit binary substring				Decoded value	Actual value
1	1	0	0	0	8	5.33
2	0	1	0	0	4	2.67
3	0	0	1	0	2	1.33
4	0	0	0	1	1	0.67
5	1	1	0	0	12	8.00
6	1	0	1	0	10	6.67
7	1	0	0	1	9	6.00
8	0	1	1	0	6	4.00
9	0	1	0	1	5	3.33
10	0	0	1	1	3	2.00
11	1	1	1	0	14	9.33
12	0	1	1	1	7	4.67
13	1	0	1	1	11	7.33
14	1	1	0	1	13	8.67
15	0	0	0	0	0	0.00
16	1	1	1	1	15	10.00

7.2.3 Key steps in a GA

Once we have encoded the design variables into bits and strings, the other steps of GA can be performed.[9] The key steps in the binary GA are (1) creation of a *starting population* $P(0)$ from a sample P_{init}. Set generation as $k = 0$; (2) evaluation of *fitness* of population $P(k)$; (3) creation of *mating pool* $M(k)$; (4) *crossover* and (5) *mutation*. At the end of step (5), a new population $P(k+1)$ has been created and we return to the evaluation of its fitness in Step (2). Each cycle of the population going through step (2) to step (5) consists of a generation. Generally, GAs are terminated after a maximum number of generations are reached and the best fitness value during the generations is taken as the *optimal value*. Other termination criteria can also be placed to stop the GA before reaching the maximum number of iterations. For example, if there is no improvement in the best design for several generations, one can terminate the process. However, sometimes it can happen that the GA can stagnate for a few generations and then suddenly move towards the global optimum due to a fortunate *random crossover* or *mutation*.

7.2.3.1 Starting population

The first step in the development of GA is the creation of an initial population P_{init}. Each member of the population is a string of size $n \times m$ bits. Consider $m = 6$ (six-bit) strings with n design variables. The variables in binary form are attached end-to-end as follows:

$$\text{Member 1}: \underbrace{101101}_{x_{11}} \quad \underbrace{101001}_{x_{12}} \quad \underbrace{001010}_{x_{13}} \quad \cdots \quad \underbrace{101111}_{x_{1n}}$$

$$\text{Member 2}: \underbrace{101001}_{x_{21}} \quad \underbrace{100001}_{x_{22}} \quad \underbrace{001110}_{x_{23}} \quad \cdots \quad \underbrace{101001}_{x_{2n}}$$
$$\vdots \tag{7.13}$$
$$\text{Member } N: \underbrace{101001}_{x_{N1}} \quad \underbrace{101101}_{x_{N2}} \quad \underbrace{101010}_{x_{N3}} \quad \cdots \quad \underbrace{101100}_{x_{Nn}}$$

The size of the population is N and the matrix of strings has size $N \times n$. The total number of bits defining the population is therefore $m \times N \times n$. The initial population is created on a computer using a uniform random-number generator. A random bit is generated using a random number between 0 and 1 as follows:

$$\begin{aligned} &\text{If } rand(\,) \leq 0.5 \text{ put } 0; \\ &\text{Else if } rand(\,) > 0.5 \text{ put } 1. \end{aligned} \tag{7.14}$$

Such *rand*( ) functions are included in most programming languages such as FORTRAN, C and Matlab. Thus, a binary substring of length five can be easily generated using five calls to a random number generator. For example, five calls can result in (0.89181, 0.181053, 0.207156, 0.713374, 0.349893) using *rand*( ) and yield (10010) as the substring. Extending this approach to all the design variables, the binary strings for each member of the population can be created and N such strings will constitute the starting population.

A good sampling of the design space helps to greatly improve the performance of the GA. For a problem with several local minima, a large initial sample is useful. In general, it is a good idea to create an initial population that is larger than the population used for the later GA generations and keep only N best members, in terms of the cost function for future operations. This process is analogous to a competitive entrance exam. As a rule of thumb, one can use 1.2 N to 2 N as the initial population, depending on the computational expense of the function evaluations in the problem.

Most studies recommend using a randomly generated starting population. However, there are times when a random sampling can result in an oversampling of one region of the design space and a sparse sampling of another region. This problem can be alleviated by using uniform sampling of the design space. As an example, consider the problem discussed earlier in Table 7.1, where the two design variables are coded using four bits each and the decoded value ranges from 0 to 15. For two variables, there are a total of $16 \times 16 = 256$ possible points in the design space of decoded values. Noticing that the decoded values range from 0 to 15, we can sample the space in increments of five corresponding to the binary strings shown in Table 7.2. These will yield sixteen values, which are shown in Table 7.3.

Another alternative solution involves creating a random population and then taking the complements of the strings to create a complement of the random population. For example, consider a population of five strings of eight bits each:

Random string1 : 01101101

Random string2 : 11101001

Random string3 : 01000001

Random string4 : 11101111

Random string5 : 01001100 (7.15)

The complement of this population can be obtained by replacing 1 by 0 and 0 by 1 in the random strings.

Complement string1 : 10010010

Complement string2 : 00010110

Complement string3 : 10111110

Complement string4 : 00010000

Complement string5 : 10110011 (7.16)

The complement strings enhance diversity by ensuring that each bit assumes both a 0 and 1 value in the population. The user can use a combination of different strategies to create the starting population. For example, one-half of the population could be obtained

Table 7.2 *Decoded values for uniform sampling*

	Four-bit binary substring				Decoded value	Actual value
1	0	0	0	0	0	0.00
2	0	1	0	1	5	3.33
3	1	0	1	0	10	6.67
4	1	1	1	1	15	10.00

Table 7.3 *Starting population using uniform sampling for two variables*

	Decoded pair	Four-bit binary substring 1				Four-bit binary substring 2			
1	0,0	0	0	0	0	0	0	0	0
2	0,5	0	0	0	0	0	1	0	1
3	0,10	0	0	0	0	1	0	1	0
4	0,15	0	0	0	0	1	1	1	1
5	5,0	0	1	0	1	0	0	0	0
6	5,5	0	1	0	1	0	1	0	1
7	5,10	0	1	0	1	1	0	1	0
8	5,15	0	1	0	1	1	1	1	1
9	10,0	1	0	1	0	0	0	0	0
10	10,5	1	0	1	0	0	1	0	1
11	10,10	1	0	1	0	1	0	1	0
12	10,15	1	0	1	0	1	1	1	1
13	15,0	1	1	1	1	0	0	0	0
14	15,5	1	1	1	1	0	1	0	1
15	15,10	1	1	1	1	1	0	1	0
16	15,15	1	1	1	1	1	1	1	1

by uniform sampling and the other half by taking random values and their complements. This initial population of size $2N$ could then be pruned to N by taking the best N values.

We end this discussion with the caveat that for problems where function evaluation costs are high, a sparse sample of the design space is needed. Even in such cases, using the combined approach of uniform, random and complement sampling is likely to sample the design space in a better manner. A good starting population provides a head start to the genetic algorithm.

As an aside, we point out that a starting solution can also be used to generate starting points for gradient-based methods in exploring the design space for multimodal functions. An RSM- or OA-based sampling of the design space can also be used to create a starting population, along with randomly generated points.

7.2.3.2 Fitness evaluation

In this phase, real values of variables for each member are extracted from the binary representations. Sets of binary digits are read, and decoding is done using the formulas discussed in the sequence of equations (7.6–11). For example, the binary two-variable string (01110001) leads to the decoded value (7, 1) which then leads to real coordinates (4.67, 0.67), as can be seen from Table 7.1.

Once we have the real coordinate values, the function values $f_1, f_2, f_3, \ldots, f_N$ are evaluated for the N strings in the populations. Function values are called *fitness* values in the GA terminology, as fitness maximization is the goal of the typical GA algorithm. The average fitness at generation k is termed $\bar{f}(k)$ and is calculated using the equation given below:

$$\bar{f}(k) = \frac{f_1 + f_2 + \cdots + f_N}{N}. \tag{7.17}$$

In general, we expect the average fitness to increase as the generations make progress. The best value of the design variable at the current generation is obtained by finding the $\mathbf{x}^{(\max)}(k)$ corresponding to $f^{(\max)}(k) = \max(f_1, f_2, \ldots, f_N)$. Both $\mathbf{x}^{(\max)}(k)$ and $f^{(\max)}(k)$ are saved and stored.

7.2.3.3 Reproduction

Reproduction selects good strings from the population to form a *mating pool*. It is typically the first operator applied to the population. The essential idea of reproduction is that above-average strings are picked from the current population and their multiple copies are inserted in the mating pool in a probabilistic manner. Two popular approaches for reproduction are roulette wheel selection and tournament selection.[8]

(1) *Roulette wheel selection* In this approach, a string is selected for the mating pool with the probability proportional to its fitness. The steps are as follows:

(a) Select the ith string in the population with a probability proportional to its fitness value f_i. Since the population size is kept fixed in simple GA, the sum of probabilities of

Table 7.4 *Roulette wheel selection*

String j	Fitness (f_j)	$p_j = f_j / \sum_{k=1}^{N} f_k$	$P_j = \sum_{i=1}^{j} p_i$
1	25	0.21	0.21
2	15	0.126	$= 0.21 + 0.126 = 0.336$
3	46	0.3865	$= 0.336 + 0.3865 = 0.7225$
4	13	0.109	$= 0.7225 + 0.109 = 0.8315$
5	20	0.168	$= 0.8315 + 0.168 = 1$
	$\sum_{j=1}^{N=5} f_j = 119$		

each string being selected for the mating pool must be 1. So the probability of selecting the ith string in the mating pool is given by the following:

$$p_i = \frac{f_i}{\sum_{j=1}^{N} f_j}, \tag{7.18}$$

where N is the population size.

(b) The roulette wheel mechanism makes $f_i/\bar{f}$ copies of the ith string in the mating pool where the variables are defined as follows:

$$\bar{f} = \sum_{j=1}^{N} \frac{f_j}{N}. \tag{7.19}$$

The selection is based on first creating the cumulative probability of each string being copied which is obtained by adding the individual probabilities as shown in Table 7.4 for a population of five strings with different fitness values.

(c) We see that the ith string in the population has a cumulative probability between P_{i-1} and P_i. Thus the first string represents the cumulative probability between 0 and P_1. The cumulative probability of any string lies between 0 and 1. The cumulative probability of the Nth string must be 1.

(d) To choose N strings from the population to form the mating pool, create N random numbers between 0 and 1. Select the string j corresponding to the cumulative probability range within which the random number lies. For example, if the random number is 0.5687, the cumulative probability is between 0.336 and 0.7225 and therefore string 3 is added to the mating pool. As a numerical experiment, we obtained the following five random numbers and selected the strings as shown in Table 7.5.

We can see that the roulette wheel selection selects more copies of the fitter strings 1 and 3. Also note that strings 4 and 5 have been discarded and the average fitness of the population has gone up. The mates can now be selected by taking the strings corresponding to random number 1 and 2 (strings 1 and 3), random numbers 3 and 4 (strings 2 and 1), assuming that only 80 per cent of the population is earmarked for the process of crossover and mutation. The strategy of keeping the best string unchanged (string 3 corresponding to

Table 7.5 *Creation of mating pool using roulette wheel selection*

No.	Random number	Cumulative probability range	String selected for mating pool	Fitness value
1	0.129834	0–0.21	1	25
2	0.568717	0.336–0.7225	3	46
3	0.222259	0.21–0.336	2	15
4	0.193974	0–0.21	1	25
5	0.70199	0.336–0.7225	3	46
				$\sum_{j=1}^{N=5} f_j = 157$

random number 5) is typical of *elitism*. In general, elitism leads to better results with GA, though in some cases it can lead to a loss of diversity in the population.

Unfortunately, roulette wheel selection as discussed until now has two problems. The first problem is encountered if the population contains an exceptionally fit string. A situation like this can happen in a constrained optimization problem where all designs except one or two are infeasible. In such cases, simple application of roulette wheel selection will result in formation of a very large number of copies of the fit string in the mating pool. The diversity of the mating pool is then reduced and the GA will stagnate. The second problem is met when the population contains several equally good points. Such a situation can occur after several generations of GA runs. In such cases, each individual is copied to the mating pool which hardly changes from generation to generation.

The two problems: existence of one exceptionally fit string or several equally good strings can be addressed by using a linear transformation:[8]

$$S(x) = af(x) + b. \tag{7.20}$$

Here $S(x)$ is a scaled fitness function, $f(x)$ is the original fitness function and a and b are constants which are defined to (1) give the best string in the population a predefined number of copies in the mating pool and (2) give an average string one copy in the mating pool. This linear transformation when performed at each generation eliminates the two shortcomings of the roulette wheel selection method.

There are several other methods for creating the mating pool. For example, tournament selection is another effective strategy, which we discuss next.

(2) *Tournament selection* In tournament selection, a subset of s individuals is randomly picked from the population and the best string from the subset is selected for the mating pool. Binary tournament selection ($s = 2$) is often used with the idea of closely modelling mating competition which is seen in nature, The tournament selection is performed as follows:

(a) The whole population is shuffled randomly to remove any *ordering* which may have crept in due to other operations.

(b) The first s strings $(1, 2, 3, \ldots, s-1, s)$ are picked from the top of the shuffled list and the *best string* is chosen for the mating pool. Since binary tournament selection is most commonly used, we take the first two strings and then select the best among these two.

(c) The next s strings $(s+1, s+2, s+3, \ldots, 2s)$ are then selected and the best string is selected for the *mating pool.*

(d) The process is continued for all the members of the population selected for mating. As discussed earlier, the best value in the population may be left untouched based on *elitism.*

(e) The whole population is then *shuffled* again and the process is repeated until the mating pool is formed.

To illustrate how tournament selection works, let us consider the problem in Tables 7.6 and 7.7. These tables depict the scenario when the population is shuffled twice to create the mating pool.

Based on these two tournaments, we can select (1, 3) and (2, 1) as the two mates. If we have selected an 80 per cent crossover rate, we can perform operations on these four strings while keeping the fifth string as the best value (string 3 in this case) unchanged.

From the discussion until now, we see that (a) *modified roulette wheel selection* using a linear transformation of the fitness function and (b) *tournament selection* are good approaches for selecting a mating pool. Generally, tournament selection is recommended as the better approach. To summarize, good strings in a population are assigned a larger number of copies for the creation of the mating pool. It should be noted that *no new strings*

Table 7.6 *Tournament selection – step 1*

String j	Fitness (f_j)	Best among two
1	25	25 (string 1)
2	15	
3	46	46 (string 3)
4	13	
5	20	

Table 7.7 *Tournament selection – step 2*

String j	Fitness (f_j)	Best among two
4	13	15 (string 2)
2	15	
1	25	25 (string 1)
5	20	
3	46	

are created during the creation of the mating pool and therefore *no new points in the design space are explored*. New strings are created using the crossover and mutation operators discussed next.

7.2.3.4 Crossover

Once the mating pool has been formed, genetic information between two strings is exchanged to create a *new population*. This process of exchange of information between two strings is called the *crossover process*. Crossover is the process by which the genetic algorithm moves across the design space as new strings are created. Typically, two parents are allowed to create two children so that the population remains constant.

The simplest crossover is the *single-point crossover* which is performed by randomly choosing a crossing site along the string and then exchanging all the bits to the right of the crossing site. We will call the two strings selected for crossover as the *father* and *mother* strings. The two strings resulting after crossover are called the *child strings*. An example of one-point crossover for four parents represented with eight-bit strings is shown next. Consider the two sets of parents:

Father1 : 00110101

Mother1 : 11110110 (7.21)

Father2 : 11000100

Mother2 : 01010011 (7.22)

Since the string has $m = 8$ bits, we can select any number between 1 and $m - 1 = 7$ as the crossing site. This is accomplished by generating a random number between 1 and 7 and then rounding off to the nearest integer. For example, if a and b are the minimum and maximum values of the random number r', we can use a random number generated within $0 \le r \le 1$ and then calculate $r' = (b - a)r + a$. For example, we got two random numbers 0.329883 and 0.895658 between 0 and 1, which lead to 2.979298 and 6.373948 between 1 and 7. This yields 3 and 6 as the two crossover sites. The children of the pair in (7.21) following crossover at site 3 are then as given below:

Father1 : 00110|101

Mother1 : 11110|110 (7.23)

Child1 : 00110|110

Child2 : 11110|101 (7.24)

In the above equations, we have simply swapped the bits of the three rightmost bits between the father and mother strings. The children of the pair in (7.22) following crossover at site 6 are then obtained:

Father2 : 11|000100

Mother2 : 01|010011 (7.25)

$$\text{Child3} : 11|010011$$

$$\text{Child4} : 01|000100 \tag{7.26}$$

Here we have swapped the six rightmost bits between the father and mother strings.

Since the crossover is done at a randomly selected site, the child strings may or may not be better than the parent strings. If good strings are created, there will be more copies of them in the next generation. On the other hand, bad children will have less or no copies. In general, crossover can be either beneficial or detrimental. It is therefore better not to use all strings in the crossover. A few good strings can be preserved in the mating pool without any changes. Typically, a crossover probability p_c is used. A p_c value of 0.80 implies that 80 per cent of the mating pool undergoes crossover and 20 per cent remains unchanged. In our simple example with a population of five used for illustrating the selection of the mating pool, an 80 per cent crossover means that four individuals are selected for mating and one is kept unchanged. We can take the best value and some other randomly selected values in the population to get the $(1 - p_c)100$ per cent strings which are to be copied into the next generation without change following the elitism philosophy.

The single-point crossover discussed until now does not provide good search capability in cases involving a large number of design variables. The problem occurs because single-point crossover has a bias towards the rightmost bits of the string and ignores the leftmost bits. Consider a case of four design variables:

$$\mathbf{x} = \{x_1, x_2, x_3, x_4\}. \tag{7.27}$$

Assuming a four-bit coding, the corresponding string looks as shown below:

$$s = \{0110, 1100, 1111, 0011\}. \tag{7.28}$$

A single-point crossover is much more likely to change variable x_4 than variable x_1 because the bits corresponding to x_4 get swapped every time a site to the left of bit 4 is selected. This problem becomes increasingly important as the number of design variables becomes larger.

The *multipoint crossover* avoids this problem of bias towards some design variables by choosing two crossover sites along the string length and swapping the bits inside these two sites. Consider the two strings shown below:

$$\text{Father} : 0110, 1100, 1111, 0011$$

$$\text{Mother} : 1101, 1001, 0110, 1010 \tag{7.29}$$

We generate two random numbers between 1 and 15; let us say we get 4 and 13. Using these two crossover sites at 4 and 13 we get the two children as follows:

$$\text{Child1} : 011|1, 1001, 0110, |0011$$

$$\text{Child2} : 110|0, 1100, 1111, |1010 \tag{7.30}$$

In this example, we see that the multipoint crossover has not changed the rightmost string but the leftmost string. In general, it is a good idea to use multipoint crossover whenever possible.

7.2.3.5 Mutation

Parent selection and crossover operation may result in somewhat identical individuals who may not be fittest. Thus the genetic algorithm can get *stuck* after some time. New genetic information is brought into the population by simulating the process of mutation. *Mutation* is a random operation for changing the fitness and is used sparingly.

The mutation operator changes 1 to 0 and 0 to 1 with a small mutation probability p_m. Every bit of a member of the population is visited. A mutation probability p_m of 0.005 to 0.1 is typically used. A random number r is generated in the range 0 to 1. If $r < p_m$, a bit is changed to 0 if it is 1 and 1 if it is a zero. Otherwise, the bit is left unaltered. Another, more efficient way to implement mutation is to modify $p_m \times m \times n \times N$ bits in the population by changing 1 to 0 and 0 to 1. For example, for two design variables with four-bit strings and a population of five, the strings can be written as follows:

String1 : 01101101

String2 : 11101001

String3 : 01000001

String4 : 11101111

String5 : 01001100 (7.31)

The total number of bits is $4 \times 2 \times 5 = 40$. Taking $p_m = 0.05$, $40 \times 0.05 = 2$; therefore, we should modify two bits. We randomly generate two numbers between 1 and 5 for the five strings (let us say we get 2 and 5) and between 1 and 8 for the eight bits (let us say we get 3 and 7). Thus, we change the bit in (string 2, bit 3) and (string 5, bit 7) to the complement to get the mutated population. Here the bits are measured from the right to the left of the string. The new population is then as given below:

String1 : 01101101

String2 : 11101101

String3 : 01000001

String4 : 11101111

String5 : 00001100 (7.32)

While crossover is the mechanism by which the designs move around over relatively large distances in the design space, mutation is the phenomenon which leads to local movements around the current solution. Mutation adds *diversity* to the population. However, note that mutation often decreases the average fitness of the population. An example of a situation where mutation can help in improving the solution can be seen as follows. Consider five strings:

String1 : 0110011

String2 : 0011100

String3 : 0101010

String4 : 0111111

String5 : 0101110

All the strings above have a zero in the leftmost bit, which cannot be changed by the crossover approaches defined until now. If the optimum requires a 1 in the leftmost bit, it will never be attained if we do not use mutation. Fortunately, mutation allows a finite probability of changing the leftmost bit from zero to one.

Since mutation generally results in a decrease in fitness of the population, the best string is sometimes shielded from mutation based on the elitism philosophy.

7.2.3.6 Evaluation

Following the completion of the three genetic operators, the population has changed. The population is evaluated using the ideas in Step 2 of Section 7.2.3. The highest fitness value in the population, $f^{(\max)}(k)$, and the corresponding design variable, $\mathbf{x}^{(\max)}(k)$, are found and stored. A generation of the GA is now complete. If the number of generations finished until now exceeds the maximum number of generations, then the algorithm is stopped and the best function value and the corresponding design point is selected as the optimal point.

In some cases, the user may want to put in some other convergence criteria besides the maximum number of generations permitted. If there is no improvement in the best function value, $f^{(\max)}(k)$, for several generations, one could terminate the algorithm. This kind of situation can either mean that the GA has found a solution or that it is stuck in a *local minimum*. It may be possible that a random mutation or crossover may result in the solution suddenly improving. However, if the best point does not improve for about ten generations, it may be a better idea to terminate the GA and run it again with a new starting population.

Genetic algorithms are quite sensitive to the proper selection of population size, crossover and mutation probabilities. Many studies have been performed by researchers with different sets of test functions and problems. In general, it has been found that the optimal parameters for a GA depend on the problem at hand. However, based on an analysis of the literature, values such as population size of 20–30, crossover probability of 0.75–0.95 and mutation probability of 0.005–0.01 can be recommended. The user may want to experiment between these values.

7.2.4 Philosophy of GA

The strength of GA comes from the use of probability through random numbers at every step of the algorithm and working on a population rather than on one point as is done in gradient-based methods. The philosophy behind GA can be outlined as follows.

1. Create an initial population of random and other strings.
2. Take a subset of the initial population consisting of the best strings to start the algorithm.
3. Reproduction favours the good strings, and a mating pool is created using a random approach.
4. Crossover combines the good strings in the hope of creating better strings in a random manner.

5. Mutation randomly alters the strings locally in the hope of creating better strings.
6. Neither crossover nor mutation is guaranteed to give only good strings. However, bad strings will be removed in the next generation.
7. Several runs of the GA should be done and the best point from the runs taken. Since each run starts from a different random population, the chance of locating the global optimum is high if several runs are done.

Due to the use of random numbers at nearly every stage of the algorithm, GA is also called a probabilistic or stochastic optimization method. The use of probability in the method is the source of both its strengths and weaknesses relative to the gradient-based methods.

7.2.5 Binary genetic algorithm

For computer implementation, we can write the algorithm as follows:

Step 1 Choose a coding to represent problem parameters, a selection operator, a crossover operator, and a mutation operator. Choose population size, N, crossover probability, p_c, and mutation probability, p_m. Initialize a random or semi-random population of strings based on the move limits of the design variables of size $1.2\,N$ to $2\,N$ and take the N best values for population, P_{init}. Choose the maximum allowable generation number, $k_{\max}$. Set the current generation, $k = 0$.

Step 2 If $k > k_{\max}$, select $f(\mathbf{x}^*) = \max(f^{(\max)}(1), f^{(\max)}(2), \ldots, f^{(\max)}(k_{\max}))$ and the corresponding $\mathbf{x}^*$ as the optimal point and stop; evaluate the fitness function corresponding to each string in the population $P(k)$. Save and store the best fitness function, $f^{(\max)}(k)$, and the corresponding design variable, $\mathbf{x}^{(\max)}(k)$.

Step 3 Perform selection operation to form the mating pool, $M(k)$, while keeping the best value unchanged. Use the modified roulette wheel or tournament selection.

Step 4 Perform a two-point crossover on selected strings in the mating pool.

Step 5 Perform a random mutation on selected strings in the mating pool.

Step 6 Set $k = k + 1$, then go to step 2.

Example 7.1 In a 10 bar truss problem, the cross-section of each member is a design variable. It is decided that the members are to be made with a circular cross-section, with the diameter of the circles as the design variables. This diameter can take a value in the range (5, 30) mm. What is the minimum overall string length for a binary coding of the problem to achieve a solution of up to three decimal places of accuracy?

Solution: The design variable has the following move limits in mm:

$$x^L = 5, \qquad x^U = 30.$$

We can find the bits needed for three decimal places of accuracy using the equation:

$$x_i = x_i^L + \frac{x_i^U - x_i^L}{2^m - 1} Dv(s_i).$$

Using a value of $m = 2$, we get,

$$\frac{x_i^U - x_i^L}{2^2 - 1} = 8.33.$$

Proceeding in this manner we get $m = 14$ as the value, where

$$\frac{x_i^U - x_i^L}{2^{14} - 1} = 0.0015.$$

To get to an accuracy of about three decimal places, 14 bits should be used for each variable. Since we have 10 design variables, we need a 140-bit string.

Example 7.2 In a GA simulation, the following is observed at generation four:

Strings	Fitness
0101101	10
1001001	8
1010110	14
0111110	20
1110111	2
0111100	12

Find the mating pool using roulette wheel selection. Use the random numbers in [0, 1] for 6 trials: 0.119928, 0.942023, 0.546047, 0.862064, 0.343616 and 0.400329.

Solution: Based on the fitness of the strings, the probability and cumulative probability can be obtained as follows:

String j	Fitness (f_j)	$p_j = \frac{f_j}{\sum_{k=1}^{N} f_k}$	$P_j = \sum_{i=1}^{j} p_i$
1	10	0.1515	0.1515
2	8	0.1212	0.2727
3	14	0.2121	0.4848
4	20	0.3030	0.7878
5	2	0.0303	0.8181
6	12	0.1818	1

Here $\sum_{k=1}^{6} f_k = 66$ has been used as total fitness of the strings. To perform the roulette wheel selection, we form the following table:

Random no.	Cumulative probability range	String selected for mating pool	Fitness value
0.119928	0–0.1515	1	10
0.942023	0.8181–1	6	12
0.546047	0.4848–0.7878	4	20
0.862064	0.8181–1	6	12
0.343616	0.2727–0.4848	3	14
0.400329	0.2727–0.4848	3	14
			$\sum_{k=1}^{6} f_k = 82$

The strings selected for the mating pool are 1, 6, 4, 6, 3 and 3. Note that strings 2 and 5 have been discarded in the mating pool. The strings with higher fitness have more copies. The total fitness of the population is now 82, up substantially from 66.

Example 7.3 Consider the function $f(\mathbf{x}) = x_1^2 + 2x_2^2 + e^{-x_1-x_2}$. Perform one generation of a GA to minimize this function. Consider a starting population of 20 random numbers between the move limits $[-1, 1]$ and use an eight-bit representation for each design variable. Take the ten best values from the initial population of 20 for the GA. Perform binary tournament selection to get points for the mating pool and keep two best strings unchanged. Then perform two-point cross-over with $p_c = 0.8$ and mutation with $p_m = 0.005$. Find the best point after one generation.

Solution: The problem is to maximize

$$F(\mathbf{x}) = \frac{1}{1 + x_1^2 + 2x_2^2 + e^{-x_1-x_2}}.$$

Step 1 Starting population

The first step in the development of the GA is the creation of an initial population. It is generated on a computer using a uniform random number generator *rand*( ) as follows:

If *rand*( ) ≤ 0.5 put 0 else if *rand*( ) > 0.5 put 1.

Once the population has been created, the decoded value and actual value of the points in the population are obtained. The results from these simulations are shown in the following table.

String no.			Decoded value		Actual value	
	x_1	x_2	x_1	x_2	x_1	x_2
1	10101100	10111100	172	188	0.3490	0.4745
2	11010010	00010001	210	17	0.6471	−0.8667
3	01011011	01011100	91	92	−0.2863	−0.2784
4	00101010	11101111	42	239	−0.6706	0.8745
5	10001101	10110111	141	183	0.1059	0.4353
6	11101001	10010010	233	145	0.8275	0.1373
7	00110100	01111001	52	121	−0.5922	−0.0510
8	10110100	01011110	180	94	0.4118	−0.2627
9	00101101	00110110	45	54	−0.6417	−0.5765
10	01101000	00010011	104	131	−0.1843	0.0275
11	00010011	10000011	19	121	−0.8510	−0.0510
12	10100100	10110000	164	176	0.2863	0.3804
13	10100100	00100011	164	35	0.2863	−0.7255
14	00101111	00101110	47	46	−0.6314	−0.6392
15	00001010	00010001	10	17	−0.9216	−0.8667
16	11100110	00111101	230	61	0.8039	−0.5216
17	10111011	01011001	187	89	0.4667	−0.3020
18	10011111	00111100	159	60	0.2471	−0.5294
19	10011111	00101011	159	43	0.2471	−0.6627
20	11101101	11011101	237	221	0.8588	0.7333

Step 2 Fitness evaluation

The value of $F(x)$ at these points is then calculated.

Sl. no.	String no.	Actual value		$F(x)$
		x_1	x_2	
1	1	0.3490	0.4745	0.4973
2	2	0.6471	−0.8667	0.2400
3	3	−0.2863	−0.2784	0.3338

Table continued next page

Table continued.

Sl. no.	String no.	Actual value		
		x_1	x_2	$F(x)$
4	4	−0.6706	0.8745	0.2635
5	5	0.1059	0.4353	0.5070
6	6	0.8275	0.1373	0.4754
7	7	−0.5922	−0.5010	0.3069
8	8	0.4118	−0.2627	0.4610
9	9	−0.6471	−0.5765	0.1824
10	10	−0.1843	0.0275	0.4535
11	11	−0.8510	−0.0510	0.2384
12	12	0.2863	0.3804	0.5306
13	13	0.2863	−0.7255	0.2713
14	14	−0.6314	−0.6392	0.1730
15	15	−0.9216	−0.8667	0.1072
16	16	0.8039	−0.5216	0.3396
17	17	0.4667	−0.3020	0.4480
18	18	0.2471	−0.5294	0.3392
19	19	0.2471	−0.6627	0.2895
20	20	0.8588	0.7333	0.3315

Average fitness of the population $\bar{F} = 0.3395$. We select the ten best strings for the starting population. We will retain the string number based on the original initial population.

Step 3 Reproduction

The ten best strings from the population are given in the table:

Sl. no.	String no.	$F(x)$
1	1	0.4973
2	3	0.3338
3	5	0.5070
4	6	0.4754
5	8	0.4610

Table continued next page

Table continued.

Sl. no.	String no.	$F(x)$
6	10	0.4535
7	12	0.5306
8	16	0.3396
9	17	0.4480
10	18	0.3392

The average fitness of this population of 10 best strings is given by $\bar{F} = 0.4385$. In this, we will use binary tournament selection as the reproduction operator.

Sl. no.	String no.	$F(x)$	Best among two
1	1	0.4973	0.4973
2	3	0.3338	(string 1)
3	5	0.5070	0.5070
4	6	0.4754	(string 5)
5	8	0.4610	0.4610
6	10	0.4535	(string 8)
7	12	0.5306	0.5306
8	16	0.3396	(string 12)
9	17	0.4480	0.4480
10	18	0.3392	(string 17)

This process has given us 5 good strings but we need more strings. Therefore, the whole population is shuffled and the tournament selection is performed again.

Sl. no.	String no.	$F(x)$	Best among two
1	3	0.3338	0.4754
2	6	0.4754	(string 6)
3	10	0.4535	0.4535
4	16	0.3396	(string 10)
5	1	0.4973	0.4973
6	18	0.3392	(string 1)
7	17	0.4480	0.5070
8	5	0.5070	(string 5)
9	12	0.5306	0.5306
10	8	0.4610	(string 12)

These 10 strings now form the mating pool.

Step 4 Crossover (two-point crossover)

Since $p_c = 0.8$, we retain the 2 best strings and perform two-point crossover on the remaining 8. The mating pool we get is shown in the table below.

Sl. no.	String no.	$F(x)$
1	1	0.4973
2	5	0.5070
3	8	0.4610
4	12	0.5306
5	17	0.4480
6	6	0.4754
7	10	0.4535
8	1	0.4973
9	**5**	**0.5070**
10	**12**	**0.5306**

Average fitness of the population after tournament selection is $\bar{F} = 0.4908$.

Generate two random numbers between 1 and 15 and what we get are 13 and 9. Using these two crossover sites, we perform a two-point crossover.

Father1 : 10101100, 10111100 (String1)

Mother1 : 10001101, 10110111 (String5)

Child1 : 101 |0110| 0, 10111100 (Child1)

Child2 : 100 |0110| 1, 10110111 (Child2)

Similarly, generating two random numbers for the crossover sites, we get 10 and 3:

Father2 : 10110100, 01011110 (String8)

Mother2 : 10100100, 10110000 (String12)

Child3 : 101101 |00, 10110 |110 (Child3)

Child4 : 101001 |00, 01011 |000 (Child4)

For crossover sites 12 and 4,

Father3 : 10111011, 01011001 (String17)

Mother3 : 11101001, 10010010 (String6)

Child5 : 1011 | 1001, 1001 | 1001 (Child5)

Child6 : 1110 | 1011, 0101 | 0010 (Child6)

For crossover sites 7 and 2,

Father4 : 01101000, 00010011 (String10)

Mother4 : 10101100, 10111100 (String1)

Child7 : 01101000, 0 |011111 |11 (Child7)

Child8 : 10101100, 1 |00100 |00 (Child8)

The population after crossover is depicted by the table below:

Sl. no.	Before cross-over	After cross-over	8-bit binary substring		Decoded value		Actual value		
			x_1	x_2	x_1	x_2	x_1	x_2	$F(x)$
1	String1	Child1	10101100	10111100	172	188	0.3490	0.4745	0.4973
2	String5	Child2	10001101	10110111	141	183	0.1059	0.4353	0.5070
3	String8	Child3	10110100	10110110	180	182	0.4118	0.4275	0.5084
4	String12	Child4	10100100	01011000	164	88	0.2863	−0.3098	0.4352
5	String17	Child5	10111001	10011001	185	153	0.4510	0.2000	0.5540
6	String6	Child6	11101011	01010010	235	82	0.8431	−0.3569	0.3875
7	String10	Child7	01101000	00111111	104	63	−0.1843	−0.5059	0.2825
8	String1	Child8	10101100	10010000	172	144	0.3490	0.1294	0.5634
9	String5	String5	10001101	10110111	141	183	0.1059	0.4353	0.5070
10	String12	String12	10100100	10110000	164	176	0.2863	0.3804	0.5306

Average fitness of the population after crossover is $\bar{F} = 0.4773$. Now, we need to perform the mutation step.

Step 5 Mutation

Given: mutation probability ($p_m = 0.005$), number of variables ($n = 2$), variable with ($m = 8$) 8-bit strings and ($N = 10$) population size equals 10. The number of bits to be modified $= p_m^* n^* m^* N$:

$= 0.005^*2^*8^*10$

$= 0.8 \approx 1$ bit.

Randomly generating two numbers between 1 and 10 for the 10 strings and between 1 and 16 for 16 bits, we get 8 and 3, respectively. Thus, we change the bit in child 8 and bit 3.

Child8 : 10101100, 10010000

Mutated Child8 : 10101100, 10010100

Step 6 **Evaluation**

New population after three generic operations is evaluated as in step 2.

Sl. no.	**Children after crossover**	**8-bit binary substring**		**Decoded value**		**Actual value**		
		x_1	x_2	x_1	x_2	x_1	x_2	$F(x)$
1	Child1	10101100	10111100	172	188	0.3490	0.4745	0.4973
2	Child2	10001101	10110111	141	193	0.1059	0.4353	0.5070
3	Child3	10110100	10110110	180	182	0.4118	0.4275	0.5084
4	Child4	10100100	01011000	164	88	0.2863	−0.3098	0.4352
5	Child5	10111001	10011001	185	153	0.4510	0.2000	0.5540
6	Child6	11101011	01010010	235	82	0.8431	−0.3569	0.3875
7	Child7	01101000	00111111	104	63	−0.1843	−0.5059	0.2825
8	Mutated Child8	10101100	10010100	172	148	0.3490	0.1608	0.5637
9	String5	10001101	10110111	141	183	0.1059	0.4353	0.5070
10	String12	10100100	10110000	164	176	0.2863	0.3804	0.5306

The average fitness of the population after three generic operations is $\bar{F} = 0.4773$. Best points after one generation are $x_1 = 0.349$ and $x_2 = 0.1608$.

7.3 Real Coded GA

There are many problems in optimization where the design variables are continuous and we want to know their optimal values to full computer precision. In such cases, binary GA requires a large number of bits to code each variable and a better approach is to code each variable as a floating point or *real* number. This approach is therefore called real coded or continuous GA.[9] The real coded GA also needs less storage when compared to binary GA, since a single floating point number represents each variable instead of a large number of integers. As the number of bits needed in binary GA increases, the computer storage requirements can become large. We have seen from Example 7.1 that a large-sized string is needed to represent design variables to a high level of precision.

7.3.1 Representation of design variables

We have already noted the complicated process of encoding and decoding used in binary GA. In real coded GA, the design variables are represented as floating point numbers. If a problem has n design variables, then the design vector can be represented exactly in the same form as used for gradient-based methods:

$$\mathbf{x} = \{x_1, x_2, x_3, \ldots, x_n\}. \tag{7.33}$$

Note that in binary GA, the design vector was represented by a string and the elements $x_1, x_2, \ldots, x_n$ were each represented as binary substrings of m bits each. In real GA, we use n floating point numbers while in binary GA, we use $m \times n$ bits to represent the design vector. The real GA can use single- or double-precision arithmetic depending on the computer. Since real GA is a search algorithm which starts from a population of values, move limits need to be designed for each design variable to bound the design space. Just like for binary GA, these move limits have the form $x_i^L \leq x_i \leq x_i^U, i = 1$ to n.

The fitness value of the function is calculated using

$$f(\mathbf{x}) = f(x_1, x_2, x_3, \ldots, x_n). \tag{7.34}$$

Real GA therefore saves us from the complexity of using the encoding and decoding operations of binary GA.

7.3.2 Starting population

The starting population is created by taking a floating point number within the design space for each variable. Thus, the starting population with all design variables lying between 1 and 10 may be expressed in the form using random numbers with up to eight decimal places.

$$\begin{aligned}
&\text{Member 1}: \underbrace{2.34527849}_{x_{11}} \; \underbrace{1.34272192}_{x_{12}} \; \underbrace{1.23972398}_{x_{13}} \; \cdots \; \underbrace{7.23582302}_{x_{1n}} \\
&\text{Member 2}: \underbrace{7.54989200}_{x_{21}} \; \underbrace{3.04011890}_{x_{22}} \; \underbrace{2.18998363}_{x_{23}} \; \cdots \; \underbrace{5.82990872}_{x_{2n}} \\
&\vdots \\
&\text{Member} N: \underbrace{9.82019902}_{x_{N1}} \; \underbrace{4.02384002}_{x_{N2}} \; \underbrace{5.77810282}_{x_{N3}} \; \cdots \; \underbrace{0.12927494}_{x_{Nn}}
\end{aligned} \tag{7.35}$$

The initial population is therefore a matrix of real numbers of size $N \times n$. Note that random sampling can also be enhanced by uniform sampling to make sure that all parts of the design space are adequately sampled. In addition, a complement approach could be used by subtracting the population of each design variable from its upper bound.

Just as in binary GA, it is advantageous to have a larger initial population compared to the population value used in the GA generations. Thus, if we start with a population of $1.2\,N - 2\,N$, the N best points can be selected for further operations such as reproduction, crossover and mutation operators. However, in real GA, some of these operators need to be defined in a new manner compared to binary GA.

7.3.3 Reproduction

Roulette wheel selection can also be used for real GA. Consider Table 7.4 and replace string j with design variable j. The fitness function and cumulative probability can then be calculated in exactly the same manner as for binary GA. Just as in binary GA, we can select the mating pool members as 1, 3, 2, 1 and 3. The mates can then be paired as (1, 3) and (2, 1) assuming 80 per cent crossover. The only difference in the reproduction operations for real GA is that string i is replaced by design variable i which is the design vector $\{x_{i1}, x_{i2}, x_{i3}, \ldots, x_{in}\}$. We also see that the scaling correction and tournament selection can be applied to real GA. The reproduction operator does not create any new points.

7.3.4 Crossover

The crossover operator used for real GA is different from that used for binary GA. A simple approach we may follow is to take two sites along the parent as the crossover site and then exchange the variables inside the crossover sites. For example, if there are two six-variable parents as given below:

$$\text{Father} = \{x_{f1}, x_{f2}, x_{f3}, x_{f4}, x_{f5}, x_{f6}\},$$
$$\text{Mother} = \{x_{m1}, x_{m2}, x_{m3}, x_{m4}, x_{m5}, x_{m6}\}, \tag{7.36}$$

we select two crossover sites randomly and get 1 and 3. The children are then as shown in the following:

$$\text{Father} = \{x_{f1}, x_{f2}, x_{f3}, |x_{m4}, x_{m5}, |x_{f6}\},$$
$$\text{Mother} = \{x_{m1}, x_{m2}, x_{m3}, |x_{f4}, x_{f5}, |x_{m6}\}. \tag{7.37}$$

The above strategy works well with binary GA where the variables are coded strings. However, in real GA the simple swapping of design variables does not introduce any new information. We need a method to create new design variables. One approach for creating new design variables is to use the blending method and define the children:

$$x_{\text{new}}^{(1)} = \beta x_{mn} + (1-\beta)x_{fn},$$
$$x_{\text{new}}^{(2)} = \beta x_{fn} + (1-\beta)x_{mn}. \tag{7.38}$$

In the above, $\beta \in (0, 1)$, x_{mn} is the nth design variable in the mother design vector and x_{fn} is the nth design variable in the father design vector. The limiting case occurs when $\beta = 0 \Rightarrow x_{\text{new}}^{(1)} = x_{fn}, x_{\text{new}}^{(2)} = x_{mn}$ and when $\beta = 1 \Rightarrow x_{\text{new}}^{(1)} = x_{mn}, x_{\text{new}}^{(2)} = x_{fn}$, where the child is a clone of one parent. When $\beta = 0.5$, the two children are the average of the two-parent design variables and are essentially identical twins. In general, it is a good idea to take a random number $\beta \in (0, 1)$ and find the values of the two children. This method is also called the *blending method* since it combines information from both parents to get the children and therefore simulates nature. However, the blending method described in (7.38) now interpolates between the parent values and is not capable of extrapolating into the design space.

Blending approaches to crossover which extrapolate have also been proposed by some researchers. One such approach is called the *linear crossover* where three children are created using two parents as follows:

$$x_{\text{new}}^{(1)} = 0.5x_{mn} + 0.5x_{fn},$$
$$x_{\text{new}}^{(2)} = 1.5x_{mn} - 0.5x_{fn},$$
$$x_{\text{new}}^{(3)} = -0.5x_{mn} + 1.5x_{fn}. \tag{7.39}$$

Here the first child is interpolated while the second and third children are extrapolated. A problem with extrapolation is that sometimes a child may go outside the bounds of the design variable. In such a case, the child is not selected. The best two children among the three are selected for further operations. As an example, consider $x_{mn} = 1, x_{fn} = 2$. Then, the children are given by $x^{(1)}_{\text{new}} = 1.5, x^{(2)}_{\text{new}} = 0.5, x^{(3)}_{\text{new}} = 2.5$. Thus we see that the linear crossover both interpolates and extrapolates using the parent values.

A further generalization of the concept of linear crossover is needed to ensure that more than three children can be created in case more than one need to be discarded because they lie outside the move limits for the design variable. We can define any number of children of two parents using *heuristic crossover*:

$$x_{\text{new}} = \beta(x_{mn} - x_{fn}) + x_{mn}. \tag{7.40}$$

This approach allows generations of children both inside and outside the parent range depending on the value of the random number $\beta \in (0, 1)$. Heuristic crossover also introduces an element of randomness in the crossover process which is absent in linear crossover.

As an example of implementing the two-point heuristic crossover, consider the two-parent design vectors, shown below:

$$\begin{aligned} \text{Father} &= \{2.762, 4.384, 1.236, 0.524\}, \\ \text{Mother} &= \{7.310, 8.236, 5.426, 4.316\}. \end{aligned} \tag{7.41}$$

Here each design variable has a bound of (0, 10) as the lower and upper limit. Using a random number generator, we pick two crossing sites, 2 and 3. Again, we generate three random numbers $\beta \in (0, 1)$ and get 0.1783, 0.8264 and 0.3123. Using these values and heuristic crossover, we get three children:

$$\begin{aligned} x^{(1)}_{\text{new}} &= 0.1783(8.236 - 4.384) + 8.236 = 8.9228, \\ x^{(2)}_{\text{new}} &= 0.8264(8.236 - 4.384) + 8.236 = 38.0745, \\ x^{(3)}_{\text{new}} &= 0.3123(8.236 - 4.384) + 8.236 = 9.4389. \end{aligned} \tag{7.42}$$

The second child is outside the move limit of the design variable and is not selected. We then take the other two values to form the children:

$$\begin{aligned} \text{Father} &= \{2.762, |8.9228, |1.236, 0.524\}, \\ \text{Mother} &= \{7.310, |9.4389, |5.426, 4.316\}. \end{aligned} \tag{7.43}$$

The two-point heuristic crossover is a good approach to use for real coded GA and is recommended for applications.

7.3.5 Mutation

As in binary GA, mutation is needed in real GA to ensure that the algorithm does not get *stuck* or converge to a *local minimum*. To apply mutation with probability p_m, we change $n \times N \times p_m$ design variables in a random manner. Recall that $n \times N$ is the number of real numbers in the population. As an example, consider design vectors of size $n = 6$ and $N = 10$ to make up the population. Taking a mutation probability, $p_m = 0.05$, we need to change three design variables, that is $(6 \times 10 \times 0.05 = 3)$. To do this, we randomly select three variables from the population and replace them by a random number lying between the move limits corresponding to these variables.

In summary, we point out that many problems involving a low level of discretization can be solved using binary GA, even when the variables are real. However, as the desired accuracy of the optimal point increases, real GA becomes advantageous in terms of storage requirements. Recent research literature shows a growing popularity of real GA over binary GA.

7.4 Hybrid Genetic Algorithm

The genetic algoritm has good global optimizing properties compared to gradient-based algorithms. However, the use of GA does not guarantee convergence to global minima because of its poor exploitation capabilities. It also has other drawbacks such as premature convergence which occurs because of the loss of diversity in the population. Another problem with GA is the need to properly select the starting population size, crossover probability, mutation probability and the maximum number of generations. Considerable human time, besides computational effort is needed to select these parameters using numerical experiments. One more shortcoming of GA is the lack of a good convergence criterion. For gradient-based methods, the norm of the gradient can be used as a descent function and should decrease as the iterations progress and becomes very small at the local optimum point. However, in the GA method it is not possible to ascertain when exactly the optimal point is reached, particularly for engineering problems where the point is not known in advance. Because of this ambiguity in the definition of convergence criteria, engineering software mostly use gradient-based methods which offer a clear (though often local) optimal point.

One approach to develop a good optimization algorithm is to combine the best of both techniques: GA and local optimization algorithms (LOA). This approach, known as the *hybrid GA* (HGA) approach can be divided into three types:

1. The first type is the *pre-hybridization* approach in which the initial population of GA is generated using LOA.
2. The second type is the *organic hybridization* approach in which a LOA is used as one of the operators of GA for improving each member of the population in each generation. However, such hybridizations often reduce the global optimizing properties of the HGA. It has been found that while organic hybridization is computationally more efficient than a GA, it offers little assurance of global minima and also lacks a proper convergence criterion.
3. The third approach of *post-hybridization* uses the GA to provide an initial design of the LOA. This kind of hybridization seems to be the best way of combining the finest characteristics of the two approaches, as no compromise is made on the global and local optimizing characteristics. The basic problem of gradient-based methods of getting a good starting design can also be addressed using this method.

Many possible HGA concepts are possible. At the simplest level, one can use the solution obtained by GA as the initial point of a gradient-based algorithm such as the conjugate-gradient method. The ideal situation would occur if we can locate the region where the global minimum lies using GA, and then use a gradient-based method to make

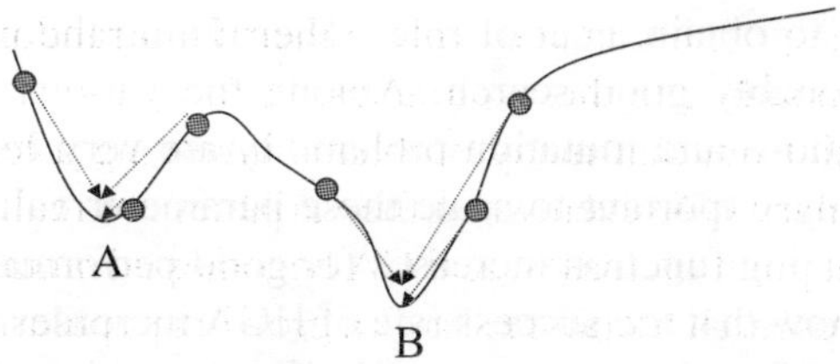

Figure 7.1 *Initial guesses and their effect on the gradient-based method*

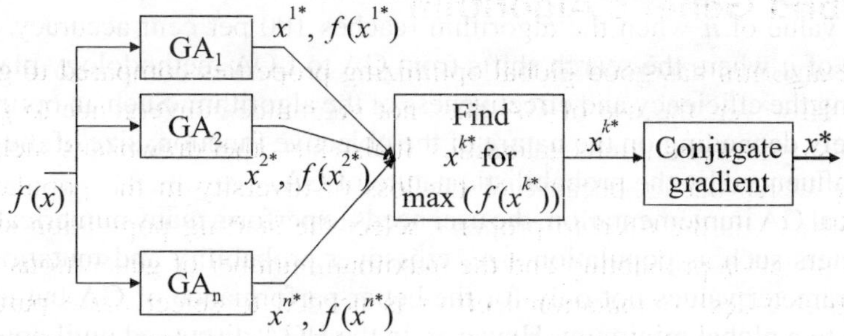

Figure 7.2 *Schematic representation of a hybrid genetic algorithm*

the algorithm converge rapidly to the optimal point. However, it is not easy to get a good starting point from function values alone. For example, Figure 7.1 shows how different starting points can lead to different minimum points in a multimodal optimization problem. It is clear that the global minimum can be located only if the starting design lies around the valley containing point B. In order that the starting design is near point B, the GA must *almost converge* to the global minimum and the gradient search is simply used to complete the local search and yield the minimum quickly.

It is a known fact that GA show better global optimization capability when they are run several times for fewer number of generations rather than run a few times for many generations. Such a behaviour is due to the well-known weak points of the technique: premature convergence and weak exploitation capabilities. Thus GAs tend to prematurely converge to a local minimum owing to loss of diversity in the population or hover around the global minima for many generations without converging. Therefore, instead of using the GA only once, a bank of n GAs may be used with the same population size; crossover and mutation probabilities and number of generations. The best point obtained from these n GAs is then used as the starting design of the conjugate-gradient method, a gradient-search method. Any other gradient-based method can also be used. In the computer implementation, a GA subroutine is called n times with a different random initial population and the best solution obtained is used as an initial condition for the gradient-based method subroutine. The number of generations is kept constant for all the n runs. The architecture of the algorithm is shown in Figure 7.2.

In the case of difficult multimodal problems, HGA reaches the global minimum at a larger value of n. The performance of HGA is better when each GA is able to carry out a reasonably good search so that it is able to reach the global optima in one of these runs. As we have discussed before, the choice of GA parameters is critical and varies from problem to problem. The behaviour of the GA depends on appropriate selection of these parameters.

However, it is possible to obtain a set of rules determining the parameter values so that the GA can do a reasonably good search. Among the various parameters, population size, number of generations and mutation probability are very important for multimodal problems. It is especially important to scale these parameter values appropriately as the dimension of the optimizing function increases for good performance of the GA.

Numerical studies show that the success rate of HGA increases as n is increased. At the same time, the number of function evaluations also increases, increasing the computational cost and reducing the computational efficiency of the algorithm. Therefore, an optimal value of n that converges to global minima while using minimum computational effort will be the smallest value of n when the algorithm reaches 100 per cent accuracy. Therefore, a proper value of n where the search shifts from GA to LOA methodology plays a key role in determining the efficiency and effectiveness of the algorithm. Such an optimum value of n varies widely depending on the nature of the objective function, size of the design space and is also influenced by the probabilistic nature of GA.

For a typical GA implementation, the user needs to perform many numerical experiments with parameters such as population size, crossover probability and mutation probability to obtain parameter values not only for the better performance of GA but also to ensure convergence to a global minimum. However, in the HGA discussed until now, we transfer the problem of selecting GA tuning parameters to that of selecting n. Even though HGA takes more computational effort than a GA with optimal parameter values while converging to the global optimum, it is more efficient in the sense that it saves considerable human effort.

7.5 Automated Hybrid Genetic Algorithm

A key variable in the hybrid approach discussed above is the number n of GA runs that are used to obtain the starting point for the CG method. One approach to automate the selection of n is to use the familiar GA criteria that if the optimal function value does not change for several iterations, then the global optimum may have been reached or is near.

In the automated hybrid genetic algorithm (AHGA), the GA subroutine is called separately for fb_i number of times, where fb_i is the ith term of the Fibonacci series. The Fibonacci series is defined as follows:

$$fb_i = fb_{i-1} + fb_{i-2}. \tag{7.44}$$

Here $fb_1 = 1$, $fb_2 = 2$. Thus the resulting series is the following:

$$1, 2, 3, 5, 8, 13, 21, 34, 55, 89, 144, \ldots, fb_i,$$

and f_i is the best function value obtained after fb_i number of independent searches are carried out using GA. The algorithm is said to have converged when the following condition is satisfied:

$$\frac{f_i - f_{i-2}}{f_i} \leq \varepsilon, \qquad i \geq 5. \tag{7.45}$$

This criterion is a measure of the fact that the optimal function value predicted by GA has stopped improving for some time. The best search point obtained is fed to the gradient-based method as the initial estimate of the solution. Due to the random nature of GA, using the Fibonacci series ensures that the best point selected by the GA bank has settled down and is therefore close to a global minimum. The use of the gradient method from this point should result in rapid convergence to the optimal point. The key problem of finding a good starting design for the gradient method is also addressed.

Problems

1. Write a computer program for binary GA. Using the program, find the minimum point of the following function:

$$f(\mathbf{x}) = \frac{3}{2}x_1^2 + 2x_2^3 + \frac{3}{2}x_3^2 + x_1x_3 + 3x_2x_3 - 3x_1 - x_3 + 10.$$

Use move limits $-10 \leq x_i \leq 10, i = 1, 3$ and 8-bit coding. Use binary tournament selection, a population of 40, crossover probability of 0.80, mutation probability of 0.005 and maximum generation of 100. Try multiple runs of the program.

2. Use the binary GA program to find the minimum point of the function:

$$f(\mathbf{x}) = x_1^2 + 2x_2^2 + e^{-x_1-x_2}.$$

Use move limits $-1 \leq x_i \leq 1, i = 1, 2$ and 5-bit coding. Use binary tournament selection, a population of 40, crossover probability of 0.80, mutation probability of 0.005 and maximum generation of 100. Try multiple runs of the program.

3. Using the binary GA program, find the four minimum points for the *Himmelblau function:*

$$f(\mathbf{x}) = (x_1^2 + x_2 - 11)^2 + (x_1 + x_2^2 - 7)^2.$$

Use move limits $-10 \leq x_i \leq 10, i = 1, 2$. Use 5-bit coding and 100 maximum generations and other operators and probabilities of your choice. Try multiple runs of the program.

4. Write a computer program for real GA. Using the program, find the minimum point of the following function:

$$f(\mathbf{x}) = \frac{3}{2}x_1^2 + 2x_2^3 + \frac{3}{2}x_3^2 + x_1x_3 + 3x_2x_3 - 3x_1 - x_3 + 10.$$

Use move limits $-10 \leq x_i \leq 10, i = 1, 3$. Use binary tournament selection, a population of 40, crossover probability of 0.80, mutation probability of 0.005 and maximum generation of 100.

5. Use the real GA program to find the minimum point of the function:

$$f(\mathbf{x}) = x_1^2 + 2x_2^2 + e^{-x_1-x_2}.$$

Use move limits $-1 \leq x_i \leq 1, i = 1, 2$. Use binary tournament selection, a population of 40, crossover probability of 0.80, mutation probability of 0.005 and maximum generation of 100.

6. Write a computer program for real coded GA. Using this program, find the four minimum points for the Himmelblau function:

$$f(\mathbf{x}) = (x_1^2 + x_2 - 11)^2 + (x_1 + x_2^2 - 7)^2$$

Use move limits $-10 \le x_i \le 10, i = 1, 2$.

7. Consider the Himmelblau function:

$$f(\mathbf{x}) = (x_1^2 + x_2 - 11)^2 + (x_1 + x_2^2 - 7)^2.$$

Consider twenty different random starting points for a conjugate gradient method and find the minimum points. Use move limits $-10 \le x_i \le 10, i = 1, 2$. Does this approach yield the four local minimum for the problem? How do the function evaluations compare with the GA?

8. Consider the Matlab peak function:

$$f(x, y) = 3(1 - x)^2 e^{-x^2-(y+1)^2} - 10\left(\frac{x}{5} - x^3 - y^5\right) e^{-x^2-y^2} - \frac{e^{-(x+1)^2-y^2}}{3}.$$

Find the minimum value of the function using the move limits $-3 \le x, y \le 3$. Use

a. Binary GA with 4-bit coding
b. Binary GA with 8-bit coding
c. Binary GA with 16-bit coding

Comment on your results.

9. Consider the Matlab peak function:

$$f(x, y) = 3(1 - x)^2 e^{-x^2-(y+1)^2} - 10\left(\frac{x}{5} - x^3 - y^5\right) e^{-x^2-y^2} - \frac{e^{-(x+1)^2-y^2}}{3}.$$

Find the minimum value of the function with move limits $-3 \le x, y \le 3$, using

a. Real GA with blending and interpolating crossover
b. Real GA with heuristic crossover

Comment on your results.

10. It is known that Wood's function, given below, has several local minima. Use the binary genetic algorithm to find the minimum points.

$$f(\mathbf{x}) = 100(x_2 - x_1^2)^2 + (1 - x_1)^2 + 90(x_4 - x_3^2)^2 + (1 - x_3)^2 + 10.1[(x_2 - 1)^2 + (x_4 - 1)^2] + 19.8(x_2 - 1)(x_4 - 1).$$

11. Find the minimum points of the following function using the real coded genetic algorithm.

$$f(\mathbf{x}) = 100(x_2 - x_1^2)^2 + (1 - x_1)^2 + 90(x_4 - x_3^2)^2 + (1 - x_3)^2 + 10.1[(x_2 - 1)^2 + (x_4 - 1)^2] + 19.8(x_2 - 1)(x_4 - 1).$$

12. Use the real coded GA to get to a good starting point for the gradient-search method on the function:

$$f(\mathbf{x}) = \sum_{i=1}^{10} i x_i^2 + e^{-\sum_{i=1}^{10} x_i}.$$

Consider move limits $-5 \le x_i \le 5, i = 1, 10$. Use the conjugate-gradient method to find the minimum point for the calculated starting point.

References

The author acknowledges the following references and recommends them for further study of the subject.

[1] Arora, J. S., *Introduction to Optimum Design*, McGraw-Hill, Singapore, 1989.

[2] Nash, S. G. and Sopher, A., *Linear and Nonlinear Programming*, McGraw-Hill, Singapore, 1996.

[3] Fletcher, R., *Practical Methods of Optimization*, John Wiley and Sons, New York, 1987.

[4] Chang, E. K. P., Zak, S. S., *An Introduction to Optimization*, John Wiley and Sons, New York, 2008.

[5] Bazaraa, M. S., Sherali, H. D., and Shetty, C. M., *Nonlinear Programming: Theory and Applications*, John Wiley and Sons, New York, 1993.

[6] Belegundu, A. D. and Chandrapatla, T. R., *Optimization Concepts and Application in Engineering*, Pearson Education, Singapore, 1999.

[7] Goldberg, D. E., *Genetic Algorithms in Search, Optimization and Machine Learning*, Addison Wesley, 1989.

[8] Deb, K., *Optimization for Engineering Design: Algorithms and Examples*, Prentice Hall of India (Pvt.) Ltd., New Delhi, 2004.

[9] Haupt, R. L. and Haupt, S.E., *Practical Genetic Algorithms*, John Wiley and Sons, New York, 1998.

[10] Myers, R. H. and Montgomery, D.C., *Response Surface Methodology*, John Wiley and Sons, New York, 1995.

[11] Ross, P. J., *Taguchi Techniques for Quality Engineering*, McGraw-Hill, Singapore, 1995.

Index